*For my father, born in Hoorn, once an important port on the Zuider Zee,*
*for my mother, born in Rostov, port on the Don,*
*for Loes, born in Yerseke, fishing port on the Oosterschelde,*
*for Marina, born in Rotterdam, the biggest port in the world.*

Han Meyer

# CITY AND PORT

Urban Planning as a Cultural Venture in
London, Barcelona, New York, and Rotterdam:
changing relations between public urban space
and large-scale infrastructure

This publication was made possible by contributions from
– the Public Fund for the Promotion of Architectural Quality
– the Architecture Department of Delft University of Technology
– the City of Rotterdam Department of Physical Planning and Urban Development, and
– the Van Eesteren-Fluck-van Lohuizen Foundation

Original title: De stad en de haven

This publication is part of the research program *Stedebouwkunde van de Faculteit der Bouwkunde 1994-1997*, and specifically the section of this program entitled *Grondslagen en Vernieuwing der Stedebouwkunde* (Fundamentals and Renewal of Urban Planning and Design).

Dust-jacket photo: Paul Martens, Nieuwerkerk a/d IJssel
Word processing: José van Os, Delft
Final editing: Henk Pel, Zeist
Translation: D'Laine Camp & Donna de Vries-Hermansader, Rotterdam
Graphic design: Marjo Starink/Studio Cursief, Amsterdam
Printing: Haasbeek, Alphen a.d. Rijn

ISBN 90 5727 020 X

International Books, A. Numankade 17, 3572 KP Utrecht, the Netherlands
Telephone +31-30 2731 840  Fax +31-30 2733 614  E-mail: i-books@antenna.nl

# Contents

# Foreword

Large infrastructural works – such as interlocal traffic and transportation networks, military defense systems, and dikes – usually leave a permanent mark on the spatial image and structure of the city. Even when infrastructure has lost its original function, when it has been written off, cast aside, or even dismantled ages ago, it leaves the urban form with a lasting impression of its presence. Whether the subject is old rural roads, demolished ramparts, dismantled railroad viaducts, filled-in waterways, or dikes no longer in use, in nearly every case these elements leave visible traces on the city map. If a city has a memory, then the legacy of discarded infrastructural works forms an important part of that memory.

Thus every design for new infrastructure or for the reorganization of existing infrastructure is imbued with a cultural quality which, in the end, is far more important than the primary function that forms the basis of its construction.

This book addresses the question of the degree to which, and the manner in which, urban planners are accountable for the cultural significance of the design and redesign of infrastructural works, and it focuses on a specific type of infrastructure: seaports. Four types of port cities are featured in this book: London, Barcelona, New York, and Rotterdam. Each type is characterized by a specific spatial form of the relation between city and port, and by a specific cultural appreciation of this form.

The process of research and writing that led to this book was not based on rational planning from the word go. It began to take shape at some point in the 1980s, when, as an employee of the Municipality of Rotterdam, I became directly involved in developing plans for old harbor areas. In so doing, I recognized the need to broaden my horizons: what kinds of plans, containing what kinds of patterns, were other cities developing, or had they developed, for the relation between city and infrastructure?

To begin with, this comparative study, made possible by a grant from the body then known as the Ministry of Welfare, Health, and Cultural Affairs, resulted in a number of articles and essays for various magazines and books.

When I transferred my activities to the University of Technology in Delft, the possibility emerged to develop the study as part of the research program being carried out by the school's Department of Urbanism. The line of approach and the presentation of the question changed during this period and, with them, the character of the argument. This book no longer focuses strictly on the future of port areas; the issue at the heart of the publication is now the discipline of urban planning. Port areas discussed here have been given the role of coat racks, on which a story of the discipline itself can be hung. This does not mean that the book is meant for professionals alone. On the contrary, it centers on a discussion of the ability of the urban planning discipline to recognize the cultural components embodied in fundamental spatial issues, such as the design or redesign of large-scale infrastructural elements. This discussion is of importance to everyone curious about or interested in the future spatial quality of the big city.

The course taken by this study can be compared to a voyage on a sailing vessel: the doldrums alternated with squalls; and currents, fluctuating winds, and sandbanks repeatedly necessitated larger or smaller corrections in the course.

Many people have contributed, directly or indirectly, to this voyage. Although most are named in the section entitled Acknowledgements, I would like to mention here the roles of my promoters, Jurgen Rosemann and Jan Heeling. They had little to do with the ship's cargo – much of which, for that matter, was jettisoned as excess ballast as time went on – but a great deal to say about the course to be taken and about the final destination. It was a pleasure to consult with them on the itinerary to be followed.

When the port is finally sighted, the captain still has to maneuver his craft into the harbor, no easy task. With their comments on the content of the first draft, Willem Hermans, Loes Verhaart, and Anna Vos made important contributions. Joke Verhaart assisted me with editorial advice.

Fortunately, after braving all the treacherous currents and storms, the home port was a constant haven, a place to catch my breath and to gain new inspiration for determining the course.

*Rotterdam, 1999*

# Chapter 1

*The Nineteenth-Century Port City
on Its Way to the Twenty-First Century*

Above: New York, Hudson Riverfront, 1987.
Center: Rotterdam, the Kop van Zuid, 1993.
Below: London, West India Docks, 1982.

# The Identity of the Port City:
# The Emergence of 'the Cultural Factor'

I

Scarcely twenty years ago, in many port cities in Europe and North America the surplus of unused, obsolete harbor sites lay like a lead weight on the shoulders of city administrators and urban planners and designers. The loss of nineteenth-century harbor areas revealed part of a process that was taking place in cities all over the Western world during the final decades of the twentieth century. Vacant harbor areas are some of the most visible exponents of the Western transition from the Industrial to the Post-Industrial Age, as well as of the consequences of this transition for the spatial and functional shape and structure of the city. The relocation of large areas of industrial production to other spots on the globe and, in particular, the emergence of completely new transportation technologies provided a reversal in the position held by industrial centers and transshipment harbors within international economic networks. The visibility of this process is manifested in large areas whose spatial features have been derived directly from the original harbor function; not only the building legacy – entrepôts, silos, warehouses, and sheds – seemed to have become absolutely useless in the blink of an eye, but also the civil-engineering infrastructure of quays, harbors, piers, and docks. And the dilapidated appearance of these areas appeared to be sucking the entire weal and woe of the port city down into a spiral of decline.

But in the course of the 1980s, cities throughout Western Europe and North America began preparing for a spectacular resurrection – referred to so nicely in Anglo-Saxon countries as the urban renaissance – in which port cities, of all things, were to play a starring role. Old harbor areas were discovered as ideal sites for the development of new urban milieus. The 'urban waterfront' became an international formula for success.

'Waterfront development' has grown into a specialty to which innumerable designers, consultancies, real-estate developers, and marketing experts now devote themselves. Professionals from all over the world keep one another informed of the most recent developments by means of international waterfront networks.[1]

In the meantime, as we approach the year 2000, the euphoria has died down to some extent. On close examination, not every formula for success is as successful as it once appeared to be. Certain large-scale waterfront projects ended up as spectacular real-estate debacles.[2] Other projects had to be trimmed down as time went on or, in some cases, radically modified. In scores of cities, the results of many years of intensive plan development are still on the drawing board.[3]

The time is ripe to make up the balance. Have various 'revitalized' harbor areas really given something to the cities, and has the wave of new plans provided a fresh, fruitful impetus for the renewal of urban planning?

In each plan and design for old harbor areas exists a noticeable emphasis on the *cultural significance* that these areas are supposed to have, to which an exceptional power is ascribed and which is deemed to be of great importance to the further development of the city. In recent decades, urban planners everywhere have tried to separate the spatial design of urban areas from functionalist principles and to pay more attention to the cultural significance of the urban form. 'Cultural identity,' 'cultural value,' and 'cultural quality' are concepts that currently saturate the jargon of urban planning. Within a short time these concepts have become criteria that are taken for granted, even though they often lack clarity of definition and the objectives they represent may be obscure. Recent plans for urban planning conversions of obsolete harbor areas are some of the most spectacular exponents of the emergence of the 'cultural factor.'

Is the focus on 'cultural quality' a new phenomenon that is giving direction in a brand-new way to the spatial development of cities and to the practice of creating urban plans, or is it rather a case of old wine in new bottles? And what do 'cultural quality' and 'identity' really mean; are they precisely defined concepts, or do they change in meaning in the course of time and from place to place? These are the questions that have led to a more detailed study of what ideas and concepts on culture and identity signify for the conversion of old harbor areas. In this first chapter, these questions are amplified and defined.


THE DIFFICULT RELATION BETWEEN FUNCTIONAL PLANNING
AND THE DESIGN OF THE URBAN FORM

To a great degree, the concepts of the practice of twentieth-century urban planning are based on what was called 'scientific urban planning'; this consisted of the close association of research, planning, and design and the attempt to create a direct relationship between the functional development of the city, according to plan, and the spatial development of the city. In the nineteenth century, the spatial shape of the city was distinguished by a universal character that allowed for the development of various functions and patterns of use. On the other hand, the twentieth-century concept of *functionalism* or *modernism*,[4] which was strongly allied with the socialist

The revitalized port: Baltimore, Inner Harbor, 1990.

movement, was advertised as the spatial exponent of the new, modern, rationally founded, planning-directed society.

Of particular interest in the recent development of nineteenth-century harbor areas is the obvious decline of functionalism in urban planning, as well as the appearance of a search for new fundamentals of plan development and design. Ever since the 1960s, a good look at scores of American and European cities has clearly revealed that old harbor areas, most of which date from the nineteenth century, have seen their better days. Initial plans for the reuse and revitalization of such areas were still based, for the most part, on the functionalist tradition. New proposals, however, couple far-reaching *functional changes* in these areas with far-reaching *morphological changes* in harbor basins, quays, warehouses – in short, the whole infrastructure underlying harbor activities had lost its function and could thus be dismantled.

Consequently, the first generation of plans for old harbor areas in the 1960s and '70s provided for harbor basins to be filled in; piers, quays, and warehouses to be torn down; and a totally new spatial shape and structure to be created. In short, modern twentieth-century urban planning seemed poised at the brink of bidding a final farewell to this large-scale, nineteenth-century legacy.

The farewell was less final than it appeared, however. For parallel to the demise of the strong position held by the Social-Democratic body of thought and of the broad consensus on economic and social planning, during the '70s, and particularly the 80's and '90s, the dominating position of functionalism in urban planning vanished as well. In this period former nineteenth-century harbor areas drew even more interest, but it was no longer focused merely on adapting the spatial shape and structure of such areas to new urban functions planned for harbor sites.

Something had changed in the relationship shared by functional planning, physical design, and cultural significance.

Rotterdam, functional city. The city center as seen from the north, ca. 1960.

An important motivation for writing this book was formed by the redevelopment of old harbor areas in a city that grew, in the second half of the twentieth century, into the city with the largest port in the world and into the paradigm of the modern, functional city: Rotterdam. As in no other city, functionalism laid the foundation for the urban planning development of Rotterdam in the decades following World War II. The postwar reconstruction of Rotterdam in the 1950s and '60s provided an example to be followed by urban planning in both Europe and the United States; it was praised by American planner Edmund Bacon, for instance, for the careful way in which 'the needs of human sensibilities were taken into account.'[5]

But in the late '60s, when the first results of the functionalist urban concept became manifest, the first doubts and criticism were also expressed openly, by 'laymen' as well as by architects and urban planners. New urban areas and ensembles, the shape of which was geared chiefly to primary functions, were criticized precisely because they failed to create a framework for 'human sensibilities.'[6]

Functionalism was undermined not only in Rotterdam, but in the entire international world of urban planning, and would lose its dominant position in the practice of urban planning and in theory development during the '70s and '80s. What emerged to replace it?

In the debate on the reorientation of the fundamentals of urban plans, an important position was taken by new conceptual approaches developed in Southern European and Anglo-Saxon countries: such approaches – with names like *projet urbain* and *urban design* – emphatically distanced themselves from functionalist concepts.[7]

Although important differences exist between the various new concepts (the kind of differences are described in this book), the common characteristic uniting them is a search for a basis for the urban plan that is not simply a derivative and that does not depend on a specific function. The common position taken is that urban planning shapes and structures can be given their own cultural significance, which does not have to change, in essence, if the use of the city changes. Urban design may be seen as a collective name for attempts to define new fundamentals for the design of a city's spatial structure and, in so doing, to create a situation in which the primary function of urban space no longer forms the obvious point of departure.

The development of the spatial shape and structure of the city may be viewed as a relatively autonomous development, with its own pace and dynamics. This interest in the autonomy of the urban form is supported by the interest that arose simultaneously, in other scientific disciplines, in the haphazardness and complexity of various, apparently coherent processes. One particularly strong influence was the new contribution made to historical sciences by the French Annales School, where Fernand Braudel was the most important instructor. His standard work, *Civilization and Capitalism*, draws a distinction among various 'layers' in history, each of which has its own dynamic, its own dimension of time, and which fulfills its own role in the culture of ordinary life in a certain region. The history of the everyday rituals of a civilization (daily routines, eating and drinking habits, family culture) is a history that follows a far slower pace (a *longue durée*) than, for example, the history of manufacturing techniques or that of political and military relations.[8]

The discovery gradually uncovered was that tenacious forms and structures can continue to survive in the city – despite a succession of various administrators, planners, and users who want to do something new with the city, time and again – and this supported the theory that the urban form, too, has its own history of the *longue durée*. This discovery represented an important legitimation of the proposition that the *design* of the urban form is an autonomous discipline, requiring a specific kind of expertise, which can lead to an insight into the field of force that influences the development of the urban form. Instead of the vast amount of attention that functionalist urban planning gave to economic and social objectives (which may be seen as aspects of the kind of 'accelerated time' that relates to specific, relatively short, historical periods), urban design focused on the urban form's production factors, which are part of a slower-paced history: the topographic treatment of the geomorphological foundation of the city and the cultural significance of urban planning structures and elements. To summarize: instead of aiming the urban plan first and foremost at current economic and social objectives, the search was on to find new legitimations of, and a good basis for, the urban plan itself.

SPATIAL DESIGN AND CULTURAL SIGNIFICANCE: THE HARD
AND THE SOFT CITY

In David Harvey's *The Condition of Postmodernity*,[9] he presents Jonathan Raban's book *Soft City*,[10] published in 1974, as a verification for the end of the dominance of functionalist urban planning and for the beginning of a new, 'postmodern' view of the city. According to Harvey, what is special about Raban's book is not so much that it takes a stand against the pretensions of functionalist urban planning. That had been done ten years earlier, with the publication of Jane Jacobs's *The Death and Life of Great American Cities*. What makes Raban's book special is that instead of criticizing functionalist aspirations based on a fear of the consequences, Raban refutes these aspirations by taking the view that it is simply impossible to control urban life with rational planning models. Because the 'soft city' is more important than the 'hard city,' the material city: 'The city as we imagine it, the soft city of illusion, myth, aspiration, nightmare, is as real, maybe more real, than the hard city one can locate in maps and statistics, in monographs on urban sociology and demography and architecture.'[11]

Raban's *Soft City* is an ode to 'the city as an encyclopedia,' where in every spot, every shape, every building, far more meanings are stored than can ever be captured on maps or in statistics. In this urban encyclopedia, every attempt to lend rational order and every attempt to replace the abundance of meanings and references with a single, new layer of meaning is doomed to fail. Raban's message is that the complexity of city life cannot be captured in rational models.

It matters very little whether Harvey is right in claiming that Raban's *Soft City* is precisely the book that marks the reversal in thought on the city and on urban planning. Another good – or perhaps even better – choice would have been Italo Calvino's book *Invisible Cities*, published in 1972 and translated into English in 1974, the year in which *Soft City* was published.[12]

This title incorporates the same sort of message as Raban's book does: the reality of urban life is formed not so much by that which is directly visible in the city but, on the contrary, by the invisible domain of meanings.

*Invisible Cities* – an even bigger best seller in the 1970s and '80s than *Soft City* – became a cult book within the world of architects and urban designers, and probably the literary publication most often quoted in the explanatory notes and descriptions accompanying recent urban plans.[13]

The crux of the matter is that both books are exponents of a new way of thinking about the city and urban planning. Following the modernism of functionalist urban planning, this new way – in which concepts like *cultural identity* and the *cultural value* of the city take center stage: the reference was to the implicit cultural and mental significance of urban forms, structures, and functions – could be called *postmodern*.[14] Meanwhile, in many European countries and in the United States, this reassessment of the cultural significance of the urban form has become a subject of government policy on both municipal and national levels.[15]

This raises the question of which goals are really being earmarked by the recent attention to culture and identity.

*Identity* is a term that has been used a great deal since the 1980s in various areas of society, not only in urban planning and architecture, but also in linguistics, historical studies, and social sciences, as well as in discussions on politics and political reforms, and so forth. To begin with, these discussions on identity all have the same source; they emanate from fear of, or concern about, the loss of certain aspects in society as a consequence of new developments such as scaling-up, internationalization, and new technological possibilities. Initially, identity seemed to be a concept used mainly to protect existing aspects considered to be characteristic of a group or situation, or even of an alleged historical situation, from the undermining results of modernization processes.[16] As yet, this new attention is not free of controversy. For how can *the* culture or *the* identity of a city be determined?

In the meantime, countless comments have been aimed at the frequent, fashionable use of the term identity, an insufficiently amplified subject.

In the poem 'Netschrift,' Octavio Paz compares the desire for identity to the mixing of ground glass through dog food: the source of the problem is external, but the result is that those involved are torn apart, slowly but surely, internally.[17]

Perhaps a bit less radical is the concept of identity that has taken root in recent years: namely, that one can speak of an 'identity' of groups, nations, cities, or locations, but that this can be seen *neither as a homogeneous nor as a static concept*.[18] A certain understanding of the identity of a place or group is not always shared to the same degree by all inhabitants of the place or members of the group. Furthermore, it is possible not only for the group or the place to change in character, but for people's *understanding* of its identity to change as well. In current rhetoric on identity, the terms identity and understanding or sense of identity are often confused with one another. Those using the word identity frequently mean the understanding or sense of identity.[19]

Complications attached to the concept of identity are summarized concisely by Adriaan van der Staay: 'The [cultural] concept of individuality – the notion of identity – prevents us from seeing reality as a dynamic process of players and elements, which is, above all, extremely varied and which derives its significance from being so.'[20] In brief, the 'cultural' criteria that have replaced 'functional' criteria as the foundation of urban design are far less self-evident and unequivocal than is often believed. What exists is more of a large-scale confusion of tongues than a new consensus on the desired renewal of urban planning.

Arguments for the realization of 'cultural quality' in old harbor areas raise two questions: what is culture, and what is there of cultural importance in old harbor areas that can serve as a foundation for urban plans for these areas?

Countless definitions of 'culture' can be found. Two differing definitions are those of De Jong and the *Winkler Prins Encyclopedia*. De Jong describes culture as 'the collection of unexpressed presuppositions that accompany communication,'[21] while the definition in *Winkler Prins* reads: 'Culture is the aggregate of human achievements aimed at providing meaning and import.'[22] There is an essential difference between the two definitions. The first interpretation places the emphasis on the self-evident, perhaps even the unconscious, quality of culture and portrays culture as a static concept (presuppositions are not likely to change if they are never expressed). In the other definition, the accent is on active, deliberate, and purposeful acts. Defined as such, culture is a more dynamic concept, since deliberate and purposeful acts can be aimed at change.

These two differences in interpretation already indicate what a precarious undertaking it is to try to find a single, comprehensive, conclusive definition of the concept 'culture.' Both definitions are applicable: that which is deemed 'culture' and 'cultural' can change in the course of time; at the same time, moreover, a diversity of concepts on culture can exist side by side. There can be an official culture, which consists of the customs and ambitions of a social elite, as well as informal cultures, which – though not recognized by the elite as 'real culture' – can play an important part in giving meaning to the daily lives of large sections of the population.

It is not the intention of this narrative to depart from a preestablished definition of culture; on the contrary, the point is to look for and find that which is considered 'culture' and 'cultural' in the practice of spatial design.

## 2  The Modernity of the Port City: Shaping the Tension of Public Space

Harbor areas now dismissed as obsolete were built, for the most part, in a period that ushered in modern times. In the course of the nineteenth century – with the introduction of the steam engine, the advent of the Industrial Revolution and of new means of transportation such as steamboat and railroad, the rise of Enlightened thinking, the creation of new forms of government and, most importantly and at the heart of all the rest, the emergence of a modern economy based on trade – the phenomenon of the 'modern city' appeared. Cities razed their walls and filled in their canals, while industrialization and mass immigration radically breached former limitations affecting manufacturing, trade, and the size of the population.[23]

'Modern times' does not denote an unequivocal, historical continuum, but consists of a succession of various phases or periods that flow together smoothly in some cases and, in others, seem to begin and end in fits and starts.

According to economist Kondratieff's so-called 'long-wave theory,' the entire period encompassing the nineteenth and twentieth centuries can be divided into *the following five phases*:[24]

– 1782-1845: the *energy revolution*; new cities arise and economic functions are liberated.

– 1846-1892: the *infrastructural era*; expanded and developing urban structure is absorbed into an evolving regional and national urban system.

– 1893-1948: *increase in (auto)mobility*; along with the reinforcement and concentration of economic activities, the basis is laid for the formation of metropolitan districts.

– 1949-1998: *globalization and internationalization of industry* arrive on the scene, accompanied by the 'office era.'

– 1999-2048: an *increasingly interwoven quality; networks*, whose structures are constantly changing, become more and more important in the Information Age.

For the most part, transitions from one phase to another occur at the same time as do both processes of transformation in port cities and changes in relations between cities and their ports. The second phase, the infrastructural era, was the period in which transit ports originated. In the largely enclosed system of the premodern port city, the harbor was the final destination on the transportation route, and the port's infrastructure was organized within the enclosed character of the city. This system was replaced by a system of maximal openness, in which the port became a link in a long transportation chain and was provided, therefore, with a largely linear form of organization. The port was no longer laid out *in* the city, but *next to* the city.

In the first place, these developments demanded a redefinition of the relation between the network of public spaces in the existing city and new, large-scale infrastructure. A new appreciation of landscape played an important role in this matter; the transit port's new infrastructure was built in the previously unspoiled rural area outside the existing city, an act that in and of itself required a redefinition of the interrelationship of city, landscape, and infrastructure.

Although there was still a sharp distinction between city and countryside in the premodern period, an era in which port-related infrastructure belonged to the domain of the city, the nineteenth century produced the urbanized landscape.

The third period, referred to as an increase in (auto)mobility, goes hand in hand with the development of transit ports into industrial complexes. For many port cities, the disappearance of their function as depot for the port and the dominance of the transit function meant that the port provided the city with little added value. Incentives offered to processing companies encouraged the processing of goods passing through the port in transit, which resulted in

Organization of the port city.                    Cityscape of the port city.

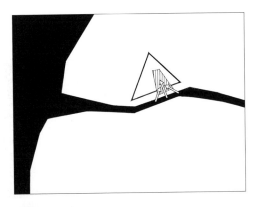

– Entrepôt port: port within an enclosed city. Goods are stored and traded in the city. Quay is also a public street. To the middle of the nineteenth century.

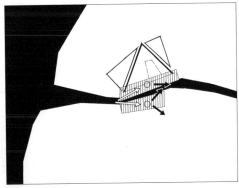

– Transit port: port alongside an open city. Flow of goods passes the city. Division of city and port has begun. From the end of the nineteenth century.

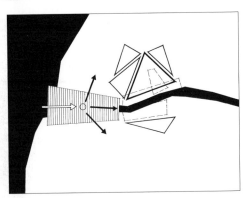

– Industrial port alongside a functional city, both as autonomous phenomena. Goods are processed in the port area. From the mid-twentieth century.

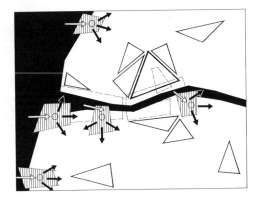

– Distribution port and network city. The port is rediscovered by the city as a part of the urban landscape; the city is rediscovered by the port as a potential nerve center for logistic organization and telecommunication.

Structure of the port city.

an extra economic advantage. Most new industrial complexes were built even farther away from the city. In many cases, a strong distinction – in terms of both policy and space – was made between the industrialized port landscape and the urban landscape.

During the fourth and fifth phases, there was increased interest in the roles played by hierarchy and by the division of tasks among port cities, which led to the development of larger ports into 'mainports' – or, in other words, into the most important ports serving large continental areas – from which goods could continue being distributed. The distribution port no longer has the linear character of the transit port, but consists of various specialized distribution hubs, which together form a network.

The city has lost its compact shape and its orientation toward the historical city center and has also taken on the appearance of a network, of which a great many components derive their quality largely from a specific association with the landscape. Neither city nor port has an unequivocal shape anymore; both are divided into specialized fragments which are spread out across the territory of the original landscape. Both port and city are entering a new relationship with each other and with the landscape: together they form an urban landscape.

This new development displays similarities to the situation in which cities in the nineteenth century found themselves: one of far-reaching developments with an unpredictable size and outcome. At the same time, areas now reappearing in the picture are the same as those that connected cities to new transportation networks in the nineteenth century: old harbor areas. Old harbor areas are assuming a strategic position as part of the new urban landscape, as a link leading to the realization of a new association between residential function and traffic function, between local network and global network.

These phases, which include various manifestations of nineteenth- and twen-tieth-century port cities, amazingly enough run parallel to changes taking place in the development of urban planning as a discipline. The birth of urban planning as a discipline and the evolution of plan development within urban planning, including plan development for a new type of transit port, took place, for the most part, in the second phase (second half of the nineteenth century). The emergence and dominance of modern, functionalist urban planning is mainly a phenomenon of the third phase (first half of the twentieth century), in which the development of industrialized port landscapes occurred. The fourth phase, in which distribution ports and urban networks appeared, is characterized by a transitional situation: the slow decline of functionalist urban planning and the search for new methods of plan development.

Typical of urban development in these three phases, in which it differs in essence from urban development prior to 1850, is the creation of a *field of tension* that explicitly comes to the fore in the development of harbor areas from the second half of the nineteenth century on: the disappearance of the quay as intermediary between international and local scales, and the development of the city – the port city in particular – as a permanent source of tension between two diverse spatial systems, which function on two extremely different scales.

Construction of large-scale harbor areas in the nineteenth century represented, in the extreme, the transformation of the city from an enclosed to a modern, open system. From time immemorial, the port has been the area in which the network of the city is confronted with the network of international transportation. Prior to the nineteenth century, this hub was controlled and dominated in many respects – for military and political reasons – by the city. With the elimination of the military necessity of a spatial boundary around the city and the simultaneous onset of the industrial and transportation revolutions, new nineteenth-century ports became areas consummately suited to connect the city to new, world-wide transportation networks. In many cases, these were locations that had been areas of fortification prior to the nineteenth century, areas meant to *protect* the city from the threat of the outside world. In the nineteenth century they were transformed into territories offering accommodations for modern transportation, areas now meant to *open* the city to the outside world.

Port areas became the meeting ground of extremely diverse networks; it was here that international shipping traffic came face to face with local urban networks.

For that matter, an age-old tradition already existed in 'premodern' port cities. The main function of quays in Dutch ports was the mooring, loading, and unloading of ocean-going ships that were, as such, part of a world-wide infrastructural network. But, at the same time, these quays were lined with housing and other urban facilities; used as urban traffic routes and promenades, Dutch quays were an inextricable part of the city's network of streets. The quay functioned as an *intermediary* system that blended together two different networks – international and local – which functioned on two extremely different levels of scale. This blending occurred within a situation that featured a trade-based economy under the rule of an elite group of city merchants. Although seventeenth-century elites in various port cities were quite diverse in structure and nature,[25] they had a number of common characteristics, including their complete immersion in the ins and outs of the city – whose main administrative functions were in their hands – and their control of most of the international trade to and from the city. The quay, as a blend of urban and international networks, was a direct spatial reflection of the blend of urban socioeconomic relations and international trade. The quays of most consequence in the shipping trade were, at the same time, the centers most vital to public city life and the places in which the most important institutions of urban administration, trade, and religion were located. This certainly applied to the principal ocean superpowers of the sixteenth and seventeenth centuries: Venice, with the Riva degli Schiavoni and, next to it, Plaza San Marco; Genoa, with the Piazza Caricamento; and Amsterdam, with the Damrak and, next to it, the Dam.

The emergence of the new trade-based economy and new transportation technology in the nineteenth century brought with it, however, a fundamental change in the significance of cities in their broader context.

Vlissingen, ca. 1900. Maintaining the existing interwoven nature of city and port is becoming more and more difficult owing to the increasing size of ships.

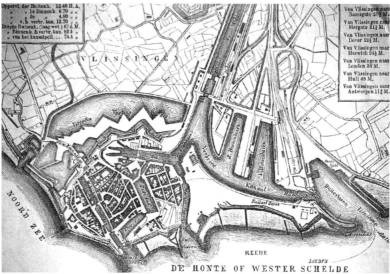

Vlissingen, the transformation of city fortifications into harbor works. Fragment, ca. 1870.

To begin with, the new transportation networks that emerged focused primarily on transporting raw materials and products from one new industrial center to another. This created a need for a new type of port, which would no longer function as a *center* of international trade but, for the most part, as a *transshipment site* within a transportation chain. The traditional blending of international infrastructure and urban fabric no longer had a place within this framework. The rapidly growing dimensions of modern steamships, desirable connections to railroad yards, and the altered nature of port activities (from storing and trading goods to transshipping and forwarding them as fast as possible) were new conditions that required a new type of port.

But the changing economic context of cities implied even more: namely, the

Canaletto, *Venice: Riva degli Schiavioni,* eighteenth century.

Anonymous, 1797. Amsterdam: the Damrak and the Dam, featuring City Hall, the Weighhouse and, in the foreground, the fish market.

disappearance of close ties between a city's established merchant elite and the new transportation-based economy. This, too, made a continuation of the traditional blend of city and port into an anachronism.

Following the emergence of the new transportation-based economy, the relation between the large-scale, international traffic infrastructure and the urban network assumed other, fundamentally different forms. This does not alter the fact that new urban planning concepts pertaining to the relation between city and port were given serious thought. This experimentation was not entirely hit-and-miss; the organization and designing of large, nineteenth-century spatial transformations was, for the most part, the work of new agencies established at this time: municipal departments in charge of public works, which organized and supervised plan development for these transformations. The development of new relations between large-scale transportation networks and local networks was an important objective of these new departments. Originally, the two most important aspects of the work done by these departments were: the creation of a city map on which networks at various levels of scale were recorded, and the design and organization of either the networks themselves or public space. In the course of time and to one degree or another, two tasks were added to those mentioned: the regulation of building practices and the supervision of the spatial-functional organization of the city.[26]

### PUBLIC SPACE AS SPACE FOR THE CITY'S PUBLIC REALM

The emergence of a field of tension among various spatial systems pertains not only to port areas; it is a general characteristic of the modern city and one that is connected to the new status of public space.

In the nineteenth century, the strict distinction between public and private was the most important formal and juridical principle underlying the new liberal and republican forms of government that originated during this period.

The distinction between public and private was also the primary principle of the practice of modern urban planning; the most important tasks of municipal departments of public works were to design, realize, and supervise exclusively public space, and to establish regulations and conditions to be applied to that part of the private domain (the use of land owned by private parties) considered to be in the public interest.

Which function did the new public space of modern times fulfill? In *Parade der passanten*, Jan Oosterman identifies five different historical manifestations of the public realm, each of which was highly influential during a certain historical period in urban society: public space as sacred space, as secure space, as democratic space, as commercial space, and as heterogeneous traffic space.[27] The new dimension of modern times, however, allowed public space to fulfill all these various functions simultaneously: new public space was the place where business could be transacted while the latest news was being discussed, where public administration buildings were located alongside cultural facilities, while traffic flowed through on the way to every conceivable destination.

It was precisely this universal character of modern public space that formed the condition for the many different meanings and types of use of public space.

The new significance of public space and the flourishing of a new kind of urban life was accompanied by various evaluative approaches to this public realm, varying from its cultivation and glorification to fear and vilification. The nineteenth-century French poet Charles Baudelaire is the personification of the cultivation of modern public urban life. Walter Benjamin finds in Baudelaire the prototype of the city dweller who sees the new urban lifestyle of modern times as a fascinating experience, as a source of the permanent euphoria to which he surrenders himself completely in Paris, the 'capital of the nineteenth century.'[28]

Benjamin describes the new public space of Parisian boulevards as a space where the traditional was confronted with the new and where freedom made it possible to attribute all sorts of meanings to that which was seen on the boulevard. As an illustration, he presents the figures of the *flâneur* and the ragpicker, personifications of the protest against unequivocal meanings ascribed to public space. While the boulevard was commended by the Parisian bourgeoisie for allowing 'fast' traffic (horse-and-buggy in those days) to flow unimpeded, *flâneurs* demonstrated their opposition to the dominance of speed by strolling leisurely along, sometimes conspicuously emphasizing their point by parading a turtle on a leash. And as a contrast to the cultivation of display windows by the new shops and department stores lining the boulevards, this 'showcase of modern material capitalism,' Benjamin offers the ragpicker, a person totally uninterested in the merchandise on display and occupied only with rags and rubbish left on the street. These rags, of no value whatever to others, are *signs* to the ragpicker; they are significant because they hold references for him, vestiges; they tell, or at any rate evoke, a story.

Benjamin considers these differences – the diversity in the use and interpretation of public space – to be the essential characteristic of the new public realm of the modern city.

But the emergence of this modern public realm introduced, at the same time, a need for new forms of seclusion, which must now be organized in the private sphere. The elimination of the physical seclusion offered by the walled city was compensated by the creation of the new seclusion of bourgeois privacy, which grew in importance in the nineteenth century as a 'safe haven,' 'a refuge for demoralized individuality, threatened on all sides and joggled black-and-blue in the overfull streets of the city.'[29]

From the very beginning, however, this new public realm was also burdened by the fear of potential dangers and uncertainties inherent in the realm itself. Learning to deal with the public realm, an unavoidable task for modern society, has once more become the subject of debate in the second half of the twentieth century, and its reappearance has been prompted in part by American authors such as Hannah Arendt, Marshall Berman, and Richard Sennett.

In the 1950s philosopher Hannah Arendt set the tone for a debate on the necessity of the public realm as a basis for an open, democratic society, a debate that also included the necessity for learning to deal with the public realm. Arendt sees the essence of the public domain as an opportunity offering a maximum of different experiences and as a chance to view the world from as many perspectives as possible.[30] The survival of the public domain as such assumes that citizens who move in this domain remain open at all times to new experiences and impressions and, in principle, exclude no one from entering and using public space. It means accepting the possibility that everything could change tomorrow because, as Marshall Berman puts it in his wonderful book on the rise of modern times and modernism, 'all that is solid melts into air.'[31]

Suddenly age-old geographical, ethnic, national, religious, and class relations were broken down and became subject to constant change: a permanent undermining of existing identities.

'Being modern' presupposes a willingness to remove oneself from an existing context, the willingness to relinquish a past and an identity. The exile, the foreigner, and the immigrant are figures presented by Arendt and Sennett as representatives par excellence of the new, modern culture: persons who were forced to leave their homelands, or who left voluntarily, and are ready to begin a new life under entirely new conditions.[32]

It is precisely this acceptance of disengagement and permanent change, in which nothing seems certain anymore, that is the most difficult part of 'being modern'; from this well springs fear of the public realm.

Arendt accentuates the act of learning to deal with the public realm, which she sees as the political task of every citizen living in a democratic society. Authors such as Berman and Sennett, whose publications tread in the footprints made by Arendt's shoes, also emphasize the necessity of learning to deal with modernity and the public realm, but they focus on something else at the same time: namely, the inability of the public realm to function by the grace of the savoir-vivre of free citizens,[33] and the simultaneous need for *space* in which the public realm can exist among optimal conditions and which is recognized as 'public space' – space in which the exile and the foreigner may feel equal to others around them and in which no one really notices, or even cares, whether someone is an autochthonous resident or a chance passer-by.[34]

## CONTRADICTORY MEANINGS: CULTIVATION AND MARGINALIZATION OF THE MODERN PORT CITY

Originally, new nineteenth-century port areas formed outstanding examples of the new public space, of contradictory experiences and meanings evoked by the modern city. These cities became transshipment stations serving a rapidly growing international network of passenger and freight transportation. Harbor districts became the sites of an unprecedented blend of activities, people, and functions: districts housing immigrants and seamen were located right next to the spectacle of ocean liners and bumboats arriving and departing, and offered a range of new experiences, bars and cafés, exotic eating houses, dance halls, and bordellos.

The nineteenth century and the beginning of the twentieth century saw a steady cultivation of new harbor areas, as well as the denigration of such areas and the resulting disdain.

The concept of the port as a large expanse of water in the city but directly connected to the sea, and the international character of large port cities – filled with sailors on liberty, new immigrants, emigrants passing through, as well as ships, goods, and products from distant lands – became fashionable topics of educational and, at the same time, sensational discussions taking place among the bourgeoisie. In the course of the nineteenth century, the idea of the renaissance in which the city represented civilization, culture, and safety; and the countryside

George Morren, 1926. Dance hall in a harbor district in Antwerp.

S. Hugill. Sailors' districts in (left) New Orleans and (right) New York.

ill-breeding and danger; gradually vanished. With urban density on the rise and cities becoming increasingly industrialized, and with the miserable living conditions of the new, large urban proletariat and the disappearance, as a result of rapid urban expansion beyond city walls, of rural areas surrounding cities, the idea experienced a complete reversal. The idea of nature as a source of danger and darkness was replaced by the idea of nature as a source of health and well-being. And *water* in particular – especially the ocean – took on an important role in this change in the thinking of Western civilization. Water in nature, in the form of natural springs, was one of the most important aspects of the new nineteenth-century health craze,[35] in which the ocean also played a special part. French historian Alain Corbin describes how at the end of the eighteenth century the idea of the ocean as a source of danger, noxious vapors, monsters, and evil spirits began to change into an idea of the ocean as a wholesome element, and how the vastness of the ocean was no longer viewed as something frightening or threatening, but as challenging and as a majestic natural element, invulnerable to urbanization.[36] This notion resulted in renewed appreciation for port and waterfront, the visible representatives of the ocean in the city and an ideal symbiosis of city and landscape. The manifest presence of rivers, estuaries, bays, and their unspoiled quality – that is, their lack of development – along with their vastness, and their connections to immense networks of water, all made the waterfront into one of the few possibilities left for portraying any direct relation at all between the city and larger structures found in nature.

Since then, this theme of the waterfront as an element within which city and landscape can confront each other or, on the other hand, can be brought together in harmony has been a leitmotif throughout the history of modern, nineteenth- and twentieth-century urban planning: weaving its way through romantic nineteenth-century sidewalk cafés, plantations, and waterside promenades; Le Corbusier's modernist visions for Algiers, Buenos Aires, and Rio de Janeiro; Rotterdam's 'Window to the River,' included in the city's postwar reconstruction plan; and still visible in the current focus on the waterfront as an attractive urban milieu par excellence.

In the nineteenth century, visiting a port city meant becoming acquainted with a microcosm that seemed to include all nationalities, cultures, and ethnic groups; a visit to a port city was an introduction to the world. Ports such as London, Amsterdam, and Marseilles became popular destinations for ordinary people as well as for the intelligentsia, who viewed and studied port areas as 'living' museums of cultural anthropology.[37] But it was the wonder of technology, which in the maritime world of shipping, harbor installations, and bridges was so manifestly apparent, that made ports into an unprecedented spectacle. Port cities became the shimmering theaters of the modern world. The cities themselves took full advantage of the growing popularity of the harbor world. Distinctive facilities were created to make a visit to the port as complete and spectacular as possible, such as train and underground railway lines through port areas of London and Liverpool; meant originally for ships' passengers and dockworkers, these lines were soon being used as special attractions to allow the traveler to become acquainted with the marvel of the modern port in comfort. In Barcelona, the same idea led in 1929 to the construction of a cable-car system above the port. In Genoa and Antwerp special pedestrian terraces were built along quays where goods were loaded and unloaded; from this perspective, strollers had a good view of shipping activities. If Paris had had a real port in the nineteenth century, it would certainly have been one of Baudelaire's favorite places.[38]

On the other hand, and occurring at about the same time as this cultivation of the modern port, life in harbor areas became the subject of moral condemnation and indignation. In the nineteenth century large port cities saw not only their ports rapidly growing in size, but also the urban population. Attracted by the prospect of work and prosperity, thousands of farmers and other agricultural workers flocked to the cities. The lack of any kind of collectivity among the brand-new city residents, or of any common social and cultural codes, was reinforced in port cities

Liverpool Overhead Railway, late nineteenth century.

Barcelona, cable-car system above the port.

by the continuous, chaotic influences of the port: in the form of port activities, characterized by irregularity and uncertainty, and dictated by the whims of the shipping industry; as well as in the form of seamen and immigrants, who were unfamiliar with local regulations and customs. Charles Dickens is one of the first, and surely one of the most famous, authors to describe London's new harbor neighborhoods not as an astonishing microcosm but as a desolate, immoral, and impoverished world in which stench, licentiousness, and crime reigned, rather than exotic tableaux and technical wonders. This perception of the modern port as a dangerous factor able to seriously undermine city life became more and more dominant in the course of the nineteenth and twentieth centuries.

These opposing concepts attached to nineteenth-century ports – varying from fascinating microcosm to frightening hotbed of marginality – gave expression to the field of tension that existed between the two levels of scale confronting the nineteenth-century port city.

The paradox of both cultivating and condemning the port city reached its peak in the twentieth century. Just as Paris was the paradigm of the modern, cultivated city of nineteenth-century industrial capitalism, in the twentieth century the city of Tangier became the paradigm of the cultivated port city. In the course of the nineteenth century, the Western world of diplomats and prominent merchants

discovered Tangier and found it to be an attractive and strategic location. The city was one of the few spots on the African continent that combined advantages such as a mild climate and close proximity to Europe, while also fulfilling the role of an international hub of trade and shipping routes. From 1923 to 1956 the city (which covers an area of 380 square kilometers, including immediate surroundings) was declared an international zone and was governed by an international supervisory board, in which Morocco and eight European countries were represented.[39] Tangier became a free port, and virtually everything was tolerated there: anyone, regardless of his or her history, could set up shop in the city, and anyone could practice any type of activity without a license, diploma, or certificate of any kind. The only thing forbidden, and thus supervised by the police force, was the perpetration of bodily or material harm. Hence Tangier became a meeting place for economic adventurers, political refugees, criminals, and smugglers.

This Tangier appealed to the imaginations of artists and intellectuals who found the political climate in their own countries too oppressive. In his *Journal du voleur*, Jean Genet, the *enfant terrible* of French literature, described his stays in cities such as Antwerp, Barcelona, and Gibraltar. He saw the port city as the sultry spot in which one may give free rein to all those hopes and desires that are reprehensible according to society's prevailing rules and codes. Living there among whores, pimps, rogues, and pickpockets, he was able to gratify his deepest desires in this world. The ultimate objective of his wanderings, however, was Tangier, the 'queen of port cities.'[40]

American writer and composer Paul Bowles, whose literary and musical work is dominated completely by confrontations between traditional cultures and the emergence of modern Western culture, found the ideal exponent of such confrontations in Tangier and, from the late 1940s on, spent the rest of his life there.[41]

And Dutch author and physician J. Slauerhoff, constantly in search of an escape from the narrow-mindedness of 'Cheese Country,' settled down for awhile in Tangier in the 1930s. He described the city as the 'pearl of the East' and: 'A place in which various undertones of East and West come together, located on one of the greatest shipping routes of modern world traffic, accommodating all peoples and yet a place with its own character, this is Tangier.'[42]

Tangier is number one on the hit parade of port cities with mythical reputations, a fact that makes the city – other than a theme in reputable literature – the scene of the action in countless adventure movies, boys' books, and comic strips.

VARIOUS TYPES OF PUBLIC SPACE: SOCIALIZED AND
TECHNOCRATIZED PUBLIC SPACE

In the course of the twentieth century, the perception of the modern port as a factor that could seriously undermine urban life became more and more dominant in most port cities, and formed not only the basis for a social policy aimed at those living in harbor districts, but also a foundation for urban plans attempting either to isolate harbor areas or to eliminate them from the urban context. In part, this perception was supported by practical, economic reasons. But these reasons are not a satisfactory explanation for the radical division that took place in the twentieth century between diverse types of public space. Ideological considerations played a vital role in this process as well.

This development can be traced to the introduction of functionalist urban planning and to the socialist body of thought that was so closely related to it. In the socialist movement, which focused on bringing an end to the unequal distribution of wealth and power, and on organizing various forms of 'collective wealth,' these efforts were translated into a policy that aspired to the *socialization* (or *collectivization*) of the private as well as the public domain.

In comparing ancient Greek society to modern Western society, Hannah Arendt explains that a typical aspect of modern society is the existence of another important domain in addition to those referred to as public and private: namely, the social or collective domain. The social domain forms the transition area between the wholly open nature of the public domain and the strictly enclosed nature of the private domain, and it is based on the principle of 'Like attracts like.'[43] The social domain prevents the individual – as he steps out of his front door, for example – from being swept along by the maelstrom of modernity. In comparison with the uncertainty of modern life, the social domain offers a number of certitudes which enable a person surrounded by the modern masses to carry on. The social domain can assume various forms: family, neighborhood, cultural society, private school, and so forth.

Originally, stark differences dominated the ways in which social domains were organized in various countries. In North America's immigrant society, from the very beginning one's country of origin played a vital role in the formation of social groups and social domains; even in the nineteenth century, big cities like New York and Chicago were geographically divided into clearly defined groups of Jews, Germans, Russians, Chinese, Italians, Irish, and others. In England it was the class difference in particular that would play a dominant role far into the twentieth century, a situation that led to a curious phenomenon in public bars, which had a separate section for each social class.

In the Netherlands, the social domain is directly related to the compartmentalization along sociopolitical-denominational lines. Since the end of the nineteenth century, each sociopolitical group and religious denomination (Roman Catholic, two branches of Dutch Reformed, Socialist, and Liberal) has been attempting to create its own social domain. Because of the major role played by Christian denominations, a term sometimes heard is the 'parochial' domain.[44] Separate schools of architecture represented the architectonic and urban design of these social domains; each school was associated with a specific group or denomination.[45]

The essence of the social domain is that it is based on an individual's freedom of choice and that it inevitably includes an element of discrimination. In and of itself, the latter does not have to be a bad thing, as long as there remains a clearly identifiable public domain in which no form of arbitrariness or discrimination exists. A fundamental premise is that the social domain as a whole is the responsibility of social groups, each of which forms its social domain on its own initiative and on the basis of the voluntary nature that lends form to the social domain, while the government (national or local authorities) is responsible for strictly public space.

It is no coincidence that Hannah Arendt's book appeared in 1958. In nearly every Western democratic country, the 1950s was a period in which the government began interfering with the social domain more and more often. In writing this book, Arendt protested vehemently against this development; government intervention into the social domain is, principally, not only a question of undesired interference, but also – and this is the target of Arendt's strongest warning – a precursor of the neglect of, and the eventual loss of, the genuine public domain. Mixing the public domain together with the social domain will produce a public domain that no longer enables citizens to see the 'simultaneous presence of innumerable perspectives and aspects,'[46] but that creates a domain in which the world can be seen from one, or from a limited number, of perspectives.

This is what happened as Western welfare states evolved in the course of the twentieth century, countries in which primarily Social-Democratic ideas on the socialization of society began to play a major role. The public domain was no longer considered a domain available to free citizens, but was seen increasingly as a means by which the population could be urged to adopt a desired sociocultural pattern of thinking and behaving.[47] And the public domain was not the sole target; the private domain was also subjected to drastic government intervention and made to become a part of the social domain.

In the twentieth century the development of the public domain was governed

CITY AND PORT

by ideas on planning, which were emerging in all sectors of Western European and North American society. These ideas on the necessity for, and the possibility of, economic and social planning formed the basis of Social-Democratic politics in Western Europe and of President Roosevelt's New Deal.[48] In the 1930s America's New Deal became an experimental garden and the model for an economic and social order to serve the postwar Western world, an order also referred to as the 'Social-Democratic consensus' and based on three points of departure: social security, full employment, and a mixed economy.[49]

Politicians, economists, and 'captains of industry' from virtually every Western democracy in the postwar period were able to find one another in this arrangement. Social security in this arrangement was more than a number of new systems of social insurance and the like; the term also covered a comprehensive cultural and educational policy aimed at establishing a new system of norms and values to be applied to the organization of society. Backed by this political offensive, governments launched large-scale interventions into matters previously belonging exclusively to the realm of the social and private domains.[50]

In the Netherlands, this process greatly affected the areas of public housing and urban planning, among others. A large number of studies and publications have already been devoted to elements found in the Social-Democratic socialization policy, such as the regulation and standardization of floor plans for housing, the institutionalization of public housing, and the deployment of urban planning concepts within the scope of 'community development.'[51]

During the postwar decades, the design of new residential districts benefited from the highly interwoven quality of urban planning and the whole system of establishing standards, issuing regulations, and subsidizing public housing; while in the area of designing the city as a whole, and city centers in particular, spatial form played no significant role whatsoever anymore.[52]

Large-scale government intervention into the private domain of housing, and the strong accent on public space surrounding this housing as a continuation of the social domain of domestic atmosphere (often called 'housing environment' rather than 'public space') has led to a lack of clarity with regard to the importance of a well-defined distinction between private and public domains, as well as to the importance of providing a well-functioning public domain.

In the twentieth century a distinction has been drawn between a socialized public domain and a purely functional public domain, a distinction in which the design of the socialized part of the public domain is seen as a task for urban planning, and in which the design of the functional part – or 'technocratized public space' – is left to civil engineers.

The division of social and technocratized public space coincides, to a large extent, with the distinction between local spatial networks in new residential districts and large-scale interlocal networks, such as highways, modern port complexes, and airports. Nineteenth-century harbor quays and boulevards still formed integrated systems (belonging to both international and local networks) that were significant on various levels of scale and very important as public space precisely because of their versatility. In modern urban planning, efforts to combine various scales have largely disappeared.

The 'socialized' public space of the Bijlmermeer. Drawing in a municipal information brochure on the Bijlmermeer as 'city of the future,' 1965.

The 'technocratized' public space of the highway network.

To be sure, these developments did not occur without a struggle. From the 1930s to the 1960s, countless design proposals were made for new architectonic and urban planning typologies capable of creating a connection between modern housing types and modern infrastructure. A few of the more famous are Le Corbusier's designs for Algiers, produced in the 1930s, in which housing and highway were integrated into one structure; proposals made by Bakema in the 1950s for Rotterdam's Alexander Polder, which included 'mammoth apartment buildings' linked to the highway network; and proposals by the Smithsons for a new intermingling of highway- and pedestrian-related infrastructure in the Golden Lane Project for London. Not to mention Louis Kahn's proposals for Philadelphia, in which he literally used the traditional infrastructure of waterways and harbors as a metaphor for a new typological coupling of city and infrastructure in the form of large apartment buildings with parking garages.

Nonetheless, nearly all these proposals remained, for the most part, theoret-

Algiers, Plan 'Obus,'
Le Corbusier, 1934.

Philadelphia. Plan for
housing with parking
garages: design by Louis
Kahn, 1958.

Expressways are like **RIVERS**
These **RIVERS** frame the area to be served
**RIVERS** have **HARBORS**
**HARBORS** are the municipal parking towers
from the **HARBORS** branch a system of **CANALS** that serve the interior
the **CANALS** are the go streets
from the **CANALS** branch cul-de-sac **DOCKS**
the **DOCKS** serve as entrance
halls to the buildings

ical concepts and produced a mere handful of incidental prototypes of a new
building typology.

Experiments with the introduction of new typological concepts also occurred
in the area of the infrastructure of public space itself; examples are parkways[53] in
the United States, England, and the Netherlands.

In the decades following World War II, however, the design of large-scale infrastructural elements, as well as of the way in which these elements relate to the city,
ultimately became the responsibility of disciplines other than urban planning. On
the one hand, this situation was the result of the privatization and institutionalization of those government bureaucracies specializing in the design and realization of
large-scale infrastructure; on the other hand, it could also be blamed on vanishing
efforts by urban planning itself to play an active part in infrastructural design.

The distinction between the social-public domain and the technocratized public space of large-scale infrastructure was accompanied by a division in plans for the twentieth-century city: a division between the organization and design of the city. One side of the equation concerns the development of large-scale traffic and transportation networks, which determine the structure of the city as a whole: harbors, waterways, roads, and railroad lines. Here the word 'structure' is used to indicate the system of elements that determines the composition of the urban form as a whole. For a long time, urban planning had no grip on such structures as a whole (and thus no grip on the urban form as a whole), or on the design of their individual parts (port, highway, and so forth).

Urban planning became more and more limited to those parts of the city that belonged to the social domain. One of the more dramatic examples of this restriction is the 1960s design of the Bijlmermeer, intended as a paragon of modern urban planning. The radical division realized here consists of a social domain, on the one hand, which includes housing combined with a ground-level area intended for pedestrians and cyclists, and, on the other hand, the traffic infrastructure, a totally autonomous system that provides access to the apartment buildings. At that time, the degree of precision with which urban planners applied themselves to the design of the social domain was equaled by the degree to which they distanced themselves from detailed plans for the traffic infrastructure, floating here above the green world at ground level like an alien element. The autonomy of the traffic infrastructure is, of all things, the element recognized in recent years as one of the essential mistakes made in the urban planning organization of the Bijlmermeer.[54]

In the process of a radical division of networks at various levels of scale in the twentieth-century city, nineteenth-century harbor areas remained an incongruity, a relic from a period in which such a division was far less apparent.

In the twentieth century, the significance of water for the composition of the urban plan became a subject of conflicting opinions. One side demanded the use of water for the purpose of infrastructure, which was deemed incompatible with social efforts to achieve community development. The other side promoted the cultivation of water as a territorial characteristic of the landscape, which made water the consummate contribution to the reinforcement of a culture of community development.

From the beginning of the 1980s, however, the Social-Democratic consensus began to diminish and was eventually superseded by neoclassic ideas on the controlling effect of the free market, and on the necessity for the privatization and deregulation of sites exposed to a great deal of government intervention. The success of the new free-market ideology appeared immediately and unexpectedly after a final, intense revival of the Social-Democratic consensus in the 1970s: in the United States, Carter's Democratic administration was succeeded by that of the Republican Reagan; in England the Conservatives, under Thatcher's leadership, assumed the power from Labour; and in the Netherlands, following Den Uyl's Social-Democratic administration, a long, denominational-Liberal period of government, headed by Lubbers, began its reign. Conditions were different only in Spain; it would not be until 1976, the year of Franco's death, that something like a Social-Democratic consensus emerged. From the very beginning, however, it differed in character from that found in the United States and in Northern Europe.

For larger port cities, most of which – as old bulwarks of Labour – were still governed by Social-Democratic administrations during the 1980s, the new free-market ideology meant new political and economic conditions that required a certain precognition. At the level of national government, the consensus on the necessity of intervening into the social domain no longer existed in the 1980s, a change expressed in the demolition of collective facilities. Government intervention into public housing declined rapidly in the '80s in the Netherlands, England, and the United States.

Therefore, while public and social domains were closely interwoven within the design culture of urban planning in preceding decades, from the 1980s on, the social domain has no longer been an obvious area of government intervention. The questions are: What does this mean for the public domain and for urban planning concepts aimed at the design of the public domain? Has a public domain even existed since the 1980s, and if it has, what does it look like, and how should it be designed? And within this continuing evolution, what significance does water have for the design of the city plan?

3    # On to the Twenty-First Century: Disappearance or Renewal of Public Space?

Changes in dominant political ideologies are an important, but not the only, condition that has confronted urban communities and urban planners since the 1980s. These changes are accompanied by, and also help to express, a number of far-reaching processes in technology, economy, and social organization which have been around much longer and which have a profound effect on the position and spatial structure of cities, and most certainly on the position and structure of port cities.

Which processes in today's urban society play a role in these developments, and what is the significance of these processes for old harbor areas?

## METROPOLIZATION AND URBAN TRANSFORMATION

When we discuss various sorts of infrastructure and wonder if the mutual integration of these various sorts is still possible and desirable, a bit of insight into the nature of modern infrastructure is advisable. This is an area subject to rather a lot of change.

The departure of the shipping industry from old harbor areas is related not only to the ever-rising increase in scale in the twentieth century; even more important is the port city's gradual assumption, in the postwar era, of a completely new position with regard to international networks. After the port city was transformed from depot to transit port in the second half of the twentieth century, it then experienced a transformation from transit to distribution port. This change was due, first and foremost, to economic and technological developments on a global scale. Thanks specifically to the emergence of new technologies in electronics and telecommunication, a new type of economic order has evolved, which is organized at the global level and which includes new financial and industrial centers. In the 1980s, both in the Netherlands and abroad, an extensive series of publications appeared in which this development was described in detail and analyzed.[55]

The reorganization of economic networks at the global level manifested itself in the form of the withdrawal of industrial corporations from traditional industrial centers, a shifting of the center of world economy in the direction of countries surrounding the Pacific Ocean, the emergence in Europe and North America of new centers for the advanced manufacture of high-quality technological products, and the concentration of financial transactions in a limited number of metropolises. This process was accompanied by the suburbanization of open space outside the cities, space to accommodate the urban middle classes as well as new centers of facilities.

These developments, which occurred at various levels, resulted in a simultaneous increase *and* decrease in scale.

## AN INCREASE IN SCALE AND 'TECHNOLOGIZATION'

To begin with, those formulating a theory on the consequences of these processes focused on the *increase* in scale. From the 1960s on, they realized that the spatial-functional organization of coherent urban systems was no longer confined to that part of the city defined by its official boundaries, but that it had spread out over a much larger area.

In the early 1960s American geographer Jean Gottmann predicted that in the Post-Industrial Age, with the decline of the relative importance of the city as a place of production, the significance of the city as a marketplace and as a hub of networks on various physical levels of scale would begin to increase once more.[56] The interesting part of Gottmann's analysis is that he looks at the transition from the Industrial to the Post-Industrial Age not so much as the start of an entirely new period, in which the city takes on a new meaning, but rather as the end of a historical intermission. According to Gottmann, the Industrial Age is a deviant chapter in the history of Western society; following the 'conclusion' of this chapter, the leitmotif carrying the original meaning of the city can be reintroduced.

The reassessment of the city's function as a hub goes hand in hand with a reassessment of the concept of *complexity*, a characteristic of every situation in which a market exists: that is, in which the freedom to exchange goods, services, and ideas is present, as well as the freedom of supply and demand. In the practice

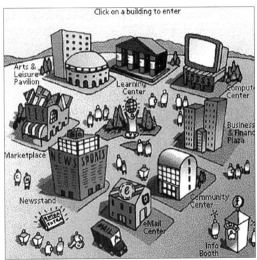

The influence of modern technology on the perception of the city, according to Mitchell. Left: Rome in an eighteenth-century drawing by Nolli. Right: Late twentieth-century e.World: design by Apple-Macintosh.

of design and plan development, this reassessment has led to various approaches that offer new conditions for an urban complexity.

This complexity no longer reveals itself, however, exclusively at the level of the 'classic' city. In discussing the development of the American East Coast, Gottmann alleges that the area is no longer a number of individual cities within an open landscape, but rather a more and more diffuse form of a modern metropolis, or perhaps even a 'megalopolis.' The city's renewed function as marketplace and hub can no longer be as clearly and unequivocally identified with concrete geographical places as once was the case with the market square and the harbor quay.

This proposition is underlined by Melvin Webber, who studied the issue during the same period as Gottmann, and who went even farther in his thinking. According to Webber, the city and the 'urban realm' are no longer tied to a certain spot but consist of a combination of diverse activities, which are, theoretically, 'footloose' and, thanks to modern technologies of transportation and communication, still within arm's reach at all times. This urban realm has assumed the character of a 'nonplace urban realm,'[57] which should convince urban and physical planners to free themselves from 'the obsession of placeness.'[58]

This argument has surfaced again and again in the 1980s and '90s, supplemented with the proposition that the 'technologization' of society[59] has caused traditional elements of the public domain to lose their significance. To be specific, the public street, as well as public facilities such as schools, museums, and theaters, have increasingly lost their significance, because their roles have been taken over by new digital networks, by the introduction of the 'electronic highway' into the home, and by the large-scale use of new methods of transportation, such as the airplane and the high-speed train. Physical distance is becoming less and less important and is being replaced by time-related distance; and in addition to genuine reality, virtual reality is assuming an increasingly more important place in everyday life.[60]

In short, in the era of cyberspace the necessity to step outside the door has become almost nonexistent (work, shopping, social intercourse – everything can be done on the digital highway), while the opportunity now exists to reach any destination in the world within the space of twenty-four hours.

According to Mitchell, the emergence of the electronic highway will have the same kind of revolutionary consequences for the process of urbanization as did the building of boulevards in the nineteenth century and of highway networks in the twentieth century.[61]

The big question is, however, whether technological innovations are a *replacement* for, or an *addition* to, the existing, 'traditional,' public domain.

### A DECREASE IN SCALE: THE REARRANGEMENT OF CULTURAL, SOCIAL, AND ECONOMIC LIFE

Remarkably, opposing the arguments of Webber and others are renewed pleas for the *design* of the urban realm, pleas that have led to a renaissance of an 'obsession of placeness'; in other words, an increasing amount of attention is being given to the new significance of the individual components that make up new metropolitan regions.

Does this imply that the public domain is going through an active process of rehabilitation after all? We can only wait and see. Forming the basis of the new 'obsession of placeness' are cultural, social, and economic developments.

### 'CULTURALIZATION' OF THE CITY

Processes accompanying an increase in scale have led, as far as traditional city centers are concerned, to the disappearance of the centrality of these centers. Or, as a 1980s study of the development of city centers in the United States and Europe put it: 'Central Business District activities, in short, are no longer either Central or Business.'[62] The traditional function of city centers as essential concentrations of activity and facilities has shifted, or is shifting, to other places within metropolitan regions, where far better market conditions are found with regard to land prices, as well as to accessibility and a broad customer base.

As a counterbalance to offset this development, attempts are being made to develop traditional city centers as centers of a 'culturalized' urbanism by making room and creating initiatives for cultural, touristic, and recreational activities: museums, galleries, theaters, festivals, and a commercial environment conducive to 'fun shopping.' The target group at which this development of renewed city centers is aimed is the new middle classes, the backbone of a new 'postmodern lifestyle' and a new metropolitan elite for whom life in the city is to be an ongoing, fascinating experience.[63] The revival of a genuine culture of *flâneurs* and sidewalk cafés in the 1980s and '90s,[64] and of phenomena like the 'festivalization of the city'[65] and 'fun shopping,' all point to an intensified use of inner cities and to a mass revaluation of what may be called the 'urban experience.'

Developing the conditions needed for this 'culturalized urbanism' is more than just an important way to make new residents feel at home in the city; it also helps to create an attractive climate for new businesses, which is, in turn, a step toward restoring the centrality of city centers.[66]

Since the 1980s, emphasis on the city as a center of culture has become an inextricable part of urban renewal strategies whose aim is to provide the city with a new look and a place on the new map of international networks composed of 'Global Cities' and 'Informational Cities.'[67] This emphasis focuses on 'the city as a work of art' – the idea that the spatial appearance of the city itself can be seen as a culturally interesting phenomenon – as well as on 'the city as a cultural capital' – the idea that a city can offer a range of facilities, including art, sports, recreation, and tourism. This renewed accent on the cultural role of the city is invariably tied to an accent on the specific, unique character of this cultural role, and both are used for the express purpose of presenting the city in comparison with other cities: in reports on and analyses of urban renewal, the words often used to sum it all up are 'the specific *cultural identity* of the city.'

Within this framework, attention focused on the *'quality of public space'* in the 1980s and '90s has become an important political issue, which has led to a marked increase in the amount of attention paid to the design and organization of public areas in inner cities. The question, however, is whether a true renewal of public areas – one that reinforces and renews public life – is taking place, or whether this renewal is nothing more than a 'beautification' meant to reinforce the city's *corporate identity*. The frequently artificial character of organized activities in new public areas and the influence of commerce on this trend have led to the development being referred to in the United States as 'variations on a theme park.'[68]

What these terms implicate, in essence, is that the current culturalization trend will lead to a privatization of urban activities and large sections of the urban territory and, ultimately, to the end of public space as such. This will have been caused not only by the commercial exploitation of the culturalization trend, but also by the way in which this trend is being supported and promoted by local authorities. New cultural festivals and the new design of public space will be focused on certain target groups that the city finds desirable and will exclude other groups. If this is true, little indeed remains of the public character of public space. The question, however, is whether it *is* true and, specifically, whether it is true at all times and in all places, or whether it is an inevitable process of modern times.

At the same time, cities in the '70s and '80s were confronted with other socioeconomic and sociocultural processes: the disappearance of industrial activities and changes in the job market have led to high unemployment rates among the urban working population, and especially among semiskilled and unskilled laborers, while decolonization and migration have created an urban population augmented by new groups from different ethnic and cultural backgrounds.

Thus far-reaching economic and physical changes in urban areas are accompanied by social and cultural changes, and as a result, the big city is being transformed, at an accelerating pace, into a domain accommodating various groups of city dwellers: besides those who have lived there since the postwar era and have never moved to the suburbs, 'new urbanites' are showing a renewed interest in the city, and migrants are moving there as well.[69]

The social effects of a new urban policy that places a strong emphasis on attracting new activities as part of a plan to develop an 'informational city' are already a subject of extensive research and discussion. Such studies point out – and warn against – an increasing polarity of 'metropolitans' and 'locals' within various population groups.[70]

Current American literature features urban planning projects that function mainly as autonomous enclaves that have no impact on everyday urban life. On the contrary, the 'militarization of urban space' implies a safeguarding of such projects against the undesirable influences of the ordinary city.[71] These projects are actually new social domains, well-demarcated and secure, accessible to specific groups and inaccessible to others.

New projects are becoming exclusive urban islands, which makes it increasingly difficult for the rest of the city to link up to the networks toward which these projects are oriented. One result is a new definition of the word 'ghetto.' The ghetto-like character of today's urban district is determined less by how well its buildings are maintained, or how 'green' it is, than by the degree to which the district is still linked to and assimilated into the most important networks.[72]

These spatial networks have the sort of character that makes them more accessible and useful to some than to others, and they have led to a development that anticipates, according to some, 'the end of public space.'[73]

## NEW BLENDS OF ECONOMIC NETWORKS

Technological innovations have also had a major effect on the development of economic activity. Remarkably, this is the exact area in which processes involving an increase in scale go hand in hand with arguments for combining new, large-scale networks with local networks. Developments in port and transportation technology are a prime example of this phenomenon.

In the 1960s a process that began with the introduction of containers and with initial experiments in the automation of shipping and transshipment ultimately led to an important qualitative change in the role and position of seaports.

The development and perfection of containerization, as well as of automation and telematics, have resulted in a freight trade that is focusing more and more on the efficiency and speed with which goods can be transported, from manufacturer to retail establishment. The word 'logistics,' coined at some point in the '70s, became the buzzword of the new transportation-based economy in the '80s.[74] With the introduction of the concept of the port as logistic hub, the situation shifted from maintaining and expanding the competitive position of the port as a single point for the transshipment of goods from ocean-going vessel to barge, for example, to acquiring a central position in transportation networks on land, sea, and in the air. Vital to a seaport is not an optimal competitive position in relation to airports, railroads, and highways, but a solid connection and good coordination with the various transportation networks. Subsequently, the 'logistic hub' is not a place that transships the most freight, but the place in which the total flow of goods within a country or region is coordinated and directed.[75]

In the development of new logistic hubs, the role played by 'traditional' infrastructure – linked to land, water, and air – has been augmented by the role of a new type of infrastructure continuously growing in importance: telecommunication and information technology, the 'electronic highway,' without which the direction and coordination of the international flow of goods has become inconceivable. Hence the heart of the new competitive struggle within a transportation-based economy – a conflict among cities, countries, and regions that first flared up in the 1980s – includes not only an optimal integration of various 'traditional' networks but also, and to an increasing degree, the development of the strongest possible position in the new network of the electronic highway.[76] In a spatial sense, this means that a strong accent now lies on developing so-called 'teleports': the cores of new electronic ports linked directly to and supported by headquarters or branches of multinationals.

To begin with, nineteenth-century harbor areas do not seem to be the most logical sites for the development of this new type of electronic port. After all, the expansive growth of the whole transshipment system in the postwar era has taken place far beyond traditional urban centers. This applies to seaports as well as to airports, which increase in importance every day.[77] The most logical solution seems to lie in the creation of a direct spatial interconnection of modern transshipment sites and new logistic coordination centers. The boom of activity in the immediate vicinity of airports and highway junctions – a phenomenon found in virtually every European country, as well as in North America, since the 1980s – may be seen as the spontaneous anticipation of such an interconnection, a process that governments can easily participate in by regulating and coordinating various operations to stimulate a first-rate development of this interconnection.

Thus old harbor areas and, more generally, traditional city centers are finding themselves competing, at the very least, with new 'boom towns' when it comes to the creation of a good climate for logistic services. The most important trump card held by old harbor areas is their potential as focal points of 'culturalized' urbanism, which makes them an attractive choice for an essential role: epicenter of the new electronic port or, in other words, a good location for companies, institutions, and major players active in the development of logistic systems.

The goal of many new waterfront projects is to recapture the key position held by traditional city centers – vis-à-vis the metropolitan region and new international networks – but the question is not only whether this attempt will ultimately succeed (judged by number of visitors, real-estate proceeds, and so forth) but also how the project relates to a plan for or a concept of the city as a whole, and how the project's international aspirations relate to an improvement of urban conditions at a lower scale. From this perspective, the recent broad-based rediscovery and revaluation of small and medium-sized businesses is noteworthy. In 1987 reports published in the world's two largest seaports – New York and Rotterdam – dealt with the economic revitalization of these cities and emphasized the importance of the position of small and medium-sized businesses.[78] Each study discussed the necessity of expanding electronic communication and information technology as a basis for the city's new position as 'electronic port,' while also stressing that this position becomes truly interesting only when accompanied by the substantial presence of small and medium-sized businesses. These companies – which deal in processing, assembly, and services (including reparations, maintenance, and cleaning) – are the key to the extra economic value so highly desired in an urban society.

Consequently, both reports attached considerable importance to the creation of physical conditions favorable to the presence of small and medium-sized businesses, and to the establishment of new businesses. Besides emphasizing the need to provide sufficient opportunities for accommodating businesses in all price categories, the reports also pointed out the necessity for public accessibility to networks used by various types of companies: businesses should have the opportunity to contact one another and to develop relationships by means of both physical and electronic networks. Of particular note was the proposal to restore and reinforce the 'classic' public domain as a condition for further economic development.

# 4    Redefining the Public Domain

To what extent do the processes described here lead to the disappearance or modification of public space? Various answers to this question can be divided, in general, into two schools of thought.

In the first, the public realm is seen as a superfluous and outdated concept. This school interprets processes such as 'technologization' and 'culturalization' largely as processes that lead to a disappearance of the significance of public space. Communication and an exchange of information increasingly occur by means of electronic networks rather than 'regular' public space, and culturalized urbanism goes on more and more often at concentrated, semiprivate, and precisely programmed sites. A limited number of networks and a limited number of places are the only genuinely relevant elements remaining in the city of cyberspace and fun shopping: networks and sites where urban life takes place in increasingly condensed surroundings at a faster and faster pace.

This school of thought perpetuates the ideological and political vacuum that has emerged with regard to the meaning of public space.

Today the far-reaching effects of the longstanding socialization policy and of growing vagueness in the distinction between public and private are surfacing as a result of the collapse of the ideological structure of socialism in the '80s and '90s, and the extinction of a goal that once aimed for the provision of public housing and urban planning as part of a process of socialization. In the course of the '80s, extensive government intervention into the social domain was seen more and more as an undesirable form of bureaucratic interference, as a criticism of everyday life, and it incurred wide disapproval. Because the public domain was treated as a social domain for many decades, 'public' became a tainted word in many ways, a term associated with a mania for organization and slow-moving bureaucracies: in short, a barrier to personal development, social dynamics, and economic freedom. In the 1980s, clearing the way for the private sector and the free market in all areas of social life was the formula for the future.

When the government abandoned its concern for the 'socialized' public domain, it evidently did not rectify this lack of concern by cultivating a sense of responsibility for another type of 'purified' public domain. The end of socialization resulted in a simultaneous disregard for the entire public domain as such and a glorification of the dynamic of the private sector.

The consequences are sufficiently well known. The public sector quickly took leave of its responsibilities; former facilities, services, and institutions belonging to the public sector were privatized. In the Netherlands, the whole institutional structure and instrumentality of public housing and urban planning came to a rapid halt, in most cases with the complete cooperation of the Socialists themselves.[79]

These developments were accompanied by a new conviction that what remained of the public sector was to behave as private enterprise and that the public domain was now a product of the market. The '80s and '90s saw the emergence of a new management jargon: municipal and other authorities presented themselves as 'enterprises,' and the matters for which they were responsible were displayed as 'products.' In the meantime, the degree to which the public sector is operated as a business is often deemed more important than the degree to which the public domain is maintained and protected. After all, the former (business-like operation) can be measured, while 'public' matters have become the subject of confusion and differing opinions. This development is taking place not only in the areas of urban and physical planning; it applies to all facets of social life belonging to the public realm.[80]

In the area of urban development, city authorities seem to be more interested in 'creating a product' and in the immediately measurable economic success of that product (expressed, for example, in a net profit made on land development) than they are in the possible public relevance of the product.[81]

Under the influence of socialism, the aim for many years was to realize the *socialization of public and private domains*; the current reaction, however, calls not only for the restoration of the status of the private domain, but also for the *privatization of the public domain*. Such privatization can be taken quite literally, as seen in a proposal by the Amsterdam Waterfront Finance Company for redeveloping the banks of the IJ.[82]

But even without such a literal privatization, many recent arguments and plans for improving 'the quality of public space' can be seen as initiatives that are more in the interest of increasing the market value of real estate than of raising the public quality of public space. Hence the function of public space is shifting from marketplace to market *goods*, in support of, and as a representation of, the value of real estate.

A curious aspect of this proposition concerning the disappearance of public space is the existence of a remarkable consensus among confirmed defenders of the proposition and many critical theoreticians. The optimistic messages of those endorsing free-market thinking go hand in hand with pessimistic analyses made by urban theoreticians. In the United States, in particular, criticism of recent urban projects is dominated by a combination of indignation and fatalism. Examples are *Variations on a Theme Park*, a compilation of essays edited by Michael Sorkin,[83] and Christine Boyer's *The City of Collective Memory*.[84] In an attack on urban planning, both books denounce plan development's intense fixation on autonomous, enclave-like, privatized projects. The application of a historicizing architecture and the use of public (financial) resources largely for the benefit of private interests are described as a corruption of the public domain which is, at the same time, irreversible: the subtitle of Sorkin's book includes the telling words: *The End of Public Space*. According to Boyer, society is becoming increasingly transitory, and life in the future will be dominated even more by transitory trends that flash around the world on digital networks, leaving 'culture' tied only to a free-market fetishism of goods.

A more interesting school of thought is one that disagrees with concepts based on the actual elimination, or at least minimization, of the public domain.

Recent analyses of developments in the urban economy, such as those previously mentioned, show that the need for a physical and spatial blend of various sorts of activity, as well as of various networks, *does* continue to exist. Not long ago, this blend was 'rediscovered,' so to speak, as an essential condition for economic vitality. In the Netherlands, the Scientific Council for Government Policy (WRR) has warned that the policy pursued by urban authorities in an attempt to link up with new economic networks carries the risk of becoming overly dependent on international networks as a result of a one-sided orientation toward such networks. This dependence creates a state of economic vulnerability that is also due to the great flexibility of the service-based economy and to the increasing 'footlooseness' of factors influencing the location of new (tele)communication systems. Cities can experience a long-lasting economic recovery only if the new orientation toward international networks is accompanied by a revival of local and regional economic networks, a situation theoretically possible only with the presence of broadly based socioeconomic and cultural support.[85]

From this point of view, 'culture' is primarily a complex – but also, in part, a very public – matter. Although *the* culture does not exist, many different cultures, large and small, unite to form a complex and ever-changing entity. In a recent publication on culture in Rotterdam, historian Willem Frijhoff wonders to what extent the ambition to become a genuine *cultural city* – a desire plainly evident in Rotterdam, as elsewhere – is linked to the city's existing and constantly evolving *urban culture*, which consists of the everyday customs, traditions, and rituals of the urban population. If this link is absent, as Frijhoff suspects it is, then projects aimed at making Rotterdam into an internationally celebrated cultural city may be extremely impressive, but in time a lack of public support will smother their chances of survival.[86]

In the area of social relations, the situation in modern urban society is also more complex than one can convey by simply mentioning a dichotomy between 'locals' and 'metropolitans.' Various kinds of social processes are occurring in the city, such as the unceasing migration of population groups leaving less developed areas and moving to big cities; a steady increase in unemployment and no sound ideas that might lead to a structural reversal in this development; and the deliberate choice of large groups, particularly the youth, to assume a less restricted position in the job process, to work part-time, or to enter into brief employment contracts for the sake of more leisure time. These are processes that have led to a situation in which large sections of the urban population have opted – sometimes involuntarily, sometimes deliberately – for an 'unhurrying' of urban life.

Complementing the 'accelerated city,' in which the pressure to keep up with the latest developments never ends, the 'unhurried city'[87] accommodates those in search of a way to spend their time.[88] The boundaries separating these two worlds are often rather vague: for the social vitality of the city, as well as for its economic and cultural dynamics, it is of particular importance that these boundaries remain unclear, that people can 'cross over' from one world to the other. When they do, it proves that something like a public domain still exists, a place in which both worlds (that of the accelerated city and that of the unhurried city) have an interest.

Although this point of view places new emphasis on the importance of the public domain as a space in which new forms of coherence, harmony, and public life can be created, at the same time, the concept clearly covers more than simply the reinstatement of the traditional public domain. Both the institutional organization of the policy and supervision of public space, and its urban planning typology, are in need of change and renewal.

In the area of institutional organization, the WRR has pointed out the necessity for a drastic change in Dutch administrative culture. On the one hand, for decades municipal administrations have been accustomed to taking a 'wait and see' attitude with regard to the central government (their source of financial resources and authority) and, on the other hand, to watching over the population like a broody hen and to assuming all responsibility for economic, social, and cultural developments. At the moment that financial resources diminished and the ideological basis underlying the implicitness of these relations weakened (and that 'moment' was, roughly speaking, the 1980s), a vacuum appeared in the administrative culture for which an immediate alternative was not available.

This alternative would have to be sought in the development of a 'civic culture,' a term that implies that diverse groups and parties in a city feel involved in and responsible for urban development as such, not merely from the standpoint of moral solidarity, but primarily because 'various parties and groups realize that they have been imposed on one another.'[89] The argument that the WRR made for a civic culture may be seen as a continuation of Arendt's philosophy on characteristics of the public domain. Civic culture signifies an acceptance of the heterogeneity and variability of urban culture by a diversity of urban groups and institutions, and an acceptance of the fact that the accelerated and the unhurried cities have been imposed on one another despite the innumerable controversies and dilemmas inherent in the situation. It is an argument for the definition of a new relationship linking the public, social, and private domains; and it asks, in particular, what the contemporary public domain is and which of its cultural dimensions should be recognized and encouraged.

What is needed, therefore, is not only an institutional framework for civic culture (in the form of all sorts of consultative structures involving the various parties), but also a concrete urban planning practice capable of designing the public domain: the space perfectly suited to the expression of civic culture.

The question is: what role does the practice of urban planning play in lending shape to this public domain? To what degree can this design process create new relationships between local networks and large-scale infrastructural elements, and what significance is given to the presence of water in the cityscape?

CHANGING RELATIONS BETWEEN CITIES AND THEIR PORTS:
TWO CENTURIES, FOUR CITIES

Each of the four cities featured here fulfills an exemplary role in the world of international urban planning: London, with the Docklands redevelopment project; Barcelona, with the revitalization of the historical port and seafront; New York, with Battery Park City and South Street Seaport; and Rotterdam, with the Kop van Zuid. Each of the four has a prominent position in the international debate on the redevelopment of port areas.

These cities have all been confronted with the problems attached to the changing nature of port activities, and have seen their older harbor areas, located close to city centers, degenerate, fall into disuse, and find themselves in a state of dilapidation. Each city can be seen as representing a specific type of port city: North American, English, Mediterranean, and Northwest-European.

Most North American port cities are peninsulas with a relatively long shoreline, along which repetitive systems of piers have been developed at right angles. The piers are, so to speak, the continuation of the street network into the water. New York is a splendid example of such a port.

The colossal docks seen in English port cities, on the other hand, are completely cut off from the urban context. London, with the enormous expanse of its 'Docklands,' outranks all others of this type.

Mediterranean port cities, with their bays, appear to be the most 'natural' of the ports; seen from the sea, the city often appears to be embraced by a natural bay, within which the port has been designed in greater detail.

In port cities along river deltas in Northern Europe, the position of dams or dikes built to protect cities from the danger of floods is a dominating factor: these structures form not only a division between land inside and outside the man-made barriers, but also between the city and the tidal port. The alternating relationship between 'inner' and 'outer' areas, and between city and port, is an essential characteristic of Rotterdam, a city of permanent change.

An apparent difficulty in a comparative study of these four port cities is that they differ from one another not only in terms of territorial features and typology of port infrastructure, but also in terms of the size of the cities and of the amount and development of port activities: areas in which substantial differences can be found.

Such differences are relative, however. If, for example, we wish to compare the size of the four cities on the basis of population, the first problem that surfaces relates to the various definitions of the concept 'city.'

| Population[90] | 1850 | 1990 |
|---|---|---|
| Greater Londen | 2.350.000 | 7.500.000 |
| Barcelona (city) | 190.000 | 1.600.000 |
| New York City | 600.000 | 7.100.000 |
| Rotterdam (city) | 80.000 | 600.000 |

In London, the word 'city,' in its most literal sense, refers to the City of London, which has only 5,000 inhabitants and covers just one of the 32 boroughs that make up the territory of Greater London, which had a popula-

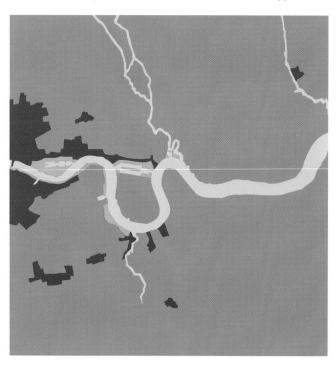 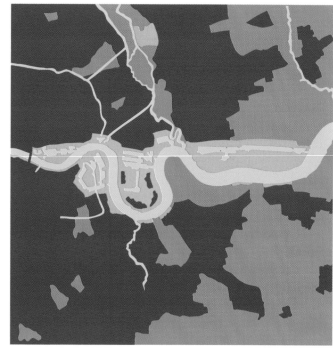

Changing relations among urban areas (red), port areas (orange), undeveloped landscape (green), water (blue), and harbor areas due for conversion (black).

tion of about 7.5 million in 1990. Down through the years various constructions have been created for the administrative coherence of this territory, only to be dissolved at a later date.

The 'city' of New York (New York City) consists of the 1898 amalgamation of five formerly independent boroughs: Manhattan (New York City was limited to the peninsula of Manhattan prior to 1898), Brooklyn, Queens, The Bronx, and Richmond (which comprises Staten Island).

The metropolitan area of a '*city*' such as New York or London is larger than the area of what is known in Rotterdam as the '*region*' of Rotterdam-Rijnmond. And in New York, the Regional Plan Association defines '*region*' as an area approximately the size of the Netherlands in its entirety.

The terms city, metropolis, and region apply primarily to various forms of complexity and concentration. 'City' means a continuous urban settlement that forms an administrative entity and has a nonagricultural economic basis. In this book, 'region' is defined as a territory accommodating a functional and spatial blend of a number of urban cores and undeveloped land.

'Metropolis' is a more detailed description of a specific type of city or region, which is distinguished from other cities and regions on the basis of spatial-functional complexity and of its international position: use of the term metropolis indicates cities that assume an important role – with regard to cultural facilities and status – within the global network of cities. London and New York are large metropolises, while Barcelona can be called a smaller metropolis. To refer to Rotterdam as a metropolis seems somewhat unwar-

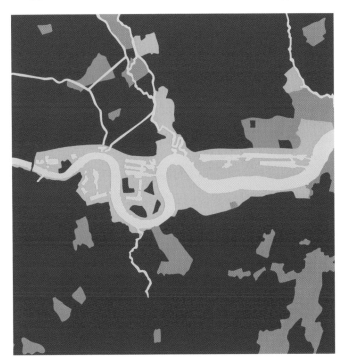
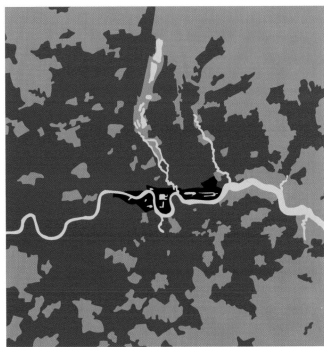

London's current port area, at Tilbury, is just outside the area covered by the map to the right.

ranted, but this hesitation has more to do with the city's relatively one-sided economic orientation and unexceptional status (so far) as a cultural city than it does with its smaller population and area.

Major differences can also be pointed out in the nature, size, and position of those nineteenth-century harbor areas that are currently the object of urban planning transformations. Inversely proportional to differences in size of population, the scale of transshipment activities in the port of Rotterdam stands out in stark contrast to that of the other three cities.

| Transshipment of goods in million of tonnes[91] | | |
|---|---|---|
| | 1979 | 1995 |
| Londen | 51,0 | 51,3 |
| Barcelona | 21,5 | 22,7 |
| New York | 115,0 | 41,0 |
| Rotterdam | 279,9 | 294,3 |

These proportions were once quite different. Prior to the sixteenth century, the network of port cities on the Mediterranean Sea represented the most important trade center in the world. Later this role was assumed by Dutch and English ports and, even later, by New York, which became the largest port city in the world in the nineteenth century. In 1961 Rotterdam finally surpassed New York in this respect. From a historical point of view, the port is an essential

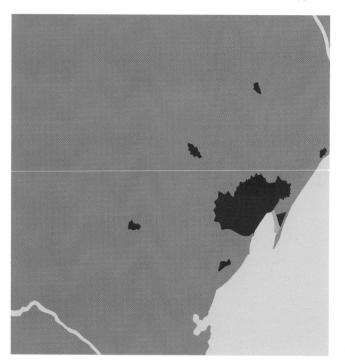 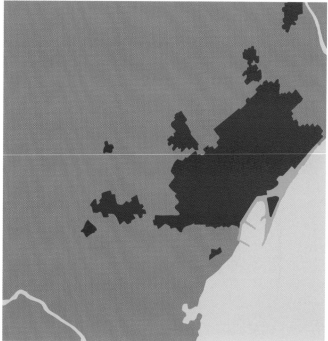

element of these cities, and even an essential reason for their existence.

Figures from recent decades imply that various processes in the area of port development are occurring in the cities in question. Although this is true, these processes are not part of an unequivocal development that produces the same results in all port cities. One city's port activities may be increasing, another's may be decreasing or even disappearing, and still another's may exhibit a fairly constant level of transshipment.

In London transshipment showed little change between 1979 and 1995, but this situation was accompanied by a total relocation of the entire port area. This operation can be compared to events in London in the early nineteenth century when the construction of new docks east of the Tower effected a radical shift of harbor activities from the section of the Thames fronting the City to the new Docklands. The recent relocation (1965-1975) of the 'Port of London' to Tilbury, 25 kilometers east of London, was every bit as radical. Docklands, which covers a total area of 20 square kilometers, now plays no role at all in the port's economy as such. Just as port activities vanished completely from the cityscape of the nineteenth-century metropolis of London, nearly all operating port and shipping industry is gone from the cityscape of the current metropolis of London.

In both the nineteenth and twentieth centuries, relocating port areas in other port cities took place more gradually.

In nineteenth-century Mediterranean ports such as Barcelona, new shipping and transshipment technologies led to an adaptation of existing

harbor bays. Later, at the end of the century and in the course of the twentieth century, port facilities along the coast expanded radically, but original harbor bays remained part of the total port area. In Barcelona the historical port continued to operate as a transshipment, fishing, and yacht marina until 1980, while the yacht-marina function grew in significance from 1970 on. Although transshipment companies left the historical port for good in the '80s, this old port area still plays an important role as fishing, passenger, and yacht harbor.

In other Mediterranean ports – such as Marseilles, Genoa, and Naples – we see a similar gradualness of the process of change affecting historical harbors.

Activities in port cities on the East Coast of the United States have not only experienced change, but have been eliminated. New York, the largest port in the world for many years, is the most dramatic example. Port cities on the Gulf of Mexico (Houston) and the West Coast (Los Angeles/Long Beach), situated more favorably with regard to new trade routes (to South American and Asia), have assumed the role once held by New York, Boston, and Baltimore as America's most important port cities.

Even so, the process of change and the elimination of port activities was much more gradual in New York than in London. An important aspect of American port cities is the great historical continuity of the type of harbors in the form of piers built at right angles to the coastline. This typology proved to be so universal that it remained in use from the eighteenth to the end of the twentieth century, despite constant changes in the size of ships and in the

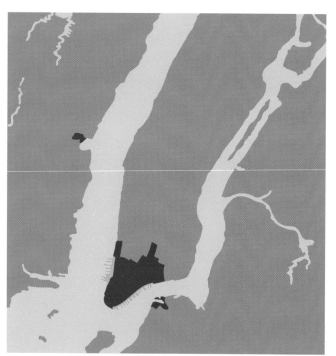
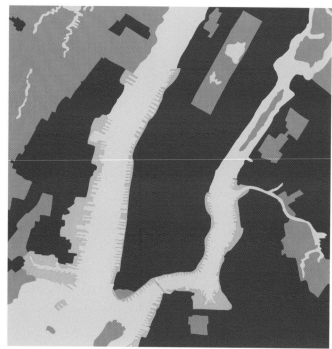

technology of port activities. The growth of port activities in the nineteenth century was made possible, in New York as well as in countless other American cities, by applying the same principle, time and again, to every expansion project realized along many kilometers of shoreline. Processes involving a decline in, or an elimination of, port activities took place just as gradually: one by one, piers were abandoned by dock industry, while elsewhere a number of piers were experiencing growth. Ultimately in New York this process of decline and shifting activity led to the current problem: relatively narrow, extremely long zones displaying rows of dilapidated or demolished piers and a desolate shoreline. The former harbor front on the Hudson River side of Manhattan alone comprises six running kilometers of shoreline.

In Northwestern Europe, the development of large port cities located in the marshy deltas of big rivers is another story. In the nineteenth century, port cities in this region, such as Rotterdam and Hamburg, developed new archipelagic areas in the indefinite peripheral zone beyond the dikes – between shallow water and marshy ground, and next to or across from the historical city; small fragments of city separated the new, large, open harbor basins. Here, too, the process of change was a slow one. While in Rotterdam, for example, the 1960s saw the most modern expansion of the port area – the Maas Plain – take place over 40 kilometers from the city center, Leuvehaven, a harbor built in direct proximity to the city center in the sixteenth century, continued to function as a port of transshipment for inland vessels.

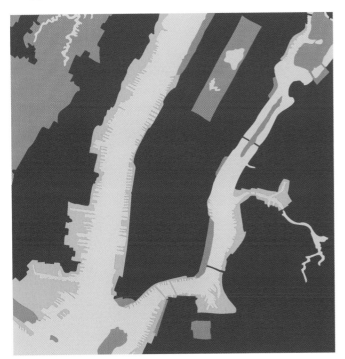
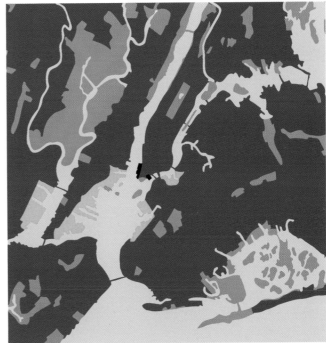

Those processes of change that apply to the relation between city and port can be explained, for the most part, by developments in the transportation-based economy and in the characteristics of the territory involved. But these factors do not fully explain why in one port city the urban planning tradition of plan development is distinguished by attempts to link city and port, while in another efforts to separate the two have been going on for centuries. This raises the question of whether plan development is influenced by other motives as well, even though at first glance it may seem as though a technical and economic issue, such as the layout of the port, is at the heart of the matter.

Nor can differences in economic developments and territorial conditions explain the recent emphasis on the 'cultural quality' of urban planning transformations of these areas. Regardless of whether port activities are relocating, declining, or growing; and regardless of whether port cities have bays, piers, docks, or tidal harbors; harbors everywhere – and especially older ones – are being discovered as areas vital to the cultural quality of the city.

For that matter, the emphasis on these motives turns out to be important not only to the discussion on revitalizing urban areas, including old harbors, but also to the creation of an image of the discipline of urban planning as a profession to be taken seriously.

This raises two questions: how important is the role played by these motives, both now and in the past, in designing the relation between city and port; and how important is the role played by the discipline of urban planning

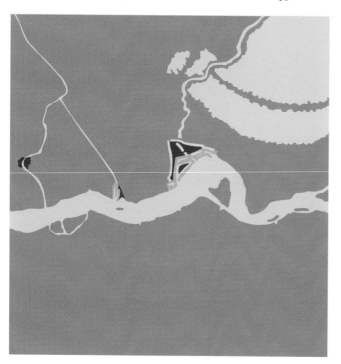
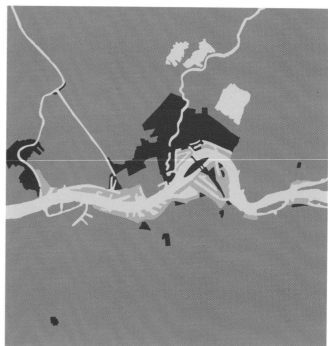

in formulating these motives and in translating them into concrete urban planning concepts?

These issues form the basis of this book. In describing the development of these four port cities, an attempt will be made to find the answers. As told here, the story of plan development for harbor areas is primarily a story of alternating ideas on the relation involving city, landscape, and large-scale infrastructure. In the case of port cities, the relation linking these three components has consequences for water's impact on the city. As a natural feature of the landscape, water (river, bay, sea) is overtly present and, at the same time, an important part of the infrastructure. With the development of modern shipping networks and ports in the nineteenth and twentieth centuries, followed by the decline and abandonment of harbor areas, comes the explicit question of how to design the relation involving city, infrastructure, and landscape. The cultural considerations on which the design of this relation is based form the object of this study.

The question addressing the relation linking city, landscape, and infrastructure can be divided into two parts: a question aimed at the relation between *large-scale infrastructure and local networks*, and a question aimed at the relation between place and program.

*a. Between global infrastructure and local network*
One characteristic concerns the function that these areas fulfilled until recently as part of large-scale infrastructural networks. Port areas, and certainly

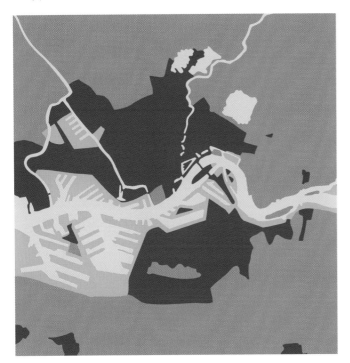
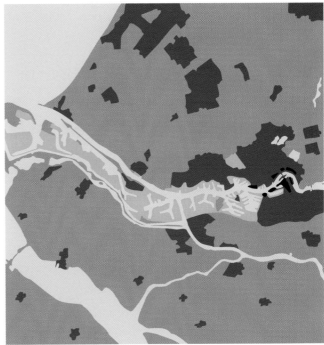

old harbor areas, are places in which two key urban functions meet and often intermingle: the residential function, or the city as a place in which to live and spend time; and the traffic function, or the city as part of an open system of interlocal traffic and transportation networks. Monographs of port cities are a search for the conscious or unconscious cultural motives (specifically expressed or implicitly suggested) that support the way in which urban planners shape the relation between large-scale infrastructure and local networks.

### b. Between place and program

The other characteristic concerns the specific relation between land and water, and possible changes in this relation as a result of the construction of port-related infrastructure. Did the bay, river, or estuary have a specific urban connotation that plan development used to good advantage? Was this connotation radically changed or, on the contrary, reinforced by the realization of large-scale harbor works in the nineteenth century? And currently, how strong is the presence of a reassessment of the local geographical and territorial characteristics of the significance of water for the (urban) landscape, as expressed by urban planning adaptations of former harbor areas?

In short, what is the meaning of a specific function (the port) for the cultural significance of the site: the territorial characteristics inherent in the natural state of land and water?

To answer these questions, the following four monographs of the port cities of London, Barcelona, New York, and Rotterdam have been prepared with the use of a uniform method, which features a chronological approach that distinguishes between:

*a.* Premodern times, or the period immediately preceding large-scale construction in nineteenth-century ports.
*b.* Early modern times, or the period in which the construction of harbor areas now considered obsolete took place.
*c.* Modernism in the port city, or the period of twentieth-century urban planning interventions into the development of port and city.
*d.* Postmodernism, or the current period, with its plans and strategies for nineteenth-century harbor areas.

Chapter 2

*The English Port City:*

# L O N D O N

*and the Wonder of Docklands*

# L O N D O N

# Between Individual Dwelling and Regional Plan

I

'Near to that part of the Thames on which the church at Rotherhithe abuts, where the buildings on the banks are dirtiest and the vessels on the river blackest with the dust of colliers and the smoke of close-built low-roofed houses, there exists the filthiest, the strangest, the most extraordinary of the many localities that are hidden in London, wholly unknown, even by name, to the great mass of its inhabitants.

To reach this place, the visitor has to penetrate through a maze of close, narrow, and muddy streets, thronged by the roughest and poorest of waterside people, and devoted to the traffic they may be supposed to occasion.'
Charles Dickens, *Oliver Twist*

The picture that Dickens paints of the London docks in 1838 was to remain the predominant image of this port area in London's East End for nearly a century and a half. In the 1960s, when the shipping industry left London's docks, the only future reserved for this part of the city seemed stripped of all hope. However, in the '70s the Greater London Council began making new plans for the area. These plans were filled with the courage of despair, or so it appeared, for who would want to live or set up a business around the docks, in the heart of the East End, the meanest, most poverty-stricken section in all of London?

Against this backdrop, it is amazing, to say the least, that after 1981 – under the auspices of Thatcher's administration, without the defunct Greater London Council, and despite its tenacious image – in barely six years this area was transformed from London's seediest district into the most promising urban renewal project in England, even in Europe, perhaps in the world.

In the nineteenth century London was clearly divided into city and port. This division was more than simply a result of technological developments in shipping and transshipping; it was also born of a desire to make the city into a distinguished, modern metropolis, an image that clashed with that of a city with a fully operating port.

The entire history of London is characterized by an age-old concern for the private atmosphere of one's own dwelling and for a harmonious relation between private domain and surrounding countryside, features that support the typical English lifestyle, which varies from the aristocratic estate to the proletarian cottage.[1] On the other hand, the spectacular economic development and enormous increase in population that led nineteenth-century London to become the largest metropolis in the world formed a constant threat to the physical condition of the English lifestyle.

London Docklands as seen from the east: In the foreground the West India Docks and Canary Wharf, in the background the Thames and the City. Below: (color) the situation in 1995 Above: (inset) the situation in 1965

Above: St. James Square as seen from the south, eighteenth century.

Center: Queen Square, Bloomsbury, 1812

Below: Cumberland Terrace, Regent's Park. W.P. Reynolds, engraving, 1814.

Early on the necessity emerged for 'comprehensive' regional plans that could be used to steer urban growth in the right direction. Established in 1888, the London City Council (LCC) – a body at a new administrative level that governed a continuous area composed of fourteen municipalities encircling a central munici-pality, the City of London – granted the status of 'borough' to these municipalities and directed them to relinquish much of their former authority to the LCC: in par-ticular, in the areas of housing and public works. The new administrative level had arrived; now for the plans.

Ebenezer Howard's Garden City [2] is the paradigm of London's duality: regional plan development as a condition underlying every Londoner's main desire: a private dwelling with a garden.

If Howard provided the theoretical concept of the garden city as a building block supporting a new regional vision of the city, then Raymond Unwin set the stage for the design of such blocks;[3] Unwin's efforts to achieve integral plan development for the London region were frustrated, however, by a lack of political and financial support from both London

City Council and national government.

Not until London really needed it, during World War II, was regional plan development tackled in a serious manner, albeit still from the perspective of Howard's concept. In 1944 Patrick Abercrombie designed the Greater London Plan, which was to form the leitmotif for the physical development of the London region for over thirty years.

The birth of the garden city phenomenon – or of New Towns, which is what these urban settlements have been called since the creation of Abercrombie's plan – and the 'regionalization' of the city are based on a solid, long-lasting tradition as well as on a shaky political balance.

In *London: the Unique City*, Rasmussen describes the division between the residential function and the City's commercial function – an essential and permanent characteristic of London – as the fundamental difference between the urban development of London and the development of cities on the Continent.[4] This process of separateness began in the eleventh century, when the royal residence was moved to Westminster, an occurrence that preceded similar moves, the most prominent of which took place in the seventeenth century, when the aristocracy

and bourgeoisie began arriving in Covent Garden and Bloomsbury, followed by their arrival in Marylebone, Mayfair, and Kensington, an area of countless squares and terraces now known as the West End. Thus a distinction was created between London's outlying areas, where the middle classes lived, and the City, which served as a business and shopping center. Thanks to this distinction, it was possible to refine the City itself into a center of trade and finance, and to develop it, by means of expansion, into the most important business center in the world.

The relation between the City and the River Thames remained a purely functional link geared to the transshipment and storage of goods, whereas outside the City, in Richmond and Greenwich, the view of the river was of great importance in designing palaces and villas. In the City itself (or, more accurately, on the Strand, an expansion of the City), the first monumental building of distinction was not realized until the eighteenth century: Somerset House, designed by William Chambers. Several years later architect-developer Robert Adams's Adelphi was erected, inspired by Diocletian's palace in Split. At a bend in the Thames where the river had been filled in and made level with the shore, a series of vaults for the storage of goods was realized. They stood at the foot of an enormous building – a city within a city – that accommodated all of London's social classes: clerks and laborers below, merchants and aristocrats above. This was the last project in which city and port were united in a monumental way within a single design.

The development of suburban areas went on for a long time without a comprehensive plan and resulted in a large number of tiny universes surrounding squares and terraces: not private, but not truly public either. Squares were intended primarily as outdoor areas for those living in the dwellings clustered around them and not for major urban activities and passers-by. In the nineteenth century, countless squares in the West End were provided with entrance gates, which were closed to the city's through traffic.

The ideas of Howard, Unwin, and Abercrombie may be seen as a continuation of this tradition, which was soon to require government-directed regional planning owing to the huge number of city dwellers in need of housing. Regional planning concepts and the design of garden cities as such were also supported by England's Conservative party, which attached a great deal of importance to the rural character of the housing milieu. At the same time, the strong Conservative accent on individual freedom carried a protest against every form of subordination of the private domain to regulation and control by a central government. These objections were underlined by the fact that the creators of regional planning and garden cities – Howard, Unwin, and Geddes – had been inspired by the utopian socialism and anarchism of the late nineteenth and early twentieth centuries. The theories of Russian anarchist Pjotr Kropotkin, in particular, were similar to the arguments of English planners. Regional planning and garden cities were seen as conditions for a society that would provide relatively small communities with a high degree of political and economic autonomy, would incorporate a direct relation and balance between industry and agriculture, and would realize a blend of city and landscape. The new phenomenon of regional planning was to eliminate disparities between industry and agriculture, city and countryside, and state and individual.[5]

Later, the utopian character of this ideological principle would be replaced by the more pragmatic ideology of the Social Democrats, who abandoned the idea of eliminating the state, while increasing the accent placed on building small urban settlements for the sociocultural benefit of community development. Thus the realization of regional plans depended on the unsteady balance among Conservatives, Social Democrats, and Liberals, a situation that has determined the political climate in England, and especially in London, in the twentieth century.

The history of the docks, which fits perfectly into this London development, is also a contrasting and frustrating element. It fits because the docks themselves were organized as an industrial variant of the enclosed square, but it contrasts and frustrates because they were also one of the biggest barriers to the completion of the postwar regional plan for London. At the exact moment that port activities left the area and the docks could be transformed into the last project of the Greater London Plan, the unsteady balance behind the consensus on the regional plan disappeared.

## 2 The Docks as a Microcosm of the British Empire

The creation of the typical English dock, and thus of the docks as a whole, plays an important role in the way in which London sees itself as a metropolis and as the center of the world.

Canetti[6] describes the Englishman as a captain with a small group of people on a ship, surrounded by and floating on the sea. The sea, though under his control, is not without danger. It is the source of the Englishman's wealth and prosperity, and the stage on which he meets enemies and allies. Life at home must offer compensation for the perils at sea: tradition and safety as opposed

to the uncertainty and dangers of the deep.

Apparently, this relation between the open sea and the safe haven at home is expressed most clearly in the distinctly English type of harbor developed in the late eighteenth and early nineteenth centuries: the dock. The English dock is a ship basin protected from the open sea by locks and often encircled by a continuous formation of warehouses or high brick walls. The dock was a bastion that offered protection against the vicissitudes and dangers of the sea; against changing tides, surging waves, and currents; but also against piracy and bands of thieves. The transshipment and storage of colonial riches could take place in a peaceful setting, away from the evil influences of the outside world.[7]

Until the late eighteenth century, London's port activities were concentrated within the small section of the Thames between London Bridge and the Tower. London Bridge was a fixed structure that allowed only the smallest boats to pass underneath (lighters, which transported goods from ships to riverside warehouses), and the Tower was the urban boundary beyond which no development or industry was tolerated. On this barely 800 meter long section of the river, dockers in the world's largest port had to load and unload ocean-going vessels, a situation that caused enormous congestion and chaos. Although the dense forest of masts was indeed an impressive sight – a rewarding subject for many an eighteenth-century artist – shipping companies found it to be an increasing source of annoyance. The biggest problem was the opportunity offered to countless pirates and bands of thieves, who were able to profit from the disorder created by ships packed together like sardines and filled to the brim with goods from the colonies. Napoleon's plans to aim a 'pistol at the breast of England' from the specially fortified ports of Antwerp and Cherbourg increased concerns about the vulnerability of the merchant fleet on the Thames.

The situation changed in the early nineteenth century. In 1802 trading companies sailing to the West Indies obtained the rights to build a new harbor complex on an undeveloped site outside the city: the Isle of Dogs. Ship basins belonging to the new West India Docks were completely enclosed by a continuous facade of warehouses, high walls, and a ring of canals; and the complex had its own police force (see illustrations on pp. 82-83).

Besides optimal protection and liberation from the congestion of the river, these docks also offered the advantage of a shorter route to the mouth of the Thames, as ships no longer had to negotiate the long curve around the Isle of Dogs. This escape from the bustle of the city led to an enormous urge for expansion in the shipping industry.

With the construction of the docks, London was confronted with a drastic spatial change originally considered spectacular but very soon the topic of negative criticism. These opposing viewpoints are still part of discussions on the role of the docks as a key factor in the revitalization of Greater London.

This port area, realized east of the Tower, was to relate to the city in an entirely different way than that of former areas which accommodated shipping activities in the middle of the city.

In the first place, the new docks looked much more monumental and imposing than any port-related structure ever seen in London, and they formed a stark contrast to the city's riverbanks, where companies of a more marginal sort still remained.

*London Docks*, an engraving from 1845.

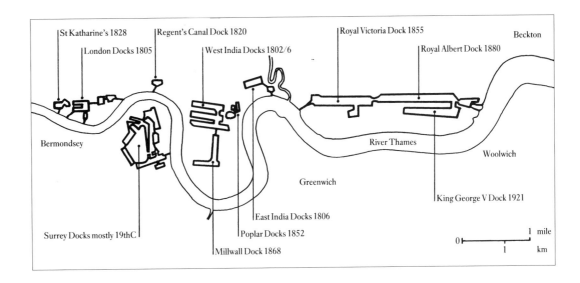

St Katharine's 1828
London Docks 1805
Regent's Canal Dock 1820
West India Docks 1802/6
Royal Victoria Dock 1855
Royal Albert Dock 1880
Beckton
Bermondsey
River Thames
Woolwich
Greenwich
King George V Dock 1921
Surrey Docks mostly 19thC
East India Docks 1806
Poplar Docks 1852
Millwall Dock 1868
0    1 mile
1    km

Not only were ship basins and warehouses of an inconceivable and unprecedented size; shipping itself, as well as shipbuilding, had the potential for unlimited growth. The port became an area in which everything was 'the biggest in the world': the biggest docks and the biggest warehouses. Together, they formed the biggest port in the world, where the world's biggest ships were built and, later, regularly moored at one of the docks.[8]

The construction of the docks also signified a new episode in London's development as a *modern* port city: it became not only the center of British merchant shipping but also, following the defeat of Napoleon, the undisputed focal point of world trade. The port was able to evolve into the world's main entrepôt, especially after the city of London decided in 1824 to relinquish its central coordinating role in the port (including the collection of groundage). The result was an enormous increase in the transshipment and storage of goods, as well as the rapid growth of the East End into a collection of neighborhoods and districts that housed dockers and seamen from every corner of the world.

The docks harbored a unique world: the wide range of activities and the social culture of dockers and sailors were a complete contrast to old London. The area became a popular destination for day trips, particularly after the completion of the London & Blackwell Railway, which ran straight through the Isle of Dogs and linked the city to Brunswick Wharf.

Both Brunswick Wharf and the railroad were spectacular innovations. The wharf was a passenger terminal on the east side of the Isle of Dogs, which used wooden platforms floating in the river as jetties. Ships mooring or casting off here were no longer dependent on the tide, as they were at the docks, which could be opened only when the tide was at a certain level. Freedom from narrow locks meant that larger ships could moor, an opportunity that companies operating passenger ships used to full advantage. In terms of passenger transportation, Brunswick Wharf became the 'gateway to the world,' bar none; a new rail line soon linked it to the city center. The London & Blackwell Railway ran across the Isle of Dogs by means of a viaduct. A ride in this train – which featured the newest devices, including an electric telegraph – provided a view of the bustling port area.

The only city to exceed the amount of passenger transportation found in London was Liverpool, which developed into Europe's main port of emigration. There, too, an

Overhead Railway along the docks evolved into a major tourist attraction.

Although the evolution of the docks went unseen in the city, the development of the Isle of Dogs, in particular, infringed on one of the city's most popular attractions. The former palace gardens of Greenwich, declared a public park in the seventeenth century, were oriented, by way of a monumental axis, toward the church at Limehouse on the north side of landed property on the Isle of Dogs. Building docks on the peninsula brought an end to this spectacular, dramatized view.

## LONDON AND THE DOCKS
## 'TWO NATIONS'

'Say what you like, our Queen reigns over the greatest nation that ever existed.'
'Which nation?' asked the younger stranger, 'for she reigns over two.'
The stranger paused; Egremont was silent, but looked inquiringly.
'Yes,' resumed the younger stranger after a moment's interval. 'Two nations, between whom there is no intercourse and no sympathy; who are as ignorant of each other's habits, thoughts, and feelings, as if they were dwellers in different zones, or inhabitants of different planets; who are formed by different breeding, are fed by a different food, are ordered by different manners, and are not governed by the same laws.'
'You speak of – ' said Egremont, hesitatingly, 'THE RICH AND THE POOR.'

Here Disraeli sketches the prevailing picture of London in the nineteenth century, an era in which it was the largest city in the world by far.[9] In 1851, with a population of 2,350,000, London had nearly two and a half times more inhabitants than Paris, the world's second largest city. London was more than the political, financial, commercial, economic, cultural, and social center of England; it fulfilled

many of these roles in a global sense as well.[10] London was the 'Workship of the World,' the greatest existing industrial center, and a laboratory for new production methods, industrial techniques, and labor relations.[11]

Everything that characterized the modern world manifested itself to the greatest degree, and certainly in the most massive way, in London. This applied to the phenomenon of indigence as well: London was also the 'capital of poverty' and hence the 'capital of extremities.' Nowhere else in the world could such great differences between rich and poor be found in such close proximity to one other.

In her book *The Idea of Poverty*, Gertrude Himmelfarb claims that the average standard of living in London's poorer districts did not compare unfavorably – but perhaps even favorably – with that of other big cities. The reason for London's infamous reputation as the 'capital of poverty' was not based on how poor people were but on how many people were poor, on the tremendous amount of poverty, and on the contrast between the impoverishment of the masses and the wealth of large financial institutions, mercantile houses, the bourgeoisie, and the royal family.[12]

This enormity and the sharp contrast made London into a 'City of Two Nations': two different populaces, who seemed to have nothing to do with, and to have no knowledge of, each other.

Particularly the latter aspect – no knowledge of each other – was the basis of London's popularity among journalists, writers, and other intellectuals, who began studying the city's working-class districts and describing them as a true *terra incognita*. The 'traveler in the undiscovered country of the poor' became a concept reserved for a select group of journalists and writers. The best-known was journalist Mayhew; his countless newspaper articles on the unknown, fascinating world of London's working-class districts was a major source of inspiration for Dickens's novels.[13]

Gradually, this contrast between two worlds – with its accent on the total disparity between poor districts and posh areas, such as the City and the terraces of the bourgeoisie – evolved into a kind of general entertainment. In 1849 *The Spectator* encouraged its readers to explore working-class districts on their own, where they might find 'an area stranger to you than Brussels, Lyons or Genoa.'[14]

The areas that became the most popular in this respect were the East End and the docks. The terms used to portray these sections of the city were the same as those used to describe excursions to Africa or Australia. 'Old' London – the City and the West End – was to the East End as London was to the world.[15]

The East End became a microcosm of the whole world, with all of the accompanying associations. It was said to be just as vast and endless as the world itself, just as multinational and varied, just as unknown, unfathomable, and dangerous as Africa's darkest jungles. Such descriptions painted an ambiguous picture of the new urban area: a place of the novel, the spectacular, and the imposing; but also of the barbarian, the unhealthy, and the dangerous – words related to the jungle, with its wild animals and savages. The darker picture gradually became the prevailing image.

When it came to portraying nineteenth-century London, the undisputed master was Charles Dickens. The London of his stories and books is a backdrop replete with the kind of rewarding material that adds to a tale's suspense, captivates the reader, and sends a shiver down the spine. The unknown perils that dominate his stories surface at the most unexpected moments, suddenly appearing amid fog or twilight. A remarkable number of Dickensian tales are filled with darkness, gloom, and fog.[16]

Dickens presented a picture of London that conflicted with the reality of the times, according to Olsen, and that contributed substantially to the concept of early Victorian London as a squalid, unhealthy city.[17] The truth, he claims, is that London had some of the highest standards of hygiene in the world, including first-rate facilities in the areas of running water, sewerage, and street lighting; and the broadest streets in Europe. Nonetheless, Londoners felt quite inferior when comparing their city with other emerging metropolises. Dickens himself greatly favored Paris, a city that appears in some of his books. To him, Paris represented a combination of a new social élan still vividly associated with the French Revolution and a stimulating cultural climate.[18] When Dickens compared London with Paris in 1863, he found Regent Street and Trafalgar Square sadly lacking in contrast to Parisian boulevards and squares, but what agitated him the most was how people looked: 'The mass of London people are shabby ... Probably there are not more second-hand clothes sold in London than in Paris, and yet the mass of the London population have a second-hand look which is not to be detected on the mass of the Parisian population.'[19]

Besides the technical infrastructure of ports and railroads, and the infrastructure of social areas like squares and terraces, London had a third spatial system, which gained significance mainly as a public domain: the system of former country estates converted to city parks. In the nineteenth and twentieth centuries, this system continued to remain the heart of the public domain. With their Speaker's Corners, these parks were centers for the formation of public opinion on political issues and prime examples of public urban space.

In the nineteenth century, several monumental urban areas were added to the park system. In the early 1800s, architect-

CITY AND PORT

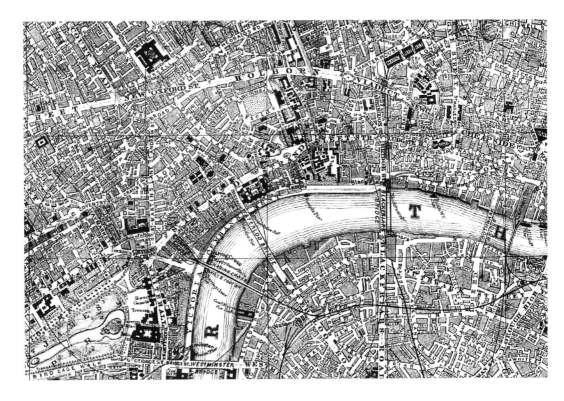

Above left: View of London and the Thames as seen from Somerset House, 1817.

Below left: View of London and the Thames as seen from Somerset House following the construction of the Victoria Embankment. John O'Connor, 1874.

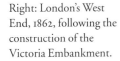

Right: London's West End, 1862, following the construction of the Victoria Embankment.

developer John Nash laid out Regent's Park and Regent Street, a boulevard linking city center and countryside. The city also got a face lift in the nineteenth century, when a large section of the Thames riverbank was revitalized. The construction of large-scale underground infrastructure (underground railway and sewerage) along the Thames, for which old harbor areas between Westminster Bridge and Blackfriars Bridge had to be demolished, enabled the realization of the Victoria Embankment – a 'lid' atop the underground network of tubes and pipelines – along this elegant bend in the river. The river changed from a traffic artery into an element that gave the city spaciousness, stateliness, and grandeur; it was no longer the place where the poorest workers sweated and slaved, and the dirtiest warehouses jostled for space, but the place that best represented the city as a national, and especially as an international, center of government and trade.

Unlike the situation in Paris, with which London was so often compared, urban face lifts in London were not implemented by an authoritarian central government. Initiated by the national regime but realized in close collaboration with investors and developers, such projects were the first examples of what is now known as public-private partnership. Projects of minor interest to developers were sometimes ignored. In the well-known case of Regent Street, problems concerning the acquisition of land forced Nash to modify the original route and, ultimately, to take on the role of developer himself in order to complete the project.[20]

Even the Victoria Embankment was little more than a decor that blocked the city behind it from the river rather than connecting the two.

Thus as early as the nineteenth century London already had four distinct systems of public space: an infrastructure of technical facilities, such as harbors and railroads; an

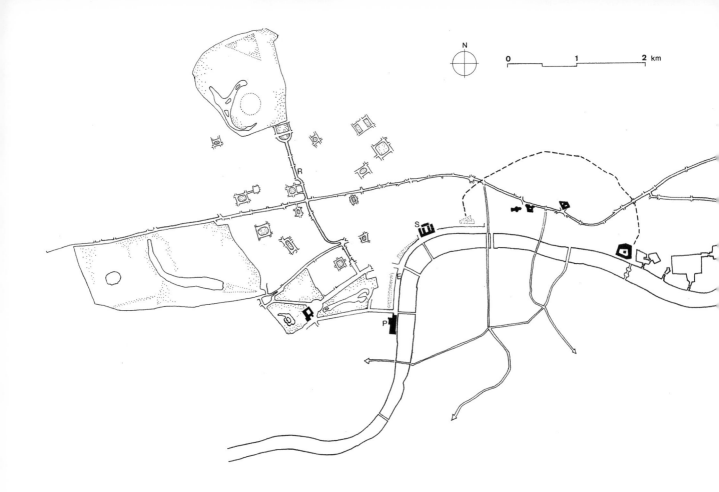

Nineteenth-century London: the 'City' is in the center, and the residential district of West End – with its squares, terraces, and parks – is to the west, along with Regent Street (R), Victoria Embankment (E), Somerset House (S), and the Houses of Parliament (P). The east side includes the East End, with the docks and Greenwich Park (G), which is axially oriented toward the Church of Limehouse (L) to provide a fine view.

infrastructure of social areas, such as squares and terraces; a system of parks which served mainly as public space; and a (modest) system of monumental boulevards with a chiefly representational function. All but the first of these systems were spatially interconnected, and of these three the parks, in particular, played an essential role in the development of the entire West End.

This triad contrasted sharply with the infrastructure of the harbors in the East End. While ever since the eighteenth century the city itself had derived its imposing image largely from the flurry of shipping activities on the Thames, shipping was now at the heart of a world that the city was trying – of all things – to relegate to the background. The idea of docks with monumental harbors

exuding international allure and modernity made far less of an impression than that of docks filled with soot, sweat, stench, and danger.

The East End was not only a *terra incognita* at the edge of an illuminated London, but also a symbol of deviation and lawlessness, of prostitution, of bars that stayed open 'after hours' and, most of all, of rebellious dockers.

The contrast between the reconstructed City and the East End meant that contempt once aimed at London as a whole could now be shifted to the East End. The City and the West End once more represented London's world-wide omnipotence; the flip side of the coin, however, was that the East End represented London's world-wide tyranny.

CITY AND PORT

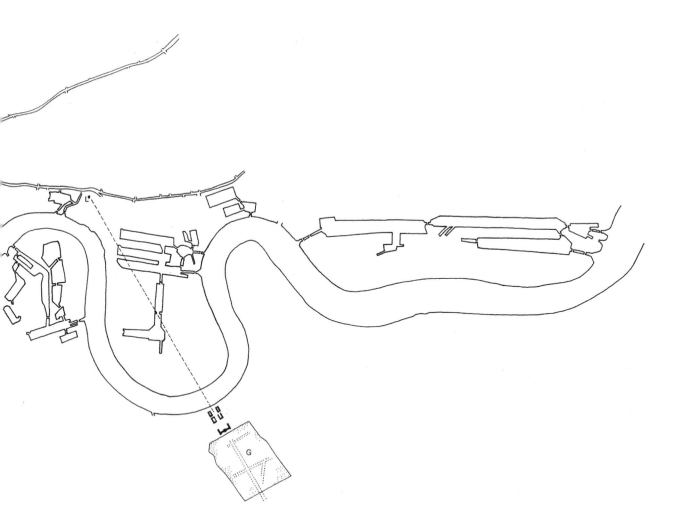

## THE DOCKS AS CENTRAL FOCUS

Opposing this image that the outside world had of the docks as the antithesis of the City and the West End is the idea that the docks could be seen as a structural variant of the West End's enclosed squares: in a spatial as well as a social sense, the docks also consisted of a cluster of small, relatively enclosed communities. Meanwhile, a great deal of material related to this concept has surfaced, particularly with regard to the Isle of Dogs.[21]

In the course of the nineteenth and early twentieth centuries, this peninsula evolved, both socially and culturally, into one of the most multifaceted and amalgamated parts of London, with a strongly developed collective sense of identity. Docks and wharves played

an important part in this evolution, not only as places of employment but also, and especially, as the spatial poles of new, 'modern' forms of social and cultural activity, of community life.

The explosive growth of harbor activities and shipbuilding drew people from all corners of Great Britain. Unskilled Irish workers, Scottish marine engineers, contractors, and financiers settled on the Isle of Dogs. Thanks to them, even today one can see a nearly complete range of English nineteenth-century housing types in this area: from typical English speculative building, garden villages, and cottages, to large manors and directors' villas. In a social sense, a great variety of neighborhoods emerged – such as those housing

Above: Isle of Dogs, Manchester Road and Millwall Dock, ca. 1920.

Below: Isle of Dogs, harbors and street plan, 1933.

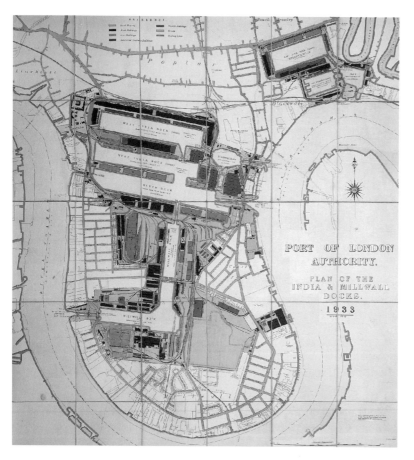

laborers, the middle class, engineers, and prominent citizens – while in a cultural sense, distinct differences could be seen among Irish, Scottish, Welsh, and Chinese neighborhoods. In this fragmented society, docks and wharves were soon playing a major role as the pivots around which new social and cultural life was organized. They undergirded the collective sense of identity found on the Isle of Dogs. During the first forty years of the twentieth century in particular, this very close-knit, stable and, at the same time, open community re-volved around the docks. It was stable in size (approximately 21,000 inhabitants), composition, and economic consistency: over 75 percent of the population worked for local companies during that time. The rise of trade-union conflicts greatly influ-enced the local population in its identifi-cation with the docks. The East End in general, and the Isle of Dogs in particular, grew to be bulwarks of England's trade unions and of the Labour party, a symbol of

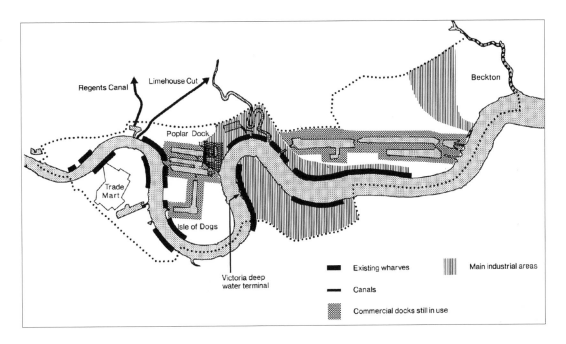

Docks as central hubs and wharves as extended ribbons along the river.

everything that socialism stood for: militant strikes, strong internal organization, and international solidarity.[22] In addition to their significance as bastions of a strongly organized working-class population, after working hours the docks became points of social contact: each dock had its own cafés, sports clubs, and so forth.[23]

A strange situation thus emerged, in which the docks – once built to isolate port activities from the surrounding world as well as possible – acquired significance as focal points of this new section of the city and, moreover, as a connection to the whole world.

The spatial structure of the port area that evolved – with the Isle of Dogs at its core – manifested three dominant characteristics: the docks as concentric hubs of port activity; a ribbon of wharves along the river, intercon-

nected by Manchester Road; and Sailortown in the north, where the hamlet of Limehouse formed the link between the docks and the City. In the nineteenth century Sailortown, an entertainment quarter for seamen, became a depot of low-paid Chinese sailors.

When the area was hit and literally shattered by German bombs and v-2s, the stable situation surrounding the docks for over forty years came to an end. Limehouse, in particular, was devastated. From a spatial point of view, this neighborhood was the most important connection between the docks and the City; furthermore, as London's Chinatown, it was one of the attractions that drew the most sightseers. After World War II, the majority of the Chinese population moved to less expensive areas of the West End, leaving Limehouse in desolation.

World War II not only had a devastating effect on the docks; it also left its mark of destruction on London as a whole. In bombing London, the Germans unintentionally achieved that which had been a topic of discussion for the past fifteen years. Having been commissioned by the London City Council (LCC), Raymond Unwin was the first to propose a regional plan for London and surroundings. Unwin even recommended a large-scale slum clearance and suggested the allocation of a broad strip of verdure to encircle the city: the 'Green Belt,' within which the urbanization process could be contained. Further urban growth, including the relocation of inhabitants from the cleared slums, would take place in expansion areas in the form of small cores and New Towns to be developed outside the Green Belt.

Unwin's proposals never got off the ground, however; in 1932 the LCC withdrew so much financial support from Unwin and his colleagues that the money remaining did not even cover Unwin's salary.24 But German bombardments resurrected Unwin's suggestions: the proposed slum clearance was implemented by German V-2s.

To begin with, the situation created the practical need for relocating tens of thousands of homeless people. But perhaps even more important, according to Rasmussen, is the broad social support that it generated for the original idealistic promotion of 'community development' voiced by people such as Howard and Unwin. On the battlefield, but especially in London air-raid shelters during the Blitz, when German warplanes bombarded the city for fifty-seven nights in a row, the atmosphere of fraternization that emerged among the various

social classes was to underpin arguments for the reconstruction of a new London, a city that would reserve an important place for building on this community development.25

In 1943 the LCC commissioned Patrick Abercrombie to design a new plan for the County of London, and a year later the central government commissioned him to design a plan for Greater London. Abercrombie actually created only one plan, composed of two complementary parts. His plan followed the line of Unwin's proposals perfectly and consisted of three main components.

The first pertained to directing and regulating the pattern of settlements. The territory of Greater London was divided into four rings within a concentric model: the Inner Urban Ring (broadly corresponding to the territory covered by the County of London), later called Inner London; the Suburban Ring, later called Outer London; the Green Belt Ring; and the Outer Country Ring, later called the Outer Metropolitan Area (OMA). Abercrombie anticipated the need for 618,000 people to be housed outside the territory of the LCC as a result of the bombardments, as well as the need for further slum clearance and the required expansion of urban open space. In addition, he expected a long-term population increase of over 400,000 people (in retrospect, an extremely low estimate).26 For these million plus residents, several New Towns were proposed for the Outer Country Ring.

The second component was the first official designation of open green space as a structural element of the metropolitan region. This essential part of Abercrombie's plan was formed by the Green Belt, the maintenance of existing park systems, and the creation of new systems on both sides of the Green Belt.

The third was infrastructure designed to interconnect the various parts of the region. Abercrombie's inspiration for this component was based on American parkways[27] created by Robert Moses and by German autobahns (!). Abercrombie wanted London's new road system to correspond closely to the city's green structure.

The Greater London Plan can rightfully be called a comprehensive plan, owing to the detailed attention paid to all its various aspects and levels of scale. Like Unwin, Abercrombie had been an architect originally; his interest in spatial design on every scale is apparent in the Greater London Plan. The design for Greater London is not only a regional map displaying the meticulous siting of settlements, parks, and roads; it also includes carefully developed designs for New Towns, parks, and roads.

The Greater London Plan was the first, but also the last, document in which so much attention was given to various levels of scale.

In implementing the Greater London Plan, however, coherence among scales was abandoned. In the 1950s and '60s, the plan's primary result was the virtually unqualified realization of Abercrombie's proposed distinction between settlement patterns and open space.

In most cases, the realization of individual small-scale components showed a lack of coordination and little coherence with the regional level. Two reasons can be named.

First: A separation of disciplines occurred in the '50s and '60s. In 1950 English universities removed regional planning from the design disciplines and made it one of the social sciences.[28] This separation can be seen in later planning documents for Greater London, in which nearly every idea of the spatial *shape* of the city has disappeared.

Second: Changes in political relations also played an important role. Abercrombie's plan was supported to a large degree by the assumption of a strongly controlling government and a free market held firmly in check. In the preceding decades, this free-market situation was precisely what had led to the intolerable conditions which, in the end, had produced the Greater London Plan. These ideas were underwritten by Labour, in particular, which held the majority in the LCC and was part of the national government during the war. After the war, Labour gained an absolute majority in the House of Commons and maintained its political power until 1951. In the beginning of the postwar era, an important part of the Greater London Plan was regulated by law: the New Town Act of 1946 stated that New Towns were to be developed by special Development Corporations operating under direct government authority. This mandate bypassed city councils representing village cores designated as New Towns, local bodies largely dominated by Conservatives, who opposed such expansion plans. Two years later a special law pertaining to the Green Belt prohibited all building activity within this ring of verdure.

In 1951, however, Labour lost its power to the Conservatives, who thought that infringements on the free-market economy had gone too far. In particular, they disliked having the housing policy geared to a rigidly controlled regional plan. Not only had the LCC lost its government support; action was also being taken to strip the LCC of its authority. At the last moment, one year before Labour regained the majority in the House of Commons in 1964, the Conservative government managed to divest the LCC of its power.

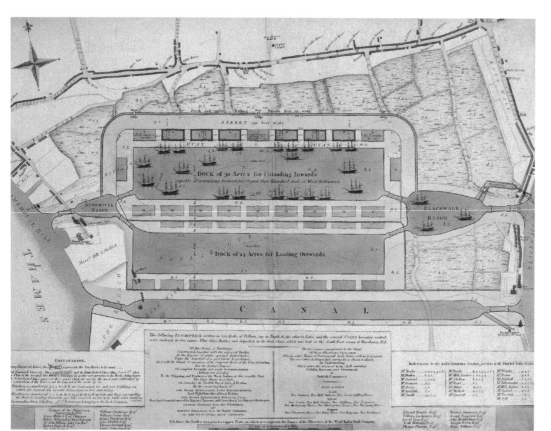

Above: West India Docks
as depicted on map drawn
by John Fairburn, 1801.

Below: West India Docks,
bird's-eye view by William
Daniell, 1805.

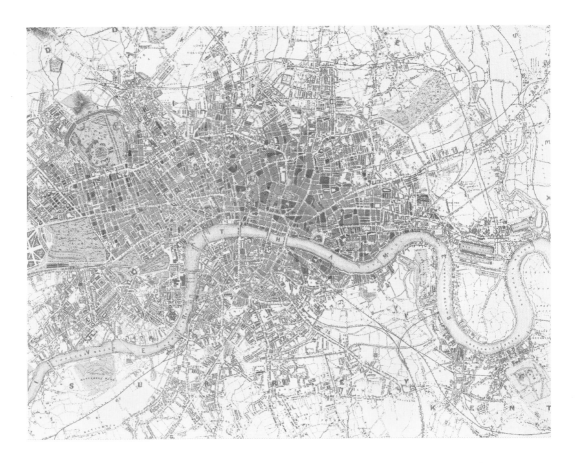

The LCC had been dominated by Labour since the 1920s, without a break. However, in the suburbs of Outer London the Conservatives had a majority of the votes. From 1945 on, it was clear that a coordinated realization of the Greater London Plan would necessitate a new administrative structure in the London region, as the LCC covered only part of the territory of Greater London. During the first postwar years, however, no quick changes were made in the administrative structure of London, since such changes would mean the loss of Labour's dominance in the London region and the obvious disturbance of the entire Greater London Plan.

With the Conservatives in power, relations in the London region could be straightened out.[28] In 1963 the LCC was disbanded and replaced by a new administrative body, the Greater London Council (GLC), which was given authority over the entire area within the Green Belt, a territory composed of thirty-two boroughs. The Conservatives enjoyed only a brief period of power in the GLC, however, as Labour obtained the majority in this administrative body in 1973.

This political aspect – the battle for political power in the English capital's most important administrative body – is an ever-present factor that dominates the policy on physical planning and the administrative structure of the city. This factor also played an important role in the 1980s.

In the area of housing, rather than the dominance of low-rise, single-family dwellings proposed by Abercrombie, high-rise construction was introduced on a large scale. Multistory apartment buildings made up a full 50 percent of the housing production between 1945 and 1970.[30] A large majority of this construction occurred in the East End, where the housing supply had suffered the most damage during the war. But in England, of all places, where so much value is attached to the single-family dwelling with garden, modernist concepts of mass housing were a highly controversial topic from the very beginning. In response to this development, Rasmussen closes his book on the 'unique city' he so admires with a pessimistic chapter entitled 'A most unhappy ending.'[31]

The Green Belt and radial park systems, intended as coherent green elements, are still largely recognizable on the map, but those using the city on a daily basis experience little of the continuity of green zones originally intended.

The biggest gap between plan and realization, however, lies in the traffic infrastructure. Peter Hall remarks that, broadly speaking, the road system serving the London region is still characterized by the same shortcomings that Abercrombie observed in 1944, while the number of cars in the intervening fifty years has multiplied tenfold.[32] In Abercrombie's plan, the main road system was intended not only as a functional network, but also as a design strategy to mark the borders of individual communities and to indicate relations between communities. In the 1960s road builders failed to understand this aspect, as did those in the '70s who protested the disastrous effects of road construction. The result is a road system that has wrought destruction rather than given a more refined shape to large parts of the urban fabric and open landscape; on the other hand, it remains incomplete and contains large gaps. An important goal of the Greater London Plan of 1944 was the integration and 'civilisation' of the car in the city. Instead, however, the road system has become an autonomous network that functions inadequately, moreover, because of the many hiatuses.

One of the most interfering elements

blocking completion of the structural concept of the Greater London Plan was the docks, a vast wedge that hindered the logical completion of the concentric and radial structure of Greater London. This deterrent is seen most clearly in the case of the proposed road system, which had two concentric beltways as its main elements. Of the two, only the outermost – projected in the Green Belt – was built. The inner ring, which was to cross the Isle of Dogs, was never realized. With regard to the green structure, the public transportation network, and housing, the 1944 plan warned that the docks and the north bank of the Thames should not succumb to one-sided use by port and industry: 'All the river frontage is not suitable for and can never be used wholly for industry.'[33]

As for what exactly *should* happen in the dock area, the Greater London Plan was extremely vague. The area remained a blank page in Abercrombie's long-term perspective, as a number of diagrams of the eastern part of London demonstrate quite literally. In particular, the significance of the Thames as a landscape-related element was not well explained. While water elements – notably the various tributaries of the Thames – were to play an important role as central features of the green corridors, when it came to the Thames, and especially the north bank, the Greater London Plan remained uncommitted.

The reason for this vagueness lay not only in the careful position taken in relation to that which was seen as an economic cork of the city. Of even greater significance was the presence of a separate administrative body in the dock area, an organ that possessed an autonomous status: the Port of London Authority (PLA). Clearly, it would not be easy to subjugate this powerful body to the objectives of general regional planning. Evidently, Abercrombie was unwilling to take on the PLA or at least

did not have the opportunity to do so.

As part of the reconstruction of the East End as a whole, in the 1960s on the Isle of Dogs, in Limehouse, and around the Royal Docks, several housing complexes were realized on sites that had been occupied by residential districts before they were destroyed by bombs. But these complexes remained isolated enclaves within a world of harbors. New neighborhoods on the Isle of Dogs displayed highly austere, function-alist architecture. Their presence also altered the function of the docks, because in the urban planning concept underlying the creation of community development in these new neighborhoods, the docks were seen as borders. The Isle of Dogs was developed in such a way that two 'neighborhood communities' arose on opposite sides of the centrally located docks.

These activities took place under the authority of the Greater London Council. The GLC was forced to face the fact that certain developments deviated from prognoses made by the Greater London Plan of 1944. The size of the population within the Green Belt had decreased, to be sure, even more so than Abercrombie's plan had estimated: from 8.6 million in 1939 to 7.4 million in 1970. In the Outer Metro-politan Area, however, the increase in population was considerably greater than Abercrombie had predicted: from 3.5 million to 5.2 million. In brief, a signifi-cant number of residents had moved from Greater London to the Outer Metropolitan Area.

This development was the main reason behind the GLC's modification of the Greater London Plan. The new Greater London Development Plan of 1973[34] demonstrates the degree to which physical planning and physical design have parted company. The plan consists of two tomes, each containing more than six hundred pages and, in total, only three maps of

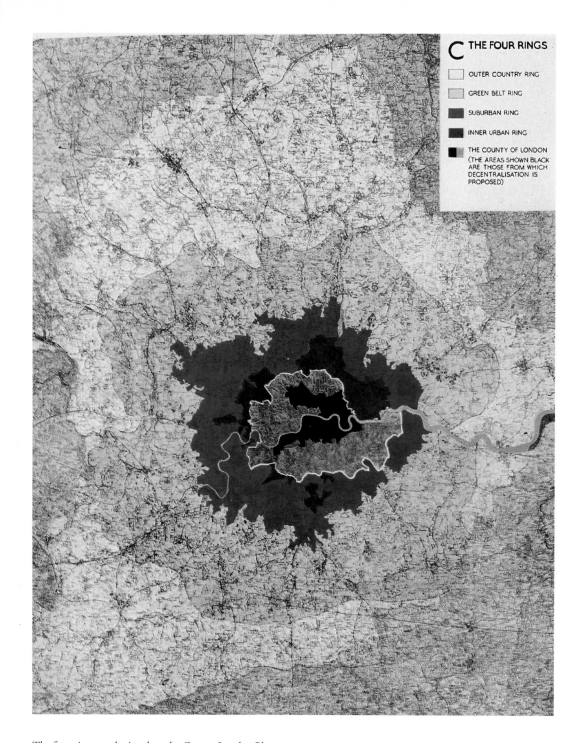

The four rings, as depicted on the Greater London Plan, 1944.

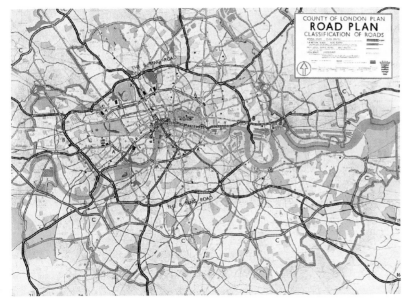

Above left: Road systems as depicted on the County of London Plan, 1943. The proposed beltway that crosses the Isle of Dogs on this map was never completed.

Above right: The 'social framework' of London's East End, according to the County of London Plan, 1943.

Realized products in the spirit of the Greater London Plan: social housing estate, Isle of Dogs, 1987.

Social housing estate with the Royal Docks in the background, 1967.

Greater London, sadly lacking in detail. The entire plan, which is merely quantitative in nature, is aimed largely at stopping the negative spiral affecting London after the departure of more than 1.2 million people. Stabilizing the size of the population had become an essential goal.

The plan offers two causes for the departure of the city's residents, many of whom belonged to the middle class: not enough housing geared to these groups and the lack of well-structured public open space in the Inner London area.

The plan ends with a plea for the allocation of 'comprehensive development areas,' within which the housing supply and open space can be augmented with the aid of integrated urban plan development. Along with Covent Gardens and the area around Kings Cross Station, the plan mentions the London docks as a principal comprehensive development area: an area that had been nothing but a blank page in the Greater London Plan.[35]

## COMPLETION OF THE GREATER LONDON PLAN

The position of the docks was influenced not only by pressure to increase housing production in London, but also by economic developments in the dock area itself. A steady increase in the dimensions of ships during the postwar era led to problems with lock gates and clearly indicated a need for the port to update its machinery. Ultimately, the demise of the docks was quite abrupt and, for the city, unexpected: in the mid-'60s, while the Port of London Authority was preparing plans to build new harbors on the Isle of Dogs, shipping companies and stevedores decided to end their operations in the dock area and to concentrate on Tilbury, 25 kilometers closer to the mouth of the Thames. Following the sudden disappearance of big shipping companies from the area, the gigantic docks remained behind, vacant and inglorious.

Between 1970 and 1973 the Conservatives, who had come to power in 1970, commissioned the first studies on possibilities for the dock area. Proposals resulting from these studies recommended the development of luxurious residential districts and accompanying facilities, such as yacht marinas. The boroughs involved – all of which were dominated by Labour and strongly oriented toward the preservation and restoration of the significance of the docks as a housing and employment area for blue-collar workers – opposed these proposals from the very beginning.

In 1973 the Greater London Council (GLC), then headed by Labour, presented initial proposals for revitalizing the docks in collaboration with the boroughs in question, now acting together as the Dockland Joint Committee (DJC).[36] Both institutions – the GLC and the DJC – were given a boost in 1974, when Labour regained the majority in Parliament as well. In 1976 these proposals were concretized in the London Docklands Strategic Plan.[37]

The key points of this plan consisted of large-scale housing production (23,000 dwellings), expansion of the London Underground to benefit the infrastructure, maintenance and reorganization of existing industry, and additional public recreation area in London, a function suitable for the banks of the Thames in the dock area. Most ship basins were to be filled in, and built-up infrastructure consisting of warehouses and entrepôts was to be demolished. The majority of the housing production (55 percent) was allocated to the free-market sector.

In the area of economic activity, an attempt was made to compensate for jobs lost when port-related industry left the area by convincing companies to move to Docklands instead of to sites outside the Green Belt. The DJC succeeded in making agreements with a number of newspapers (among which the *Daily Telegraph*) and chain stores (notably ASDA Superstores) regarding their future relocation to Docklands. Later these concerns turned out to be key players in the new economic development of Docklands.

In the context of Greater London's functional structure, the development of Docklands served primarily to reinforce the radial structure of London: the Thames was designated as the new green corridor, and a new underground line was to run in an easterly direction from the City straight through Docklands.

With the development of Docklands, the biggest obstacle hindering the Greater London Plan would be eliminated after all, and the structure of a city of radials and rings would be complete. The Docklands area itself would be a novel version of a New Town – not at some distance from London, but in the middle of the city.

However, the degree to which this modern-style, inner-city New Town would qualify as a true competitor of suburbs in the Outer Metropolitan Area remained unclear. The policies of the Greater London Council suffered badly here as a result of the separation of the disciplines. The global zoning plan for Docklands lent a general sense of order to the area's various functions, but failed to offer a clear picture of the spatial manifestation to be realized here.

Only later, at the end of the '70s, was an attempt made to develop a concept of Docklands as an area that was more than simply another part of the city. This development was related directly to a debate conducted in England in the '70s, within both left- and right-wing political camps, that focused on the blurring of the national identity and the accompanying increase in the national government's bureaucratic centralism – trends rooted in international developments and in how the English government tried to respond to them. Originally, most of those engaged in this debate were found in and around the Labour party, whose New Left movement, in particular, developed a perspective calling for greater local autonomy as a defense against the loss of job opportunities and social facilities in cities, and for the pursuit of a cultural policy that corresponded to the altered needs and lifestyles of the English population.[38]

Gaining ground within the Labour party was the view that the time had come to abandon the still predominant ideology of community development, a 1940s concept that was forming an increasingly sharper contrast to the growing social and cultural diversity of the English population. Labour's New Left movement promoted the standpoint that a good cultural policy needed to take this very diversity as a point of departure and that a stronger emphasis should be placed on the unique identities of various population groups. A group's identity could be based on ethnic origins, socioeconomic kinship, a sense of commitment to local circumstances, or a combination of such factors. At the same time, Labour sought the means needed to pursue a policy of mutual solidarity: a policy that would emphasize the unique identities of

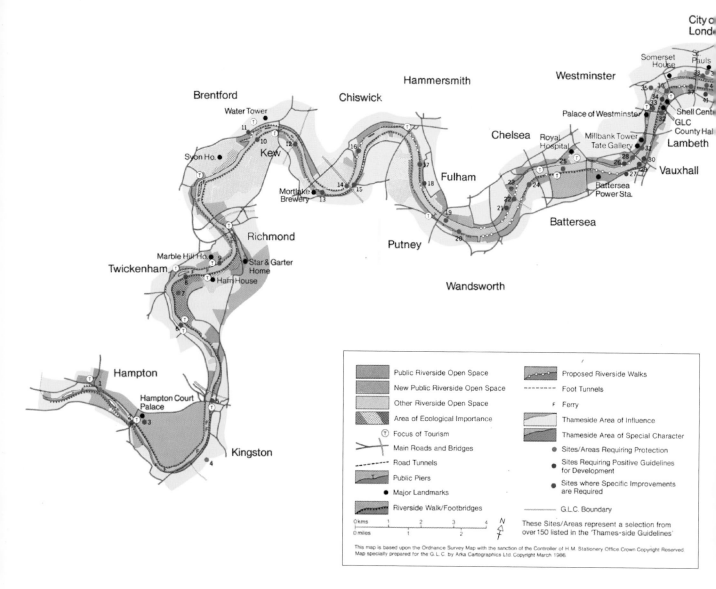

Design Guide for Thames Side, Greater London Council, 1981.

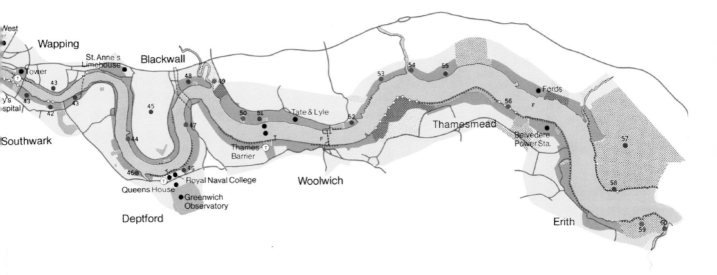

Below: Definitive image of the spatial-functional organization of Docklands
according to the London Docklands Strategic Plan, 1976.

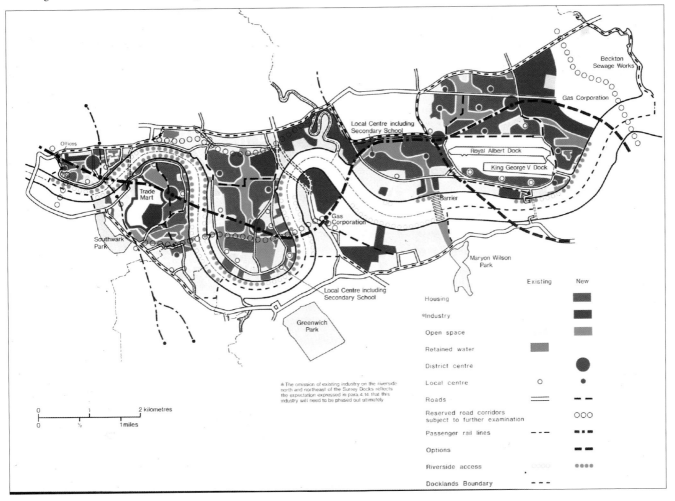

diverse groups, but would also create new forms of solidarity among groups.

In the late '70s, renewal programs were launched in various big cities governed by Labour: namely, London, Liverpool, and Glasgow. London, in particular, became an experimental garden of new ideas on Labour's cultural policy, especially after the introduction in 1980 of a completely rejuvenated Greater London Council which bore the signature of the New Left.

## NEW PROSPECTS FOR THE THAMES AND DOCKLANDS

The new Greater London Council wished to reopen the discussion on the development of Docklands: the Docklands area was to be used as more than a remedy for the shortage of housing, employment, and public verdure; the importance of the area to the East Ender's sense of identity was to play an equally major role in the council's new plans.

The East End was a prime example of the desolation, dismantlement, impoverishment, and fragmentation of England's industrial centers; but it had always been one of the most radical bulwarks of England's Labour party as well. In those years, any approach to the docks – the 'heart' of the East End – had to both exemplify *and* verify the methods that England's left wing planned to use in implementing the economic, cultural, and social renewal of the city.

Building on the symbolic significance that the docks held for the unique cultural identity of the area, the heritage of docks, warehouses, and industrial and civil engineering structures was earmarked to play an important role in creating a new, 'positive' sense of identity for the East End.

The program established by the Greater London Council in 1980 and 1981 was aimed at developing this heritage, as well as possible, into a public facility: buildings were to be used for diverse public functions and ship basins, along with quays and riverbanks, for public space.[39] The 'discovery' at the heart of this work was that the history of the docks embraced more than marginality; more than mud, stench, and sludge; more than rot and decay. Instead of 'forgetting' the area's past for good and beginning with a clean slate, this very history was called upon to reinforce the East End's sense of identity and to exploit the area's characteristic past as a special attraction.

At the same time, a search began for new ways to link Docklands with other parts of London. The solution seemed obvious, but from a London perspective, it was an absolute premiere: the Greater London Council proclaimed the Thames a spatial element capable of playing a role as a connective, integrative factor within the sociocultural diversity of the city of London. The council's plan focused on developing the Thames as one, nearly 27-kilometer-long, recreational zone meandering through the entire city. The reason the plan was such an exception for London was due to the city's administrative division into thirty-two boroughs, seventeen of which bordered the river. Only one borough, Richmond, spanned the river. In the case of the other sixteen, the river formed a border and had always been seen and used as such: 'The River Thames is the greatest peripheral area of London; it is the greatest throwaway area of all, not just figuratively but also over many decades, many centuries literally, it has been the greatest rubbish dump in London.'[40]

The Thames Plan provided for the transformation of debris-strewn riverbanks into green recreation areas; for the creation of promenades, public piers, and jetties; for the designation of ecologically valuable locales; and for a higher quality of river water. Special attention was paid to the river's relationship with historical landmarks and cultural facilities.

The plan bore a great deal of significance for Docklands, in particular: this area would be part of the new, comprehensive zone encompassing the Thames and its banks, and would thus be even better incorporated into Greater London, without losing its unique identity.

But the Greater London Council was a fraction too late in formulating its new plans and ideas. Just as the Docklands program was about to be implemented, Thatcher's brand new Conservative government divested the Docklands Joint Committee of its authority and established new conditions for developing the area.

Fortunately, however, the 'discovery' of the potential effect of the area's heritage was not ignored. Thanks to the preliminary work done by the DJC, the docks and their heritage were viewed with appreciation by the general public: London now looked at Docklands in a different light. In retrospect Labour organizations had to admit, resentfully, that the Conservatives let them do the legwork, only to claim the discovery of this heritage at precisely the right moment, after which it was privatized.[41]

This new development provided the history of the area itself with the job of attracting new businesses: the reinterpreted past of the docks was to be used as an important marketing factor.

# 4    The New Course

Docklands became the topic of heavy political conflict – in this case between Labour, which controlled local governments, and Margaret Thatcher's Conservative party, which had assumed power in Parliament in 1980. This government believed that Docklands could be England's answer to the explosive battle raging among large metropolises fighting for a prominent position in the world, or at least in Europe. The situation of this area in relation to the anticipated Channel Tunnel was deemed strategically important to England's place within a united Europe. With an eye to the competitive struggle between Paris and London for the position of Europe's cultural and financial capital, the French had already ascertained that London, thanks to Docklands, was a giant step ahead of Paris.[42]

To aid the development of the area, Thatcher's administration, referring to the New Town Act of 1946, took the opportunity to designate 'urban development areas,' which were invested with special significance for the national interest. The development of such areas was entrusted to special Urban Development Corporations (UDCs), which were answerable only to the government itself. The first two UDCs were established in 1981: the London Docklands Development Corporation (LDDC) and, for Liverpool's port area, the Merseyside Development Corporation. Since then both port areas, and especially London's Docklands, have been regarded as visible and tangible proof of the success of Thatcherism.

POLITICAL TRANSFORMATIONS

Not only did the substance of plan development differ from that of the previous period; method and decision-making differed as well. The achievement of a fast, unequivocal, and uncompromising result demanded a homogeneously composed planning body highly

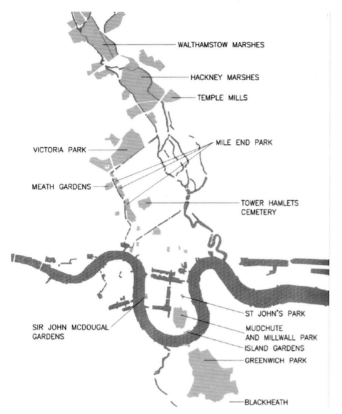

WALTHAMSTOW MARSHES

HACKNEY MARSHES

TEMPLE MILLS

MILE END PARK

VICTORIA PARK

MEATH GARDENS

TOWER HAMLETS
CEMETERY

SIR JOHN MCDOUGAL
GARDENS

ST JOHN'S PARK

MUDCHUTE
AND MILLWALL PARK

ISLAND GARDENS

GREENWICH PARK

BLACKHEATH

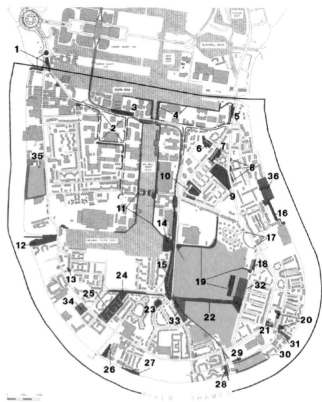

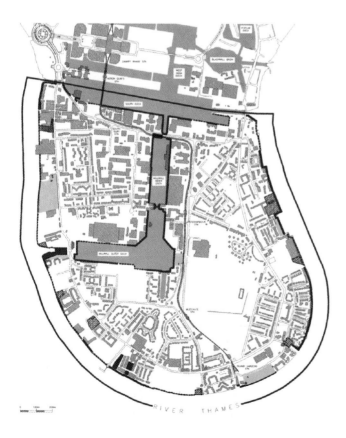

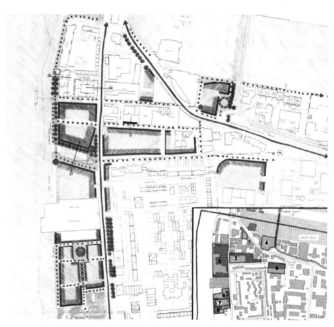

Development framework, Isle of Dogs, 1994. The Isle of Dogs as part of the structure of the East London landscape (above left); the green structure (above right) and water structure (below left) of the Isle of Dogs; design of public space (below right).

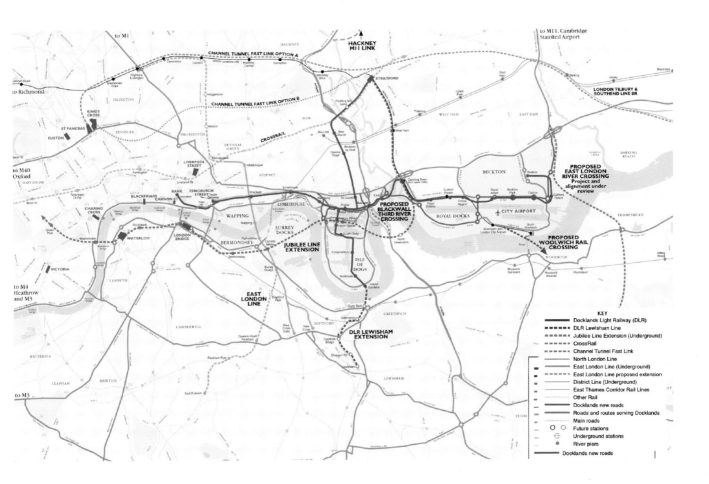

Above: London Dock-
lands, projected traffic
and public-transportation
infrastructure: 1995 plan.

Below: Canary Wharf,
1995. Mudchute is in the
background to the left;
visible across the Thames
are Greenwich Park and
the Royal Naval College.

Pages 96 and 97: Map
of London on a scale of
1:25,000.

resistant to outside influences. The LDDC satisfies these conditions: not only is it answerable only to the government; LDDC meetings are not open to the public. London boroughs are able to comment on LDDC plans only indirectly, through a new body known as the London Planning Advisory Committee (LPAC). The LPAC, established after the dissolution of the Greater London Council in 1986, is composed of representatives from all thirty-two London boroughs. However, the authority of the London Planning Advisory Committee is restricted to giving advice to the government.

The government and the LDDC have placed a permanent emphasis on the stark contrast between the new approach to Docklands and the Dockland Joint Committee's original approach. But on closer inspection, one sees that in dealing with several important points, the LDDC has built on the preliminary work of the Dockland Joint Committee: this applies not only to the 'discovery' of the potential quality of the Docklands area, with its many kilometers of riverbanks, abundance of ship basins, and monumental buildings, but also to the arrival of the first generation of new companies, which were lured to Docklands by the Dockland Joint Committee.

One difference that plays a major role in the grave political tension affecting Docklands is the drastic change in political persuasion found in London's East End. Within a few years this part of the city, an unassailable bulwark of the Labour party for nearly a century, has had to assimilate a flood of very affluent residents, most of whom favor the Conservative point of view. The boroughs, which have no influence at all on plan development, had to stand by as the composition of their councils and administrations made a radical and sudden shift from Labour to Conservative. The new Docklands area has transformed the city of London not only spatially, but also politically.

When Labour lost its footing in both borough governments and the Greater London Council, and Docklands became a Conservative bulwark, Thatcher's government found itself in the same position that Labour had been in in the 1940s, and it used the same methods that Labour had once developed to deal with the Greater London Plan and New Towns.

SPATIAL TRANSFORMATIONS: FOUR STAGES OF URBAN PLAN DEVELOPMENT

The LDDC's main task was to develop a Docklands strategy that would help government investments in the area to generate an abundance of private investments. Thus the question that first came to mind was: where should the public sector's investment policy be directed?

The LDDC had a budget of 700 million pounds at its disposal for the period 1981-1985, three times more than 'the rest' of London was able to spend on similar projects during the same period.[43]

No clear picture existed of the way in which a spatial strategy could be developed with the use of such investments. Ever since the LDDC was established, ideas and strategies concerning the physical and functional completion of Docklands have been modified time and again. In the period between 1981 and 1995, four different spatial strategies were applied to Docklands:
*a.* A balanced urban planning concept for Docklands as a whole
*b.* An urban plan restricted to the scale of an enclave
*c.* The development of a new centrality
*d.* A new relationship between the structure and shape of the city

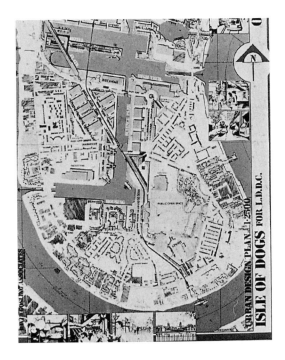

Proposal for the main urban planning structure of the Isle of Dogs, with the reinstatement of the visual axis Greenwich-Limehouse: design by Gordon Cullen, 1982.

## FIRST STAGE: A BALANCED URBAN PLANNING CONCEPT FAILS

In the first years – 1981 to 1983 – experimental urban planning concepts included David Gosling's 'comprehensive urban design study' for the Isle of Dogs. In collaboration with Gordon Cullen and the LDDC's chief architect Edward Hollamby, Gosling worked out four different concepts: two based on the development of high-tech industry directly related to water basins within the docks, a third based on the restoration of the historical visual axis from Greenwich to the church at Limehouse, and a fourth that indicated the possible implications of a development that would focus on privatizing the waterside along the docks and the river.

Formulated and developed by Cullen, the third concept, in particular, was originally presented as an important option for developing the Isle of Dogs. In a spatial sense, the design provided the Isle of Dogs with both a clear structure and a place in the urban context.

Cullen gave new meaning to the old Greenwich axis by offering a place on this sightline to Mudchute and the water basins. Mudchute, located on the south side of the Isle of Dogs, is a green hill composed of excavated soil left over after the docks were realized in the nineteenth century. A vantage point on Mudchute provides a splendid panorama of London, the Thames, the Isle of Dogs, and Greenwich. Differences in height between Greenwich Park and Mudchute, and between the church at Limehouse and basins alongside the West India Docks, formed the topographic ingredients of the basic physical structure of Cullen's design for the Isle of Dogs.

Within the main lines of Cullen's plan, a great deal of freedom remained for private developers to fill in building sites. Even so, the LDDC itself decided that these proposals were overly predeterminative and would have, therefore, an inhibiting effect on the objective with the highest priority: the stimulation of new investments and developments in the area. The corporation was afraid that potential developers and investors would see the urban planning framework as a highly restrictive factor.[44] But a second aspect, mentioned by Gosling in a later dissertation, was even more important: Cullen's plan was too much like a classic 'urban design plan' – not in the sense of his use of morphological concepts and resources, but in the sense of a relation between morphological concept and planning strategy.[45]

The plan fits into the postwar English tradition of New Town developments, in which programmatic completion (largely housing) was established beforehand. The new perspective introduced in Docklands was that the program was not preestablished, but needed to be generated by the urban plan. Cullen's design, however, contained no concrete directions for filling in the plan. It offered no clues, for instance, that might suggest where to begin the first building projects.

After the demise of the government's central planning policy – a policy that enabled postwar urban design to operate in a 'safe' way – no fresh ideas emerged to help create a new relationship between urban design and planning strategy. As Gosling ascertained in retrospect, this lack was the true cause of the crisis experienced by British urban planning in the 1980s and the real reason why the LDDC rejected his and Cullen's proposals.

### SECOND STAGE: AN URBAN PLAN RESTRICTED TO THE SCALE OF AN ENCLAVE

The LDDC itself developed a strategy which gave little more attention to the spatial coherence of Docklands as a whole or to the area's position within the greater urban context than previous proposals had given. The strategy focused on three aspects.

First, special 'enterprise zones' were allocated to foster the economic transformation of the area.

The second aspect called for the realization of transportation links to benefit the area's accessibility and, owing to the spec-tacular appearance of such links, to set the tone for recognition of Docklands as 'The Exceptional Place.'

Third, the urban plan – the creation of an integrated spatial entity of buildings and open space – was to concentrate primarily on the scale of individual housing projects.

*Economic transformations: Enterprise Zones*
The LDDC wields a great deal of power in the areas of planning and land-use policy but is not authorized to develop projects itself. Its activities are centered on creating and regulating conditions meant to encourage desirable developments and to discourage those less desirable. For this purpose the LDDC is equipped with an instrumentality based on two major elements: money and the authority to establish special enterprise zones.

Enterprise zones are areas intended to attract new companies by imposing as few restrictions as possible on those setting up business there. From a physical planning point of view, a good term to use would be rigorous deregulation: within an allocated zone, regulations applying to design, building volume, and building height are strictly limited. Running a business in an enterprise

The territory of the London Docklands Development Corporation. The dot-dash line represents the border of this territory. Enterprise zones are shown as dotted fields.

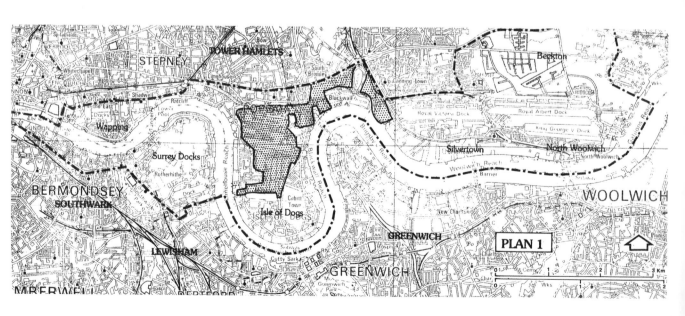

Two pictures of 'second-stage' results: Enterprise zone, Isle of Dogs, 1988.

zone has been made exceptionally attractive: during the operative period of such a zone (ten years), companies located there receive generous subsidies (frequently over 50 percent of their expenditures) when they make investments.

The largest enterprise zone realized to date (120 hectares) is on the Isle of Dogs, the location at which far and away the most new businesses are concentrated.

The original reason for creating enterprise zones was to reinforce Docklands' attractiveness as a location for advanced, relatively light and clean, industry; and as a place with a pleasant housing environment in the immediate vicinity for those employed by this industry. Building and business-establishment regulations for the enterprise zone on the Isle of Dogs were issued primarily to prevent large-scale development (maximum building height is 120 feet, or about 40 meters) and industry associated with danger and pollution. Urban planning tasks were limited to the preservation and repair of existing streets.

In the course of the 1980s, most of those opting for the Isle of Dog's enterprise zone were newspapers and others in the graphics industry, wholesale firms, assembly plants, and headquarters of distribution and transport companies. Business sites on the Isle of Dogs were grabbed up primarily by concerns

hoping to escape the congestion of London's inner city and, at the same time, to realize major organizational changes in new, modern accommodations. The enterprise zone became an experimental area for labor-extensive companies seeking to revamp their organizational structure.[46]

This industrial evolution – the disappearance of docks and dock-related industry, followed by the arrival of new businesses – has caused an enormous shift in the socio-economic structure of Docklands, the net result of which has been the loss of thousands of jobs. Although the LDDC has set up vocational programs for the local population, results have been marginal.[47]

*Infrastructure without public space*
From 1981 to 1985, the LDDC's initial investments were aimed at providing the area with a new transportation system, which would link Docklands not only to the City but, more importantly, to the whole world. At first glance, it looks fantastic: the Dockland Light Railway, which runs on an elevated line; the STOL airport for planes requiring only a 'Short Take Off and Landing'; and a fast ferry connection to the City.

The use of a large section of the nineteenth-century London & Blackwell Railway viaduct is a reminder of the revolutionary

Left: The nineteenth-
century London &
Blackwell Railway
viaduct, now part of the
Dockland Light Railway.

Right: Royal Docks as
seen from the east, with
London City Airport on
the spit between the Royal
Albert Dock and the King
George V Dock, 1995.

significance of this rail line in its day. This comparison seems complete, with the realization of the Docklands Light Railway line to the new STOL airport: London City Airport. The trip to the airport, via the automatically operated metro line, is a modern version of the nineteenth-century trip to Brunswick Wharf by elevated railway.

The new airport lies on a spit between two large ship basins and is geared to serving internationally oriented business people flying from Docklands directly to Europe's major cities. The airport's capacity is extremely limited, however, owing to the small size of STOL airplanes and to relatively infrequent flights as a result of the facility's single runway and London's congested airspace.

A third initiative concerns the new waterbus, a link between the Isle of Dogs and London's city center and, in terms of speed, a potentially formidable competitor of both car and underground. For the time being, this new means of transportation has too little capacity to take on its rivals, and owing to exploitation problems in 1995, it has been made temporarily inoperative. Although Docklands luxuriates in a surfeit of open space, public space has been reduced to a minimal infrastructure: a road network that merely provides access to housing and industrial complexes, and a functionally

inadequate public transportation system. The most important open areas, such as ship basins and riverbanks, are largely privatized.

The only undeveloped element on the Isle of Dogs is Mudchute, which since 1982 has been 'occupied' by residents of the old districts surrounding it who use the hill as an allotment garden complex and a children's farm. Thanks to this farm, school classes and families visiting the spot daily can view the wonder of Docklands from the top of Mudchute.

*Housing: new enclaves*

Most of the LDDC's attention to spatial design is aimed at housing projects. Once more, here is concern for the domain of the private home and its immediate surroundings, an English tradition greatly honored by Londoners. The LDDC realized quite well that the key to success would have to be found in building on, and in modernizing, the tradition of meticulously designed squares and terraces.

With a production of 17,000 dwellings in the first ten years (1981-1991), the amount of housing in Docklands more than doubled.[48] Small neighborhoods built years ago are beginning to pale into insignificance, as it were, amid the massive increase of new housing projects, new office buildings, and new industrial complexes.

Left: Public space in
Docklands: a leftover area
between fortified enclaves.

Right: The first exponents
of the 'third stage' under
construction: West India
Docks, South Quay, 1988.

The LDDC has paid a great deal of attention to the design and quality of housing projects. While new construction to accommodate businesses in the enterprise zone is highly deregulated, housing is subjected to even more stringent design regulations established by the LDDC. For each individual area in Docklands (Isle of Dogs, Wapping/Limehouse, Surrey Docks, and Royal Docks), the LDDC has issued special suggestions and recommendations for architectonic design and urban planning. These recommendations address not only building lines, allotment size, building heights, and desired housing types, but also the use of materials and colors, and the quality of outdoor space.

The exclusivity and closed nature of these housing projects have been emphasized by privatizing the most attractive aspects of the area – ship basins and riverbanks – and by sealing off and safeguarding new housing complexes from the outside world. Conscientious efforts being made to carry on the tradition of fortifying the docks are sometimes quite literal, as in the decision to preserve old dock walls.

By imposing strict regulations on design, the LDDC hopes to stop developers from realizing standard projects in Docklands without giving much thought to the result. Housing design should take maximum advantage of the special qualities unique to harbor quays and riverbanks, and should also emphasize the distinct character of individual areas. The design regulations mentioned apply to projects realized on sites controlled by the LDDC. Although projects on sites belonging to private parties must comply only with general land-use regulations, building lines, and building heights, the LDDC hopes that such projects will adapt to others in the vicinity.

Originally, it looked as though the new housing would accommodate, in most cases, an influx of suburbanites and affluent Londoners from residential districts outside the East End. Both price development within the Docklands housing market and LDDC policy stimulated this situation. The first housing projects became spheres of activity for so-called 'speculation nomads,' who bought houses and sold them a few months later for three or four times what they had paid, often collecting from 300,000 to 600,000 pounds for two-room apartments. This speculative market collapsed in 1987-1988, however. In addition, the LDDC was concerned about criticism that social contrasts in Docklands – between newcomers living in luxurious housing complexes provided with all the creature comforts and locals in their dilapidated public-housing estates – were becoming increasingly

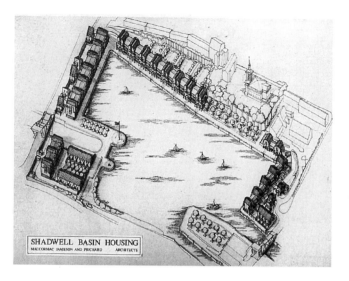

SHADWELL BASIN HOUSING
MACCORMAC JAMIESON AND PRICHARD ARCHITECTS

The Docklands equivalent of West End squares: housing estates surrounding the docks. Shadwell Basin, Wapping. Architects: McCormac, Jamieson, Prichard & Wright.

excessive. Ultimately, after local residents were granted the first option to purchase dwellings and were offered a special mortgage scheme, 50 percent of the new housing in Docklands was occupied by autochthonous East Enders.[49]

Various studies, however, have shown that this development intensified rather than lessened social segregation in Docklands: LDDC measurements have led to a fast-paced outflux of higher-income groups from older East End neighborhoods into new projects in Docklands.[50]

Generally speaking, an unprecedented degree of multiplicity exists in Docklands: a greater diversity of sociocultural groups, economic activities, and income categories would be hard to find. But the various fragments composing this complex whole have become completely isolated from one another. This disconnection is the result of the schism between urban design and urban planning: while planning has been reduced to providing a good traffic structure for the sake of accessibility, designers assume responsibility for lending shape to individual neighborhoods and industrial estates (or at least for establishing the preconditions necessary for this task).

This method produces something like a

mixture of functions, but only in the context in which urban design operates: within the confined sphere of privacy found in well guarded residential complexes, or along harbor quays equally off-limits to the public. It is in this context of privacy and enclosure that one finds the most important historical references to the area's former identity: ship basins and quays, renovated warehouses, harbor cranes still standing as decoration on certain quays – the dismantlement and 'privatization' of the historical heritage of Docklands.[51]

After 1986 the LDDC's original disregard for existing neighborhoods and population groups changed into a policy of rapprochement. Since then more than 20 million pounds have been set aside to subsidize facilities in traditional neighborhoods: schools, libraries, and community parks. But even such facilities remain, in most cases, within the confinement and isolation of these neighborhoods. Every fragment in Docklands is developing into an isolated enclave: new housing complexes with, for example, their own health clubs and cocktail lounges; and traditional neighborhoods with their own facilities, including community parks. Consequently, Housing Associations are

The Docklands equivalent of West End terraces: housing estates along the Thames. Compass Point, Isle of Dogs. Architect: Jeremy Dixon. Crowstepped gables gave the project its nickname: 'Little Holland.'

having more and more trouble maintaining public-housing complexes from the '50s and '60s, several of which have been vacated owing to exploitation problems.[52]

Although both superior and inferior qualities are present in abundance, in Docklands the two never meet.

### THIRD STAGE: THE DEVELOPMENT OF A NEW CENTRALITY — CANARY WHARF

The amorphous character of the physical development of Docklands as a whole, with the area's vast industrial estates in the enterprise zones and its series of suburban housing enclaves, provoked a discussion in 1984 and 1985 on the need for a 'city center' in Docklands: a core that would represent aspirations permeating the entire Docklands area. A proposal made by Cullen in 1982 – to designate the area of the West India Docks as Docklands's core – was revived for this purpose. In 1987-1988 new headquarters for The *Daily Telegraph* (architect: Seifert Ltd.) arose on South Quay, the south side of the West India Docks complex. Main offices for the LDDC itself were built adjacent to this building. These were the first buildings to

take full advantage of the permissible building height (120 feet), and they set the stage for the area's new urban image. For years to come, South Quay would symbolize Docklands.

During the same period, Docklands aroused an increasing amount of interest as a potential locale for financial institutions. In the mid-'80s annual rents in the City averaged six hundred pounds per square meter, twice the amount being asked for office complexes in Docklands. Originally, the American First Boston Consortium reported a plan to build a new Financial Center on the neck of land known as Canary Wharf, an office complex covering an area of 1.2 million square meters (by comparison: in 1990 traditional business districts in London, the City, and Westminster covered 2.8 million square meters of office space).

The plan was an extrapolation of the prevailing trend in Docklands to build enclosed, introverted enclaves. The neck of land was designed as an inwardly oriented bastion. Following the stock market crash of 1986, Canadian real-estate developers Olympia & York took over the initiative. A new master plan – designed by Skidmore, Owings and Merrill – places greater emphasis on orienting the center toward the water by giving harbor-basin quays a public function. Nonetheless, even this design gives Canary Wharf the character of an autonomous enclave, and in most cases the individual components of this bastion front the center's inner courtyard, Cabot Square. Located on the west side, Westferry Circus – a monumental entrance to the building ensemble of Canary Wharf – provides vehicular traffic with access to the center.

The master plan was to be developed in phases, the first of which focused on developing and putting out to tender 418,000 square meters of office space.

In developing Canary Wharf, Olympia & York introduced a 'discovery' that had been

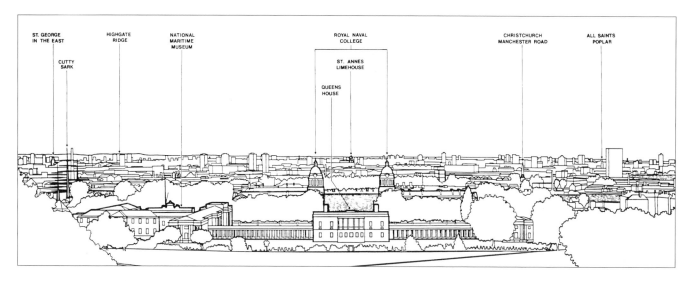

ST. GEORGE
IN THE EAST

HIGHGATE
RIDGE

NATIONAL
MARITIME
MUSEUM

ROYAL NAVAL
COLLEGE

CHRISTCHURCH
MANCHESTER ROAD

ALL SAINTS
POPLAR

CUTTY
SARK

ST. ANNES
LIMEHOUSE

QUEENS
HOUSE

Changing skyline as seen from Greenwich.
Above: The situation prior to the realization of new construction on Canary Wharf.
Below: View from Greenwich, 1996.

subjected to ample experimentation on the American market: the creation of an 'urban realm' in which even more important than image (a factor strongly emphasized by the LDDC) was a combination of image with public urban space and facilities: a blend certain to produce urban activity.

This combination was deemed powerful enough to hold its own in a competition with London's city center, and the wharf was originally provided with designs for various versions of a complete ensemble of skyscrapers. Ultimately, only the 245-meter-

high office tower designed by Cesar Pelli was realized; this building, the tallest in London (and the tallest office building in Europe), is the dominating factor in the cityscape of East London. The tower occupies a controversial position on every level of scale. On the level of East London, together with Greenwich, the tower dealt a deathblow to the age-old Greenwich axis. Even though construction on the Isle of Dogs in the 1980s had virtually eliminated the view from Greenwich Park to the church spire at Limehouse, Pelli's tower

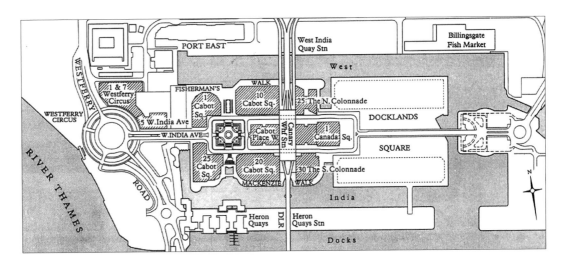

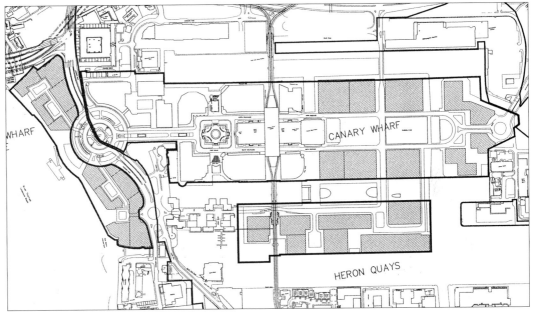

definitely drew the line of vision more to the east.[53]

The Beaux-Arts design and the building volumes refer to both Victorian London and today's Manhattan; the London skyline, increasingly dominated by high-rise buildings, was overmastered by the skyscraper on Canary Wharf. In combining these form- and image-determining means with the mass of attention paid to the area's public function, Olympia & York played their most important trump card in a bid for the success of Canary Wharf – despite major doubts about the future need for office space, and despite the relatively isolated situation of Canary Wharf in relation to the City. This isolation is augmented by the insufficient capacity of the Dockland Light Railway, built several years earlier when no one envisioned Canary Wharf as a concentrated center. While the train can carry no more than 6,000 passengers an hour, the LDDC's new policy was aimed at far more activity than originally anticipated. Of the 200,000 jobs to be created in Docklands, 50,000 are earmarked for Canary Wharf.

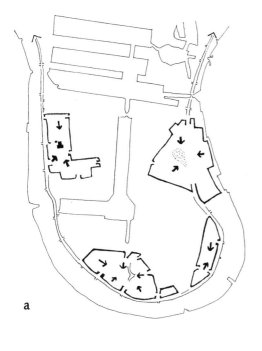

a

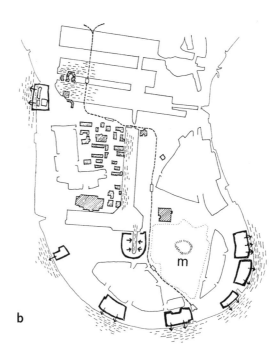

b

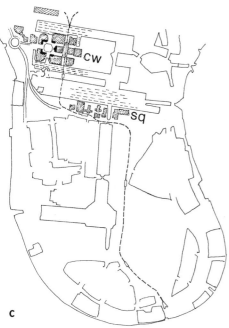

c

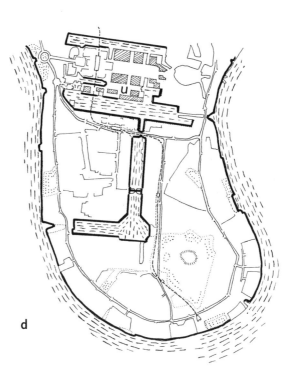

d

Four stages of urban
planning concepts for
Docklands:
*a.* The situation circa
1980: 'introverted'
housing enclaves as
autonomous elements
in relation to the structure
of riverbanks and harbor
basins.
*b.* Second-stage results:
the Dockland Light
Railway as most
important new public
facility for new housing
enclaves and the
haphazardly built
industrial estate (shaded
areas) of the enterprise
zone. River and harbors
merely play an incidental
role. Mudchute (m), as
public park, is claimed
by surrounding
neighborhoods.
*c.* Third-stage results:
South Quay (sq) and
Canary Wharf (cw) as
representatives of a new
urbanism.
*d.* Fourth-stage plans:
design for the structure
of harbor and river quays,
parks, and public roads,
Expansion of Canary
Wharf, with a new station
for the Jubilee Under-
ground line (u).

This uncertainty in the real-estate market, combined with Canary Wharf's isolated situation in relation to the City and the lack of an adequate traffic and public-transportation network, led to a debacle in 1992. Prior to this crisis Olympia & York had invested three billion dollars in Canary Wharf and had realized 70 percent of the 488,000 square meters of office space, although only 40 percent was occupied, with no hope of improvement.

Olympia & York went bankrupt in 1992. Building activities drew to a halt and the incomplete skeletons of Westferry Circus, the monumental entrance to the wharf, were left as ruins.

FOURTH STAGE: A POSTERIORI URBAN PLANNING – TOWARD A NEW RELATIONSHIP

After the Canary Wharf debacle of 1992-1993, a new course was charted. In the waning twilight of its existence, the LDDC (to be dissolved in 1998) is aiming for the development of a more solid, long-term physical structure for Docklands. After a progression of various trial-and-error projects, 'a posteriori urban planning' is being applied to Docklands after all. In 1994 this new approach was set down in documents called 'development frameworks,' one for each subarea. These development frameworks were the first urban planning exercises for Docklands that surpassed the level of individual projects since the studies of Gosling, Cullen, and Hollamby in 1982. (See illustrations on pages 94-95.)

The development framework for the Isle of Dogs is composed of three main elements:
– An improved connection to the city center, a highlight of which is the construction of a new eastern extension of the Jubilee Underground line.
– The development of Canary Wharf into a full-fledged city center surrounding the basins of the West India Docks. The plan also includes the Heron Quays spit, the north and south riverbanks, and adjacent sections of the Thames riverbanks. A specially formed consortium, Canary Wharf Ltd., largely composed of parties directly involved in the activities, will act as developer. The Jubilee Line Station – a new focal point of this central area – is being built between Canary Wharf and Heron Quays.
– A strong spatial anchorage of the Isle of Dogs – to be achieved by a good structuralization of East London's large open spaces: parks, watercourses, and basins – and more emphasis on the spatial design of such elements, which are to heighten the sense of a public domain.

The second and third points introduce a vital change to the function of Westferry Circus. On the urban scale, the new plan makes this traffic circle a central link in East London's network of public space. As part of this area of the city, the circle becomes a crucial hub within the structure of verdure, water, and main roads. On the level of the Isle of Dogs peninsula, Westferry Circus forms one of three important visual elements which orient the peninsula toward both the river and the greater urban context: in addition to Westferry Circus, which boasts a promenade with a view of river and City, the other two elements are Island Gardens, a park that presents a historical vista of Greenwich; and Mudchute Park, surrounded by differences in height that allow for a panoramic view of river and city.

This new approach is faced with a major problem, however: the legacy of earlier stages. The reinstated objective calling for the realization of a continuous ribbon of public areas along the Thames and ship basins is being frustrated at various spots by 1980s housing projects with private quays.

The expansion of Canary Wharf also faces a problem in the form of a complex of industrial buildings realized in 1985 on Heron Quays; this complex is hard to fit into the urban planning structure of the area that will accommodate the new 'city center.' In the meantime, the LDDC and Canary Wharf Ltd. have proposed the demolition of this complex.

Barely ten years after their realization, projects that once proved the success of the original Docklands strategy – a scheme based on a highly liberalized physical planning policy – are turning out to be obstacles to the development of an urban planning structure still considered desirable.

## 5  Balance: From West End to East End

Docklands may be seen as a typically English – typically London – product, which is wrestling with problems that have characterized London since the nineteenth century: the conflict between the harmonious design of the urban ensemble and the position of that ensemble in a greater urban context. For a long time such ensembles could be developed as small, autonomous universes, because they were realized outside the City and were thus removed from problems created by spatial congestion in the City. This description applies to seventeenth- and eighteenth-century squares in the West End, as well as to nineteenth-century docks in the East End.

It is London that offered the first, and most obstinate, glimpse of the concept that infrastructure within a transportation-based economy has nothing to do with the domain of urban culture. Early on, this concept was accompanied by a stringent separation between, on the city's east side, an infrastructure of technical facilities for port activities and, on the west side, a system of distinguished, socially oriented public areas in the form of squares and terraces.

Parallels between the eighteenth- and nineteenth-century development of the West End and the current development of Docklands exist in more than one sense. The most important parallel concerns the relation between the structuralization of the city, on a high level of scale, and physical-spatial design, on a lower level. New elements, such as Regent Street and the Victoria Embankment, were introduced in the nineteenth century to lend structure to the western part of London as a whole, but at the same time, these structural elements were designed down to the smallest detail. Later, especially following World War II, the higher level of scale became the domain of planning, and the design of structural elements was no longer seen as an urban planning objective. Patrick Abercrombie's Greater London Plan originally attempted to repair the cleft between technical and social public space and to integrate spatial design on various levels of scale. In practice, however, such attempts rapidly led to an even greater separation between large-scale urban plans for land use and urban plans on the scale of the district and the ensemble.

This separation was related to a separation of investments: planning strategies paved the way for large-scale public investments in land acquisition, infrastructure, and public facilities, after which the area in question was filled in with partly private, partly semipublic investments.

In fact, the LDDC's original strategies fit neatly into the same pattern. Reappearing in

Canary Wharf, 1991, with Westferry Circus in the foreground. The Heron Quays project (below right) was built in Scandinavian style during the second stage.

the form of development frameworks is an attempt to emphasize the design and material-ization of the main elements of the spatial structure. The kind of strategy being applied to today's Docklands is the same as that used in the West End in the nineteenth-century: a posteriori urban planning in the form of plans aimed at the later addition of spatial structures to districts composed of a sequence of autonomous enclaves. In the early 1800s John Nash, in designing Regent Street, tried to introduce new public space and simultane-ously add structure to the West End. When problems with landowners became too com-plex and thorny, he was forced to modify the route taken by Regent Street.

The new generation of plans for Dock-

lands, created since 1994, exhibits the same intentions and the same problems. Attempts are still being made in Docklands to intro-duce elements that will add more structure to individual subareas and will build a better relationship with the city as a whole. And such plans are also impeded by land and buildings unable to be acquired or torn down without delay. Completing the new gener-ation of development frameworks will require many adaptations and a great deal of time. The question, however, is who – which in-stitution – will find this time, since govern-ment authorities, who believe that the LDDC has done enough, plan to end this body's activities in 1998. Authority over the docks will be returned to the boroughs. Many of

View facing west as seen from Westferry Circus, with the City in the background.

the proposed spatial structures overrun the boundaries of individual boroughs, however, and London as a whole no longer has a coordinating government agency.

As this book goes to press (first Dutch edition, 1996), the implementation and completion of 'a posteriori urban planning' in Docklands remains extremely uncertain.

Another remarkable similarity between nineteenth-century London and present-day Docklands concerns the appreciation of water as an element on the city map. Efforts to provide the Thames with public quays, which would assume a major role as components in an urban network of public space, have received remarkably little attention. The Thames has always been held in high regard,

but chiefly as a factor to be used in boosting the elegance and status of an individual building or the private domain. The Victoria Embankment, a nineteenth-century project realized by the City of Westminster, stopped precisely on Westminster's border with the City of London: Blackfriars Bridge. Then as now, no higher or coordinating government body existed to authorize a continuation of the embankment along the section of the Thames fronting the City. In comparison, although riverbank areas and ship basins in Docklands are still imbued with a public character, current projects are bound to meet the same fate that once befell the Victoria Embankment: an abrupt termination at Blackfriars Bridge.

Chapter 3

*The Mediterranean Port City:*

# BARCELONA

*And the Other Modern Tradition*

# BARCELONA

# The Premodern Port City:
# The Orientation of the City Toward the Sea

Most Mediterranean port cities owe their present urban structure largely to the period in which the Mediterranean region presented itself as the first premodern network of cities in the world: the second half of the sixteenth century. In his study of the area bordering the Mediterranean Sea, Braudel explains that the Mediterranean itself is the element that creates the most vital condition required for the development of this unique network of urban hubs.[1] The sea was important not only in a technical respect – as infrastructure for shipping – but also in a political sense: as a free territory, the sea was not controlled by a feudal hinterland. The abundant presence of natural bays, protected from the hinterland by high mountain ridges and deserts, was the physical condition cities needed to organize themselves without interference from inland areas and, aided by the sea, to focus all their attention on one another.

The sea was more than just a basis on which to build a mutual network among city-states; it served the same function for networks of which the individual city-states themselves were composed. At that time, no city of any significance was autonomous; each lay at the heart of a network of villages and towns with individual functions, such as food supplier or shipbuilding center.

This network of port cities reached its peak when the Mediterranean Sea became a thriving center of both trade with the East and colonization of the West: a center with an urban network at its core. At the same time, a longstanding competition existed among Mediterranean cities, as did a hierarchical relationship that included Venice and Genoa, in particular, as age-old rivals for hegemony in the Mediterranean region.

Both cities are prototypical exponents of Mediterranean seaport culture: not only with respect to their political and military autonomy, their detachment from the hinterland, and their orientation toward the sea; but also in the way that they used the waterfront as the consummate manner in which to display the power, autonomy, and wealth of the city.

And it did not end there: in both cities the waterfront represented the city as a whole: a *pars pro toto*.

Venice is possibly the most extreme example of a Mediterranean city represented as a seaport, as a center of the sea. This portrayal appears first in pictures and on maps, and only later in the form of urban planning and architectonic intervention. Not until the sixteenth century was Venice seen as a single city surrounded by water.[2] Prior to that time Venice was depicted, in both text and

Barcelona, the old harbor front as seen from the south (inset, 1975; colored photograph, 1992).

paintings, as a collection of larger and smaller islands *along* a shipping route, the Canal Grande, whose primary function was to link the mainland with the Adriatic Sea.

This new presentation of the maritime state of Venice was related to the heightened need of various noble families to be viewed as a collective. Their need was based on two developments: the increased spatial complexity of islands that had merged into one, a situation that demanded the communal regulation of matters such as access, passage and transit, and moorage rights and privileges; and the position of Venice as the center of a great empire whose individual components were found largely in the eastern part of the Mediterranean region.[3]

Pictures of Venice dating from the early sixteenth century use three ways in which to show the city in a new light.

The first focuses on the city as a *center of the sea*: as a center of the Venetian lagoon and, later, of the Adriatic Sea. Earlier, most cartographers and painters had presented Venice as a city on the Canal Grande. The pictorial expansion of the spatial context of the city to include the lagoon, and even the Adriatic, emphasized the location of the city among complex networks that looked to the sea for both concrete infrastructure and metaphor.

The second way was to show the city as a *compact structure* amid the emptiness and openness of the sea.

The third and – with an eye to the relation between city and port – most remarkable presentation was that of the city as an *architectonic entity*. Owing to their monumentality and architectonic coherence, ensembles such as Plaza San Marco and the Rialto Bridge, together with their surroundings, were literally a *pars pro toto*: the urban entity was presented as a *Gesamtkunstwerk*, in which incongruous sections of quay structures were 'rectified' and the existence of a periphery and rear side denied altogether.

This representation of the city (on paintings, but to an increasing degree on maps as well) as an architectonic entity, as a monumental structure rising from the sea, was accompanied by architectonic interventions commissioned by private clients at strategic spots in the city, a development that pushed architect Andrea Palladio, in particular, into the spotlight. This new perception of the city as a coherent structure ultimately led the city council to adopt a policy aimed at the realization of such architectonic uniformity, to be achieved by rebuilding existing quays and building new ones, and by applying strict regulations to future quayside development.

Owing to unique topographic conditions, Venice was able to manifest itself as both a city in the sea and an architectonic entity. After all, Venice had no need for ramparts, as its means of defense consisted of the invisible difference between shallows and channels.

However, even in cities lacking such lagoons and thus largely surrounded by ramparts, it was still the waterfront, usually protected by fortifications built on peninsulas or piers, that was transformed into a coherent architectonic ensemble. A prime example was Venice's greatest rival: Genoa.

Genoa had no large public areas representing a central government, as was the case in other Italian cities. Genoa was a *compagna communis*: a city governed by a collective of several powerful, but mutually autonomous, merchant families. A few administrative buildings and several palaces belonging to the most influential of these families were grouped around the part of the city with the greatest collective significance: the port. Thus the port became the first public – or rather, collective – area in the city with a representational function.[4]

By the late sixteenth century, Genoa had evolved into not only the most important trade center but also the first financial center in the world, thanks to enormous loans made to King Philip II of Spain, who needed funds to finance his war with the Netherlands.

As a result, Genoa became a model of a new type of powerful, independent, and wealthy city-state. The cityscape of Genoa, with its characteristic waterfront, was imitated by dozens of cities, even after Genoa was no longer regarded as the most important shipping and financial center, a position later claimed by English and Dutch seaports.

Painted cityscapes, which were favored in the seventeenth and early eighteenth centuries, usually present a city from a vantage point in the harbor, at sea, or on the river; such scenes feature the port and shipping activities in the foreground, with the city and its waterfront as scenery. The 'rest' of the city is concealed behind the waterfront.

The idea of the port city as a *Gesamtkunstwerk* presenting itself to the sea is developed most consistently in the least Mediterranean city of those discussed here: Lisbon. Located on the west coast of the Iberian Peninsula, and thus facing the Atlantic Ocean, Lisbon is not a Mediterranean port in the 'true' sense, but it played a major part in the process of reorienting the Mediterranean region toward increasingly important traffic with Western and Northern Europe, and with America.

The significance of Lisbon was not always properly appreciated, however, as noted by Braudel, among others, who refers to Philip II's choice of Madrid, rather than Lisbon, as the capital of his kingdom; in making this choice, he passed up the opportunity to exert a higher degree of control over Atlantic shipping traffic.

Portuguese regents and merchants, who were more aware of the strategic position of this port city, saw their chance to highlight the relation between city and ocean when in 1755 Lisbon was hit by an earthquake, followed by a 30-meter-high tidal wave that completely inundated the low-lying city center, wiping it from the face of the earth.

This disaster made an enormous impression on the Western world. Some (including Voltaire) saw the catastrophe as a sign that the world was coming to an end. This was not the view held by the Portuguese Prime Minister, the Marquis of Pombal. In his eyes, the disaster created an opportunity to build an entirely new Lisbon, 'the first modern city in the world.'[5] Pombal's new Lisbon was to be a cosmopolitan city able to cast off the yoke of religious oppression and feudalism that seemed to be suffocating, to an increasing degree, members of the rising merchant class.

The picture of the old Lisbon was one of a maze of narrow streets lined with countless churches and parishes. The design created by Eugenio dos Santos for the new Lisbon turned its back on space occupied by the Church: the result was an austere, formal plan that ignored holy sites and introduced a modern image that 'owed nothing to the memory of stones from another era.'[6]

Unlike the old Lisbon, which had shut itself off from the ocean, the new city faced the Atlantic foursquare. All main streets converged at the new central square fronting the Tagus River, originally called Commercial Square as a reference to the commodity exchange projected at this place and as a tribute to the class that had financed the reconstruction of Lisbon.

Although the reconstruction plan was the product of an enlightened despot and seemed at first glance to promote the commercial interests of a minority group, this modern Lisbon gave the Portuguese a new sense of identity. A Portugal seen as backward, clerical, and feudal suddenly had a new face, open to the world, that radiated an enlightened spirit of commerce. The earthquake and subsequent reconstruction marked the turning point between old and new, between an *Ancien* and a *Nouveau*

Map of the Mediterranean
Sea and its surroundings,
with Barcelona's
consulates indicated,
ca. 1500.

Genoa, ca. 1845.

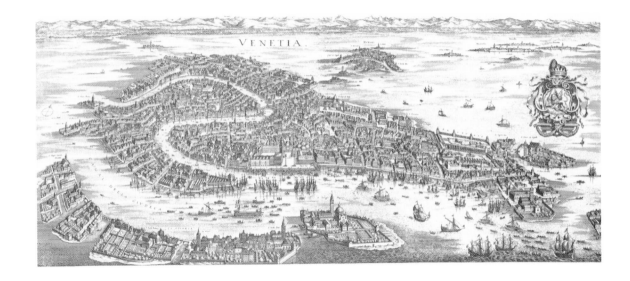

The Venetian archipelago, pictured as a single city, ca. 1500.

*Veduta di Genova*, drawn by Cristoforo de Grassi, 1579.

BARCELONA

*Régime*. With the aid of strict building regulations for development within the newly planned network of streets, the entire lower-town area was realized as one uniform architectonic structure. While the idea of the seaport as *Gesamtkunstwerk* was merely hinted at in Venice and Genoa, with their waterfront masquerades and 'rectifications' of the cityscape, in Lisbon the idea became reality.

But the perfected realization of this idea took place in an era preparing to welcome a different concept of the city. In the course of the eighteenth century, the idea of the city as a *Gesamtkunstwerk*, as an architectonic entity, began making place for an interest in the diversity and multiplicity found in, of all places, the seaport.

Venetian artist Canaletto was one of the most important exponents of a new trend in painting seaports, in which the function of waterfronts as a refined setting gave way to a fascination for the complexity and contrasts found in the world of the port city. Apart from several less well-known forerunners (including Dutch artist Caspar van Wittel), Canaletto was the first artist in Venice to see the city itself as a subject. Earlier painters, even Venetians, had used the city mainly as a background or framework for important events such as processions, gala parades, and naval pageants. These events were depicted against the backdrop of the most representative cityscapes in Venice: on or along the water, on the quay of the Palazzo Ducale, at locations along the Canal Grande lined with the finest palaces, and on the Plaza San Marco.

Canaletto grew up in a Venice whose supreme reign of colonial power lay in the past, in a city that was losing one colony after another. In 1717, when Canaletto was twenty, the Turks conquered Peloponnesus, the only remaining Venetian colony of any size. The self-confidence of the commercial center was badly battered, and artists re-ceived few commissions for paintings filled with the pride and power of the city.

Canaletto looked at his city in a different way than his predecessors did. He became fascinated with contrasts of wealth and poverty, vitality and decline. He painted the city in its ordinariness, not as a setting for organized events, but as a living entity of buildings and people. Typical of Canaletto's work are the unusual vantage points he took when painting the city: he preferred extremely unfavorable angles and made a noticeable effort to exaggerate contrasts and signs of deterioration. Canaletto's paintings show crumbling bits of stucco where, in fact, the surface was intact; and they reveal a Plaza San Marco with threadbare canopies and soiled laundry. He was able to indulge his imagination thoroughly in tableaux on and along the water, in which he depicted a jumble of activities: people buying, selling, and strolling; parade ships at anchor; farmers transporting vegetables in their little boats and shouting curses at gondolas carrying prominent parties and refusing to yield the right of way.

This emphasis on the chaos, disorder and, therefore, apparent hyperactivity of harbor life was made aesthetic, was cultivated, in Canaletto's paintings, and brought him international fame. It took him little time to find employment in what was then the most powerful port city in the world: London. There he produced a large number of paintings displaying his clients' terraces and palaces in the foreground (including Richmond Hall and Somerset House) and the bustle on the Thames as the focal point of the pictures – a mixture of cargo ships, luxury yachts, and small workmen's boats – against a backdrop of shabby working-class districts on the south bank of the Thames.[7]

The 'discovery' of the spectacle of daily life in these premodern ports became public knowledge in the late eighteenth and early nineteenth centuries. In a study of harbor scenes and cityscapes of Genoa, Poleggi reveals the drastic change in the viewpoints taken by artists at the end of the eighteenth century: they no longer painted from the viewpoint of the port, with the city as scenery, but the other way around; from a vantage point in the city, they presented the port as a living spectacle, a permanent theatrical performance for urbanites.[8]

This new fascination with the port as an exotic spectacle – as a connection to distant, unknown worlds – did not remain limited to the art of painting but became part of a new urban culture and new urban planning interventions. In 1835, on the quay in Genoa, directly adjacent to the distinguished waterfront lined with the palaces of merchants, an enormous entrepôt – the 'Terrazzi di marmo' – arose to serve the fast-growing shipping industry. The development of this structure appeared to be a manifesto for the creation of a new type of port city: the immense building blocked the previously exclusive view of waterfront palaces built by merchants, and on the roof of the entrepôt, a public boulevard was created for pedestrians, along which strolling and enjoying the vista provided by bustling international shipping traffic became a favorite activity of both residents and visitors – a public facility unequaled in the world at that time.

This principle, of uniting city and port by means of an *urban balcony*, was applied in this period – late 1700s and early 1800s – in countless other port cities, both in the Mediterranean region and elsewhere. In Genoa this urban balcony still bore the shape of an autonomous structure. In other cities, experiments were carried out to integrate the concept of an urban balcony into the network of public space. An excellent example is Barcelona.

## BARCELONA AS MEDITERRANEAN PORT CITY: BETWEEN AUTONOMY AND DOMINATION

The attachment of the Mediterranean city to an autonomous position and the pursuit of a good spatial relationship with the sea – an exponent of this autonomy – is demonstrated beautifully in Barcelona. This city has experienced two long periods in which the search for autonomy was frustrated by the policy of colonization and oppression pursued by the Spanish government: from the 1500s through the 1700s, or the precise period in which other Mediterranean cities were transforming their waterfronts into coherent architectonic ensembles; and during the Franco regime (1939-1976).

The specific orientation of the city toward the sea evolved largely in the intervening years, or 'between acts,' as it were. These were periods in which every bit of energy and enthusiasm in this city was needed to concretize the pursuit of autonomy and individual identity. Down through the ages, the city has swung back and forth between autonomy and colonization, and during various periods each form of power has left its specific mark on the spatial structure and shape of the city.

This interaction between autonomy and colonization is precisely what makes Barcelona a paradigm of the Mediterranean port city.

## THE REVITALIZATION OF BARCELONA AS AN AUTONOMOUS MEDITERRANEAN PORT CITY: THE RAMBLAS AND THE HARBOR FRONT

Barcelona, founded by the Carthaginians and later conquered by the Romans, flourished for a long time – from the 1100s to the late 1400s – as the center of a Catalan empire. In this period Barcelona developed into a typical

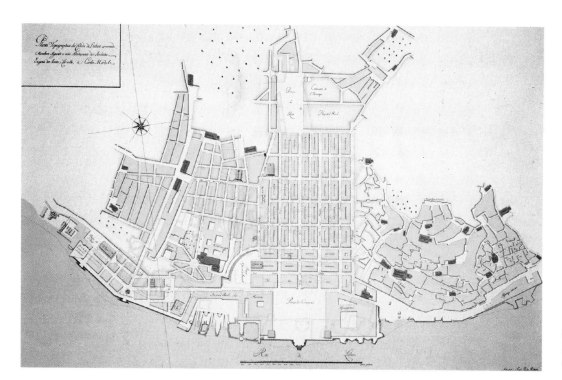

Reconstruction plan for Lisbon: design by Eugenio dos Santos, ca. 1756.

Genoa, *Terrazzi di marmo*. Painted by Carlo Bossoli, ca. 1850.

Venice, *Canal Grande.*
Painted by Canaletto,
ca. 1720.

Mediterranean seaport: that is, Barcelona's port was the center of a finely subdivided network of smaller towns and cities in Catalonia, as well as the hub of an international network of port cities that began to develop during this time. The hub itself – the port – was no more than a bay with a beach in the late Middle Ages: 'Then for three hundred years the procession of ships from the little ports of the Catalan seaboard plied ceaselessly back and forth on the Barcelona "beach," where sailing ships from the Balearics would also put in to harbour as well as boats from Valencia which was always something of a rival, Biscay whalers, and the constant flow of boats from Marseilles and Italy.'[9]

The location and shape of the city are determined, first and foremost, by specific geographical conditions: a lowland plain fronting the sea, surrounded by massifs to the south and west (Montjuich and Tibidado) that offered protection against the influences of weather and enemy forces from the hinterland. This plain was crisscrossed by countless streams, which carried water from Tibidado to the sea. While the course of the streams would have a major effect on the layout of the

city *map*, the surrounding mountains and, in particular, the elevation of the plain itself (a plateau barely above sea level) would be of vital importance to the city*scape*.[10]

The vulnerability of the harbor front called for a rampart. The fact that port activities had to take place, temporarily, in the bay and on the beach instead of on quays, with their dockside accouterments, was compensated for by the presence of large numbers of *macips de Ribera*: liberated galley slaves employed as dockworkers.[11] Barcelona's great need for dockworkers and sailors, not enough of whom were available in the immediate vicinity, resulted in a recruiting operation that covered the entire Mediterranean region and beyond. The city soon gained a far-reaching reputation as a place welcoming adventurers, buccaneers, and former galley slaves, among others, from all over the Mediterranean region.[12] In the course of time, they settled in the Barrio Ribera (coastal or riparian district) on the north side of the medieval city.

Originally, the city was not oriented toward the sea in a *spatial* sense. Barcelona had evolved concentrically around the old Roman

Left: Barcelona, the position of the Roman city within the contours of the late-medieval city.

Right: Barcelona's original watercourses.

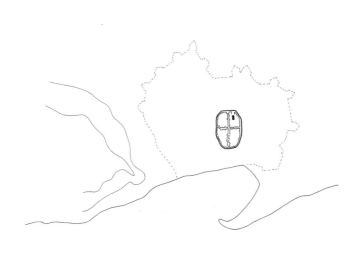

CITY AND PORT

Barcelona: the Ramblas, 1995.

expansion, which took place in the southern part of Barcelona, the city's existing southern border – formed by a system of streams ('ramblas') – was transformed into a long boulevard. In the course of time, this boulevard became a central route straight through the expanded city and a line of orientation toward the sea. Moreover, the Ramblas[15] became the most important entrance to the port for traffic arriving from every corner of Catalonia. Thus from the very beginning the Ramblas was an attractive site for various urban institutions, such as market buildings, monasteries, and the university; as well as for palaces built by affluent merchants.[16]

The Ramblas was soon seen as the focal point of the city, where one could find not only the wealth and power of the urban elite, but also a manifestation of public urban life: traffic, trade, entertainment, and festivities.

Because the Ramblas originated as a stream carrying water to the sea, its conversion into a central urban boulevard suddenly provided the city with a prominent urban area oriented toward the sea. The Ramblas ended at the old shipyard known as the Drassanes, which fronted the harbor. It seemed only logical to extend the orientation of the boulevard toward the sea even farther.

The city did not have the opportunity to realize this extension until the seventeenth century. In the second half of the fifteenth century, the city continued to present itself, with added emphasis, as an independent city-state, while in fact it belonged to the Kingdom of Aragon. In 1472 Ferdinand of Aragon decided to discipline the city by means of military intervention. The restraints imposed were more than simply administrative and military; they also affected the economy and urban planning. The marriage of Ferdinand of Aragon to Isabella of Castile united their kingdoms in 1474 and placed Barcelona under the dominion of Central Spain.[17] In the seventeenth century, King Philip IV loosened the reins somewhat and

city, and for a long time its spatial organization focused on this ancient center. In the fourteenth century, the city's *Consell de Cent* ('Council of Hundred'), which consisted of approximately one hundred representatives of both the bourgeoisie and the working class,[13] decided to build a new city hall. They, too, opted for the old city center. The harbor front was no more than the edge of town, with its rampart as military line of defense.

Another fourteenth-century building – and one of the most important symbols of solidarity between Barcelona's population and the sea – is the Santa Maria del Mar, a church built outside the Roman city center in the La Ribera district.[14] But even though this church is filled with models of ships, seascapes, and maritime tableaux, it still fails to make a physical connection between city and sea.

The initiative for this physical connection came in the fifteenth century, when the city needed to expand in order to accommodate its growing population. As part of this

Map of Barcelona, 1708.

View of Barcelona.
Joseph Friderich Leopold,
ca. 1700.

Map of Barcelona, 1806. The harbor front wedged between the fort on Montjuich and the citadel, with La Barceloneta on the cape south of the citadel.

View of Barcelona. Painted by Jacques Moulinier, ca. 1803.

BARCELONA

Barcelona: Muralla
de Mar. Lithograph by
Isidore L. Deroy, 1865.

restored, to a limited degree, Catalonia's right
to govern itself. In this period, city authorities
picked up the thread of urban renewal that
had been dropped in the fifteenth century,
after the transformation of the Ramblas, and
turned their attention to reconstructing the
harbor front.

Since a military fort built on Montjuich
now stood guard over the entire bay, the
rampart between city and port could be far
less sturdy. After demolishing the existing
rampart, the city council took advantage of
this knowledge and built a broad boulevard
– on land filled in and made level with the
shore – between the Ramblas and the city's
northern mooring place. They also had
waterfront buildings torn down and replaced
by a distinguished facade of merchants'
palaces and administrative buildings. A new
quay wall was built, but it was too high to
allow ships to tie up to the quay. The resulting
cityscape presented the city atop the plinth of

the quay wall, so to speak, and displayed a
new boulevard, the Passeig de la Muralla de
Mar, as an urban balcony overlooking the
harbor. Although this boulevard failed to
function as a quay, it did unite the port's
essential poles: in the south, the Drassanes
wharf; and in the north – in the 'crook' of
the bay – the mooring place where vessels
were loaded and unloaded.

### THE COLONIZATION OF BARCELONA: CONFINING AND EXCLUDING

People were not able to enjoy the new
situation for long, however. The eighteenth
century represented a very black page in the
history of the city. From 1702 to 1714 the
War of the Spanish Succession raged
between the Bourbon and Habsburg
Dynasties; at stake was the Spanish throne.

The citizens of Barcelona opposed Philip of Bourbon, who emerged from this war as King Philip v of Spain.

The sovereign took revenge on Barcelona by depriving the city of its open connection to the sea. He had a fortress built on the north side of the city, which together with the fort on Montjuich, kept both city and port completely under control. The new fort and the city walls would hold Barcelona in an iron grip for nearly one and a half centuries. Despite the fact that every type of urban expansion was forbidden, the population increased from 37,000 in 1717 to 189,000 in 1855: a mass of humanity crammed into an area of about 250 hectares.[18]

Besides confining the majority of the city's residents to the space within the walls, another element was kept outside: namely, the original inhabitants of La Ribera. Construction of the new citadel had required a large section of La Ribera to be torn down. Those living in the demolished part of town – fishermen, sailors, and dockworkers: Barcelona's most rebellious citizens but also the ones most needed in the harbor – were relocated to a new district on the cape adjoining the port, La Barceloneta.[19]

The central government in Madrid treated Barcelona in the same way that it treated other areas to be subdued: as a colony, not unlike Spain's many colonies in Central and South America, for example. The construction of the new district of La Barceloneta was a prototype of colonial urban planning in this era.[20] The Spaniards developed a certain type of colonial city, which was required to meet two conditions: the city's *surroundings* had to be controllable, but *the city itself* had to be kept under control as well, keeping in mind that the colonial population of such a city consisted not only of the military but also, in many cases, of convicts and exiles.[21]

Both the citadel and La Barceloneta were designed by Flemish engineer Prosper Verboom. He took a primarily military point of view in laying out the streets, which are in the field of fire of the fort on Montjuich and the citadel. This layout not only kept the district from being used as a bulwark to shelter enemy troops, but also allowed for possible rebellions mounted by the district population itself to be suppressed with ease. Furthermore, the direction of the wind played a role as well: the street network provides for maximum protection from cold easterly winds. The layout of the rational pattern of La Barceloneta is derived from the square: the square of the *casa* ('home') and of the barracks. *Casas* in the district are all based on standard dimensions: 8.40 by 8.40 meters. Different housing types – duplexes and maisonettes – were designed using variations of these dimensions. Dwellings were built on opposite sides of the public street and, in the case of duplexes, were built back to back.

From the moment the first *manzanas* ('housing blocks') were built until 1868, a regulation existed which determined, in precise detail, the dimensions and materials to be used in building *manzanas*. The result was a high degree of uniformity, not only in the size of land parcels, but also in the design of façades: portals, windows, balconies, and cornices.

In the nineteenth century the district was expanded as far as possible – to the edge of the sea – a project which built on the existing pattern of streets and which produced a triangular grid.

Thus the city of Barcelona entered the nineteenth century as a city with a double legacy: the legacy of the proud, autonomous port city, whose most precious heirlooms were the Ramblas and the Passeig de la Muralla de Mar; and the legacy of colonization, symbolized by the citadel, the medieval city's absurdly high density of

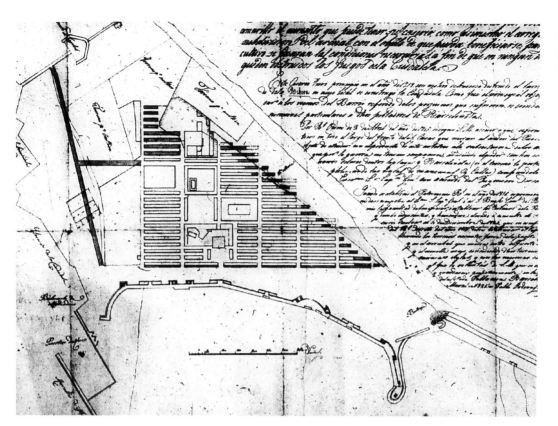

La Barceloneta, expansion plan extending toward the coastline, 1825.

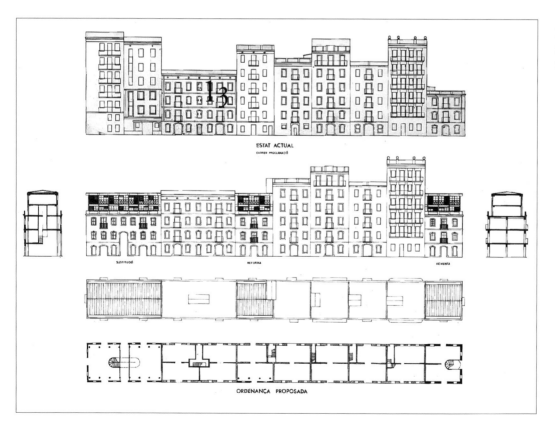

La Barceloneta, wall of facades, sections, and floor plan of a *manzana*.

CITY AND PORT

buildings and people, and the *ex-muras* enclave of La Barceloneta.

La Barceloneta played a dual role in the course of the eighteenth and nineteenth centuries. Together with the citadel, this district was the most visible product of the colonization of the city. But in its position *beyond* the clutches of the city walls, La Barceloneta also provided a 'liberated' view of city, port, and sea: a view not only from the quays, but also from the streets, of this transparent district.

La Barceloneta became a popular haven for city dwellers hoping to escape the city and a favorite standpoint for painters trying to capture the essence of the cityscape. In short, La Barceloneta also functioned as the city's 'conscience,' for in its streets the memory of the proud harbor front was kept alive.[22]

# 2 Modernity in the Mediterranean Region Barcelona as a *European* City on the Water

The Spanish government's hold on Barcelona began to weaken in the early nineteenth century. With the rise of industrialization, Barcelona once more became a city of exceptional strategic significance owing to its proximity to the rest of Europe, as well as to its favorable seaside location. Moreover, the Spanish state had no desire to frustrate the interest shown by entrepreneurs and investors in moving to and investing in this city. In the early 1800s Catalonia was responsible for more than a quarter of the gross national product.[23] New industry and population growth remained concentrated within the city walls for the time being. Various epidemics – cholera in particular – plagued the city during this period.

The grip that the city walls had on the city in the first half of the nineteenth century was broken to some extent by the realization of tree-lined promenades outside the walls: the Passeig de Gràcia, which formed a connection between the village of Gràcia and the far end of the Ramblas; the Rondas, laid out along the ramparts; and the Cami del Cementiri, which ran along the coast from the Pla de Palau to the cemetery on the city's north side. The Passeig de Gràcia and Cami del Cementiri were of utmost importance, as they helped to create a greater spatial context for the Ramblas and the waterfront boulevard.

In the second half of the nineteenth century, following a change in the balance of power in Spain in 1848, the military significance of Barcelona's fortifications disappeared, after which the citadel was vacated and, together with the city walls, demolished. The following period was of great significance to the city: Barcelona not only expanded toward the hinterland but also restored its waterfront relationship with the sea. Plans realized in the late 1800s and early 1900s put an end to the former state of confinement and transformed Barcelona into an open, modern, European city.

## EUROPEAN, MEDITERRANEAN, AND CATALAN IDENTITY

From the mid-nineteenth century on, the search for a unique Catalan identity played an important role in Barcelona's efforts to shrug off the domination of the central Spanish state.

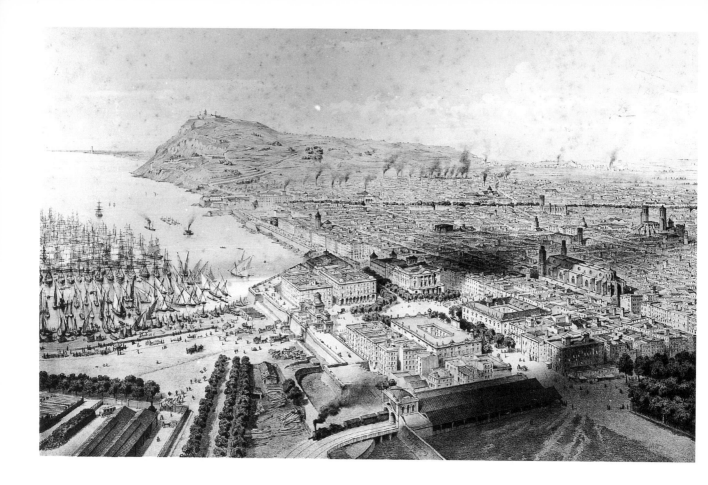

Bird's-eye view of
Barcelona, ca. 1860.
The ensemble of Plaza
de Palacio and Station
Francia is in the fore-
ground.

Over the years, many different versions of
'the Catalan identity' have passed in review.
In a cultural respect, 'Catalan' varies from an
introverted search for a completely unique
and autonomous cultural basis to the idea
of Catalonia as an (independent, to be sure)
element belonging to a greater (but definitely
not Spanish) entity – either Europe or the
Mediterranean region  – a concept in which
Barcelona plays the role of a modern, international metropolis. In a political respect,
'Catalan' varies from reactionary Catholicism
to socialism and anarchism.

From 1880 to 1936, during the first major
burst of growth experienced by modern
Catalan culture – or rather by the search for a
unique Catalan cultural identity – the focus
was on a strong orientation toward Europe,
and especially toward the Continent's big
cities: Paris, London, and Vienna.

In describing this period, Isidre Molas and
Marilyn McCully point out that this orientation dominated everything else in the areas of
both culture and economy: although one was
not the result of the other, this simultaneous
orientation did create a basis for a certain
consensus about the direction of the struggle
for independence with respect to Madrid.[24]

Orientation in the field of visual arts was
aimed largely at Paris, where many a Barcelona artist spent longer or shorter periods of
time gathering inspiration for the subsequent
design of a unique Catalan cultural movement that came to be known as *modernismo*.

In the area of music, the focus was on
Vienna. Molas mentions that in Barcelona
Viennese opera was more popular than
Italian opera, another example of Barcelona's
attempt to display a European, rather than a
Mediterranean, image.

As for architecture and urban planning, Barcelona developed its own *architectonic* culture, which gained world fame thanks to the work of Gaudí and Domènech, among others.

The bourgeoisie saw its economic future on the Continent. Catalan industry, whose past dealings had been confined to Spanish colonies like Cuba and the Philippines, was forced to find new markets in the late 1800s, when Spain lost these colonies. Essential exponents of this new orientation were world's fairs held in 1888 and 1929, events which were to raise the status of Barcelona to a level enjoyed by London and Paris, cities that had hosted such exhibitions in the past.

Politically speaking – and this includes Liberal Catalan Republicans, as well as anarchists, Socialists, and Communists – the most prominent ideas adopted were those arriving from Western, Central, and Eastern Europe, not from the Mediterranean region.

Although Barcelona's political, economic, and cultural life did remain extremely diverse, and although various interpretations of a 'Catalan cultural identity' continued to exist, a common denominator was present as well: namely, the orientation toward the Continent and the idea of Catalonia as part of a modern, industrialized Europe rather than as part of a backward, feudal, clerical Spain.

### URBAN HARBOR FRONT VERSUS AUTONOMOUS PORT

In the mid-nineteenth century, Barcelona welcomed the renewed opportunity to reorient the city toward the port, and especially toward Europe, by means of a large-scale urban planning project at the moorage site in the crook of the bay. Here, surrounding the Pla de Palau, a new urban planning ensemble arose, together with the realization of the Estació França railroad station, which created a rail connection with France. The combination of port and station – along with the formal, monumental character of the new ensemble – made the site into the main entrance to the city; at the same time, it formed an inset between the old city and La Barceloneta. In the years that followed, the district of La Barceloneta was provided with fine beaches, restaurants, and other facilities for Barcelona's beau monde.

In 1888 the significance of the city's new main entrance was reinforced when the despised citadel next to it was demolished. The site accommodating the citadel – the very spot that once prevented the city from having unrestricted relations with the outside world – was converted into a park for visitors to the 1888 World's Fair, an event intended to draw the attention of all Europe to Barcelona. When the boulevard was beautified with rows of palm trees, the Passeig de Colom – together with the Pla de Palau – would be 'the most urban and international boulevard of Barcelona.'[25]

Barcelona in 1888: the city is oriented toward the port by means of a connected series of public areas.

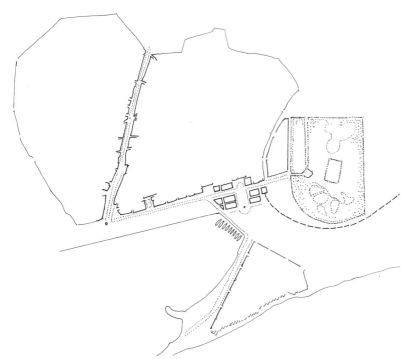

Barcelona was given little time, however, to enjoy its new image as 'the city on the water.' A concurrent development was to lead, of all things, to a new separation between the city and its waterfront. This development was related to the establishment of a new means of power, the Port Autonom, which was created by the national government in the nineteenth century as an independent organization authorized to control the territory of the port. The municipality of Barcelona had a limited number of seats in the Board of Governors; the majority were allocated to diverse national ministries and the Chamber of Commerce. With the introduction of the Port Autonom, Barcelona again faced an external, largely Madrid-dominated, source of power with control over the very thing that the city so badly wanted to control itself: the port.

At the turn of the century, the Port Autonom decided to build the Moll de la Fusta, a broad (un)loading quay, by filling in waterfront land and making it level with the shore, a project that would also bridge the difference in height between the boulevard (Passeig de Colom) and the water. Large harbor-related buildings that rose along this new quay were indeed vital to the expanding port economy, but they also relieved the Passeig de Colom of its function as an 'urban balcony' with a view of the water. The Moll d'Espanya, a large harbor pier that started at the crook of the bay, also stripped the Pla de Palau of its role as main entrance to the city.

This new barrier between city and water was followed at the turn of the century by plans for a series of docks which were to extend north from the coast of La Barceloneta. These plans remained on paper, however, and ultimately the port realized the needed expansion in a southerly direction.

All of which fails to change the fact that the coastal strip north of La Barceloneta was filled in with a substantial amount of industry during the early decades of the twentieth century.

Still another attempt was made to re-create a connection between city and port. This time, as in 1888, a major event laid the basis for a spatial transformation. The International Exposition of 1929 was held on Montjuich. This event – the focus of global attention – eliminated the city's last military bastion and produced another city park as well. Efforts were made to restore ties between the city and La Barceloneta by realizing a cable-car system and by radically expanding the beaches, thus providing comfortable seashore accommodations for international visitors.

The exposition prompted the completion of the first transformation of Barcelona's waterfront: from a militarized zone to a series of public areas combined with port and industrial activities.

This new system of public space on Barcelona's port side, realized in a period extending from the late nineteenth century to 1929, was meant to express a new economic and cultural élan in the city, and a strong orientation toward the rest of Europe. The port area was supposed to symbolize the city's openness, its eagerness to face the rest of the world or, in any case, Europe.

The creation of this new spatial system was accompanied by major problems, however. In particular, investments in the 1929 exposition on Montjuich caused the city serious financial problems,[26] which left no financial leeway for the municipality to invest in and maintain public areas and facilities in the 1930s. As a result, exhibition buildings, pavilions, and facilities such as the cable-car system and cog tramlines, originally intended only for temporary use during the expo, continued to be used afterward. Hence the city was not left completely empty-handed.

Although the cable cars became a popular tourist attraction, they were unable to prevent La Barceloneta from returning to its isolated position with respect to the city. La Barceloneta's beaches and the park that had once been the site of the citadel could not stop various elements – port, railroad, and industry – from going in separate directions and from evolving into physical barriers between city and sea. Warehouses blocked the view of the city from the port, and railroads formed a new barrier between the old city and Barceloneta.

URBAN EXPANSION, FURTHER MARGINALIZATION OF THE WATERFRONT

The demolition of the city walls not only enabled the spatial transformation of the harbor front, but also provided an opportunity to release throngs of city dwellers and urban activities from their cramped quarters. However, despite the eagerness of authorities who jumped at the chance to expand the city, the occasion would also lead to an even graver marginalization of the waterfront, which already showed signs of decline.

In 1859 Barcelona's city council organized a contest for an urban design for future urban expansion: *ensanche* in Spanish, and *eixample* in Catalan. The council chose a design by Antoni Rovira i Trias, whose work was organized along several radials, with the old city as the focal point.

Historians have never found a satisfactory answer to the question of why the Spanish government intervened and ordered the municipality to implement a design by Ildefonso Cerdà. Cerdà was no less Catalonia-minded than Rovira and certainly could not be considered a figurehead of Madrid, as confirmed by Hughes,[27] so the government's choice could not have been due to his political orientation. In any case, of relevance to this story is that Cerdà's plan implied an entirely different relation between city and sea than the design by Rovira. The latter had organized the whole city around the historical urban core as city center. Thus the harbor front of the old city would still be the most important element forming a connection between city and sea.

In Cerdà's design, however, the historical city no longer assumed a key position, and neither harbor front nor extended coastline played a major role. Cerdà envisioned the city developing in a northerly direction: the best opportunities for growth were in the north, with its readily available and easily developable space, and it was also the direction leading to the rest of Europe, to the target of Barcelona's strong economic and cultural orientation.

Cerdà was pervaded by the idea of an egalitarian society, which was to be expressed in the spatial organization of the city. His city would exhibit an even distribution – from one end to the other – of rich and poor, facilities and industry, parks and markets.

The ingenious character of Cerdà's plan is found in his ability to combine a mathematical, orthogonal, organizational pattern with important existing geographical and topographic constants, and to make all elements agree: he used the city's east-west orientation, which followed the original course taken by Barcelona's many streams, as a basis for the orientation of his grid pattern.[28] This allowed for the fairly easy incorporation of important existing routes – such as connecting roads between the village of Gràcia and Barcelona, and between the hamlets of El Clot and Icaria – into the seemingly quite rigid and neutral grid.

Two prominent diagonals that transected the grid formed elements which, together with an extra broad east-west boulevard

Above: Expansion plan
(Ensanche) for Barcelona,
design by Antoni Rovira i
Trias, 1859.

Below: Expansion plan
(Ensanche) for Barcelona,
design by Ildefonso
Cerdà, 1859.

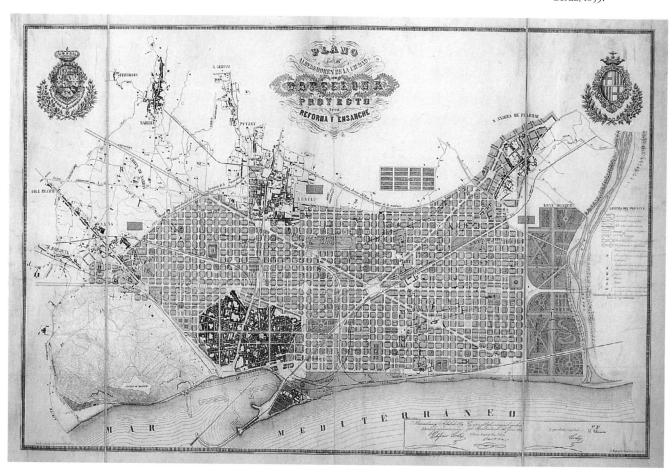

(Passeig de Gràcia) and an equally broad north-south boulevard (Gran Via), lent greater detail to the design of the city as a whole. At the point where the two diagonals and the Gran Via converge, plans were made to build the city's new administrative center.

The neutral grid of the design was subdivided into districts of about 5 square kilometers each (twenty housing blocks to a square), provided with their own facilities. In this plan, the old city was simply one more district and thus lost its significance as Barcelona's city center.

This northward urban expansion meant that the city's total coastline would measure nearly 6 kilometers, only 1 kilometer of which was the old harbor front. In Cerdà's design, however, this long coastline was not developed in greater detail as a special urban element. The city simply ended there. For that matter, the existing coastal railroad line made the development of a special seafront quite difficult.

More important in Cerdà's plan was the view of the sea provided by virtually every east-west street in the city's orthogonal street network. Only in the south was this view obstructed by the presence of the historical city. Cerdà compensated for this lack by twice breaching the old city, on opposite sides of the Ramblas. He believed that in time, when they had experienced the advantages of the new city, both population and administrators would turn their backs on the old city. At that point, the historical city could be torn down completely and transformed into one of the 'normal' districts of the Ensanche. Cerdà's plan made no provision for the projected seafront. Instead, the accent in the late 1800s and early 1900s remained on the old city's harbor front.

The implementation of Cerdà's plan differed from his expectations. His design assumed a precisely planned realization phase, with strict municipal supervision of the density of housing blocks and of the social composition of those living in each block. He had established building regulations that allowed inner courtyards next to housing blocks to be organized as communal 'social' areas which would form a transition between the public nature of the street and the private nature of the home: areas directly adjacent to the 'real' public space of the street network but chiefly intended as outdoor space for residents of the individual blocks.

Cerdà's urban plan was based on the conviction that urban planning should focus on four things: the city plan, which should indicate a network of public areas and the pattern of building sites to be allocated; the design of open space; the establishment of building regulations; and the establishment of regulations for social open space (the actual design of which may be realized by the private sector).[29]

From the beginning, however, Cerdà's plan functioned mainly as a building-line plan: municipal authorities assumed responsibility for the infrastructure of the street network, while all development within building lines was the result of private enterprise. The municipality lacked the perseverance and resources needed to carry out the regulatory tasks proposed by Cerdà. His egalitarian city was to remain a dream.

The primary result failed, in nearly every sense, to follow Cerdà's proposals for building density and the realization of 'social' areas. Only in a few housing blocks can Cerdà's ideas still be found. Of the four objectives of urban planning, as defined by Cerdà, only two were implemented: the city plan and the design of strictly public space.

The heart of urban development did not emerge north of the historical city, but west. The existing Passeig de Gràcia was the

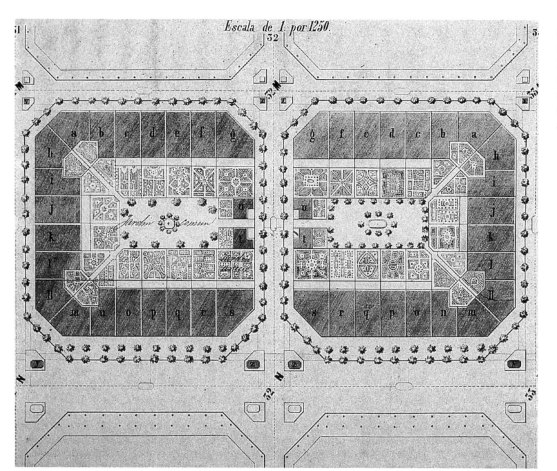

Escala de 1 por 1250.
32

Prototypes of housing blocks in Cerdà's Ensanche, with street network as public space and (semiopen) inner courtyards as 'social' space.

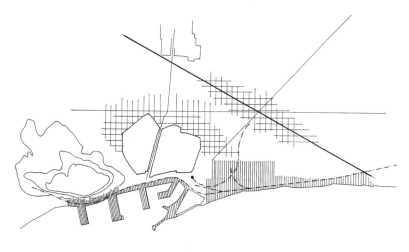

Early twentieth-century Barcelona, with the coastal strip as an industrial zone and the city cut off from the sea.

'magnet' along which the first building initiatives were developed and around which the grid of the Ensanche was filled in during the first decades after 1860.

The connection between the Passeig de Gràcia and the Ramblas was formed by a new square, the Plaça de Catalunya, which would evolve into Barcelona's central square in the twentieth century.

In the early 1900s the part of the Ensanche between the old city and Gràcia was filled in completely, while the northern area remained largely vacant. The only development was next to the railroad line that now ran along the seafront, where a limited amount of industry was realized.

In the second half of the nineteenth century and the first part of the twentieth, the relation between city and sea, and between city and port, acquired a new form. This form was defined by a new series of public areas, from Montjuich and the Passeig de Colom to Pla de Palau and Parc de la Ciutadella. The significance of these public parks, quays, and squares was emphasized mainly by the practical opportunities they provided for traffic and entertainment.

At right angles to the Passeig de Colom are the Ramblas, which centuries earlier had acquired the form of an urban space in the same way, and the Via Laietana. Of Cerdà's two recommendations for streets designed to breach the old city, Via Laietana was the only one realized. It became, therefore, the only east-west street of the Ensanche to offer a clear view of the sea: a goal that Cerdà had envisioned for the Ensanche as a whole. In the northern part of the plan, where this transparency was supposed to have been fully developed, nothing came of his intentions.

Of great import was the fact that the site of the citadel, despite its conversion into a city park, remained a mental cutoff point between the central part of the city and the urban area to the northeast. The words 'behind the Parc de la Ciutadella' (referring to the northeastern part of the city) are still charged with emotion in Barcelona.

This cutoff point was reinforced by the presence of the coastal railroad, now lined with industrial development realized without strict adherence to building lines prescribed by the Ensanche and with no thought to a view of the sea, which such development has totally obstructed.

Hence Barcelona marched into the twentieth century surrounded by just as much equivocality as it had taken into the nineteenth century: accompanied, on the one hand, by a series of initiatives for urban revitalization projects meant to reconfirm concrete efforts to orient the city toward port and sea and, on the other hand, by the frustration of such initiatives as a result of the professionalization of the port, under the leadership of the Port Autonom, and of the industrialization of the coastal strip of the Ensanche.

## 3  The Uncompleted Project of Modernism – Spatial Form or Building Form?

The strong orientation of Barcelona's intellectuals toward European culture created a climate receptive to the concepts of modernism. Catalan architects who felt an affinity for these ideas established the GATCPAC (*Grup d'Arquitectes i Tècnics Catalans per al Progrés de l'Arquitectura Contemporània*), the Catalan branch of CIAM. GATCPAC initiated studies aimed at a radical reorganization of the entire city. In 1934 these studies led to a comprehensive plan for all of Barcelona which was based on a supergrid derived from Cerdà's grid for the Ensanche. In fact, this was the second attempt following Cerdà's plan to incorporate the old city into a larger, neutral structure. Typical is the radical separation of urban structure and urban shape, a significant characteristic of modernist European urban planning from 1930 to 1965.[30] While the road and street network – although not designed in detail – follows the structure of the grid, the city takes its shape mainly from its buildings, which are designed as autonomous objects.

The harbor front was to be revitalized as well: one harbor area was to be filled in to augment the new grid with an extra strip of land, 400 meters wide, along the old water-

Bird's-eye view of the Macià Plan. Gouache by Torres Clavé, 1936.

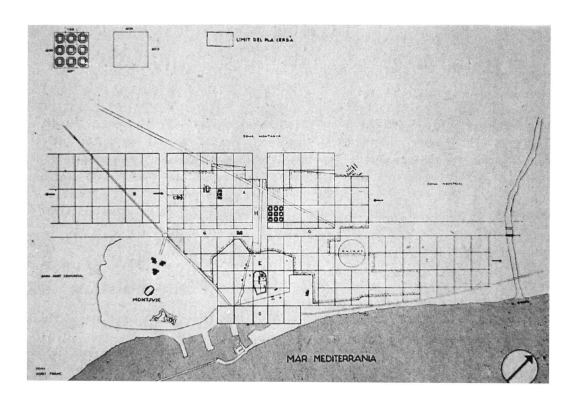

Design for a new city map of Barcelona, GATCPAC (Macià Plan), 1933.

front. This strip would provide space for several large apartment buildings with collective facilities. GATCPAC had the full support of the Catalan government – the Generalitat de Catalunya – whose president, Frances Macià, was largely responsible not only for GATCPAC's existence, but also for bringing Le Corbusier to Barcelona to serve as an adviser during the development of the plan.

In introducing both Le Corbusier and the plan, the Generalitat added yet another dimension to the desire to make Barcelona into a *modern* city oriented toward the rest of Europe. The new harbor front was based on the same concept that Le Corbusier had applied in Algiers a few years earlier and would apply later in Buenos Aires: the concept of a large-scale superbuilding that allowed for variation on the scale of the individual dwelling while remaining a wholly uniform entity responsible for lending expression to a new collectivity in modern urban society.

With this emphasis on the *building form* as a representation of the city, the Catalan government and urban planners set off on a new course, unlike the one followed in previous decades during which the focus

had been on designing a new *spatial form* for the harbor front.

Despite broadly based political support for GATCPAC's modernist plans, they were never realized. Not only were they thwarted by the economic crisis and the destitute situation in which Barcelona found itself but also, and even more so, by the Spanish Civil War, which started in 1936 and ended with Franco's victory in 1939. The war eliminated GATCPAC's political support. Public investment in the city came to a virtual halt, and private enterprise was given top priority.

In the period that followed, urban development in Barcelona would be determined almost entirely by the laws of a free market and of speculation. The existing city was marked by serious neglect, deterioration in the old inner city, an enormous increase in building density in the Ensanche and La Barceloneta, and the development of new expansion areas based on nothing but speculation.

During Franco's regime, both harbor front and seafront assumed a marginal position. The Moll de la Fusta, which was used wholly and exclusively for port activities, blocked any view of the city from the port. The Passeig de Colom was redesigned as a thoroughfare, which ultimately had twelve lanes linking the new port and industrial area – Zona Franca, south of Montjuich – with the north. On the side facing the city, La Barceloneta became totally immured by industrial and railroad complexes, and the seafront of the Ensanche was fully occupied by industry.

As a result, the harbor front all but lost the function it had acquired in the seventeenth century and developed to an even greater degree in the 1800s and early 1900s: as a central area for public urban life.

In the late 1960s, a relative thaw in the dictatorship led to a revival of functionalist urban planning and, at the same time, to a resurgence of criticism aimed at functionalism, which heralded in turn the onset of new urban planning practices.

Prominent architects who were part of an informal, more private circle began to revaluate urban planning and architectonic methods used between 1860 and 1930, and to criticize GATCPAC's modernist principles and proposals. The heart of this criticism was a belief that GATCPAC plans – in this case, the Macià Plan – would force the city into an overly comprehensive international straitjacket and thus fail to express the unique identity of the city and the region. Moreover, the separation of shape and structure would eliminate both a sense of significance and the means needed to generate an urban atmosphere.

The original source of this criticism, as well as of the renewed interest in turn-of-the-century achievements, was a number of architects united in an alliance called 'Grupo R.' Their initial objective was to develop a uniquely Catalan style of architecture. One of the founders of Grupo R was Oriol Bohigas, a professor since 1963 at the Escola Tècnica Superior d'Arquitectura de Barcelona (ETSAB), the architecture department of the Polytechnic University of Catalonia. Thanks to Bohigas, the study of the formal characteristics of architecture and urban planning in Barcelona acquired a key position in ETSAB courses and associated research. Urban planning aspects, in particular, were given an increasing amount of attention in the 1960s. This focus was institutionalized in 1969 when Manuel de Solà-Morales and Joan Busquets established the Laboratorio de Urbanismo.

These developments ultimately played a large part in Barcelona's urban planning policy after Franco's death brought an end to dictatorship in 1976.

In the first place, the situation at the university in the 1960s had produced an entire generation of architects – a genuine 'Barcelona school' – who had carried out extensive studies of the city's formal architectural characteristics and urban planning traditions and who were highly like-minded on the significance of such traditions.

Of special interest is the continuity found in the theorization and design practices of the Barcelona school throughout a period of more than twenty years, a continuity supported and personified by, in particular, the designers mentioned: Bohigas, de Solà-Morales, and Busquets.

The first open confrontation between the two urban planning practices (those of the municipality and those of academicians belonging to the Barcelona school) concerned, of all things, the city's seafront.

The spot at which the original expansion plan (the Ensanche) seemed to indicate the most open relationship between city and sea ultimately produced the largest barrier: the Poble Nou zone, located between the Parc de la Ciutadella and the Besos River. In Cerdà's original plan, the citadel was to have 'dissolved' completely within the pattern of the new grid. Instead, the special position taken by the site of the citadel remained

Somorrostro, a village of barracks on the beach at Poble Nou.

Nou into a zone for apartment buildings, offices, and hotels. The plan was created for the Catalan power company, which owned a great deal of land and many outdated structures in the area, and thus wanted to find new types of land use.[31]

The new morphology of the plan – which preserved the broad, sunken railroad line between coastline and Ensanche – and the exclusive character of its new functions would make Barcelona, behind the railroad tracks, even more isolated from the coast than it already was. La Barceloneta, the part of town with the strongest ties to sea and port, would disappear.

The main objective of the Ribera Plan was to raise the value of land and real estate. The traffic infrastructure, in the form of a dual route followed by rail line and thoroughfare, created a concrete boundary between the existing city and the new area.

The plan was received favorably by the majority of entrepreneurs and landowners in the area in question, as well as by municipal authorities, and seemed on its way to becoming an important part of the new structure plan that the city council asked the urban planning department to develop in 1969. After thirty-five years, authorities were finally backing a seafront policy based on the content of the 1934 Macià Plan. In collaboration with La Barceloneta's federation of district organizations, however, the Catalan Collegi d'Arquitectes launched a counteroffensive in 1971, in the form of a design competition for the area. The group that won the competition was headed by Manuel de Solà-Morales and called itself the Laboratorio de Urbanismo. Their preliminary study included spatial, architectonic, social, and economic developments in the district.

The winning design for La Barceloneta preserved both the historical structure of the existing district and the proposed route for a

recognizable, and even after this site was transformed into a city park as part of Barcelona's urban development, it continued to function as a cutoff point.

Poble Nou had become a dumping ground for clusters of railroad infrastructure and industry, which together formed an impenetrable barrier that separated city and sea. In the 1950s an entire district of illegally constructed barracks appeared on the beach at Poble Nou: housing for migrants from the countryside.

This situation was reinforced when the economic heart of the city began shifting southward around 1960. The southern part of the Diagonal had been one of the most popular business locations for some time, a fact expressed in the price of land, which was higher in the south than anywhere else in the city. The price of land in La Barceloneta and Poble Nou, on the other hand, was the lowest in the city.

In 1967 former GATCPAC architect Antoni Bonet Castellana designed the Ribera Plan, which covered the entire coastal strip from La Barceloneta to the Besos River and proposed transforming the industry-dominated shoreline of Poble

new beltway. Furthermore, the design projected the development of a new structure of large-scale housing blocks on the north side of the district, which were to create a link between La Barceloneta and the grid of the Ensanche, as well as to integrate the new beltway into the urban fabric.

This new structure was to be the first phase in the future urbanization of the coastal zone. The designers also strongly recommended the preservation and revitalization of La Barceloneta and most of the Ensanche, thereby emphasizing the essential value of the historical structure of these districts to Barcelona's urban culture and to life in the city. In other words, Barcelona would not be Barcelona without La Barceloneta and the Ensanche.

This logic did not apply, however, to the structure of the seafront zone north of La Barceloneta. Even though this zone was also part of the original Ensanche and even though it still displayed part of the original street pattern, its use as an industrial zone and its association with the railroad had stripped it of the allure attached to the Ensanche. The relocation of industrial activities and the realization of a beltway were to create conditions for entirely new typologies of urban areas and buildings: frameworks for the development of new urban programs and for the creation of a specific significance for the area.

Hence the design by the Laboratorio de Urbanismo was not opposed to magnitude and modernity per se; its aim was to introduce a new, large-scale urban form

Above: The Ribera Plan, design by Antoni Bonet Castellana, 1967.

Below: Alternative Ribera Plan: this design by the Laboratorio de Urbanismo was the winning entry in a competition organized by the Collegi d'Arquitectes.

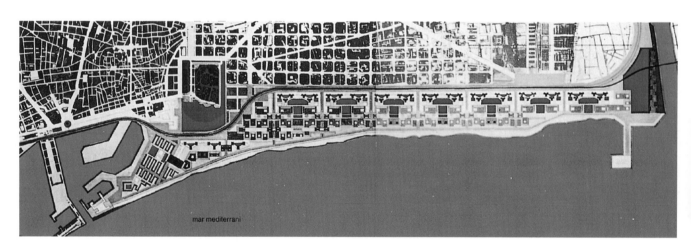

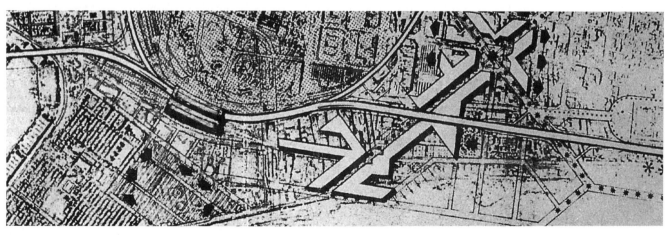

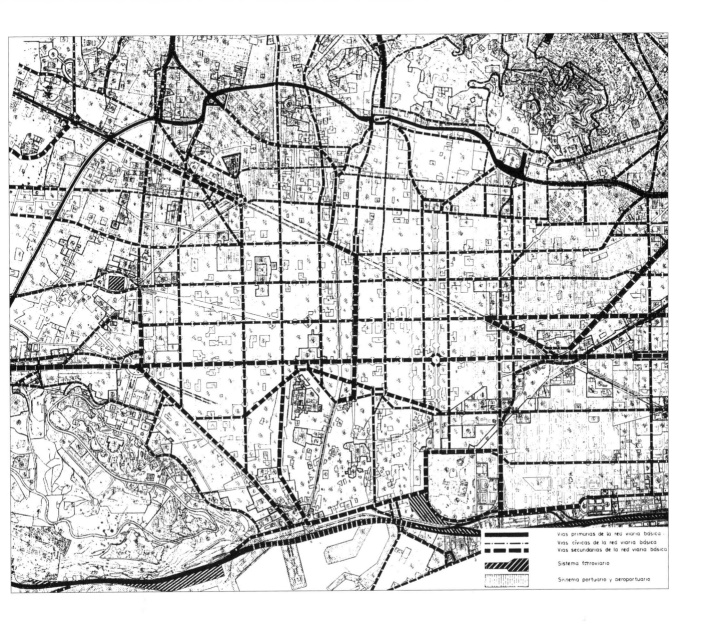

The Plan General
Metropolitan, 1976.

capable of corresponding to the scale of the beltway, as well as to the scale and shape of the historical structure of La Barceloneta and the Ensanche. The designers focused most of their attention on this capacity to correspond, which relied largely on the significance and treatment of the main traffic infrastructure. While the Ribera Plan used the route of the new beltway (Cinturon) to destroy historically developed structures and to reinforce the physical separation between city and coastal zone, the design by the Laboratorio de Urbanismo

tried to create a new urban composition by combining the new traffic route and the existing urban planning context.

The design by de Solà-Morales and associates was, in fact, an urban planning manifesto that took a stand on two important issues which had been dominating the debate among Catalan architects and planners for some time.

The first was the issue of historical continuity: what significance should a design give to historical urban structures vis-à-vis the necessity to introduce new spatial typologies in the city?

The second was the issue of spatial continuity: to what extent and in what way can a design create coherence among various urban planning fragments and elements?

In the case of both issues, the basic assumption was that a general consensus existed with regard to criticism of the modern GATCPAC tradition, which had raised such a furor and of which the Ribera Plan could be seen as a belated exponent.

Despite seemingly broad support for those criticizing modernist urban planning, however, the alternative for this practice was less unequivocal.

The Laboratorio de Urbanismo's design was based on the following principles:
– Historical structures are important in that they provide a spatial framework for everyday urban life.
– When historical structures become a hindrance to urban vitality, the situation calls for a drastic change.
– New infrastructure is needed to keep the city open and accessible, and to introduce new relationships.
– A city should provide space for new typologies of urban areas and buildings, which are essential to new urban programs.

Although these principles formed a fine preamble to the transformation of the seafront scheduled for the 1980s, the plan still faced a great deal of revision.

For the time being, the controversy between the Ribera Plan and the design by the Laboratorio de Urbanismo remained a debate on paper. In 1969 the municipality had commissioned the urban planning department to develop a new structure plan for the city, with the assurance that a considerable part of the municipal budget would be reserved for the implementation of this plan.

In 1976 the new Plan General Metropolitan (PGM) was approved by the city council. In several ways, the PGM may be seen as an attempt to pick up the thread of plan development at the place where Cerdà and GATCPAC had dropped it. This applies in particular to the desire to breach the old city to an even greater degree, and to an improved method of adapting both harbor front and seafront to the infrastructure of the entire city. These goals were to be met by newly designed traffic routes and nothing else. A street that would breach the old city was proposed south of the Ramblas, and both harbor front and seafront were made part of a beltway around the city.

The PGM was limited to a selection of routes and profiles for streets and highways, on the basis of which land could be acquired and building sites could be allocated. The plan provided no details on the *shape* of the city, which remained a matter of minor importance.

# 4 Barcelona's *Urbanismo.* Recapturing Public Space

Accompanying the democratization process that went on after Franco's death in 1976 was a renewed opportunity for Barcelona to concentrate all its efforts on achieving political and cultural independence from Madrid and on stimulating economic growth. From the beginning, however, Catalonia's regional government, dominated by Conservatives, had very different ideas from Barcelona's municipal government, controlled by Socialists.

The Generalitat de Catalunya focused most of its attention on shaping the city of Barcelona into the industrial and commercial center of Catalonia. Top priority was given to improving the traffic infrastructure, as determined by the Plan General Metropolitan of 1976, and on developing Zona Franca, an industrial area on the south side of Montjuich. Barcelona's airport had been built close to Zona Franca at an earlier date. The realization of the new beltway was deemed highly important, as this route would provide Zona Franca and the airport with a faster connection north (to France and the rest of Europe). The coastal route, which ran along the old harbor front, also played a major role in these plans.

The city council was also very eager to see an improvement in the traffic infrastructure, and not only because of the direct economic interests involved. If there was anything that would visually represent social change in the wake of Franco's death, it was recapturing public space, making the street a domain in which everyone could feel like a free citizen again. For forty years public streets had been an area in which the right to assemble was banned, in which people had to watch what they said and to be on their guard at all times,

alert to the political terror of the central government. The end of this period and the beginning of a time in which the street would be used once more as an arena for free speech was visible not only in the explosion of events organized by political parties and labor unions, but also in the restoration of traditional folk festivals and in the return of the Catalan language to public life, on public signs and announcements, in shopwindows, and so forth.

The new city council, in which Leftist parties had gained the majority in 1979, assigned top priority to the restoration of public space, and not simply a formal restitution of the public realm, but a reinstatement of what public space means mentally: a restoration of the opportunity for city residents to identify with public space and to attribute to public areas a meaning associated with freedom and (Catalan) autonomy.

This accent on having the urban population reidentify with the city was also considered necessary to prevent Barcelona, now developing new economic stimuli owing to closer contacts with the European market, from facing the imminent loss of residents and economic activities to the surrounding region.

Because of restrictions formed by natural boundaries (Montjuich, Tibibado, and the sea), Barcelona – with 1.7 million inhabitants within about 100 square kilometers – was already one of the most densely populated cities in Europe. Maintaining the size of this population as well as possible called for maximum efforts to create a 'compact city.'

To keep Barcelona's enormously concentrated population within this limited territory, the city council found it advisable to develop a policy that would provide the people with a new faith in, and an identification with, the city.[32]

The implementation of this policy was launched in 1979, when Bohigas was appointed supervisor of the urban planning department. After all, for years Bohigas had been the personification of the key role played by architecture and urban planning in the debate on Catalan culture.

After Bohigas was appointed, the big questions were: which strategy and which resources shall we use to approach the task of revitalizing and reorganizing public space, and what kind of role remains for the structure plan – Plan General Metropolitan (PGM) – formulated a few years ago? For that matter, the PGM placed both city council and Bohigas in a paradoxical situation. On the one hand, the intentions of the PGM were at odds with what Bohigas and his colleagues had in mind. Bohigas believed that the new network of traffic 'breaches' would have a destructive effect on the city's social climate and would cause even more residents to leave town.[33] On the other hand, the PGM was a reality on which a great deal of energy and financial resources had been spent since 1976. Large operations aimed at procuring land and other real estate for the sake of these new breaches had taken place. Furthermore, the PGM was a political reality as well, in view of the Catalan government's great interest in the plan. The former director of the urban development department, J. Solans i Huguet, who was responsible for the creation of the PGM, was now director of the department of land use of the Generalitat de Catalunya and, as such, in a position to monitor the implementation of 'his' PGM.[34]

Bohigas solved this paradox by establishing an urban planning policy which left the main urban structure proposed by the PGM intact, but which made the design and layout of individual elements (such as traffic routes) its most important priority. As a result, the next job was not to develop a new and complete structure plan, but to develop a new relation between the structure and shape of the city.

This new relation was based on two main points: the link needed to connect the structure of the city to the shape of individual districts and public space; and the principles to be used in designing public space.

City authorities gave absolute priority to the part of the new policy that dealt with public space: in the years 1980-1983, 62 percent of the municipal budget was spent on public works.[35]

'URBANISMO' AND REGIONAL IDENTITY

The prominent place that architecture and urban planning occupied in the debate on the cultural development of Catalonia and of the city in general was largely the consequence of involvement in the city by the architecture faculty of the Polytechnic University and the Laboratorio de Urbanismo. One venue at which this high regard was expressed was the Congres de Cultura Catalana, organized in 1978 by the Generalitat de Catalunya. Those attending this important congress drafted a program for the restoration and reinvigoration of the Catalan culture; in addition to language and theater arts, architecture and urban planning were essential aspects of this program.[36]

In this debate, an increasingly greater accent has come to lie on Catalonia's geomorphological and topographic qualities, and on the specific forms assumed by urbanization in this region, whose greatest exponent is Barcelona. In 1979 the magazine *Lotus international* published a special issue dedicated to a detailed study, carried out by Laboratorio de Urbanismo, of the morphological and structural characteristics of the Catalan region.[37] This study showed a direct connection between recent and abrupt democratization and decentralization processes in Spain and the development of conditions needed for people to identify with the region. In his introductory article, Manuel de Solà-Morales claims that efforts to achieve political autonomy and democracy can be made only in the presence of a *culture* that recognizes and appreciates regional characteristics. He says that such a culture is based on two important aspects: a *cartographic culture* of the territory, which is a condition for seeing and knowing the territorial characteristics of the region; and an urban planning culture, or *culture of working the territory*, which considers specific territorial features and uses them in the design of urban space. The second aspect is a form of *urbanismo* that does not look first and foremost to the architecture of buildings in developing the identity of city and region, but to the way in which a territory's geomorphological and topographic features can be used in this development.[38]

*Urbanismo* in Barcelona, with the Laboratorio de Urbanismo's plan for La Ribera as its first manifesto, symbolized the city's position in the Southern European debate on architecture and urban planning.

A key moment in this debate came in 1959, when an Italian urban planning competition was organized for an expansion project in Mestre, located in the Venetian lagoon. After many years in which the modern movement had dominated the international debate on urban planning, designs by Saverio Muratori and Ludovico Quaroni, in particular, demonstrated two different attempts to establish new principles for the design of a new city in the immediate vicinity of the paradigmatic historical city: Venice.

Muratori used his entry to show how a study he had developed in the 1950s of the morphological and typological characteristics of the city (in this case, Venice) could be used as a basis for the design of an urban expansion project. By reducing the many morphological and typological variations found in Venice, Muratori actually designed a sort of archetypal version of Venice.

Quaroni's design, on the other hand, was not a total rejection of the modern tradition. He tried to combine several principles of modern urban planning – such as the development of completely new building and infrastructural typologies capable of providing space for new urban programs – with specific conditions related to landscape and topography.

Quaroni's criticism of modernism was aimed less at the typology and enormity of buildings in designs by Le Corbusier and colleagues than at the lack of a relation between new building typologies and their territorial, topographic context. He saw Venice's old city not as a point of departure on which to build, but as part of the topographic context to which he wanted to react with his design. With his large c-shaped apartment buildings, Quaroni explicitly built on new building typologies, such as those that Le Corbusier and Louis Kahn had developed for, respectively, Algiers and Philadelphia. Quaroni's buildings, however, were not introduced as models for general use but, on the contrary, as a means to emphasize territorial characteristics – the specific peculiarities of the lagoon landscape – and, thanks to their orientation, they also created a connection to Venice.[39]

While in the years, and even decades, that followed, Muratori's approach would assume a dominant position in urban planning theorization and practice in Southern Europe, and later in Northern Europe as well,[40] the Laboratorio de Urbanismo based its approach more on the views espoused by Quaroni.[41]

The competition design for La Barce-

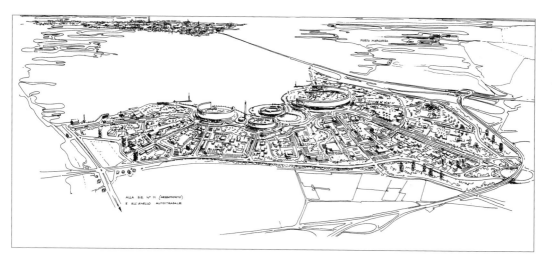

Ludovice Quaroni, bird's-eye view of the design for Las Barene de S. Giuliano, Mestre, 1959.

loneta is not actually a plea for a radical alternative to modernism; it is more of an attempt to continue modernist urban planning in a critical way. To achieve this critical continuation, Manuel de Solà-Morales turned to the work of Quaroni, in particular, a man to whom he had dedicated a monograph in an 1989 issue of the magazine *Urbanismo Revista*. Several years earlier he had published an article entitled 'Another Modern Tradition,'[42] in which he claimed that the modern movement was a heterogeneously composed movement in which the work of Le Corbusier and Giedion had captured a major role largely on the basis of personal charisma and power politics. For the most part, Le Corbusier and Giedion used two different levels of scale in applying their concept of the modern city: the regional plan and the autonomous architectonic structure. As a result, the modern tradition remained bogged down either in general schemes for the spatial organization of the city or in a fixation on the development of new building typologies.

What was lacking – and this included even a lack of interest, according to de Solà-Morales – was, of all things, 'the intermediate scale': the scale that offers an opportunity for negotiations between large-scale interventions and the existing topographic and historical context: in other words, the scale at which urban space can be designed. The influential modern movement led by the 'Giedion-Le Corbusier front' was more interested in general planning principles than in specific solutions, however, and more involved in the shape of buildings than in the shape of public space.

*Another* modern tradition – to which the title of the article referred – was that of designers who had lost the international tug of war surrounding CIAM, but who had developed (in the opinion of de Solà-Morales) highly interesting urban planning innovations on the very scale ignored by others: the intermediate scale of *el projecto urbano*. Mentioned as representatives of 'another modern tradition' were Ludovico Quaroni, Cornelis van Eesteren, and Leslie Martin from, respectively, Southern Europe, Northern Europe, and the British Isles.[43]

In the words of de Solà-Morales, the key to this other modern tradition lay in 'an architecture of the city that is the opposite of an urban architecture of the buildings themselves, but which is an architectural organization of the city's physical body.' To achieve 'the definition of urban form,' urban architecture had to focus on two main things: specific territorial features and 'the major works of urban engineering, railways, canals, skyscrapers, avenues.'

From the beginning, therefore, attention aimed at Barcelona's port and seafront was based on the position of the waterfront both as the city's most explicitly territorial feature and as the hub of 'the major works of urban engineering.'

*Urbanismo* is specifically defined as 'urban planning = land division + urbanization + building.'[44]
– Land division: the creation of a city plan indicating the distinction between public and private space, and between open and developed space
– Urbanization or urban design: the design and organization of public space in combination with public facilities, to be done in such a way that public space can become a significant element of urban culture
– Building: the establishment of building regulations.
These three activities do not necessarily make an unequivocal, coherent whole, however, and in most cases are not implemented simultaneously. The activity to be emphasized varies from situation to situation.

In the existing city, which had received most of the attention since the early 1980s, regulations for new construction were of minor importance, while the Plan General Metropolitan had just provided the city map with a new structure. Urbanization was the missing element: the practice of urban design aimed at the detailed design and organization of structural elements found in the new city plan. This aspect, urban design, is thus the activity emphasized most in the 1980s.

The practical strategy for implementing the urban design made use of two aids: the designation of clearly defined *projects* and the *authorship* of the urban design.

*The project: the intermediate scale*
From 1980 onward, the spotlight was on a decentralized approach to various areas with specific spatial, programmatic, and social characteristics. 'From plan to project' was the key to this new approach, a slogan that meant the idea was not to deal with the PGM as *plan* by changing or replacing it, but to translate the components of the PGM into well-organized *projects* limited in terms of time and space.[45] The most important aid needed to achieve this goal was largely organizational in nature: namely, the establishment of a special municipal Department of Urban Projects (*Projectes Urbanes*), which would be responsible for both the design and the integral realization of the lengthy series of public-space projects to be developed in Barcelona in the 1980s.

The main objective in realizing individual projects for the design and organization of public areas was the creation of conditions for new economic, social, and cultural vitality: 'Acting as a motor for regeneration of the surrounding area through the initiative of its own residents, it can even produce a new demographic balance.'[46]

The way in which Barcelona planners dealt with this balance was explained by Josep Acebillo, director of the Department of Urban Projects.[47] What it boils down to, according to Acebillo, is that urban areas are truly urban only if they are capable of providing space for complex and unforeseeable forms of use. He claimed that urban areas designed to be used for and associated with only one specific kind of function are fatal to the development of urban life within public space. He urged practicing designers to make certain that an area's main function did not dominate its shape and spatial organization. The consequences of this point of departure applied chiefly to urban areas required to handle heavy traffic. Instead of treating urban planning as 'just another' discipline, subordinate to predetermined traffic regulations, traffic was incorporated into the urban planning design. Acebillo said that every site calls for a specific appraisal to be made of qualities that represent the 'repertoire of the city' and qualities that emphasize the specific identity of the area in question.

Acebillo's views reveal that the way in which a relationship is created between the coherence of the city as a whole and the individual project is not categorical. This relationship depends not only on how the location of an individual project site relates to the urban network, but also and especially on the interpretation of the designer granted *authorship* of the project. In the early '80s, in particular, this freedom of interpretation led to enormous variation in the design and organization of squares, parks, streets, and boulevards: a variation that generated skepticism, in certain cases, about the way in which the 'repertoire of the city' was incorporated into, and made subservient to, heightened attention to the unique identity of the site, which included specially designed light fixtures and street furniture for each project.

A repetitive theme was the 'dual orientation' of projects, most of which were sites on the borders of distinctive districts that formed part of important, or potentially important, main arteries within the city's traffic infrastructure. In many cases, this dual orientation led to a division of the project into two separate components, which together produced a coherent spatial composition. One component is tied directly to the highly public urban domain of the main infrastructure and is expressed primarily by the use of stone-like materials. The other component is linked to the 'social' domain of adjacent neighborhoods and is expressed by a more park- and garden-like layout, often combined with facilities for sports and games, education, community culture, and so forth.

This duality of public and social domains forms one of the most distinguishing marks of Barcelona's approach to public space in the 1980s.

## TOWARD NEW FUNCTIONAL AND SPATIAL COHERENCE

Originally, other than in the strictly functional character of the Plan General Metropolitan, coherence among individual districts was defined most often in conceptual and spatial terms. Important themes in this concept were the accentuation of the city's natural location, surrounded as it was by the sea, Montjuich, and Tibibado; and better utilization of these natural elements as facilities for the entire city.

Only in the second half of the 1980s, when Bohigas had been succeeded as supervisor of the urban planning department by Joan Busquets, were these conceptual themes for the entire city connected to plans developed in the meantime for individual districts and incorporated into a new planning document for the city as a whole.[48]

This new city plan raised questions about the city center, which covered – as it had since the realization of the Ensanche (more than a hundred years earlier) – the zone between the Ramblas and the Via Laietana, from the harbor front to the intersection with the Diagonal. This zone accommodated every important public administration center, as well as the city's greatest concentration of office buildings, hotels, and shopping facilities. Beginning in the early 1970s, many in Barcelona became convinced that this central zone could maintain its position only if conditions were created for enlarging the city center and making it more easily accessible. The 1976 PGM saw the solution in a drastic expansion of the main traffic network and an enlargement of the central zone itself, to be achieved by designating many sites in and around the historical inner city for large-scale reconstruction projects.

When modifying the city plan in 1987, instead of using areas adjacent to the existing central zone for reconstruction projects, authorities chose sites throughout the city which were due to be renewed anyway: they designated traffic hubs lined with development, such as the Plaça de les Glòries Catalanes and the Plaça de Espanya, as well as extensively used zones on the urban periphery, as *Àrees de Nova Centralitat*. Improvement of the main traffic network was no longer aimed simply at making the central zone accessible, but at interconnecting new 'central urban areas.' Both the *àrees* and the lines connecting them became main components of Barcelona's urban design.

This new strategy had important consequences for the function that the entire coastal zone was destined to fulfill in the future city. The introduction of *Àrees de Nova Centralitat* removed much of the pressure being put on the historical inner-city harbor front to become a location for large-scale office development. Insistence that the traditional central zone should be enlarged at all cost disappeared and, with it, demands that the harbor front be seen primarily as a potential building site.

Three *Àrees de Nova Centralitat* were to be waterfront sites: the historical harbor front, the Poble Nou industrial zone and, in the north, a zone in which the Diagonal reaches the coast. Only the Diagonal zone was given a largely commercial program of office buildings, which are scheduled for long-term implementation that will be geared to future developments in the office market.

In the first two zones – the historical port and Poble Nou – activities focused on developing the waterfront as an attractive place for people all over the city. In addition to reinforcing recreational quality by improving public space and by transforming Poble Nou into a housing area with hotel accommodations, new projects also attempted to strengthen the importance of the waterfront zone for the city as a whole by improving traffic infrastructure.

The design of the main traffic infrastructure – and especially of the new Cinturon

beltway, which was to accommodate about 120,000 vehicles daily – was a key component of Barcelona's urban design.

All things considered, clearly the redesign of the harbor front did not headline a program of buildings, but a program of the use of public space: the harbor front had to be transformed into part of the beltway and, at the same time, into an attractive public area.

### THE RENEWED WATERFRONT AS TEST CASE

Beginning in the early 1980s, the renewal of the total waterfront was realized by means of a connected series of four individual projects.

The first was the area in which the old city fronted the harbor, the Passeig de Colom with the Moll de la Fusta; and the second the harbor front of La Barceloneta, the Moll de la Barceloneta. These two projects combined to form the framework of the old port: Port Vell. The third project was La Barceloneta's coastline and the last the seafront of the Ensanche, with the Poble Nou industrial zone as its core element.

At the same time, projects were also developed to reinforce the connection between city and waterfront: vital in this respect were a number of east-west lines that intensified the city's orientation toward the sea.

In what way have the ambitions of these projects, as described here, been put into practice?

*Moll de la Fusta: reestablishment of the balcony overlooking the water*
The transformation of the old city's harbor front was launched thanks to an agreement between municipal authorities and the Port Autonom. When transshipment activities left the old port, the opportunity arose to fully reorganize Port Vell. The Port Autonom's

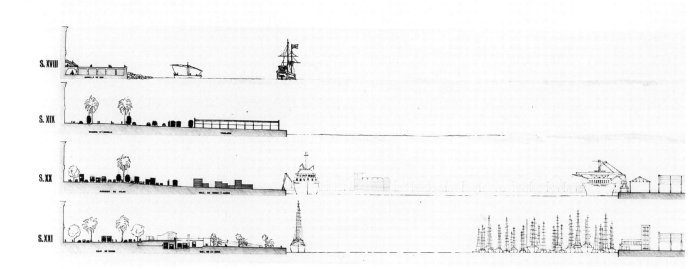

Above: Harbor-front
sections: eighteenth to
twenty-first centuries.

Below: View of the Passeig
de Colom – Moll de la
Fusta, design by Manuel
de Solà-Morales.

consent was not without conditions, how-ever: the territory involved was to remain under its control, and the converted Passeig de Colom was to be large enough to accom-modate 80,000 vehicles daily (later increased to 120,000). The Passeig de Colom's traffic function was of vital importance to the Port Autonom, since this street would form the main connection between the modern port, on the south side of the city, and Northern Spain and France, the destination of most of the city's transport operations.

In 1980 Manuel de Solà-Morales was commissioned to design this plan, as well as to implement the plan for La Barceloneta that he had developed together with the Laborato-rio de Urbanismo in the 1970s.

The task of transforming the harbor front was an extreme example of the paradox that planners were wrestling with during this time. On the one hand, the harbor front was seen as one of the most meaningful and historic urban areas, which along with the Ramblas had oriented the city toward the sea for centuries. Converting the harbor front was to be the first step in restoring this

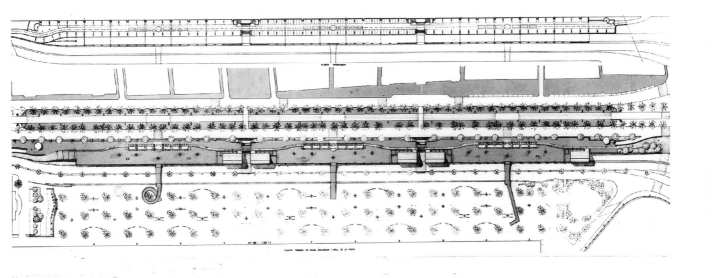

Plan for the Passeig de Colom – Moll de la Fusta: design by Manuel de Solà-Morales.

Moll de la Fusta.

orientation. On the other hand, the very same area was supposed to offer room to the modern reality of a new beltway, the very function – harbor front as major twelve-lane highway – that since the '60s had contributed significantly to eradicating Barcelona's orientation toward the sea.

Not only the harbor front of the Moll de la Fusta, but the old port's entire basin – Port Vell – was seen as one integral design project. By emphasizing Port Vell as a spatial entity, designers could also make La Barceloneta an instantly visible part of the city.

Highlighting the overall area of quays and harbor basin as one *open* space had a second objective: to encourage interest in, and the use of, existing buildings along the harbor front and in La Barceloneta. A revived Port Vell was to give a new boost to the whole infrastructure of cafés, restaurants, beaches, and the aquarium in La Barceloneta.

De Solà-Morales's design was based on two important interventions.

First, the Moll d'Espanya harbor pier was to be demolished in part and the remaining island made into a center for maritime activities (mainly cruises). This intervention would reemphasize the Pla de Palau as a key location: the place at which the connection between city and port is organized and also at which the city is linked to La Barceloneta. The latter link was strengthened when an expansion project for the Pla de Palau made use of an underground tunnel for through traffic.

The second intervention restressed differences in height – clearly creating a distinction between higher and lower zones – in a quay area that originally sloped gradually toward the port. This intervention underscored the unique topography of this waterside zone: the difference in height between the basal area of the city and the water level of the sea. The result was the development of a contemporary version of the situation prior to 1878, when quay walls, together with the Passeig de Colom, formed an 'urban balcony.' At the same time, the high, uninterrupted quay wall placed the city on a 'plinth,' as it were, which created a spatial coherence that united the entire harbor front. This intervention was important to the spatial organization of the area, as well as to the image it presents.

With regard to spatial organization, the introduction of two levels allowed for complex usage without reducing the inter-

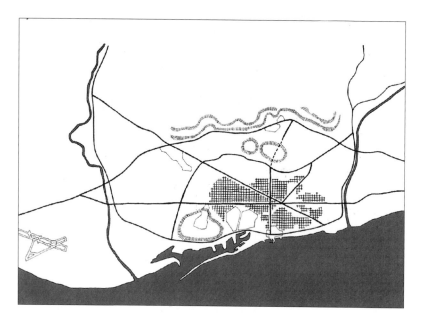

Barcelona 1990: main traffic network, with beltway (Cinturon).

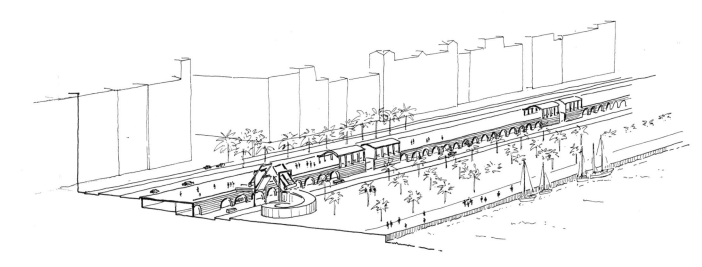

Bird's-eye view and section of the Passeig de Colom – Moll de la Fusta.

vention to a simple differentiation between areas for vehicular and pedestrian traffic. The two levels represented a distinction between two different domains: one level obviously still belonged to the domain of urban culture, while the other, lower level belonged to the large-scale world of port and sea.

The former, which provides space for urban traffic, is dominated in terms of design by a precisely differentiated profile, in which the emphasis lay on a broad strip of outdoor cafés, pavilions, and an elegant balustrade:

this strip is the city's new 'balcony,' which offers a view of the world of port and sea, while also forming a definitive border. The latter, which accommodates through traffic, is dominated by the emptiness of a 75-meter-wide esplanade that relates to the port in both size and use of material. Behind arched arcades located beneath the 'balcony' lies part of the through traffic artery, as well as a parking garage.

In designing the port as an area of public space, planners looked to public space itself:

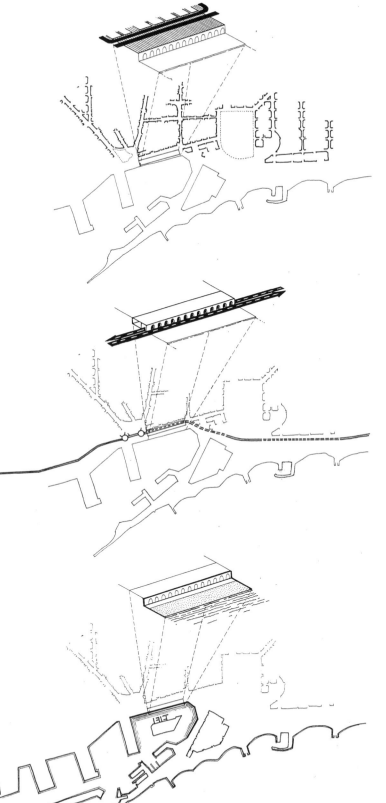

Harbor front as part of the local network.

Harbor front as part of the beltway.

Harbor front as part of the seaside landscape.

Completed 'fun city' on
the Moll d'Espanya, 1994.

they used quays as space-shaping elements
in their treatment of water and emphasized
differences in height by employing heavily
accentuated arcades as an architectonic
element. In so doing, they made the shape
of the port as public space relatively independent of the shape and architecture
of buildings along the Passeig de Colom.
The new harbor front builds on the historic
significance of this part of the city and on
specific territorial conditions found here. On
the other hand, however, the goal was also to
design an urban area that responds to contemporary city life, a way of life that includes mass motorized traffic.

The way in which this design was
combined with the plan for the Moll de
la Fusta caused controversy in Barcelona.
Architecture critic Kenneth Frampton
called the plan for the Moll de la Fusta an
extreme version of a 'Neo-Haussmannian'
approach: a logical continuation of nineteenth-century urban planning concepts.
As a contrast he mentioned a new focus on
neo-modernist design in Barcelona, and
gave Pinon and Viaplana's design for Plaça
dels Països Catalans, a new station square,
as an example.

De Solà-Morales replied to this
criticism: 'Some people think a space is

modern because it contains modern objects.
This is a big mistake. For example, certain
critics find squares in Gràcia [urban district
in Barcelona] quite modern, owing to the
shape of the objects. But in my opinion,
these are old urban areas that function in the
same way they did a hundred years ago. But
now some objects have been placed there,
and the traffic is hidden under the ground...
In the case of the Moll de la Fusta, the crux
of the matter is not objects within an urban
space, but the urban space itself: this is a
completely new area that never existed
before. What is new or, if you prefer, modern
about this space is an unprecedented
combination of various urban functions.
Something totally new is happening in this
place, thanks to a new organization of space.
In filling in and adding detail to this new
area, maximum use has been made of
generic, existing elements, which make the
new space immediately recognizable as part
of the existing city. It is nonsense to design
new elements for every new urban area: new
lampposts, new benches, new balustrades.
These are the very elements that can
reinforce the continuity of the city and thus
should not look different in every area.'[49]

The realization of Port Vell as a whole
proceeded somewhat differently than had
been expected. After the Moll de la Fusta
proved its success and the Olympic Games
were hosted by Barcelona in 1992, the
situation changed.

Both quays and piers remained under the
authority of the Port Autonom, which had
made an agreement with the municipality
on the reorganization of quays that did
not apply, however, to piers. It had been
clear for some time that other options
existed for the Moll d'Espanya besides the
partial demolition it faced according to
the original plan. As early as the mid-'80s,
American real-estate developer Enterprise
Development Corporation (EDC)[50] had

proposed the creation of a complete 'fun city' on this pier. A grateful Port Autonom borrowed this idea and went on to realize a complex at the end of the pier – with shops, restaurants, a new sea aquarium, and a number of movie theaters – as well as a hill to call attention to the pier.

To a certain extent, this intervention enervated the original concept of Port Vell, and especially of the Moll de la Fusta. Instead of an emphasis on the spatial entity of the port as a whole, a hill on the pier now obstructs the view between the Moll de la Fusta and La Barceloneta more than ever. Instead of the restoration of the Pla de Palau as foremost crook in the bay, a new urban fragment has been developed in the port. Instead of a new concentration of public urban life on waterside quays and around the Pla de Palau, the Moll de la Fusta has been demoted to an access area to the new fun city in the water. And instead of the original accent on the significance of the Pla de Palau as the link between the old city and La Barceloneta, a Gordian traffic knot has been created by the Port Autonom's failure to recognize the necessity of a tunnel to accommodate through traffic at this spot.

The result also differed from the original concept in a programmatic respect. The primary intention had been to reorganize Port Vell and thus prompt private parties to invest in new functions for existing buildings surrounding the port; these parties were now investing in the new enclave in the middle of the water.

The present predicament is rooted in the power of the Port Autonom and in the failure to adequately legalize the urban plan by means of an official document or a political contract between municipality and Port Autonom.

The realization of a fun city on the Moll d'Espanya is a fascinating incident that proves the municipality's continuing inability to fully implement an urban planning policy based on its own concept. This development may be viewed as a stubborn move on the part of the Port Autonom, which promoted a project that nullified both the original intentions of the design and the anticipated investments. But it can also be alleged that the realization of a fun city on the Moll d'Espanya is testimony to the original lack of attention paid to the considerable significance of contemporary projects such as this, even though American developer EDC had introduced a similar proposal a decade earlier. In 'The Urbanization of the Private Domain as a New Challenge,' a review of ten years of urban renewal in Barcelona, de Solà-Morales responded to these accusa-

Left: Original concept for Port Vell, showing the port as a central open area, with emphasis on visual openness, and a perceptible connection between the inner city and La Barceloneta.

Right: Port Vell after completion of the renewed Moll d'Espanya, showing the pier as a new central area, with an accent on the Moll d'Espanya's visual spectacle.

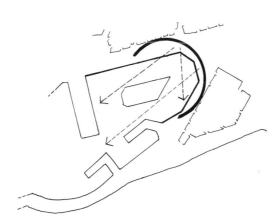
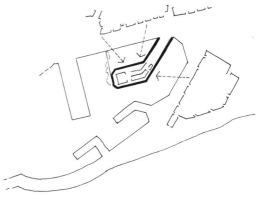

tions.[51] He confirmed that the design of the public domain was lagging behind the way in which new elements – 'supermall,' soccer stadium, amusement park – had been developed within the frameworks of the private domain and had become a highly significant part of urban life. Up to this point (1992), phenomena such as these had led to an 'internalization' of urban life, to an inward orientation of urban activities, which were played out within the walls of the private domain. The situation was based partly on the wishes of private clients, but also on the inability of urban planners to cope with these new phenomena. The Moll d'Espanya is a striking example.

*Moll de la Barceloneta*

As for La Barceloneta, projects there built largely on Laboratorio de Urbanismo's 1971 design, although introducing new large-scale elements on the north side was not feasible since the area covered by the plan was limited to the district of La Barceloneta.

In his approach to La Barceloneta, de Solà-Morales made a distinction between the main structure of public areas, which were important to the city as a whole, and the more internal structure of the district, which functioned chiefly as a *social* domain. To end La Barceloneta's isolation, the accent was placed on reorganizing the main structure of public areas, which consisted of the borders of the district – the Moll de la Barceloneta and the beach – and the places at which these borders were connected to the urban network. The goal of this reorganization was to exploit La Barceloneta's potential urban qualities (both quay and beach were an important and attractive part of the city's network of public space) and to provide the local economy with space and a clientele on which to base future development.

The uniform morphology and typology of the 'interior' of the district was so strong that functions could be changed and housing needs met in a relatively simple way.

De Solà-Morales's original design provided for the preservation of monumental waterside warehouses on the Moll de la Barceloneta and of dozens of fish restaurants in largely ramshackle and illegal structures on the beach: the *chirinquitos*. Port buildings were given public functions such as market buildings and library, while the fish restaurants were moved into better, and legal, accommodations under an elevated boardwalk. Both aspects were meant to reinforce the significance of the district periphery: new facilities in port buildings, together with the row of fish restaurants, were to stress the public character of the periphery, which was of essence to the whole city and would benefit the economy and culture of the district as well.

Both components of the plan were eliminated, however: the Port Autonom feared the amount of operating costs associated with rebuilding port structures, and the Ministry of Transport and Communications prohibited building on the beach.

The monumental entrepôt in the crook of the bay, however, was able to be preserved by converting it into new accommodations for Catalonia's Ministry of Social Affairs.

Ultimately, Olga Tarasso and Jordi Heinrich designed La Barceloneta's entire periphery as open space. As was the case with the Moll de la Fusta, the reorganization of the Moll de la Barceloneta seems to have built on the role it played two centuries ago: an informal strip of landscape that offers a view of the cityscape atop a 'plinth' formed by the Passeig de Colom. Thanks to slopes, along with a step-by-step change from formal elements on the 'city' side of La Barceloneta to more informal elements on the 'port' side, the transition from an urbanistic to a landscape-related atmosphere is gradual, fluid, and less sudden than the transition found on the Moll de la Fusta.

The concept of the entire port as a spatial entity bordered on two sides by broad, open, public quays was strengthened by this design.

### La Barceloneta's 'urban beach'

Perhaps the most modest, but also the most spectacular, project of the series designed for Barceloneta's waterfront was the plan for La Barceloneta's beach, another design by Olga Tarasso and Jordi Heinrich. A paved area of natural stone forms the transition from district street network to beach; the pattern of the pavement, which corre-

sponds to that of the street system, abuts on a wooden boardwalk that runs along the shore. The austere, formal character of this design was softened by planting palms throughout the entire zone, sometimes alone and sometimes in groups, both in the paved area and on the beach.

Nowhere else in Barcelona is the social domain (of which the natural-stone pavement forms an extension) linked so simply and yet so effectively to a structuralizing public domain, emphasized by the boardwalk.

Nowhere else does the autonomous power of a well-organized public area resonate so forcefully: although the ends of building blocks facing the beach form a frayed edge, so to speak, the beautifully designed public area provides this side of the district with a strong sense of unity and allure. Here a genuine urban beach has been created. Furthermore, the original

La Barceloneta linked to the city by the reorganization of public space.

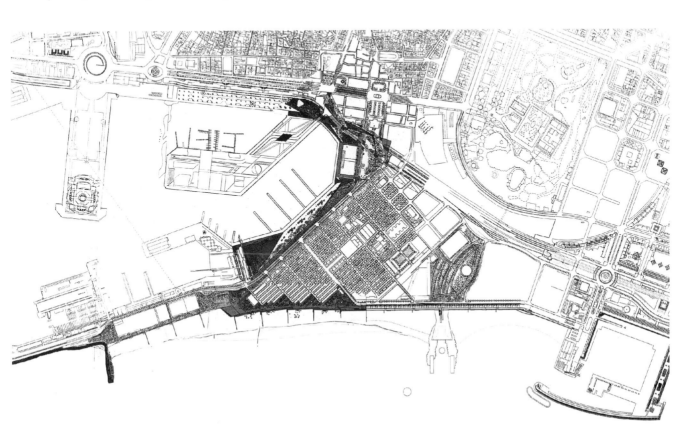

Passeig de Colom – Moll de la Fusta as seen from the north prior to the revitalization project.

Passeig de Colom – Moll de la Fusta as seen from the north after the revitalization project.

The old port in the foreground and the new port in the background, as seen from the north, 1990.

Above: The beach at La Barceloneta, with dozens of *chirinquitos* lining the shore, ca. 1980.

Below: The beach at La Barceloneta after the revitalization project, 1995.

transparency of the district has been restored. Despite its relatively narrow streets, La Barceloneta is the only district in which one can experience the openness of the sea so powerfully from the heart of the district.

*Poble Nou:*
*intersection of Ensanche and waterfront*
When Barcelona was given the opportunity to host the 1992 Olympics, the city continued a tradition that began with the World's Fairs of 1888 and 1929: namely, the use of large events as a motor to power a desired spatial transformation. In this case, the goal was to speed up the transformation of the coastal zone of Poble Nou by building the Olympic Village there. Authorities hoped that locating the village on this site would result in a definitive breach in the aforementioned mental cutoff point represented by the citadel.

However, de Solà-Morales's 1971 proposal for developing a new urban planning structure for the coastal zone was to be modified considerably.

The design of Poble Nou saw Oriol

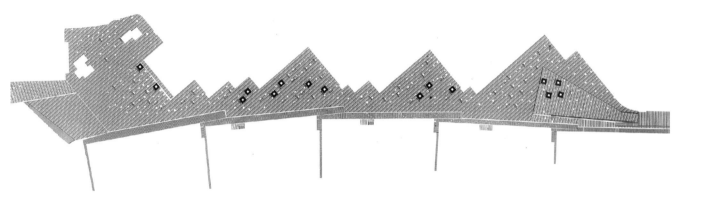

Plan for the coastline of La Barceloneta: design by Olga Tarassò and Jordi Henrich.

Bohigas in a major role once more, since 'his' firm, MBM (Martorell, Bohigas, MacKay and Puigdomènech), was commissioned to design the plan.

The urban planning design for the Olympic Village had to provide 2,500 apartments, 60,000 square meters of office space, and 185,000 square meters of facilities. In addition to a complex relocation operation to remove existing industry from the site, the project consisted of four distinct tasks:[52]
– Main infrastructure: incorporation of the remainder of the Francia Station rail line and of the new beltway, the Cinturon, running along the coast
– Seafront: realization of a new public seafront, as a continuation of the earlier development of the harbor front
– Ensanche: continuation of the structural principle of the Ensanche
– Housing typology: creation of space for new building typologies of the same caliber as those previously considered feasible only on the urban periphery and in suburban milieus

Methods used to develop these four points are visible in the four layers of which the design is composed. The first, or infrastructural, layer consists of the rail line and the Cinturon, both of which lie, for the most part, in a tunnel. The second, or waterfront, layer accommodates a series of parks, a beach boulevard, and two tall towers precisely on the axis of the Passeig de Charles I. In the third layer, the pattern of the Ensanche is transformed into a number of superblocks that incorporate the fourth layer, a series of new, 'free' building typologies: low-rise housing, small towers, and a 'crescent.' The combination of these various layers was an attempt to anchor the project fully into the urban context; the final result, however, left ample room for criticism.

Originally the first two tasks, infrastructure and seafront, were closely interwoven. The 150-to-200-meter-wide zone between the wall of facades formed by the superblocks and the beach was to feature tripartite spatial articulation: the Cinturon was designed as a parkway, and a 'transparent screen' formed by a row of six high-rise towers was meant to create a contrast to the beach boulevard, the Passeig Maritim. This series of towers would provide the seafront with a new shape, geared to the scale of the metropolis as a whole. This scheme represented a definite break with goals envisioned by the Ribera Plan of the 1960s. Instead of an autonomous enclave, separated from the city by an infrastructural cluster, the new seafront – together with the parkway and the contiguous part of the Ensanche – would be designed as a single urban planning composition.

Both towers and parkway, however, were eliminated from the plan. The towers were

A reorganized Moll de la Barceloneta:
design by Olga Tarassò and Jordi Henrich.

The beach at La Barceloneta after the reorganization project, 1995.

The beach at La Barceloneta after the reorganization project, 1995.

The beach at La Barceloneta after the reorganization project, 1995.

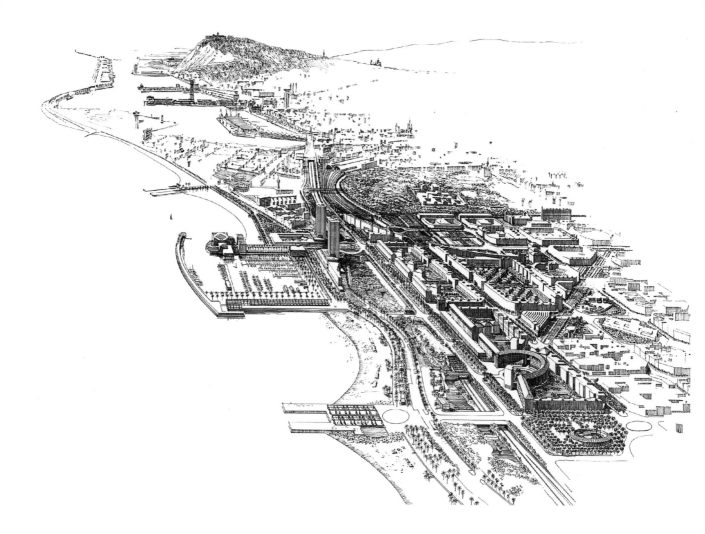

Bird's-eye view of Poble Nou: design by MBM.

unacceptable to the Spanish Ministry of Public Works, which found the seacoast too instable to support buildings within 200 meters of the water's edge. The construction of two towers was permitted only behind the yacht marina, which also functioned as an extra means of protecting the coast.

Subsequently, the Catalan traffic department declared that the capacity of the Cinturon was to be increased to at least 120,000 vehicles a day (instead of the original prognosis of 80,000). This amount of traffic was considered too high to be combined with pedestrian traffic and was sure to produce an excess level of noise pollution that would affect adjacent

housing. Owing to a lack of funds, only part of the hastily designed tunnel was realized completely below ground level, and as a result, an approximately 2-meter-high dike stands between the Olympic Village and the sea, depriving the village of a view of the Mediterranean. A single broad area eventually replaced the planned multiarticulated zone. This robbed the Cinturon of much of its charm as a pleasant coastal road, and the dike continues to form a barrier between the Olympic Village and the beach.

The third and fourth layers of the design, the superblocks and the new building typologies they contain, formed a second controversial aspect of the plan.

Many analyses of the Ensanche have been published since the late 1980s.[53] A common factor found in all these publications is surprise at the ingenious combination of, on the one hand, urban planning clarity and simplicity and, on the other, architectonic and programmatic richness. Even today, the dimensions of building blocks and street profiles seem to have the capacity to incorporate new urban developments related to architecture and building typology, as well as to traffic.

Cerdà's original plan offered dozens of variations on the construction of individual building blocks; only several variations were realized, not all of which still exist. Famous are housing blocks crisscrossed internally by alleys lined with low-rise housing fronted by gardens; the result is a virtually village-like atmosphere amid the bustle of the big city. Of special note is the status of these 'internal' alleys, which differs from that of the public street. Although they frequently function as public streets (especially during the day), these alleys are not an official part of the public domain but the collective property of homeowners whose dwellings are accessed by these streets. Consequently, these areas enjoy a much higher degree of social control than that found in the streets of the urban grid. A stark contrast exists between the strictly *public* domain of the public street and the internal territory of these alleys, which is not absolutely public but open, nevertheless, to outsiders who respect the codes of those living there: a territory that may be referred to as the *social* domain.[54]

Plan of Poble Nou: design by MBM.

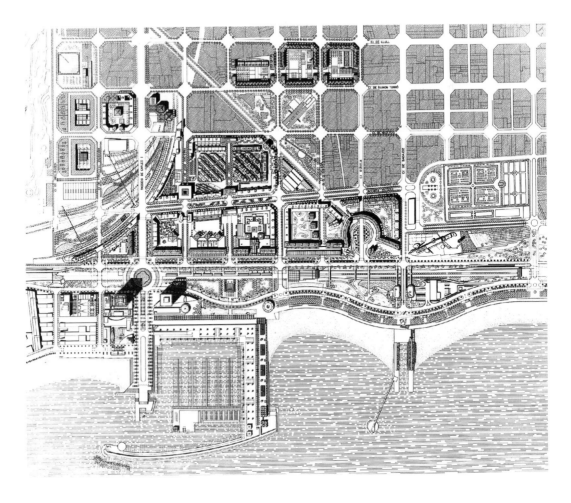

Arees de Nova Centralitat, 1987.

Right: Barcelona's new
seafront, part of the city's
network of parks.

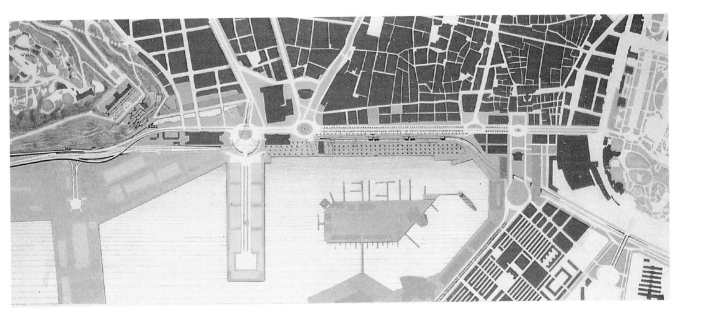

Plan for Port Vell: design by Manuel de Solà-Morales.

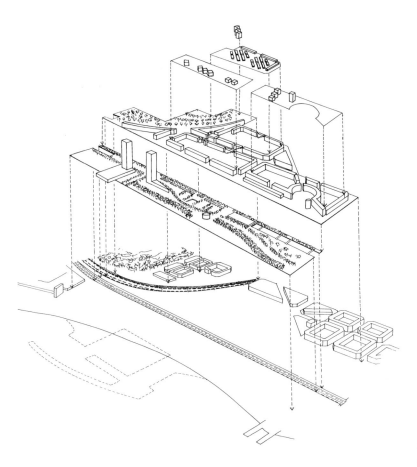

proposed the development of a new urban morphology, which was to be the symbiosis of qualities found in both classic and modern cities.[55] The basic elements of this new morphology were described as 'îlots presque fermés et rues presque corridors' – nearly closed building blocks and nearly urban streets – which were to give planners a chance to enrich urban morphology with a greater diversity of housing types, thus allowing for many different kinds of dwellings and lifestyles within the city.

By uniting blocks found in the Ensanche, three superblocks were created: elements meant to produce a combination of perimeter blocks and free land division, as well as a combination of urban avenues and spatial types of a more suburban nature.

At first glance, the variety of housing types and urban milieus seems to be a continuation of nineteenth-century experiments with avenues carried out according to the Ensanche. Larger building blocks set the stage for the realization of diverse types of suburban land division within the sizable inner areas formed by these superblocks.

In a 'mental' sense the same kind of distinction is present in the Olympic Village: a distinction between the atmosphere of city streets lined by superblocks and that of the inner areas, which suggests a largely social domain that offers a high degree of individuality, security, and intimacy in the immediate proximity of the dwelling.

The difference between city streets and inner areas is heightened by developing an unambiguous image of buildings lining city streets – not only in terms of building volume but also with respect to the architectonic execution of exterior walls – and by creating inner areas that accommodate a great variety of building typologies and architectural diversity. The realization of architectonic uniformity in the streetscape of urban areas included a prescribed use of materials.[56]

Poble Nou: four-layered plan analysis. Bottom to top: *a.* urban and landscape-related context of the design; *b.* large-scale structural elements; *c.* 'superblocks'; *d.* suburban infilling.

Experiments from the Ensanche which focus on the design of housing blocks are relevant to efforts by MBM to build on these experiments by applying a 'modern interpretation' of Cerdà's grid to the design for Poble Nou.

Bohigas also gave a great deal of thought to the creation of new spatial typologies capable of combining traditional and modern forms of use. In his case, however, the primary focus was always on building typology and, to a lesser degree, the typology of new kinds of infrastructure.

The theme of a combination of 'traditional' urban and 'modern' suburban typologies has permeated the work of MBM for over twenty years. In a discussion on the controversy between the 'classic' city and modern urban planning in a 1973 article in *L'Architecture d'aujourd'hui*, Bohigas

Unlike the situation in the nineteenth century, however, the distinction between the domain of city streets and the domain of inner areas was not established legally. In a strictly official sense, therefore, inner areas are just as public as big city streets; indeed, four of Barcelona's seven thoroughfares leading to the sea run straight through the superblocks and thus through the inner areas.

The result is twofold: both the character of inner areas and the potential for a well-organized social domain are adversely affected; and the public sphere, along with the accessibility, of thoroughfares leading from city to sea is undermined. For residents of an inner area, the general public use of a thoroughfare that runs through their superblock interferes with a need for peace and security; for urbanites, the route to the sea, which takes them straight through an inner area, is an involuntary confrontation with an intimate world.

Hence the question: to what extent is the new Poble Nou really a link between city and sea, or should it be seen as an exclusive enclave? This question became even more intrusive when the original plan for Poble Nou was greatly reduced to its current size. The first comprehensive project for Poble Nou consisted of many more building blocks than are now anticipated, a significant number of which were earmarked for public housing. This approach was deemed necessary for the integration of the area into the city, socioculturally and otherwise, and for its successful reception. When the plan was pared down to the scale of the Olympic Village, the result was an exclusive enclave[57] surrounded by a belt of blocks and building sites, most of which still have no function.

*From city to sea: a new park system*
The attempt to make seafront sites into an important part of the public-space network has gone beyond the simple creation of a symbiotic relationship with the Cinturon. A number of projects based on the internal structure of the city have also been developed to anchor the seafront to the city. Such projects focus mainly on reinforcing a number of long lines in the Ensanche. A few lines with extremely broad profiles were redesigned as spacious green avenues; examples are the Passeig San Joan and the Carrer Prim (each about 80 meters wide).

Certain lines interrupted in the past by railroad lines or other development have had their former continuity restored. One of the most spectacular projects in this category is the new bridge over the Sagrera Station railroad complex, a connection that reunites the Carrer Felip II and, with it, the whole district of San Andreu with the seafront.

Attention paid to specific territorial features of the city was expressed not only by working with differences in height along the seafront and by revaluating the street network based on the original system of streams, but also by highlighting structural relief, the city, and the larger scale of the urban periphery. At places in which landscape is unmistakably present in the form of mountain peaks or vast expanses of water, and in which the city uses the landscape productively as sites for relaxation and pleasure, a number of new beacons have arisen that symbolize the link between city and landscape, as well as between city and modern communication networks: telecommunication towers on Montjuich and Tibibado (both mountains offer a wide range of facilities for sports and entertainment), and hotel and office towers in Poble Nou, with its beach as a brand-new urban facility. This approach allows Barcelona to be seen – on the scale of the city as a whole – as a man-made, twenty-first-century urban landscape and as a response to the shapelessness and disintegration of the twentieth-century city.

o                    1 km

# 5 Balance: The Ongoing Spatial Organization of the City

Early on, the city of Barcelona underscored the shape and structure of a number of important public areas essential to the urban planning coherence of the city per se, as well as to a coherent connection between the city and large-scale networks.

Large structuralizing areas developed on an urban level of scale were the Ramblas, in the fifteenth century, and the harbor front (Passeig de Colom), in the seventeenth century. These interventions, which oriented the city as a whole toward the water, were unique in the context of the Mediterranean region. In the fifteenth century, the only city with a large urban area comparable to Barcelona's – an area that lent structure to the city as a whole and also helped to connect it to large-scale networks – was Venice. The role played by Venice's Canal Grande is similar to the one fulfilled by the Ramblas in Barcelona.

The Ramblas and the Passeig de Colom share a number of remarkable features.

The first is their enduring recognizability and the emphasis placed on their specific territorial characteristics: the direction and irregular pattern of the streams, of which the Ramblas is the most striking result; and the difference in height between the 'urban front' and the water level of the sea.[58]

A second similarity lies in the organization and use of space, activities largely *unrelated*, in both cases, to the function and appearance of buildings. Instead of a situation in which buildings determine the shape and function of an urban area, the opposite is seen here: the buildings that line the Ramblas and the Passeig de Colom were erected to fortify the significance of these structuralizing areas.

The third feature is the *multifarious use* of these areas: although they have been the city's most important traffic connections from the very beginning, they are also its most important public areas and esplanades.

Unlike London, for example, public space in nineteenth-century Barcelona was characterized by the strong interconnectedness of various functions: the Ramblas and the Passeig de Colom, in particular, simultaneously functioned as technical infrastructure, public domain, and urban area of distinction.

Two important urban planning developments that occurred in the nineteenth century proved to be vital to every subsequent seafront project: the design of two parks to augment the harbor front and Cerdà's expansion plan, the Ensanche, which represented in turn a redevelopment of the unique territorial topography. With the two parks on opposite sides of the port– Montjuich and the Parc de la Ciutadella – the harbor front became part of a series of important urban areas. Developing the Ensanche prefigured a potential expansion of this series of public areas along the coastline; furthermore, the orientation of the city toward the sea, introduced in the fifteenth century with the realization of the Ramblas, became a general planning principle that took shape in the form of many east-west oriented streets.

Initially, the comprehensive development of this system was frustrated by two factors: the autonomy of the port, which was no longer under the jurisdiction of the municipal government and which carried out its own policies; and the extensive period of Franco's dictatorship, a time in which the municipal government had virtually no operational urban planning resources. The heart of the city shifted toward the southwest during this era, away from port and sea.

The changed orientation of urban development: before (above) and after (below) 1980.

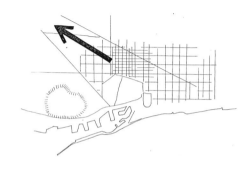

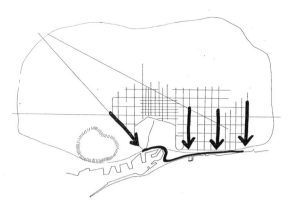

Except for attention given to main elements of the city's technical infrastructure, public space was badly neglected for a long time. Since public areas were not being developed as social areas, public space in Barcelona soon evinced a contrast between areas that were an essential part of major traffic and transportation networks, and areas neglected so badly that some of them – particularly in districts built in the 1950s and '60s – were not even paved.

The late 1970s saw not only the end of Franco's regime; this was also the period in which harbor activities left the old port and relocated to other sites. Finally the time had come to pick up the thread dropped in the nineteenth century.

In Barcelona's recent urban design activities a distinction can be seen between emphasis placed on essential elements found in the network of public space and emphasis placed

on the various neighborhoods and districts tied to this network but, at the same time, imbued with a more or less private, autonomous character. The current planning approach, dating from about 1980, focuses chiefly on designing the main elements of the network of public space, a task closely connected to designing the periphery and areas adjacent to the more autonomous districts.

The approach to the urban seafront as a whole is a prime example. The plan for the seafront was determined by two considerations: the function of various sections of the seafront as strictly public domain and the significance that such sections have for surrounding districts, whose internal character resembles that of social or private domains. The entire coastline and the part of the beltway that follows the coast have become the focal point of the urban design. The new plan for the harbor front zeroes right in on the detailed design needed to combine the territorial singularity of the 'balcony' overlooking the sea with the task of incorporating the flow of traffic on the Cinturon and other public-space functions into one 'major work of urban engineering.' Urban architecture here is, first and foremost, an architecture of public space: an architecture that takes a brand-new urban phenomenon like the Cinturon and integrates it into the urban fabric.

As a result, in a functional sense the harbor front once more assumes the role of a highly complex area: most functions clustered here, such as technical traffic space and the public domain, have a public nature. In addition, combined port functions involve both land use and water use. Port Vell fulfills a function as an open expanse of water, but it also accommodates a fishing harbor, a passenger harbor, and a yacht marina, and is part of the still operational port complex of Barcelona.

Augmenting Barcelona's waterfront with

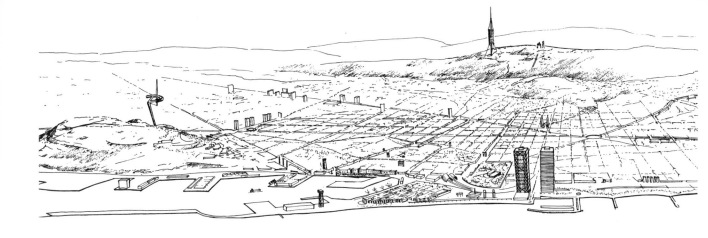

Panorama of Barcelona.

Passeig de Colom – Moll de la Fusta, 1995.

Poble Nou and the borders of La Barceloneta, and upgrading the city's east-west lines, which lead to the sea, ultimately produced a waterfront endowed with far-reaching spatial continuity.

In its entirety, the route of the beltway links various urban fragments. From south to north, these are: piers belonging to the modern port; the old inner city on one side of the Moll de la Fusta and, on the other, the converted piers of Port Vell; La Barceloneta; and Poble Nou. Fragments differ in character, and the way in which they function depends on various conditions. For example, La Barceloneta still retains the air of a close-knit social community, which uses its own district organizations and housing corporations to steer, in particular, the internal structuralization process. Overlapping components of the redesigned network of public space and the reorganization of La Barceloneta are revealed primarily in the design of the district's borders. These should support the public character of both quay and beach and, at the same time, have a beneficial effect on La Barceloneta itself. Efforts have also been

made in Poble Nou to introduce a distinction between the urban public sphere of areas bordering thoroughfares and the relatively private, internal world behind these areas, where private clients should have greater freedom to shape their own 'social domain.' Although this difference – between external borders and internal world – does exist in Poble Nou, it remains undivided in an urban planning respect. The district has become more of a theoretical manifesto than the product of a consistent difference between the treatment of 'public' borders and a 'social' interior.

Radical interventions into Barcelona's public space were based on a broad consensus, in both an economic and a cultural respect. Such interventions were also aimed at reinforcing and expanding the economic life of the city. This applies to the completion of the beltway, which makes the modern port area and the Zona Franca industrial area more accessible, but which also benefits the development of new industry along the seafront, thanks to the conversion of this area into a coastal strip offering entertainment and beach facilities. Instead of going to beaches elsewhere in the vicinity, Barcelona's residents can now enjoy the beach in their own city. Barcelona is perhaps the most successful example of a city that has realized a radical orientative reversal in barely ten years time.

Three principles form the basis of Barcelona's urban design: *historical continuity*, in which territorial characteristics play a major role; *spatial continuity*, in which the port area takes its place within various spatial systems simultaneously; and *functional complexity*, in which public space fulfills various functions at the same time.

With regard to the third principle, it is important that the design does not give the most emphasis to the primary function. Because it does not, the autonomous status of the spatial quality of public space is stressed: a spatial quality that is not dependent on the primary function. When vehicular traffic is curtailed as a result of an oil crisis, for example, the Moll de la Fusta will still be a splendid and valuable public area.

Of importance in a cultural respect is the position held by Barcelona's urban design practice within a broad cultural and political movement that has dominated the most important positions in urban political and cultural institutions without interruption since 1979. In the 'postmodern' world of the West, it is this solidarity that may be unique: around 1980, when urban planning everywhere had lost sight of its own tasks, along with its credibility, Barcelona's *urbanismo* – following decades of preparation – became a key element in the new city council's reformist politics.

Identity has also been a central concept of Barcelona's urban planning practice in the '80s and '90s. It is primarily associated with geomorphological qualities in the area and with the design of public space. The identity of the city is, therefore, an identity open to various interpretations and to continuous change. In the '80s and '90s a struggle arose concerning who has the right to call themselves the true protectors and heirs of Barcelo-na's identity.[59] On one side are the Conservatives, who crack the whip in Catalonia. They point to the age-old tradition of prominent Catalan festivals, which dominate the street scene in various districts for days on end and which are supported and promoted by subsidies from the Conservative government. On the other side are the Socialists, who hold the reins in the city council. They point to the wealth of architecture, which is being maintained and augmented thanks to their policies on preservation and new construction. Both interpretations of the city's identity can be presented and maintained thanks to the clarity and continuity of public space, which provides room for celebratory festivities and also offers a great deal of freedom to an enormous diversity of building styles. Here the design of urban space has not produced just one kind of cultural identity, but has allowed for the creation of various interpretations of the identity of the city, and various ways of forming a sense of identity.

Chapter 4

*The North American Port City:*

# NEW YORK

*A Boundless Urban Landscape*

NEW YORK

# The 'Pure' Modernity of the American City: Between Cultural and Economic Principles

One of the most remarkable aspects of port areas in American cities, in comparison with their European counterparts, is the initial absence of striking contrasts in spatial form and use between the site of port activities and the rest of the city. The dissimilarity and contrast exhibited by nineteenth-century European port areas in relation to the existing urban fabric found an antipode in the consistency with which nineteenth-century American waterfronts were interwoven with city life. This antithesis was due largely to the expansion of city and port during this period, a task that rarely presented the American city with the problem of how to conquer the historical ballast of fortifications.

But even more important was the development of a principle of city planning unique to American society. In designing the American city, urban planners interpreted the social basis of economic freedom and political equality in the form of a grid, which tolerated no deviations, theoretically, not even encounters with natural boundaries like waterfronts.

This does not mean that urban development based on a grid-like network was a self-evident matter in American urban planning from the very beginning. On the contrary, from the moment that the largest grid plan of the nineteenth century – the 1811 Commissioners Plan for New York – was adopted, it was a continuing subject of debate and

criticism, and many attempts were made to supplement, modify, break through, or dismantle the grid. The position of the waterfront, as a special zone within the grid, assumed a major and ongoing role in the development of both debate and plan development.

A classic and pertinacious picture of the United States of America is that of a society which promotes the absolute supremacy of individualism, and thus an emphasis on private profits, and which manifests a total absence of history or, at least, any interest in history.

As early as 1920 historian J. Huizinga, basing his comments on personal impressions gathered during a trip to America, pointed out the inadequacy of this classic image.[1] Indeed, he said, the way in which individualism and the desire for a new future take shape in America is new, just as everything in this country is new. But that does not mean that individualism and hopes for the future are all that exist. What is new about America is that a new *relationship* is being developed between 'man and mass,' between the individual and shared interests, and between hopes for the future and an awareness of history.

Without a doubt, individualism and the desire for a new future were and are the primary motivation of most emigrants arriving in the New World.

New York: Manhattan as seen from the south (inset, 1950; colored photograph, 1987), with Battery Park City on the left and South Street Seaport's Pier 17 on the right.

In America – a land of immigrants, exiles, and foreigners – the condition of modernity looms larger than anywhere else. The ocean plays a vital role in fostering the process of detachment. The decision to cross the ocean was strongly influenced by a desire to better oneself and to make a radical break with the existing social context, which seemed to offer no possibility for a higher quality of life. Far into the twentieth century, the voyage by ship was the only way in which to act on this decision, and at the same time it paved the way for an even greater acceptance of the break with the past and an identification with the *New* World. The importance of the chastening effect of a voyage lasting seven days or more was described recently by Jonathan Raban in his search for the roots of the American mentality.[2] Sailing for days on end across an infinite expanse of water, together with thousands of fellow sojourners, stimulated mental detachment from the world left behind. At the same time, the emptiness of this watery expanse aroused curiosity and a desire for something new. And the contrast between a vast, empty ocean and the first sight of the New York skyline was always overwhelming and compelling, regardless of whether the panorama was or was not enhanced by a robust row of skyscrapers.

Nevertheless, this mass of individualists had a common interest as well: namely, the right of each individual to the *freedom* of economic, social, and cultural development, which could be guaranteed only by legally establishing the fundamental equality of every individual. These basic rights of political equality and economic, social, and cultural freedom do form, in fact, the foundation of American society, as set down in 1776 in the Declaration of Independence.[3]

But the establishment of this duality of political equality and economic freedom also introduced the question of how to give this dyadic quality concrete form in the constitutional organization of American society and in the physical planning of city and country.

The leitmotif that pervades the history of American society *and* American urban planning is a search for a way to balance and lend shape to the relationship between political equality and economic, social, and cultural freedom: in other words, the relationship between public and private interests.

Beginning in the early years of the United States as an independent nation, even before the nineteenth century had arrived, Americans debated about the most desirable *amount* and *form* of future urbanization in this New World.

A point to note in studying the debate on the 'right' *amount* of urbanization is that from the very beginning the image of *New* and *Unknown* possibilities was related primarily to the land itself, a country whose natural scenic beauty embodied completely new forms and dimensions, a nation that appeared to be an inexhaustible spring of productivity and natural resources. Maintaining and cultivating the country's rural qualities and living in harmony with the natural landscape have always been important considerations in the debate on urbanization. The argument against the kind of urbanization that produces big cities and urban agglomerations has left its mark on page after page of American history. In their book, *The Intellectual Versus the City*, Morton and Lucia White describe this tradition, beginning with Thomas Jefferson – who saw the development of big cities as an unnecessary encroachment on, and a neglect of, the natural wealth of the land – and following the theme all the way through to Frank Lloyd Wright and his designs for Broadacre City.[4]

In an attempt to create a foundation for a collective, American, republican sense of identity, this tradition has focused not only on developing and exploiting the American countryside, but also – and especially – on *experiencing* nature.[5]

When in the course of the nineteenth

century the growth of big cities could no
longer be stemmed, an apt question arose:
how can big-city dwellers be given a chance
to enter into the collective experience of
America's scenic beauty? The answer was the
development of parks and large-scale park
systems, which became a key factor in efforts
to realize a collective American identity.

Along with the issue concerning the amount
of urbanization, another continuing subject
of debate has been the *form* to be taken by
urbanization. In this case, American repub-
licanism seems to have created a dichotomy:
on the one hand, an emphasis on theoretical
political equality and the related attempt to
achieve a new collective cultural identity
and, on the other hand, the principle of free
economic, social, and cultural development.

This duality has produced two different
urban planning methods of approach: one
that stresses the design of the city as a cultural
monument to the new republican society, and
one that stresses an urban planning layout
that provides optimal opportunities for the
development of private enterprise.

A late-eighteenth-century manifesto for
the former approach was a plan for Washington designed in 1792 by Pierre Charles
L'Enfant and Andrew Ellicot. As the young
nation's new capital, Washington was to
become a symbol and example of the new
republican identity of the United States,
represented by the classicistic European
repertoire of grand boulevards and monumental buildings proposed by L'Enfant and
Ellicot. Except for the realization of several
elementary principles of the plan, such as the
central position of the Capitol and a few large
boulevards, Washington never became the
monumental city that L'Enfant envisioned.
Political and cultural support needed for the
success of the plan simply did not exist.[6]

About a century later Daniel Burnham
(in collaboration with Edward Bennett) made
a similar attempt with his design for Chicago,
which was to become a 'Paris by the lake,' a
city in which the architecture of the buildings
was meant to enhance the desired monumental image of boulevards, avenues, and
squares.[7] Here, too, only one part of the
plan was realized: Lakefront Boulevard.

The urban planning approach that stressed
the principle of an optimal development of
private enterprise took shape spectacularly in
1811 in the form of the Commissioners Plan
for New York. Never before had a completely
uniform grid been developed for such a large
territory: no less than 35 square kilometers.

The uniformity and continuity of the
street network theoretically guaranteed that
the government would treat public areas
equally and that all parts of the city would be
accessible to all citizens. The initial absence of
any kind of restrictions applied to the area
occupied by a building site also guaranteed a
maximum economic development of private
enterprise.

The American grid city:
no city center, no hard
boundaries.
Bird's-eye view of
Quanah, Texas.
Lithograph by Thaddeus
M. Fowler, 1890.

Below: Fragment of a map
of New York and vicinity
by B. Ratzer, 1776.

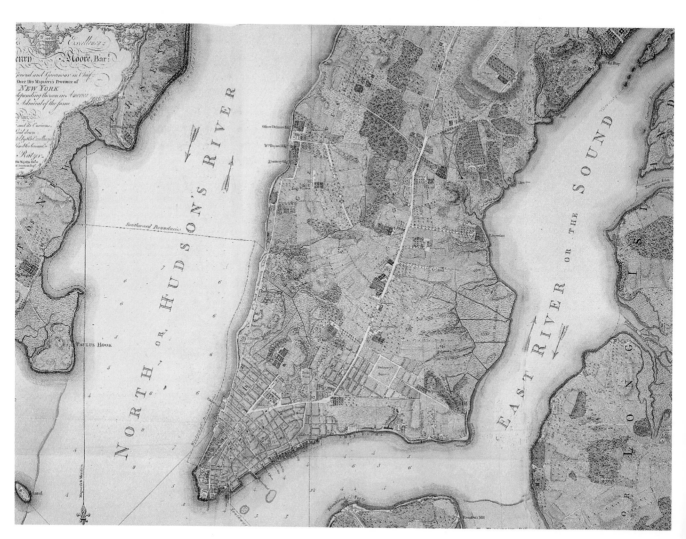

Map of New York by
G.W. Colton, 1865.

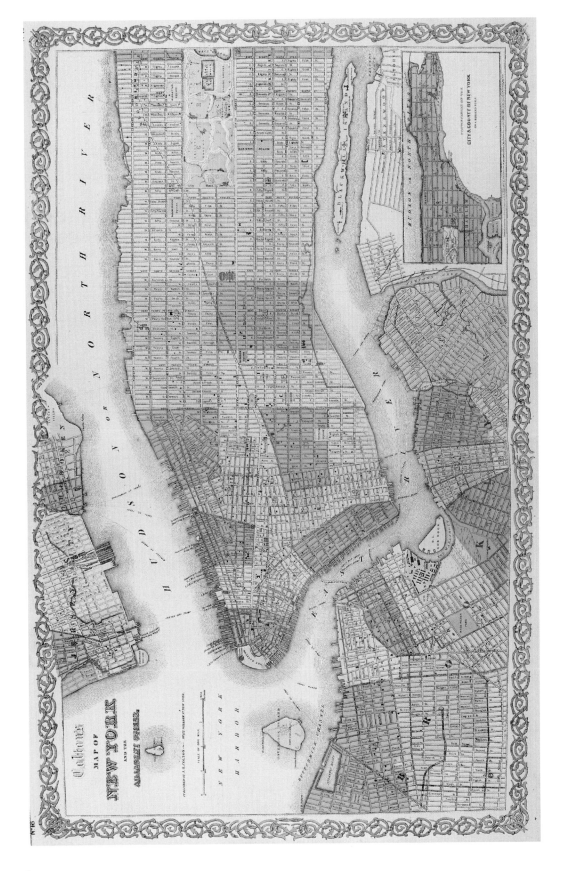

NEW YORK

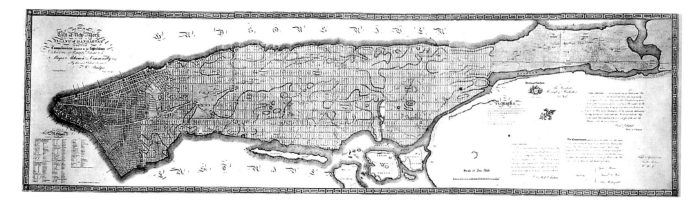

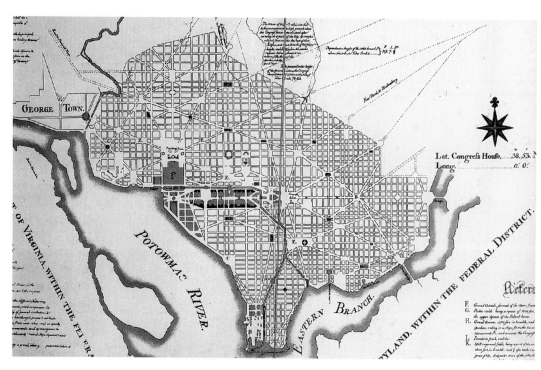

Commissioners Plan for New York, 1811.

Plan for Washington by Pierre Charles L'Enfant, 1791.

In his explanatory remarks, the commission secretary emphasized that the most important advantage of the plan was 'to afford facilities for buying, selling and improving real estate on New York Island.'[8]

In the nineteenth century, the dispute that pitted the type of urban planning based on a desired cultural identity against the type based on maximum economic freedom was decided, initially, in favor of the latter approach. Despite arguments for living in harmony with nature, cities grew tremen-

dously. And the example being followed was New York, not L'Enfant's Washington.

Even so, cultural movements working for strong ties with the countryside – as the foundation of a collective, republican sense of awareness – and for a closer and more monumental connection between architecture and urban planning remained a dogged element within America's urban planning tradition. Such movements were to contribute a great deal to the further development and differentiation of grid cities, in which the position of waterfront areas was at stake.

At various times, the waterfront has been a consummate battlefield of opposing concepts and approaches. Although it has always been a source of economic development, of trade and transport, the waterfront and its expanse of open sea is also a plainly visible symbiosis of city and unspoiled nature.

At the same time, the significance of the waterfront is linked to that of the frontier, an important part of the American self-image.[9] The history of America's development is the history of crossing one unknown threshold after another: those braving the frontier have been men and women who gave their all and, in so doing, displayed the true American mentality. The frontier has become a quintessential American myth, a metaphor for a never-ending flood of new opportunities, new discoveries. The waterfront is indeed a typical American concept, the most recognizable and timeless representative of the frontier, the mythical symbol of a line precisely on the border between land already conquered, already civilized (the city), and the immensity and boundlessness of a world *still to be* discovered and conquered (water, the ocean). This myth has both a collective interpretation (the frontier as the border of the new American society) and an individual interpretation (the frontier as the opportunity to transcend the limits of one's own capabilities). Consequently, beginning in the nineteenth century both public and private approaches to urban planning in America treated the waterfront as a highly significant feature.

# 2 The Modernity of the Port City: The Port Area, From Neutral to Marginal Zone

Characteristic of the American grid city was an initial absence of any hierarchy in the network of public areas, a network within which each street potentially played a role on every level of scale. Public streets linked each lot directly to the neighborhood, as well as to all parts of the city, the region, and even the world. Theoretically, after all, streets and avenues had no boundaries. Natural boundaries like hills, valleys, and rivers were simply covered by the grid, sometimes after being eliminated (leveling hilltops, for example). Riverbanks and shorelines were not considered definitive boundaries either.

Most American port areas consist of a series of piers positioned at right angles to quays, forming a comb-like structure. This structure allows streets composing the grid to run straight into the water, so to speak, and creates the possibility for the grid to be expanded into the water. This interwovenness of port and street network assumed various forms.

Philadelphia, founded in 1682 as the capital of William Penn's new colony of Pennsylvania, became one of the first port cities to realize such a pier. The pier was built in 1685 for primarily practical reasons: constructing a wooden jetty like this one was relatively simple and inexpensive, compared with the complexity and high costs of building a quay along the river. Private shipowners could construct a wooden pier without difficulty, and it was, above all else, an easily managed element clearly distinguishable from the public nature of the riverbank. The

Plan for Chicago by
Daniel Burnham and
Edward H. Bennett, 1908.

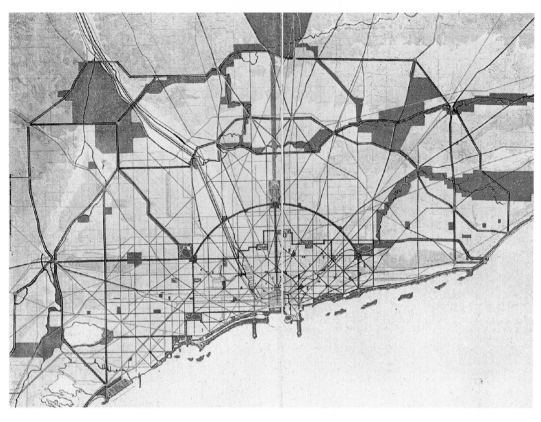

Waterfront section of
the Plan for Chicago by
Daniel Burnham and
Edward H. Bennett, 1908.

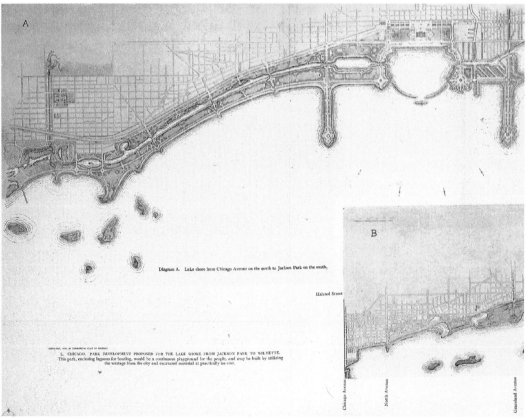

Diagram A. Lake shore from Chicago Avenue on the north to Jackson Park on the south.

L. CHICAGO. PARK DEVELOPMENT PROPOSED FOR THE LAKE SHORE FROM JACKSON PARK TO WILMETTE.
This park, enclosing lagoons for boating, would be a continuous playground for the people, and may be built by utilizing
the wastage from the city and excavated material at practically no cost.

New York: Lower Manhattan skyscrapers, which represent centrality. Schoolroom illustration, ca. 1930.

principle was imitated on a large scale: a hundred years later Philadelphia's waterfront was marked by sixty-six piers, and other port cities – including New York, Boston, and San Francisco – had also developed this type of port.

Admittedly, the process was not always as matter-of-course as it appears in retrospect. In nineteenth-century New York, for example, proposals were developed for the construction of docks based on those in English port cities.[10] The principle of piers prevailed, however, owing to efficiency, fast and cheap implementation and, in particular, flexibility. Building a series of waterfront docks would have created a sharp boundary, an 'edge' to the city. The east-west streets of Manhattan's grid were designed to link the two banks of the island: in creating the grid, designers foresaw intensive traffic between the two waterfronts and included a large number of east-west streets. In many cases

■ 1650
◪ 1776
◪ 1850
◪ 1973
■ 1980

Manhattan's expanding shoreline, 1650-1980.

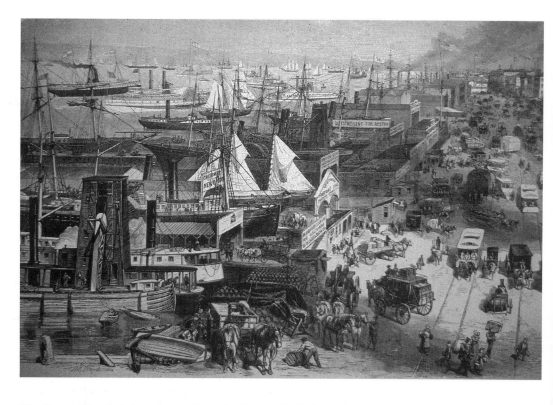

West Street in New York drawn by A.R. Waud for *Harper's Weekly*, September 1869.

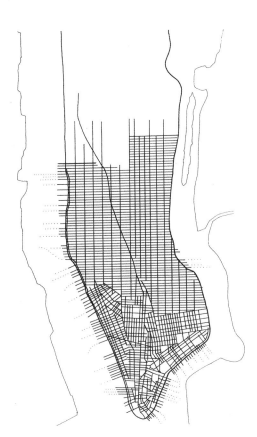

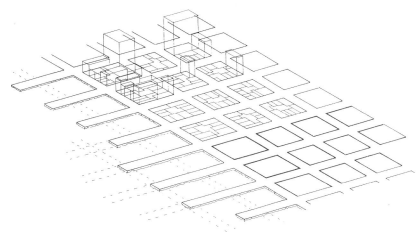

The grid: no city center, no hard boundaries.
The port zone is a continuation of the grid into the water.

this traffic infrastructure experienced a smooth transition with that of the river, especially at places boasting ferry connections to New Jersey, Queens, or Brooklyn. Manhattan had about twenty-five ferry connections of this sort in 1900.

In various locations port cities literally expanded, by way of their piers, into the water. In the late 1700s, development along one of Boston's main streets was continued on the adjoining pier, a project that transformed the pier into a breakwater. Piers were converted into dams, water separating these dams was filled in (usually with ground from leveled hilltops), new waterfront sections were created, and future piers were built even farther out into the water. This 'landfill' process caused waterfront areas in cities like New York, Boston, and San Francisco to edge increasingly farther away from the original shoreline, thus allowing the city to expand its territory significantly.

This blend of city and port was quite the opposite – the reverse image, so to speak – of the blend of city and port found in sixteenth- and seventeenth-century Dutch cities, which welcomed a network of waterways that penetrated deeply into the urban fabric. In American port cities, on the other hand, networks of public streets penetrated deeply into the water.

Early in this developmental process, quayside streets formed the center of public urban life: it was here that immigrants disembarked and goods were transshipped, and here that the first buildings were realized. In Philadelphia, Front Street fulfilled this role in the early nineteenth century; in New York it was South Street. The use of these quays, as well as the piers, was highly diverse: they functioned both as worlds of traffic and activity, and as spheres of amusement, entertainment, and facilities.

Brooklyn Bridge.
Lithograph, 1883.

In nearly every nineteenth-century port city, these quays or the areas bordering them accommodated the busiest public markets, where farmers, fishermen, and small-scale manufacturers could offer their wares without the use of middlemen. Far into the twentieth century, public markets such as these remained not only important facilities fulfilling the daily needs of a large part of the urban population in dozens of cities but also, according to a study carried out by Philip Langdon, 'organizers of urban community.'[11] This important function – harbor front as marketplace – has been a typical feature of the American port city for a long time: South Street Market in New York continued operating until 1980 and Faneuil Market in Boston until 1972, while the latter's Broadway Market, along with Pike Place Market in Seattle, are still open for business.

In addition, in the course of the nineteenth century 'amusement piers' began appearing in cities like New York: piers with swimming pools or a hospital with a floating sun deck. The combination of harbor world and urban life was seen as both a fascinating and salubrious attraction.

Originally, a specific urban planning concept for the waterfront of the American port city was nonexistent. The general neutrality of the grid concept allowed for enormous diversity along the waterfront, with respect to both building typology and usage, which included ferry service, marketplaces, and amusement piers.

The picture that emerges from all this is that of an American harbor front *spatially* connected to the characteristic structure of the American grid city and *functionally* linked to, and an obvious part of, public urban life.

## RECONCILIATION OF CITY AND COUNTRYSIDE

The ability of the port zone to develop into the American seaport's informal city center was due largely to the neutrality and uniformity of the grid-shaped street network.

Nonetheless, as early as the nineteenth century spatial developments occurred that undermined the neutrality and uniformity of the grid and that introduced forms of hierarchy and centrality into the spatial structure of the city which greatly affected the position and significance of urban waterfronts.

First, despite the apparent denial of historical structures, grids did indeed prove to have tenacious historical elements of special significance to the various cities.

A second development was the construction of new infrastructural facilities – particularly railroad stations and cross-water connections – which boosted the importance of certain sites and routes; these sites and

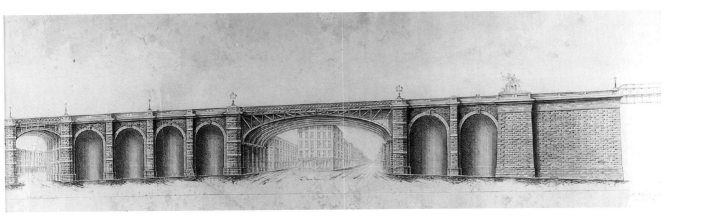

The approaches to Brooklyn Bridge: structures within the urban grid pattern.

routes went on to assume special positions within the urban context.

And third, from the mid-nineteenth century on, deliberate efforts – in the form of designs for park systems – were made to develop large-scale structuralizing elements for various cities.

*Old networks*

Certain boulevards and squares in New York, which were linked to or built on forms and structures that had evolved historically, began to play a special role in urban life: namely, Fifth Avenue, Washington Square, and Broadway.

Washington Square was a distinctively designed transition from old city to new, located on the spot at which several existing grid elements met the new grid. Fifth Avenue was Manhattan's main street, which led precisely to the center of Washington Square. Here, at Washington Square and Fifth Avenue, were the homes of the city's most prominent families, as well as elegant shops and establishments.

And then Broadway, the pivot that seemed to draw all facets of urban life together. When the grid for Manhattan was designed in 1811, most of the street now known as Broadway was called Bloomingdale Road, a country lane lined with farms, pig farms, and inns. While the grid plan was being filled in, little

by little, this road was the only route that continued to serve traffic moving across the island diagonally and which was, at the same time, already lined with buildings on both sides. Its existing rural and agrarian functions became part of the new urban context: farms were converted to clothing factories and inns to hotels and theaters.

Throughout the nineteenth century, as more and more buildings were added to the grid, public appreciation increased for the contrasting character of Bloomingdale Road, which became an extension of the original Broadway in the late 1800s, at which time the entire route became known as Broadway. Many people found the orthogonal pattern of streets and avenues monotonous and unimposing. Preserving, extending, and even broadening Bloomingdale Road-cum-Broadway at certain places was largely a result of this critical view of the grid and of appreciation for Broadway's disparate dimensions, orientation, and profiles. Broadway became New York's first central boulevard, a position reflected by the name originally given to the northern section of the route (north of 42nd Street): Grand Boulevard.

This capital deviation from the grid was, of all things, the element destined to develop into the focal point of urban life and an archetype of public space in the modern city: a boulevard that embraces the entire complex scale of modern life in the city. Broadway

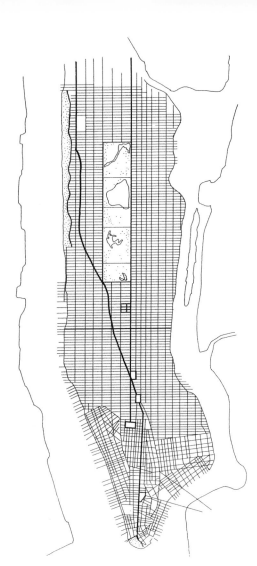

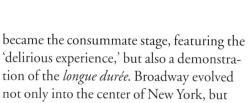

became the consummate stage, featuring the 'delirious experience,' but also a demonstration of the *longue durée*. Broadway evolved not only into the center of New York, but also into 'the heart of the world.'[12]

### New infrastructural elements

The port was an important, large-scale, infrastructural element in the nineteenth-century American city, but not the only one. The construction of railroad stations and cross-water connections also meant that sites and routes linked to these new facilities would claim special places on the city map.

When Grand Central Station was erected in New York, 42nd Street assumed a central position, which was reinforced by providing this street with a broader profile, making it one of the most important connections between port areas along the East River and those along the Hudson River. And a legend unparalleled in the city arose at the intersection of 42nd Street and Broadway, a spot known far and wide as *the* center of New York, though this was never planned: Times Square.

The first major cross-river connection between Manhattan and Brooklyn, the Brooklyn Bridge, not only highlighted the

Central Park. Aerial
photograph, 1946.

tion of the approaches to these viaducts and
the existing street network. The grid was
respected and preserved wherever possible.

*Park systems as bearers of a collective
republican identity*

Although the special significance imparted
to historic elements such as Grand Central
Station and the Brooklyn Bridge may have
been 'spontaneous' at first, from the mid-
nineteenth century on an urban planning
culture emerged in America which made a
deliberate and systematic attempt to inject
new order, structure, and hierarchy into the
nation's cities by introducing park systems.

The Commissioners Plan of 1811 still
reserved center stage for the development
of private enterprise, and the structure and
organization of the street network was determined by rational motives such as opening up
areas and improving accessibility and traffic
circulation. The concept of the Commissioners Plan called for New York to be developed
first and foremost as a seaport, which
demanded a concentrated and uninterrupted
network of east-west connections between
the island's two harbor fronts, a network that
permitted no deviation.

In 1811 the commissioners argued that
since quay areas had always been used as a
recreational facility, which offered an unobstructed view of the river, large open areas in
the grid plan were unnecessary.[13]

In the second half of the nineteenth century,
Americans recognized the need for urban
areas capable of playing a major role in the
communal life of the city, as bearers of a new
collective identity. The American city was
characterized by a rapidly growing population boasting an unprecedented diversity:
people from every corner of the world, each
with its own social and cultural features.
Furthermore, the Civil War that raged in the
1860s may have ended, militarily and polit-

importance of feeder roads, but also – owing
to its architectural monumentality and its
prestige as a central icon of the city – placed a
strong accent on the essential significance of
the East River, its quays, and the boroughs of
Manhattan and Brooklyn.

A remarkable feature of these nineteenth-
century infrastructural interventions was the
way in which they merged directly with the
network of the grid, despite their enormous
dimensions. When an element like the
Brooklyn Bridge, which rises 40 meters into
the air to allow ships free passage, needed
long viaducts to span existing streets, extra
care was given to a well-designed combina-

ically, in 1865, but in a mental sense it continued to fester.

Within this situation, the phenomenon of the city park became a hot topic in the debate on urban development. Landscape architects like Andrew Jackson Downing, Frederick Law Olmsted, and Calvert Vaux were given a great deal of attention, not only because of their qualities as designers, but also because of their strong views on the significance of the city park for the development of a collective republican identity.[14] Their opinions endorsed the previously described American tradition, which saw an awareness of natural scenic beauty as an essential factor in the development of a collective, republican sense of identity. Now that the massive growth of big cities clearly indicated that millions of Americans would no longer have the chance to experience this beauty directly, the argument for *introducing the landscape into the city* intensified.

Downing was the ideological godfather of the concept of public facilities, and particularly the park, as the core of republican awareness: 'Open wide, therefore, the doors of your libraries and picture galleries, all ye true republicans! Build halls where knowledge shall be freely diffused among men, and not shut up within the narrow walls of narrower institutions. Plan spacious parks in your cities, and unloose their gates as wide as the gates of morning to the people.'[15]

Downing may have established the new ideology of the park, but his pupil Olmsted and Olmsted's companion Vaux were the foremost executors of the concept of the new city park. The project that set the stage for their renown was the design and realization of Central Park. For years Downing had harped on the subject of a large city park in New York. Only after his death in 1852, however, was his proposal adopted by the city council, which commissioned Olmsted and Vaux to design the park.[16]

Like Downing, Olmsted believed that the purpose of the park was to make 'a contribution to a truly republican society.' He thought this goal was feasible, since the park would represent a common interest of all Americans: the scenic beauty of their nation – 'The park must be the country in the city.'[17]

Olmsted and Vaux designed Central Park as a naturalistic, scenic park; their approach was based on the tradition of the formal English landscaped park, with its aesthetically elegant paths, differences in height, boscages for enhanced depth perception, ponds, and unexpected vistas. A visitor strolling along the paths of Central Park becomes acquainted with the spectrum of the American countryside, with 'the beauty of the fields, the prairie, of the pastures and the still waters.'[18]

The gigantic park represented a major interruption of the continuity of the street network. However, this network was provided with four sunken roads straight through the park, leaving the visual coherence of the verdant landscape unimpaired.

Central Park provided New York with more than a huge facility (800 by 4,000 meters); it also gave the city a structuralizing element on the scale of the city as a whole. The park attracted not only people in search of peace and relaxation, but also real-estate projects: the park worked like a magnet on developers of quality apartment buildings, offices, and hotels. Central Park became more than a park; it became an urban center.

In the years that followed, this aspect – the use of a park design as a structuralizing element of the city – was developed in greater detail. Olmsted and Vaux's design for Prospect Park in Brooklyn was accompanied by proposals for a system of parkways that were to connect the park, as a formally landscaped urban facility, with boroughs farther away. The proximity of the park was to be apparent from every part of the city.

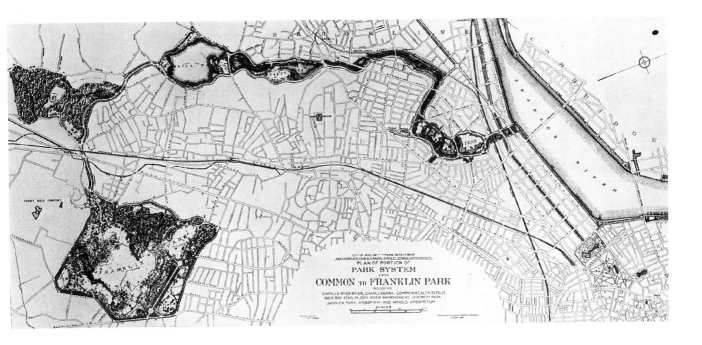

The most consistent development and implementation of this concept was found in the Boston park system, realized in the late 1800s. Taking advantage of the presence of various ponds and bogs, Olmsted and Vaux designed a differentiated system of individual parks linked by parkways. This system, which meanders through the various grid patterns of the city, ultimately reaches stately Commonwealth Avenue on the way to its final destination: Boston Common, once a central tract of grassland, now a city park. The system developed into a network whose individual parks imbued each of Boston's districts with a unique identity, while at the same time functioning as a single system to provide the city as a whole with a central, collective structure.

Olmsted and Vaux's primary contribution to the story told here is their 'discovery' of the waterfront of American port and river cities as a structure obviously eligible to become – if guided by principles of landscape architecture – a cardinal component of an urban park system. In 1875 they were given the chance to demonstrate this concept in New York by creating a prototypal design for part of the

Boston Park System, design by F.L. Olmsted, 1885.

Hudson River shoreline of Manhattan, between 83rd and 140th Streets. Riverside Park, designed for this site, set the stage for similar treatment of riverbanks all over Upper Manhattan and the Bronx. The presence of a vast expanse of water transcended the idea of a phenomenal scenic attraction in the form of a continuous element that would characterize the many sections of Riverside Drive as it encircled the city. Thanks to their significance as the collective destination of countless immigrants to the New World, waterfronts and water itself could fulfill an important role in the concept of raising republican consciousness. This design for New York's riverbanks would provide a system 'with a view to utilize, in the greatest degree practicable, the advantages offered by the territory, *as a whole.*'[19]

The design provided for a system of elegant avenues and paths, intended for 'pleasure drives' and walks, and an undulating building line of distinguished residences to represent the city on the waterfront. Of note in the plan for Riverside Park is thought given by the designers to the construction and maintenance of harbor and railroad

Map of Riverside Park, New York: design by F. L. Olmsted, 1875.

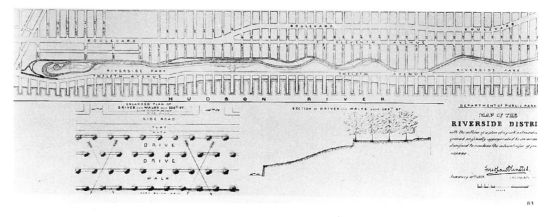

Impression of Riverside Drive. Cover of an advertising brochure promoting the sale of building lots, 1888.

functions. Making use of differences in height in this section of the riverbank area, Olmsted and Vaux designed Riverside Park with a clear view of the water, while maintaining port and railroad functions at a lower level.

For the time being, the experiment was restricted to this prototype for Riverside Drive, since real-estate interests in zones accommodating port terminals in the rest of Manhattan were too powerful to yield to a park system.

Olmsted and Vaux had created quite a stir, however. In the decades that followed, Manhattan's waterfront became a constant subject of debate and the focus of a great many proposals.[20]

The most integral application of Olmsted's concept for the waterfront was not

realized in New York, however, but in the vicinity of Chicago, where in 1868 Olmsted was given the opportunity to design a plan for Riverside, an entire urban district along the water. The exhibition of this design at the Chicago World's Fair of 1893 brought Olmsted public recognition and was a stepping stone to his involvement in an initiative by Chicago business leaders to develop a plan for their city 'that will make Chicago so beautiful it will outrival Paris.'[21] Olmsted did not live to see this plan completed by Burnham and Bennett. Although it remained largely a plan on paper, one important element was realized: Lake Front Park, part of which was based on Burnham's theories. He borrowed directly from Olmsted, however, in his design of the avenue through the park, the greenery, and especially the water-related components, which are situated like a lagoon in the park landscape.[22]

The development of park systems in the city provided city officials with a new means of introducing structure and differentiation into the urban area without making radical interventions into the architectonic shape of buildings. On the contrary, the large scale and careful organization of park systems furnished the network of public space with new structure, which injected a great deal of individuality and irregularity into building typologies and the use of open space. Park systems permitted urban land to be used with a high degree of flexibility, as demonstrated in the design for Riverside Park, in particular, whose architects anticipated the maintenance and expansion of port functions during the design phase. But Central Park was also to be a demonstration of the combination of a continuity of the

park itself and flexibility in the use of the land around it, a concept expressed in the great variety of building typologies along the borders of the park. In other words, the introduction of park systems, along with the development of the skyscraper, led to the creation of a new relationship between public space infused with new shape and structure and expressing collectivity and continuity, and a new building typology that allowed for an even stronger emphasis on individuality and freedom of private enterprise.

This approach to urban design, best exemplified by developments in New York, began functioning as an important alternative to starkly contrasting concepts promoted by the City Beautiful movement, which called for a high level of conformity in the design of public space and buildings and, consequently, strict regulations to be applied to architecture and buildings.

Daniel Burnham's 1909 plan for Chicago

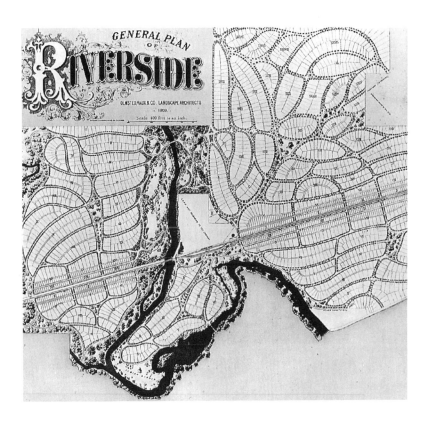

Plan for Riverside, Chicago: design by F. L. Olmsted and C. Vaux, 1869.

was an important manifesto for America's City Beautiful movement. In this plan, Burnham not only added a new system of radial and diagonal boulevards to the grid, but also proposed that regulations be applied to building design for the purpose of forging street profiles and adjacent buildings into a coherent urban image. The salient feature was the shoreline of Lake Michigan. Essential to Burnham's plan was the preservation of most of the existing grid; filling it in, however, especially with regard to the development of building sites, was subjected to design regulations of a more specific nature.

The ideals of the City Beautiful movement did not go unchallenged. Lewis Mumford, who was to play a major role in American urban planning in the following decades, called the plan an example of 'urban cosmetics' and later compared it to the urban concepts of totalitarian regimes.[23]

Mumford saw in Burnham's plan an undesirable restriction of free private enterprise stemming from overstrict building regulations, while noting that these same regulations provided the city with a cosmetic layer that drew attention away from Chicago's serious social problems.

Ultimately, time would prove Olmsted right. For while City-Beautiful showpieces, such as New York's once prominent Pennsylvania Station complex, were subjected to demolition long ago, Olmsted's park systems remain distinctly dominant elements, which lend shape and structure to those cities in which his designs were realized.

The 'timelessness' of concepts and designs created by Olmsted and colleagues is expressed not only in the physical structure of cities, but also in the formulation of ideas within the discipline. These park designs have been exceptionally relevant to an American sense of cultural awareness and to theories on the development of the American city. Countless observations, analyses, and reviews

have been devoted to Olmsted's work.[24] A complete Olmsted bibliography would probably equal that of a highly regarded American president.

Olmsted's concept of the park as a representation of the countryside and as a timeless phenomenon immune to fluctuation and caprice, and ultimately as a plea for a reconciliation between city and countryside, made an enormous impression and, even today, more than a century after his death, assumes a prominent place in American urban planning. In particular, as this story will tell, his concept of the waterfront as a pivotal element within a structuralizing park system remains a constant theme in the debate on urban design in American cities. Interestingly, Olmsted's considerable influence applied not only to converting urban areas into parks, but also to designing and organizing these areas into formally landcaped, naturalistic parks. Because the idea was, and is, not simply to add 'a bit of greenery' to the urban area, but to bring America's scenic beauty into the city.

## INTROVERSION OF THE CITY

*The skyscraper as a sign of centrality*
The structuralizing effect of new park systems in American cities was expressed primarily in the use of parks and parkways by people from all walks of life. True to Olmsted's predictions, parks became sites that demonstrated the collectivity and equality of the urban population.

But park systems also had a powerful structuralizing effect on the image of the city as a whole, as well as on the development of the price of land. Developers of both quality apartment buildings and skyscrapers were attracted by the new park systems.

Despite the tenacious myth that the skyscraper was born of a lack of space and overblown land prices, various authors have proved beyond a doubt that quite the opposite is true: skyscrapers are not the result, but rather the cause, of congestion and a drastic increase in land prices.[25] In the late 1800s and early 1900s, New York had room for all sorts of building projects, especially in harbor areas, where land and other forms of real estate were relatively inexpensive. Nonetheless, New York's skyscraper boom did not occur along the waterfront.

The first clients to opt for the type of building known as a skyscraper based their choice on the prestige involved: they saw the building as a 'profane cathedral' and, consequently, as a world-famous trademark advertising their company.[26] The choice of location depended on a combination of an available building site and, high on the list of priorities, the proximity of new parks, avenues, and squares.

The new structure of public areas, which was based on local government initiatives, and the new trend toward high-rise buildings, which was based on private enterprise, reinforced each other and produced a common result: a new centrality and hierarchy in the city.

### Waterfront slums

Designers' efforts to transform urban waterfronts into parks had only limited success. In most cases, both waterfront and port area were labeled 'marginal' or 'peripheral'; harbor districts were the first areas in America to acquire the status of slums.

The significance and image of the slum changed substantially in the course of the nineteenth and twentieth centuries. The origin of the word *slum* played a major role in the 'secularization' process of urban poverty: *slum* no longer indicated a certain population group or a collection of individuals, but an area, a location in the city, which was seen initially (in the nineteenth century) as an obvious phenomenon of urbanism. Warner explains that originally the term *slum* had more than a negative connotation.[27] It may have signified poverty amid overcrowded circumstances, but the tenants themselves saw this as temporary and matter-of-course: life in the slums was a first step toward discovering the New World.[28] According to Warner, this definition displayed an optimism that existed all the way up to the 1930s.

Having arrived in the slums, the brand-new immigrant became familiar with the rules of the New World. Writing of the slums, the classic American police reporter, Jacob Riis, described the Lower East Side as a place where new immigrants found hospitality, understanding, solidarity, and support from hordes of those who had arrived earlier, as well as from the many relief organizations set up to help them.[29] Life in the slums was also a recurrent theme in American novels set in this era.[30]

Outsiders saw the slums as a curiosity, an exotic and exciting part of town at variance with the rest, where those looking for diversion might spend a day or an evening. 'Going slumming' was a popular activity among nineteenth-century urbanites, who were drawn mainly to harbor areas and immigrant neighborhoods, the prototype of which was New York's Lower East Side, soon to be known around the world as the 'mother of urban slums.'

The negative, pessimistic connotation of slums – as areas of dire poverty, dilapidation, and apathy – became prevalent only later, at a time when slums were no longer seen as a starting point, but as the end of the line, a final haven for *losers*. This change in the definition and image of slums meant that instead of being the obvious destination of those arriving in the New World, they represented a contradiction, a stigma: slums became the antithesis of the land of unparalleled opportunity.

Slums and skyscrapers: although at first the Lower East Side and Lower Manhattan seemed to form a duality, they eventually evolved into two different worlds increasingly at odds with each other. Thus in about 1900, the American port city displayed a distinction between presentation and representation.

In a spatial-functional respect, the waterfront and adjacent districts still played a major role in city life. This area accommodated a concentration of countless urban functions, mixed with various sorts of traffic. This remained the place in which the city 'presented itself' to a large extent.

The relatively indeterminate shape of urban space in waterfront zones, however, formed an increasingly greater contrast to the way in which central, skyscraper-lined boulevards and avenues dominated the urban image. These streets represented the city. Both urban planning and architectural design turned to concentrate on these territorial, intermediate, urban zones.

For the time being, differences between the world of the slums and that of the skyscrapers emerged gradually. Thanks to continuity within the network of urban areas, people could move with ease from one world to the other and use the facilities offered by both. The distinction between the two was rarely hard and fast; clear lines of demarcation were nonexistent.

The introversion of the American city, with its highly significant park system in striking contrast to the marginalization of the waterfront, made one thing absolutely clear: a well-defined border between city and countryside has enormous potential for development.[31] The enormous popularity of areas adjacent to Central Park and of peripheral areas lining Boston's park system was due largely to a combination of two extremes: a peerless, modern, city milieu and an open, unspoiled, idyllic landscape.

The remarkable aspect was the apparent desire to create these borders only by artificial means in the middle of the city. Miles and miles of urban coastline were a far more obvious area for the design and exploitation of an attractive border area. For the time being, however, the interests of a port- and transportation-related economy posed a barrier to such an exploitation of the waterfront. But from the 1920s on waterfront development could no longer be avoided, and New York's harbor areas became the target of a large-scale urban planning transformation aimed at creating a new urban landscape.

# Modernism on the Waterfront: The City Merges With the Landscape

## HIGHWAYS AND THE REGIONALIZATION OF THE CITY

The radical transformation of waterfront areas in American port cities coincided with a chapter in American urban development that introduced a new, traffic-related infrastructural element: highways.

The realization of a vast network of highways in the 1920s and '30s, followed by an enormous expansion of this network in the decades after World War II, was the result of a policy based on a uniquely American combination of social motives (many of which were derived directly from socialist and anarchistic ideologies) and economic motives (which were aimed at achieving a fully developed capitalist economy).

Prior to the twentieth century, waterways and railroads were the two main components of interlocal and transcontinental transportation and traffic infrastructure in the United States. In those early years, the automobile was used mainly as a luxury vehicle by members of the gentry out for a pleasure drive. To a limited degree, the role of the motor vehicle as a means of transporting freight emerged as well, especially with regard to the transport of goods *within* cities and to special agricultural functions. Neither roads nor vehicles were equipped to handle long-distance, intercity transportation.

The development of the new infrastructural element – highways – which was accompanied by an explosion of automobile production, was based on two important stimuli: World War I and the New Deal.[32]

### *The economic motive: the flexibility of the truck*

After entering World War I, the American government found it necessary to call on the automobile industry for the mass production of trucks, to be used both in America and in the European war zone. Initially, the government appropriated private railroad companies to use for transporting materiel from industrial cities to seaports. When this proved insufficient, authorities introduced the mass utilization of trucks and, in so doing, not only increased freight capacity, but also discovered the flexibility of the truck: suddenly the transport of materiel was no longer dependent on either the timetables or routes of railroads. The use of this new means of transportation meant not only an explosive expansion in the automobile industry, but also the introduction of the first paved interlocal highways, which had to be designed with the total weight of trucks and freight in mind.

Within a few years, trucks had supplanted trains in the area of freight transport. Government intervention had turned out to be a double-edged sword.

On the one hand, after railroads were appropriated, transport companies were forced to switch to trucks for freight haulage. At the end of the war, there was no turning back: although railroad companies recovered their rails and equipment in 1920, most of their customers were gone for good.[33]

On the other hand, having confronted the automobile industry and road-building companies with such large and unexpected orders, the government felt obliged to support these sectors after the war was over. In 1920 it established the Bureau of Public Roads (BPR), an agency headed by the legendary

Thomas MacDonald, nicknamed Mr. Highways. The activities of the BPR, along with support measures and incentives aimed at the automobile industry, soon provided the United States with a network of interstate highways, and in the 1920s once exclusive automobiles entered the world of mass production.

Railroad companies still able to compete were bought up, in many cases, by the automobile industry and shut down.[34] This also applied to many interurban trolleys, a thriving means of public transportation prior to the 1940s.

*The sociocultural motive:
the American identity*

To a man like MacDonald, expanding the road network and increasing the production of cars was more than an economic issue, and highway transportation meant more than moving goods from one place to another. MacDonald fervently believed that the 'automobilization' of America should involve passenger traffic. The unrestricted availability of cars and of a highway network that would make the entire nation accessible to every

American would promote 'a broad Americanism.' According to MacDonald, if cars and highways had existed in 1860, there never would have been a Civil War.[35]

Furthermore, it soon became clear that mass car ownership and a vast network of highways were to form the basis of a completely new kind of urban development. Although Thomas Jefferson's historical arguments against the development of metropolises had long since fallen in the face of reality, with the arrival of car and highway America was confronted, nonetheless, with the potential disintegration of the big city. For certain people, this possibility came at a highly opportune moment.

In the early twentieth century, various groups thought the time had come to establish a new physical planning policy for the city. Arguments for the development of regional plans gained ground during this period. Patrick Geddes, who had been influenced greatly by the anarchistic theories of Proudhon, Kropotkin, and Bakunin, was seen as the spiritual father of regional planning. From the beginning, New York and its Committee on the Regional Plan of New York played a leading role in an organization set up in 1923: the Regional Planning Association of America (RPPA). Early on, explosive urbanization in and around New York had convinced a substantial number of planners, academics, and politicians to support efforts aimed at a regional plan. The most important spokesperson was Lewis Mumford, one of the founders of the Regional Planning Association of America. The expansive development of the regional plan in New York owed a great deal to the enthusiastic support of Franklin D. Roosevelt, then governor of the state of New York.

Geddes argued for a new balance between the public quality and neutrality of urban space and the freedom of private enterprise. Inspired by the attempts of anarchism to erase the discrepancy between city and countryside, Geddes claimed that this new balance could no longer be realized within the city itself, but only on a regional scale. Meticulous regional-planning research on social, economic, and spatial developments was to form a basis for a new type of plan development on a regional scale.

Ultimately, the reality of regional plan development did not live up to the expectations of Geddes and Mumford. New York presented itself as the first laboratory of regional planning. In 1929 regional-planning research proposed by Geddes degenerated into the voluminous *Regional Survey of New York*, a document that De Casseres quickly referred to as 'a survey mountain that bore a regional-planning mouse.'[36] All of which does not mean that New York never managed to develop spatial designs on a regional scale. On the contrary, New York played a vanguard role in the area of spatial designs on a regional scale. These designs, however, were completely unrelated to the research that went into the Regional Survey.

Besides discussing regulations for the appearance and height of high-rise buildings in the city, members of the Committee on the Regional Plan of New York also concentrated on regulating the *number* of towers,[37] as well as on developing a system of parkways to improve the structure of public roads. A new type of physical planning and urban design was to use this system as an important instrument that would transcend the scale of the city. Planning departments and commissions from both the city and state of New York increased their efforts to regulate private enterprise, but also to exert influence themselves – by means of new public investments – on the image and shape of the city and, consequently, to transform the city as a whole.

THE NEW DEAL AND THE CREATION OF MODERN MAN

Ideas within the intellectual framework created and fostered by the Committee on the Regional Plan of New York in the 1920s, when Roosevelt was governor of the state, gained national significance in 1933 when he was elected President of the United States. As President, Roosevelt launched a political program known as the New Deal.

Against a backdrop of economic depression, which had led to an unemployment rate of 25 percent of America's working population, the main objective of the New Deal was to create jobs. But the New Deal was more than simply a policy to provide work. The New Deal began a program of integral planning on a federal level that was unlike any other political program in American history. *Integral* referred to the proposed coordinated correlation of economic, social, cultural, and physical planning.

Integral planning of this type was never realized. At the end of Roosevelt's first two terms in office, an evaluation of the New Deal showed that efforts to implement coordinated social and physical planning on a national scale had failed, and that the

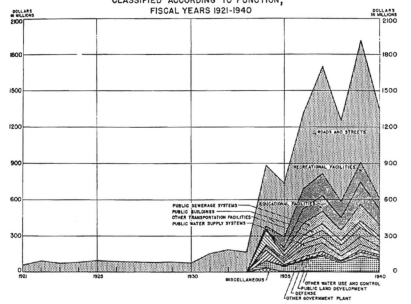

EXPENDITURES FOR FEDERAL GRANTS FOR NON-FEDERAL PUBLIC CONSTRUCTION CLASSIFIED ACCORDING TO FUNCTION, FISCAL YEARS 1921-1940

essential condition. The New Deal envisioned a new, *modern* American way of life as its goal.

The federal government's desire to combine economic and sociocultural objectives did not go unchallenged. Roosevelt and his associates were accused on a number of occasions of trying to turn the United States into a socialist – perhaps even communist – country.

A combination of government investment in public works, the industrial policy, and a new pattern of public consumption was developed most fully in the area of energy. One of the showpieces of the New Deal was the Tennessee Valley Authority, a federal corporation that realized the first hydroelectric power station in the United States. Upon its completion, millions of households were provided with electricity. Finding a practical outlet for this source of energy was a matter of offering substantial government loans to manufacturers of electric appliances. Within a few years, Americans had become dependent on the use of such items as refrigerators, vacuum cleaners, and air conditioners.[39]

The New Deal was less successful in the area of housing, at least in a direct sense. A key player here was Rexford Tugwell, one of Roosevelt's most important advisers and, as a professor at Columbia University and chairman of the City Planning Commission, a fellow New Yorker. Tugwell strongly favored regional-planning ideas propagated by the Regional Planning Association of America and the Committee on the Regional Plan of New York. He launched a plan for the realization of so-called greenbelt communities, which were to serve as alternatives to big-city slum areas. These communities were to be planned and designed by the federal government, but built and managed by local residents' cooperatives with the aid of government subsidies. Greenbelt towns were supposed to relieve the housing

main effect of the New Deal had been to turn the machinery of the federal government into a 'broker state': the government as a real-estate agent with the authority to intervene on behalf of certain powerful groups within American society, regardless of whether the interventions in question were or were not geared to one another.[38]

Originally, the New Deal was based on three programs: an energy program, a housing program, and a program for public works. All three were created to stimulate the industrial economy: the energy program was designed to provide a tremendous boost to the production of electrical equipment, the housing program to lend relief to the building industry, and the public-works program to spark road building and the automobile industry. At the same time, products emerging from this industrial policy laid the foundation needed to modernize the daily life of the American population: a life in which a house in the suburbs, complete with electric appliances and a car in the driveway, was to form an

CITY AND PORT

shortage, solve the problem of urban slums, provide better distribution of industry and employment opportunities, and create a new urban reality to support a new type of sociocultural community development. The doctrines of Geddes and Mumford were a major part of these ideas.[40]

One of the most elaborate and well-known plans based on this concept is Frank Lloyd Wright's Broadacre City, in which every American was to have his own home and a plot of ground that would allow him to grow his own food and to form voluntary cooperative associations with his neighbors. Wright presented Broadacre City in 1924, developed the idea in the 1930s, and published the plan in 1945 under the telling title: *When Democracy Builds.*[41]

At the heart of ideas found in the New Deal, and especially of new ideas on physical planning, lay the necessity for planning to focus on both public and private domains and, consequently, to introduce a new relationship between the two. The private domain was to remain the realm in which private enterprise would develop, but its growth was to be based on a common point of departure provided by the federal government: a home of one's own and, if possible, a plot of ground (as in Broadacre City).

Ideas on regulating the private domain and on providing a common basis met with broad disapproval. Roosevelt's Republican opponents referred to Tugwell's proposals as communist-inspired, as an attempt to introduce Soviet socialism into the United States. Of the three thousand greenbelt towns that Tugwell had hoped to build, only three were realized.[42]

Despite these setbacks, Tugwell's key concepts – big cities 'merging' with the countryside, and the suburbanization of America – *were* implemented. The essential condition for this implementation was the

success of the public-works program. By refurbishing public space with national parks, city parks, and parkways, advocates of this program hoped to offer Americans a new collective experience of the scenic beauty of their country. In addition, they wanted to create the conditions needed for full-scale suburbanization by opening up rural areas with new infrastructural elements – parkways and highways – and by building parkways in big cities for the benefit of slum-clearance operations. This approach was to pave the way for all-out suburbanization and the transformation of America's big cities. Ultimately, most of the federal funds generated by the New Deal were used to realize parks and highways.[43]

Rather than simply remaining part of the comprehensive program of greenbelt communities, the public-works program gained an increasingly independent status. This program also featured a combination of government investment in public works and an incentives scheme aimed at industry. The network of highways and parkways laid the foundation for a new type of traffic: mass transportation. At the same time, a system of credit and price-fixing agreements with the automobile industry ensured the actual use of the new infrastructure.

Within a short time, the New Deal's public-works program had provided the United States with a vast network of national parks, state parks, and parkways, created not only to display America's scenic beauty, but also to highlight the historic significance of certain sites and routes: many former battlefields, as well as roads taken by early explorers and pioneers. This infrastructure of parks and parkways was designed to give America and its citizens a unique collective identity: a collective identity that could be experienced individually, thanks to the family car. Car plus highway: the ideal combination of individual freedom and collective experience.

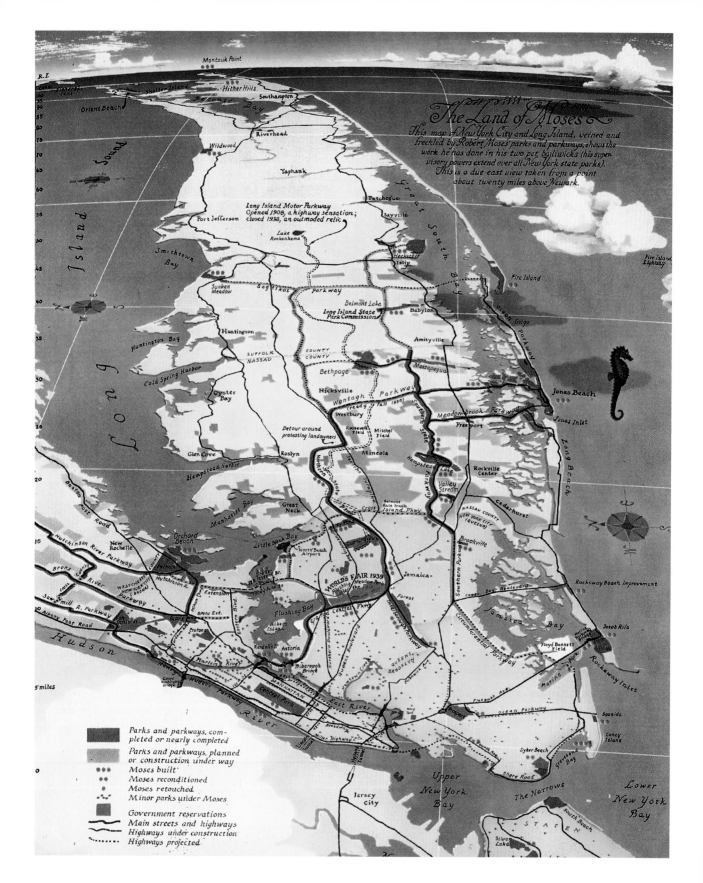

The Land of Moses
This map of New York City and Long Island, veined and freckled by Robert Moses' parks and parkways, shows the work he has done in his two pet bailiwicks (his supervisory powers extend over all New York state parks). This is a due east view taken from a point about twenty miles above Newark.

Long Island Motor Parkway
Opened 1908, a highway sensation;
closed 1938, an outmoded relic

Long Island State
Park Commission

Detour around
protesting landowners

WORLD'S FAIR 1939
(touching
finger to
the fair)

Parks and parkways, completed or nearly completed
Parks and parkways, planned or construction under way
Moses built
Moses reconditioned
Moses retouched
Minor parks under Moses
Government reservations
Main streets and highways
Highways under construction
Highways projected

Henry Hudson Parkway, as seen from the north, 1953.

Left: 'The Land of Moses': illustration taken from the June 1938 issue of *Fortune*.

While Olmsted's parkways had been urban promenades designed to create a new intracity relationship between city and nature, when the automobile appeared on the scene, the discussion on the significance of parkways gained a whole new dimension. The countryside now became directly accessible and passable for city dwellers, and the speed of the car produced a new perception of the city: sitting in a fast-moving vehicle, people looked at big buildings, still far away, with a new awareness. The modern skyline becomes a moving picture when one approaches it, or drives parallel to it, in a car. The concept of the cityscape as moving scenery was born.[44]

*Riverside parkways as a new collective experience*
Under the leadership of Robert Moses, a 'power broker' who took to the new broker state like a fish to water, the city and state of

New York managed to obtain about one-seventh of the federal funds set aside for roads in the President's New Deal. The waterfront, in particular, was to be a key player in creating the new collective highway experience and in transforming the city.

Robert Moses, 'America's greatest builder' and somewhat of a twentieth-century Haussmann, who dominated the city and state of New York for over forty years, was a man with the capacity to think big; it was Moses who fused the city and state of New York into one gigantic network of parkways, expressways, and highways.[45] Thanks to his efforts, as early as 1940 New York City had a network of expressways longer than the total length of all highways found in the 'following' five American cities.[46] He was the man who transformed the crowded metropolis of New York City into a world of new 'space, time and architecture.'

Moses, who held administrative positions on both municipal and regional levels, truly personified the fusion of the city and its greater context: from 1918 to 1963 he was president of the State Council of Parks in New York, and from 1933 to 1966 he held a comparable municipal position as City Park Commissioner.[47] In addition, he fulfilled various other administrative roles, including functions related to the New York World's Fairs of 1939 and 1964.[48]

Moses believed that a country like the United States – a melting pot of cultures, races, and ethnic groups – needed a government policy aimed at providing its citizens with a collective identity.

This sense of *collectivity*, however, was limited to those who owned a car. Moses saw the car not only as a modern mode of transportation, but also as a criterion and a method for selecting those suitable for the 'admittance policy' that he intended to create for a modern America. According to Moses, owning a car was proof of good American citizenship.

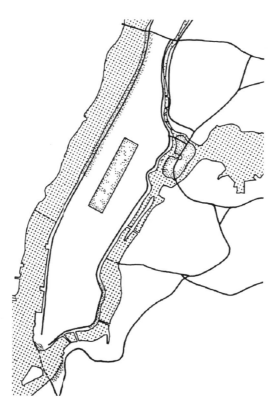

Robert Moses's parkways and expressways in New York City.

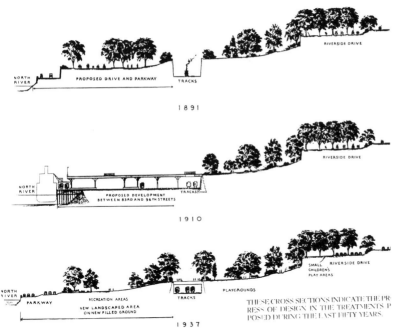

Parkways were intended explicitly for recreational traffic and were off-limits to trucks carrying freight and to public transportation in the form of buses. The general shift that the New Deal caused in the investments made in transportation networks – from railroad to road construction – was reinforced in New York by the systematic neglect of the public-transportation network during the years that Moses was in charge. Moses considered the privately owned car to be the modern materialization of the American Dream and, theoretically, available to everyone. Those lacking this basic ingredient of modern life could count on nothing but his deepest contempt and thus were deprived, if it was up to him, of the blessings of the New World.

He gained notoriety for having the viaducts of parkways on Long Island designed to prohibit access to buses. The objective was Jones Beach, a spacious coastal strip that Moses wanted to keep pristine and free of bums, a goal he perceived as the high point of his career. No amusement parks, arcades, snack bars, and candy stores on

Jones Beach: the masses that filled this beach on warm Sundays were a 'better public,' one community sharing one communal facility, but only by means of the total freedom offered by individual cars.

Moses also vetoed a plan by the Long Island Railroad Company to build a line to Jones Beach. President Roosevelt had to intervene on several occasions to overrule the more serious of Moses's excesses.[49]

Moses's prominent role in the New Deal consisted of more than simply raking in a disproportionately large share of the budget, which paid for much of the network of parks and parkways subsequently realized throughout the state of New York; his most essential contribution was to *transform the city* by situating parkways *in* the city. The beauty and expanse of the countryside was to be directly accessible and tangible to urban residents.

By the late 1930s Moses had realized 10 large city parks, 10 outdoor swimming pools, 320 playgrounds, 6 large-scale bridge and tunnel projects, 8 state parks, and 17 parkways.[50]

*Along and across the water*
One of Moses's favorite subjects was the waterside. Nothing better represented the collective experience of America as a nation of immigrants than the waterside; water was part of the vastness of the New World. Water in the archipelagic city of New York, moreover, may be seen as a divisive, as well as a *binding*, element.

These connotations of water did not originate with Moses himself; they are rooted in countless proposals developed for the waterfront as early as the mid-nineteenth century. All these proposals foundered on the feasibility factor, however, since the waterfront was a hornet's nest of big interests, an area with a concentration of ships, trains, and

Henry Hudson Parkway, as seen from the south, 1940.

Wilhelm Thöny,
Riverside Drive and
Henry Hudson Parkway,
ca. 1940.

East River Drive (currently F.D. Roosevelt Drive), as seen from the north, 1939.

other means of transportation that had to be considered. The ultimate success that Moses had in subjugating such interests shows that he fully deserved to be called the 'power broker.'

Moses was responsible for New York City's Riverside Park on the east bank of the Hudson River. Ever since Frederick Law Olmsted presented his first designs for Riverside Park in 1864, this unfinished park on the Hudson had been the subject of a disagreement between a railroad company, which claimed a substantial part of the area for a switchyard, and a number of interest groups that wanted to realize a large city park on the waterfront.

Despite the railroad company, not to mention a campaign against this company's plans led by Women's Leagues fighting to keep the waterfront accessible, Moses succeeded in building his first

parkway in New York City.[51]

Moses presented the plan as an absolute innovation: 'The Henry Hudson Parkway built properly and a great park created alongside it on what was now the mud flats of Riverside Park, the city's residents would not even have to leave the city to find beauty. They would be able to drive along the water, the river stretching to one side of them, the green of the park to the other, above the park the spires of Manhattan. It would be a public improvement unequaled in the world!'[52]

Although not anticipated, the Henry Hudson Parkway belongs to the category of highly successful parkway projects: that is, to the category of those that have stood the test of time. These are projects realized as *additions* to the nineteenth-century city. Another in this category is the Brooklyn Queens Express-

way, which runs along Brooklyn Heights. Both urban arteries fill broad zones along waterfront sections where pronounced differences in height had posed a problem to earlier attempts at development. Hence Moses had no existing buildings to demolish before implementing his new projects, and differences in height were exactly what he needed to articulate the public areas in question. Furthermore, in the case of the Henry Hudson Parkway, Olmsted's original designs for this area provided a basis for the new ones. Even today, some of the most versatile public areas in the city are the combinations of Riverside Park and Henry Hudson Parkway, and Brooklyn Heights and the Brooklyn Queens Expressway: areas that accommodate several public-space functions (through traffic, urban traffic, and recreation) and simultaneously operate on different levels of scale. These remain the most spectacular

sections of New York's highway network, and they also provide adjacent districts with beautiful riverfront parks.

This combined nineteenth- and twentieth-century city was not really what Moses had in mind. On the contrary, his goal was to dismantle the nineteenth-century city.

Moses's ultimate dream was to line every waterfront in the city with this type of parkway. Toward the end of the 1930s, he managed to realize East River Drive (now Franklin D. Roosevelt Drive) on the east side of Manhattan, which presented a more difficult task than the Henry Hudson Parkway: a large part of the Lower East Side, the immigrant district, had to be demolished to make way for this project. Moses had no regrets; in his opinion, the Lower East Side was 'the mother of urban slums.'

Attempts by Moses to link various parts of

The transformation of Manhattan's East River waterfront between 1879 and 1983.

NEW YORK

Brooklyn Queens
Expressway, seen from
the northeast, 1952.

Brooklyn Heights Esplanade.

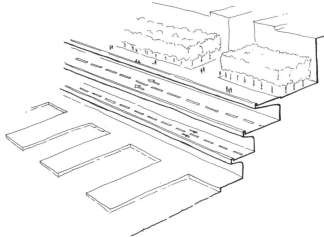

Brooklyn Queens Expressway: section of roadway bordering Brooklyn
Heights.

Belt Parkway, 1940. This parkway follows the entire southern shoreline of Brooklyn and is flanked by pedestrian walkways, bikeways, and beaches.

Pages 222 and 223: Map of New York on a scale of 1:25,000.

the city by means of a system of parkways culminated in the Triborough Bridge: a complex designed to interconnect the three boroughs of Manhattan, Bronx, and Queens. Moses wanted this bridge to be more than simply a link uniting the three island and peninsular boroughs: the Triborough Bridge was to be the preeminent symbol of mutual solidarity among the elements of this archipelagic city.

Small islands spanned by the Triborough Bridge – Randall's and Ward's Islands – were converted into a large city park with a 70,000-seat stadium. Moses had high expectations for this park, which he hoped would become *the* central park of New York City.

This project – composed of four big bridges spanning a total of 5 kilometers, and an additional 23 kilometers of access roads – was the largest bridge complex in the world. The Triborough Bridge Authority, with Moses as its president, was set up especially to supervise the realization of this mammoth project. This function, in particular, inextricably cemented Moses into the heart of

New York politics. Besides the mayor, the most important political figures in New York are the five borough presidents. When Moses assumed the presidency of the Triborough Bridge Authority, he actually became a sixth borough president: the one controlling the most strategic link in the city, not to mention huge financial resources. Soon after the bridge opened, it became clear that the profit from tolls represented a gold mine, all of which was to be managed, independently, by the Triborough Bridge Authority. Moses was free to use this money for many other projects, without relying on the limitations of municipal or federal budgets.

However, regardless of the amount of power he wielded, even Moses could not accomplish the impossible: he failed to realize his parkway dream at sites along the waterfront where port activities continued to thrive. At such spots he resorted to building elevated expressways, which offered fine views of the water and the skyline of Manhattan, but still lacked the element of greenery.

*The city as a jungle*
Moses and his projects were, and still are, extremely controversial. His interventions into the city symbolized a break with the American urban planning tradition and its predominantly orthogonal street plans, in which the relation between public space and private enterprise was established beforehand.

Unlike the parks and park systems previously added to nineteenth-century urban grids, Moses's parkways and expressways were not designed, in any way, as supplementary or differential features of the grid, but as elements aimed at *dismantling* the grid system. The irreconcilability of the new urban landscape and the existing city has had far-reaching consequences for the latter.

The simile of the city as a jungle was not coined by Moses, but he did interpret it quite

Left: West Side Highway,
1984. The viaduct, in
total disrepair, serves
as a jogging trail.

Right: Henry Hudson
Parkway, 1990.

literally. Particularly after World War II, when America's titanic war industry had switched to, among other things, the manufacture of private cars, Moses poured nearly all his efforts into building expressways, which left a trail of destruction throughout the city that was not compensated for by green, scenic parkways.

The most notorious of these new routes was the Cross-Bronx Expressway. Moses engaged one of America's most well-known jungle specialists as consultant on this project: General Thomas Farrell, builder of World War II's Burma Road. Moses sent him out to reconnoiter the area and to report his findings, which he did, in style: he described the Bronx as a dense forest of buildings grouped along a valley, an area through which traffic – like wildly churning water – struggled to force its way. He was referring to a Haussmannian boulevard known as the Grand Concourse. Farrell mapped a route straight through this rugged wilderness, along which the 'advance guard' could penetrate the city.

The construction of the expressway also followed the laws of the jungle: a straight line drawn through the hilly rock bed of the Bronx was cleared by detonating many thousands of kilograms of dynamite. The consequences reflected the method used. To the five thousand people whose homes were demolished to make way for the expressway,

another ten thousand were added when their dwellings subsided, cracked, or completely collapsed as a result of the many explosions. In one fell swoop, the realization of the Cross-Bronx Expressway changed a flourishing South Bronx into the desolate area currently considered the prototype of a city in decline.

In the wake of the appropriation and demolition activities that preceded the construction of parkways and expressways, large building sites became available for new housing projects in the Bronx, as well as in the Manhattan areas of the Lower East Side and Harlem. Having transformed the shape of the city with a new typology of public works, Moses now had the opportunity to introduce a new building typology as well.

The debate on the best way to develop Manhattan was influenced strongly by the realization of Rockefeller Center in 1929. Rockefeller Center was the first integral building complex to transcend the scale of a single building block. The tremendous scale of Rockefeller Center's high-rise buildings meant that the complex was unaffected by skyscrapers in the direct vicinity – the skyscrapers of Rockefeller Center rise in the middle of an open space. Even though these towers stand freely within open space, however, their bases form an integral part of the street network of Manhattan, where they

Left: Cross Bronx
Expressway, 1990.

Right: F.D. Roosevelt
Drive provides protection
for a slum area.

relate directly to stores, cultural facilities, and entrances to office buildings. Modern architects and urban planners of this era sometimes forgot this aspect of the design or, on the contrary, made an explicit effort to criticize it.[53]

The concept of Rockefeller Center, and in particular the plasticity of its slender towers rising amid open space, was incorporated into a 1931 proposal by the Regional Plan Association, in which the amorphous 'mountain range' of New York's skyline was replaced by a 'city of towers.'[54]

Moses, too, was filled with enthusiasm for this ideal; wherever he got the chance, he set the stage for the new city of towers, but always with a deliberate disregard for Manhattan's grid of streets. A good example of his support of this new concept are a number of residential complexes along East River Drive and East River Park: Vladeck Houses, Baruch Houses, and Jacob Riis Houses.

Certain occupants of housing blocks in the Lower East Side and the Bronx – their dwellings having been razed – moved into these new public-housing projects. The majority of those who had lived in the blocks now demolished, however, were forced to relocate to mass housing complexes that Moses had situated on Coney Island and in Rockaway Beach, far from the city.

Apart from these matters, the Cross-Bronx

Expressway was only a foretaste of what Moses had in mind for Manhattan. In 1946 he launched a plan for three 'cross-Manhattan' routes: the Upper, Mid, and Lower Manhattan Expressways, all of which were to run straight over and through the existing city from east to west. The Mid Manhattan Expressway, in particular, was to crown his career. Moses envisioned an elevated expressway, about 30 meters above street level, running straight through the sixth or seventh floor of the Empire State Building.

Although the Lower Manhattan Expressway was the most feasible of the three, it was also the one faced with a monstrous offensive organized by neighborhood groups, entrepreneurs, real-estate owners, the Chamber of Commerce, and the like.[55] In the end, Mayor Lindsay received so much support that he mustered up the courage to defy Moses. In 1966 Moses was removed from all but one of his positions. He was allowed to remain director of the Triborough Bridge Authority for the next several years, but only because he could do little additional damage to the city in that position.

*Euphoria and confusion*
Moses considered both the construction and use of parks and parkways – New York's new infrastructural elements – as activities com-

Right: Route of the Lower Manhattan Expressway.

Below: Projection of new, large-scale phenomena onto Manhattan's street plan: expressways destroy the grid, while an ensemble like Rockefeller Center leaves the grid intact.

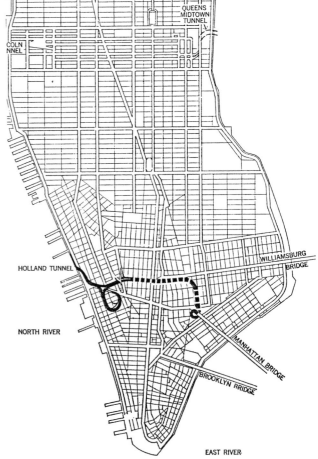

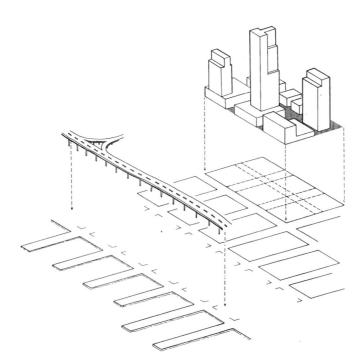

pletly within the scope of 'making a better public.'[56] His efforts to do so, however, were at odds with those of Roosevelt and Tugwell, the original architects of the New Deal. Moses's ideas on the significance and accessibility of the public domain differed greatly from the aim expressed by the New Deal: the creation of a new relationship between public and private domains.

Moses introduced a hierarchy into urban public space and its green elements, in which private interests were of minor importance. His interventions into the city ultimately robbed 250,000 people of their homes, but countless landowners, along with city and town councils, also saw certainties that they had believed would go on forever disintegrate beneath the violence of Moses's bulldozers.

Although Moses incurred the hatred of all those forced to yield to the implementation of his grand plans, workers who enthusiastically brought the new projects to full fruition, and who believed in the importance of their efforts, thought the world of him. These were not just parks to be laid out, or roads to be built: the real project was a New America. Berman claims that the realization of these works reanimated the ideals of Goethe and Marx; New York gave birth to the modern romance of a large socially minded community in which everyone eagerly and confidently joins together in working for the common good.[57]

Moses was popular not only among those who found work again thanks to the large-scale realization of parks and highways. A much broader public saw Moses – or at least the man described by the media – as an important benefactor. A good example of his popularity is a long article printed in a 1938 issue of the well-known magazine *Fortune*. A full-page photograph of Moses, with 'his' New York in the background, is captioned: 'As usual, Robert Moses, commissioner of parks, has all of New York City behind him.' Another full-page illustration – a bird's-eye view of Greater New York indicating all of Moses's projects – bears the title '*The Land of Moses.*' This Biblical reference contains only a touch of irony; throughout the entire article Moses is described as a savior of the fundamental values of the American society, as 'one of the nation's ablest and honestest public servants – or, as he himself concedes with a laugh, that he has "stayed on the side of the angels."'[58]

The new riverside parkways, and especially the Henry Hudson Parkway, were received enthusiastically even before they were open to the public: 'This magnificent exit from the city, all of it Robert Moses' doing, will not be finished until this fall, but already travelers and fascinated observers are thick along the whole length of the parkway. And what Moses has done to give utility and beauty to the western edge of Manhattan, he is also doing on a smaller scale along the island's eastern edge.'[59]

American literature described this emerging urban landscape as a new kind of natural phenomenon. The new combination of skyscrapers and parkways was portrayed as a harmonious symbiosis of human labor and divine creation, or nature; and big bridges, viaducts, ships, and farms were interpreted in a manner that underlined the alliance between man and nature.

In the early twentieth century, New York produced an entire school of photographers devoted to capturing the essence of this skyline. Their aim went beyond pictures of individual buildings; they wanted their photographs to present a collective image of buildings as one massive, majestic work of art – an aim that could be achieved by shooting the desired cityscape from a distance, from the water, for example, or from one of the bridges. The emphasis on the collectivity and magic of this skyline was strengthened when the city was cloaked in fog or darkness, which virtually eliminated the distinction between buildings, and the photograph revealed nothing but a silhouette and the massiveness suggested by thousands of illuminated windows.

The perception of the modern city as a work of art, a symbiosis of man and nature, was so universal that even authors of the most anti-urban books lauded the skyline of New York as a pastoral idyll. F. Scott Fitzgerald's *The Great Gatsby* is a prime example. When protagonist Nick returns to Manhattan Island after a drive to Long Island, he watches the promised land appear for the umpteenth time: 'Over the great bridge, with the sunlight through the girders making a constant flicker upon the moving cars, with the city rising up across the river in white heaps and sugar lumps all built with a wish out of nonolfactory money. The city seen from the Queensboro Bridge is always the city seen for the first time, in its first wild promise of all the mystery and the beauty of the world.'[60]

The way in which the city dweller identifies with the new cityscape as a natural phenomenon is described beautifully by Gay Talese in *The Bridge*, in which the reader learns to look at the city through the eyes of a couple of builders: '"It's a good life," Danny Montour was trying to explain, driving his car up the Henry Hudson Parkway in New York, past the George Washington Bridge. "You can see the job, can see it shape up from a hole in the ground to a tall building or a bridge." He paused for a moment, then, looking through the side window at the New York skyline, he said, "You know, I have a name for this town. I don't know if anybody said it before, but I call this town the City of Man-made Mountains. And we're all part of it, and it gives you a good feeling – you're a kind of mountain builder…'"[61]

At first sight the skyline is perceived as a complete ensemble of skyscrapers, which present themselves as a whole, surrounded by space; and water creates the perfect condition for this perception. The combination of skyline and vast expanse of water points out, as nothing else can, the equilibrium between what man can do and what nature has to offer. Above all, the waterside provides the opportunity to experience this modern cityscape in a modern way: from the car, driving along the highway.

The leaders of the modern movement in architecture, Le Corbusier and Sigfried Giedion, were full of admiration for the new phenomenon of parkways, especially when combined with Rockefeller Center. According to Giedion, such elements – parkways and solitary towers like those in Rockefeller Center – made New York 'the forerunner of the city of a new scale.' Giedion put his hopes in New York: 'The Parkway and the Rockefeller Center are only small beginnings, isolated growths in the immense body of New York, like the young branches of a tree.'[62] Clearly, Moses's influence reached far beyond the borders of New York.

Dozens of city councils in America asked Moses to serve as a consultant on parkway and expressway construction in their municipalities; each time he agreed to help, his preference for waterfront sites seemed to grow stronger. The Moses trademark was a Riverside Expressway.

In the 1930s, '40s, and '50s, his New York network of parkways and expressways were a popular destination of excursions taken by politicians, urban planners, architects, and engineers from all over the United States and Europe.

During the same period, European governments were building the German *Autobahnen*, the Italian *autostradas*, and the English motorways. But the big difference between the New York projects and their European counterparts was that the latter were built from city to city, from region to region, and *along* the cities, while Moses allowed his parkways and expressways to penetrate *into* the existing city, for the purpose of transforming the city itself.

In addition to euphoria, however, the creation of the modern urban landscape engendered confusion and opposition. The first generation of parkways introduced an unprecedented combination of large-scale infrastructural elements and the urban network, and an unprecedented combination of city and scenic beauty. A *combination* such as this no longer existed in the 1950s.

President Eisenhower's administration gave a new stimulus to highway programs that were to have such a devastating effect on cities that even the staunchest advocates of such programs were shaken. As early as 1957, regional planners and housing authorities called attention to the social segregation emerging in American cities as a result of building highways through urban areas: highways that quickly formed hard boundaries between affluent and impoverished urban districts. Lewis Mumford tried in vain to inject a breathing space of two years into highway programs, a period in which authorities could give serious thought to a more successful continuation of these programs.[63] Apparently, even Eisenhower was shocked when he saw, with his own eyes, the consequences of an interstate highway near Camp David, his 'summer White House.'[64]

Marshall Berman, who grew up in South Bronx, describes the confusion he felt in the 1950s when Moses built the Cross-Bronx Expressway: 'I can remember standing above the construction site for the Cross-Bronx Expressway, weeping for my neighborhood (whose fate I saw with nightmarish precision), vowing remembrance and revenge, but also wrestling with some of the troubling ambiguities and contradictions that Moses' work expressed… As I saw one of the loveliest of these buildings being wrecked for the road, I felt a grief that, I can see now, is endemic to modern life… Here in the Bronx, thanks to Robert Moses, the modernity of the urban boulevard was being condemned as obsolete, and blown to pieces, by the modernity of the interstate highway. Sic transit! To be modern turned out to be far more problematical, and more perilous, than I had been taught.'[65]

The development of the interstate-highway network led not only to the dismantlement of existing cities, but also to the creation of completely new 'instant cities.' The new highway network provided an opportunity to open up every corner of the nation; as a result, the development of utopian cities no longer depended on existing cities, but could take place far beyond them, in the unspoiled countryside. This development relied primarily on initiatives from the private sector, particularly those of dynamic real-estate developers. In the course of time, a number of these initiatives – Miami, Disney World, and the aforementioned Rockefeller Center – assumed important exemplary functions.

*Miami – city of real-estate developers?*[66]
The names of the streets in Miami reveal that this city did not build its reputation on the works of great statesmen, colonists, or industrialists. Miami's main streets and boulevards bear the names of real-estate developers, speculators, and wealthy landowners: Flagler Street, Julia Tuttle Causeway, and Collins Avenue are good examples.

For that matter, Miami's origins are not rooted in the highway, but in the railroad. During the extremely severe winter of 1894-1895, railroad magnate and industrialist

Henry Flagler discovered that the southern tip of Florida was the only unfrozen spot in the United States. When Flagler's railroad reached Miami in 1896 and his first venture in this city – the Royal Palm Hotel – opened its doors, the stage was set for this hamlet, with its four hundred inhabitants, to enter a new era. During the next thirty years, Miami was to become by far the largest and most important of Florida's instant cities.

The significance of Miami truly began to soar when Carl Fisher discovered the place. Fisher, a like-minded contemporary of MacDonald and Moses, was a real-estate developer and multimillionaire who believed in the automobile. Prior to discovering Florida, Fisher had built the Indianapolis Motor Speedway and had been involved in the development of the Lincoln Highway, America's first transcontinental route, which ran from the East to the West Coast of the United States.[67]

Fisher was not enthusiastic about Moses's collectivization ideals, however; he was a developer who loved cars, and he saw the construction of highways as a lucrative form of real-estate development and as an interesting resource to be used in developing projects in distant places.

In Miami, Fisher's interest was aroused by the elongated island that ran parallel to the shore for 16 kilometers, while barely rising above the surface of the water. After obtaining the rights to part of the island, Fisher built a 4-kilometer-long wooden bridge to connect it to the mainland, which immediately became the longest of its kind in the world. At the same time, he began raising and broadening the narrow island strip with millions of cubic meters of sand and clay pumped from the bottom of Biscayne Bay. In the meantime, he made sure than his future paradise would have an independent status and would not be part of Miami, which had grown into a fair-sized city by this time. In 1915 the new island, completely uninhabited, was incorporated as

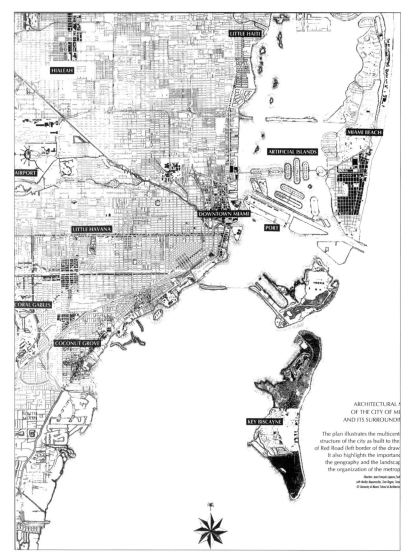

ARCHITECTURAL
OF THE CITY OF MI
AND ITS SURROUNDI

The plan illustrates the multicent
structure of the city as built to the
of Red Road (left border of the draw
It also highlights the importance
the geography and the landscap
the organization of the metrop

*Director: Jean-François Lejeune, Ten*
*with Harley Naquamache, Tom Regan, Tom*
*© University of Miami School of Architectu*

the autonomous town of Miami Beach.

In fact, Fisher applied the same principle that Flagler did: he built a complete instant city in the middle of nowhere. Flager built his city in the middle of palmetto growths; Fisher built his in the middle of the ocean. Flagler's Miami was a product of the railroad era; barely twenty years later, Fisher's Miami Beach was the product of a new, automotive era. Furthermore, Fisher did not stop after realizing the new bridge, but went on to build a new route from Chicago to Miami: Dixie Highway.

The five Miami Beach hotels that Fisher built himself were so successful that he was able to sell the rest of his property to other developers at a huge profit. In 1926 Miami Beach had fifty-six hotels. As a tourist spot, this brand-new instant city was already far ahead of the twenty-year-older Miami.

Originally, Fisher's model city was not based on a well-designed and comprehensive composition of an ensemble of buildings and other urban planning and natural elements; his city was more of a combination of isolation and exclusivity. It was, after all, an artificially developed island, whose most attractive component – the coastal strip – was reserved almost solely for developing hotels and apartment buildings. Only Ocean Drive, one small

Above: Map of Miami, 1990.

Below: The Douglas Entrance to Coral Gables; design by W. de Garmo, D. Fink, and P. Paist, 1925.

segment of the public street network, provided a direct view of, and access to, the ocean.

In the 1920s and '30s, this principle would be repeated over and over on a small scale, and as a result, a new archipelago appeared along Miami's real coastline: a collection of larger and smaller islands, floating in the water like mini-wonderlands linked by a system of causeways.

Another developer, George Merrick, discovered Miami at approximately the same time that Fisher did. Merrick was the man of the suburb. He inherited a citrus plantation, 'Coral Gables,' expanded it, and subsequently decided to use the land to create an 'urban design masterpiece.' Merrick wanted to leave nothing to chance; his new city was to be designed with great deliberation down to the tiniest detail. He put together a team of 'masters of illusion,' headed by architect Phineas Paist and landscape architect Frank Button. Their collaborative design for 'The City Beautiful' included a preponderance of Mediterranean (Spanish and Italian) style features and, to a lesser degree, French, Dutch, and Chinese influences. Monumental urban entrances on all four sides of Coral Gables accentuated the autonomy of the new city.

Sold by the lot, Coral Gables proved to be a resounding success, even though the project as initially planned was never completed after a hurricane and the impending Depression plunged Merrick into bankruptcy in 1927. Coral Gables became the El Dorado of the wealthier, more successful Americans looking for permanent homes in South Florida.

In Coral Gabels, the once neutral grid system was transformed into a differentiated layout of public areas and private premises. The goal was to take maximum advantage of the existing natural landscape in designing both street profiles and individual lots for private homes. By fully coordinating the design of public space with the typology of various sorts of housing, Merrick created a community very similar to Burnham's ideal: The City Beautiful.

The phenomenon of the real-estate developer was nothing new; the novelty lay in the phenomenon of a developer clever enough to transform such a large area, in such a short time, into a complete city covering nearly 4 square kilometers. This was the situation in the United States in the 1920s: the creation of an ideal city had turned out to be a real possibility, as long as the entire area involved was in the hands of one private owner, located in an attractive natural environment with a favorable climate, and far enough away from potentially meddlesome authorities representing existing urban communities.

The main goal of this ideal city was to create the *image* of a specific entity of architecture, urban planning layout, and existing scenery; Merrick proved that it was possible to design such a comprehensive composition *and* to realize it: the city as an architectonic megaproject.

*Disney World*
While Merrick and Fisher experimented with the development of instant cities in which they tried to fully utilize the existing landscape, Florida also provided a laboratory for an instant city designed without a thought to

Ocean Beach, a section of Miami Beach.

the topographic context, a city in which every element of the internal spatial organization corroborates every other element. This experiment is called Disney World, and its realization perfectly exemplifies urban development in the United States.

Walt Disney's attempt to reconcile a cultivation and romanticization of traditional urban elements with technological innovations and progress is more significant than his efforts to develop a completely new type of city. Disney was one of the first to recognize old-fashioned 'downtown' areas as potentially important sources of a new tourism and recreation industry.

Disney's interest in the city stemmed from his response to plans by Robert Moses for New Orleans. In 1946, having been commissioned by the city council of New Orleans, Moses designed an Elevated Riverside Expressway – what else? – for this city, which would destroy most of its historic city center. Owing to strong opposition the plan was shelved for nearly twenty years; in 1965, however, it emerged virtually unchanged.

Once more, protests rose from those trying to preserve the heritage of the old French-Colonial inner city. A counterproposal recommended rerouting the Expressway *under* the historic city center, a solution that would have cost 30 million dollars. At this point Walt Disney entered the picture with an offer to rebuild the city center at three-fourths of the full scale, in another location, for half the money needed to implement the proposed tunnel project.[68]

By this time, Disney was well aware of the possibilities of an old-fashioned city center: even in the 1960s, tourism was New Orlean's second greatest source of income. Although Disney's proposal for New Orleans was turned down, he would go on to realize the concept anyway, by creating Disney World in Florida.

Disney World is not simply an amusement-park clone of Disneyland in California.

Nearly ten times larger than its older sibling, Disney World is a complete instant city and, moreover, self-supporting in areas such as water supply, power supply, and transportation. Walt Disney set out to build a city that would boast the latest technologies for minimizing air, soil, and water pollution.[69]

*The city merged*

The period of the 1930s to the 1960s was a bizarre era in the history of the American city and American urban planning. In the course of this era, the practice of urban planning assumed an unprecedented position of power. Held in high regard by society, urban planning acquired an extensive technical instrumentality, especially in the area of public works. Taking advantage of this position of strength and the advanced techniques, urban planners attempted to gain maximum control of both the shape and function of the city. Anything uncontrolled was not tolerated. What made it bizarre is that this enormous use of power and technique, and this passion for control, led to a shapeless *non-city*.

The new world of the expressway caused city and countryside to merge in two ways. To begin with, the existing city was dismantled. The new system of urban space thus introduced differed radically from the design principles that determined the spatial qualities of the grid and of nineteenth-century deviations existing in the grid. Buildings were no longer relevant to the shape of new urban landscapes. The continuity and dimensions of the new network were based on natural elements only. Within this concept, urban buildings were to present themselves as a collection of random objects ('above the park the spires of Manhattan').

The new network of parkways and expressways created an urban world with a new spatial continuity, which bore no connection to either the existing urban world or the continuity of the grid. And besides lacking a connection between these two worlds, the world of the expressway also hacked the grid into isolated pieces, destroying its continuity.

And secondly, the world of the expressway, together with a huge increase in car ownership, granted every middle-class American a great deal of mobility, as well as independence from big cities. The countryside was accessible not only as a place of recreation; its relative proximity by car also made it suitable for residential purposes. Thanks to both car and expressway, Jefferson's eighteenth-century ideal – the symbiosis of countryside and human settlement – could be realized in the form of suburbia.

The 1940s saw the beginning of a mass exodus of people from big cities to the suburbs. Thirty-five million Americans had settled in the suburbs by 1950.

The development and success of projects like Coral Gables, Miami Beach, and Disney World proved that the nineteenth-century ideal of the City Beautiful was feasible. Mumford had accused this movement of looking to totalitarian concepts for its ideals, and indeed, these projects did appear to demonstrate that such ideals were best realized by one individual with a deed to all the land and with complete control over the spatial forms, structures, architecture, and program to be realized within the area in question. New instant cities rose on land owned by private individuals whose architectonic megaprojects seemed more like urban worlds than like conventional cities.

Remarkably, the development of instant cities flourished during a period in which the official world of planning, from Moses through Tugwell, was pursuing an explicitly anti-urban policy, which caused cities to 'merge' into the countryside. The success of cities such as Miami and Disney World showed that a majority of the American public still saw the city as a fascinating phenomenon, as a source and exponent of culture, progress, dynamics, and vitality. Miami Beach and Disney World represented the perfection of this idea of the city, a place without negative urban factors (congestion, criminality, pollution). Furthermore, Miami Beach was a version of Olmsted's concept of the reconciliation of city and countryside, realized in various projects (Boston, Chicago) with the use of lagoons. Miami Beach is nothing *but* a lagoon, with the city nestled against its side.

Disney World is the 'purest' example of an instant city that remained in private hands, even after its realization, and in which open space, streets, and squares evoke the suggestion of urban complexity, but form no official part of the public domain, since they are managed and supervised by a private owner.

Many see the success of Disney World, in particular, not only as an exponent of a new market of leisure-time exploitation, but also as an indication that private enterprise is capable of playing a major role in urban development.

In 1964, in an essay destined to become famous, Melvin Webber observed that the new world of highways, suburbia, and a hypermobile middle class represented a break between 'the urban place and the non-place urban realm.'[70] Webber believed that the city as a place had become redundant: 'For it is interaction, not place, that is the essence of the city and of city life.'

Webber's words were prophetic only in part. After all, the development of instant cities proved that the city as a place could still command center stage, which led to a situation in which not only the government but also private developers, of all people, opted to become 'guardians' of the traditional, physical manifestation of the city.

# 4  After Modernism: Cities Are Fun – Revaluation of the Complexity of the Nineteenth-Century City

The paradoxical quality of American urban planning traditions – with an accent on the dismantlement of urban complexity and, in contrast, the cultivation and beautification of a suggested complexity – meant that new developments within old harbor areas were both inspired and hampered by experiences gathered from these urban planning traditions. They are inspired by experiences that have demonstrated the possibility of developing complete instant cities as finished projects, and hindered by the legacy of the world of the expressway, which has left the waterfront of nearly every American seaport lined with enormous elevated expressways, often in a drastic state of decline.

When Moses vanished from the center of the urban planning scene in the 1960s, his disappearance coincided with the outset of an exodus of port functions from the shores of Manhattan. The once thriving waterside gradually became an area of abandoned harbor piers and expressways, beneath which a literal underworld emerged, feared and avoided by upstanding citizens and savored as a location for making crime movies.

The waterfront became the tangible symbol of the collapse of the city, which drew to a dramatic climax in 1973, when a truck carrying tar to fill the umpteenth hole in the West Side Highway sank through the surface of the road itself.

Hence the success of waterfront projects in American cities was determined to a large degree by the way in which the heirs of such legacies handled the bequests.

The ideal of the modern city à la Moses came to an end in the late 1960s, a period that witnessed great changes in the area of urban planning. Not only the spatial structure, but also the entire social and economic structure of American cities, began to experience major shifts. The departure of a great many industrial activities and significant numbers of middle-class people from big cities can be traced to the expressways themselves, since they made the place where (well-to-do) people lived and set up companies less dependent on urban life; this exodus was also caused by structural economic changes, which favored strong growth in the service sector at the expense of industry.

At the same time, from the 1960s on American cities were confronted with a new wave of immigration as a result of liberalized immigration legislation passed in 1965. The effect of this legislation on New York City's population was obvious in 1990, the year in which one-third of the city's residents were allochthonous; furthermore, the majority of these foreign-born New Yorkers were semi- and unskilled 'Hispanics' (largely from Mexico and Caribbean countries) and Asians.

While some were proclaiming the end of the city as a place in the 1960s, a simultaneous movement emerged to argue for a revaluation of the city's significance. A new generation of city plans that appeared in the late '60s and early '70s represented the desire to make a radical break with the Moses era and to reassess urban design. Prominent examples were the Plan for New York City (1969) and the Comprehensive Urban Design Plan for San Francisco (1971); equally noteworthy were new urban planning approaches gaining popularity in Baltimore and Boston.

A shared feature of the various versions of this new orientation was a search for new concepts to apply to both 'public' and 'private' urban planning.

With respect to public urban planning, the crux of the matter was to define a new relationship between various kinds of public space and between the various functions fulfilled by public space. An explicit issue was the radical separation that isolated interstate highways from traditional street networks.

Private urban planning, on the other hand, had to address the question of how to realize large-scale urban real-estate projects that would imbue public space with added value. During the 1960s it became clear that major investors and real-estate developers were starting to show interest in cities. It was not clear, however, whether this interest would lead to new instant cities that would function autonomously, without relying on other cities – such as instant cities like Disney World operated independently of their context – or whether it was feasible to introduce big real-estate projects in combination with the development of a newly differentiated structure and significance of public urban space.

In the '70s the search for new concepts and strategies began leading to three kinds of city plans:

*a.* City plans that feature a new public-space matrix, which provides room for modern city life while also respecting the nineteenth-century pattern of the city; in such plans, the waterfront is seen as the primary component of this new matrix.

*b.* Plans that introduce the experience of architectonic megaprojects into the city itself; in such plans, the waterfront is the place where megaprojects have the best opportunity to succeed.

*c.* Plans that create a relationship between the development of a new public-space matrix and the strategically located use of private investments; in such plans, waterfront projects assume the role of 'strategic pawns.'

The way in which various American cities developed these ideas differed from place to place: in certain cases the concepts are aligned with one another, in others they are complementary, and in still others they contrast with one another. Again, New York serves as a fine example of each of these schemes: the riverbanks of Manhattan are lined with prototypes of the different kinds of plans, realized side by side, with varying success.

THE WATERFRONT AS A NEW PUBLIC AREA: LOOKING FOR A SYMBIOSIS OF NINETEENTH-CENTURY PATTERNS AND TWENTIETH-CENTURY USE

Just as Giedion's book *Space, Time and Architecture* became the Bible of the modern movement, Jane Jacobs's *The Life and Death of Great American Cities*, published in 1961, may be viewed as the manifesto of the '60s movement devoted to reorienting public urban planning in the United States.[71] Jacobs, who lived in Manhattan's Greenwich Village in the '60s, was one of the driving powers behind the protest movement that opposed Moses's projects, and particularly the Lower Manhattan Expressway, which was to run straight through her neighborhood. The first sentence of her book – 'This book is an attack on current city planning and rebuilding' – is followed by a passionate plea for the restoration of street and neighborhood to their rightful position as cores of urban social culture. Jacobs presents the street as the place where one can encounter new contacts and impressions; experience the creation and re-creation of new relationships and cultures; and find a permanent source of discovery, of rejuvenation, of life. Her book may be read as an argument for a revaluation of nineteenth-century urban systems. A central concept of the book is diversity: Jacobs claims that the loss of the

American city is mainly the loss of social, cultural, economic, and functional diversity caused by the development of monofunctional districts and socially one-sided neighborhoods on the brink of becoming, or having become, slum areas.

Jacobs believes that social, economic, and cultural diversity should be stimulated down to the lowest level of scale, however, because this is where diversity forms the essence of urban culture and, in so doing, enables the uninterrupted creation of new initiatives, contacts, and networks. 'City diversity itself permits and stimulates more diversity' is Jacobs's creed, but this social, cultural, and economic diversity can exist only under the correct spatial conditions.

Jacobs reports the growing emergence of 'border vacuums': large, vacant peripheral areas that separate districts and no longer create spatial relationships between them. She finds this inconsistent with the most elementary fundamentals of American urban planning, in which the grid system represents an obvious attempt to develop a solid basis of neutrality and continuity. The phenomenon of the border vacuum attacks the essence of these fundamentals, according to Jacobs, who points an accusatory finger at the new, large-scale network of expressways, which has produced marked spatial divisions between districts once closely interconnected. Furthermore, Jacobs calls attention to a tendency of introversion in individual urban neighborhoods, whose cultural and economic functions, and important public areas (squares and parks), are increasingly concentrated in the middle of these districts, instead of at their edges.

As districts become more and more autonomous, mutual exchange among them becomes less and less self-evident, and the one-sided quality of each individual neighborhood grows stronger: a vicious circle.

Jacobs recommends transforming border vacuums into zones designed to accommodate an exchange and a condensation of urban activities; she specifically mentions nineteenth-century parks as the most important example of a similar physical-planning policy in American urban planning history. She particularly admires Olmsted's parks and park systems, elements that fulfilled not a divisive, but a binding, function. These parks, rather than being vacuums, acted as condensers of public life.

Jacobs says that a border is not necessarily a periphery, and she presents the waterfronts of cities like New York and San Francisco as examples of border areas that functioned for a long time as zones hosting a concentration and intensification of urban activities, only to become border vacuums under the dominant influence of expressways.

One striking reference in Jacobs's book concerns Rockefeller Center.[72] She describes Rockefeller Center as a successful intervention into the city that afforded a completely new, large-scale building typology while also enhancing public space with a blend of functions and a mixture of building typologies; an intervention that succeeds in particular because of its conformity with the existing network of streets and its avoidance of border vacuums. The borders of Rockefeller Center have remained important zones on the urban level thanks to significant functions established there when the project was first designed.

Jacobs's praise for this complex – an outstanding exponent of a large-scale private investment – is extraordinary, since her whole book is largely a plea for added attention to be given to the small-scale economic, cultural, and social life of the city.

Around 1960 Jane Jacobs was not the only one concerned about the future of the American city and that of New York City in particular. During this same period, the Rockefeller group was gearing up the discussion on the future of Manhattan's financial district. In 1958 the Downtown Lower Manhattan Association, headed by David Rockefeller, published a study that enumerated several problems that were plaguing the financial district: the matter of space, which meant not only too few building sites for expansion but also a system of 'canyons' between skyscrapers, which New Yorkers were finding more and more unpleasant; poor accessibility, which often led to hours of inching through slow-moving traffic on the way to one of the city's airports; and functional monotony, as seen after office hours on the empty streets of Lower Manhattan.[73]

As a result of these problems, the report observed 'a continuous exodus of long-established business and activities to areas in which they can find better working conditions and a more agreeable and convenient environment for their employees.'

Among other things, the study prompted an initiative that produced the World Trade Center, but it also led to a recommendation to take advantage of the disappearance of waterfront shipping activities by developing new expansion areas on both sides of the financial district. Appropriate sites on the east side were the old Fulton Fish Market and land newly created by filling in part of the East River. Expansion of the financial district on the west side was able to take place on an artificial fill in the river north of Battery Park.

From that time on, both initiatives were to play an important role in the debate on the redevelopment of Manhattan's riverbanks.

Building excavation for the World Trade Center, including the construction of cellars, resulted in huge amounts of surplus soil. This earth was dumped into the Hudson River, right next to the World Trade Center, a process that created a large artificial fill of more than 37 hectares. Immediately, the development of this area became a point of contention between the city and the state of New York (the latter of which owned the land in question), a debate in which the personal intervention of another family member, Governor Nelson Rockefeller, was to play a vital part.[74]

*'The highway and the community development can be planned in tandem'*[75]
Ideas promoted by Jane Jacobs, as well as those of the Rockefeller group, appeared in the first new plans designed after the Moses era: the Lower Manhattan Plan of 1966 and the integral Plan for New York City of 1969.

These plans provided for the restoration of spatial connections linking various urban neighborhoods (the elimination of border vacuums), the expansion of Lower Manhattan by filling in parts of both the Hudson and East Rivers, and a new approach to problems involving interstate highways. The third aspect was seen as an essential condition for the first two: without a new strategy for interstate highways, the city would be unable to get rid of physical barriers segregating urban districts, and the expansion of Lower Manhattan would be infeasible and pointless. The cancellation of plans for the Lower Manhattan Expressway made it even more of a necessity to maintain highway routes along Manhattan's waterfront. Of particular concern was the redesign of the West Side Highway, which was considered an absolute condition and a priority for any plan created to shape new development in Manhattan.

The Plan for New York City contained these words: 'The essential point is that the highway and the community development can be planned in tandem.' The Brooklyn Heights Esplanade, a product of the realization of the Brooklyn Queens Expressway, was presented as a positive example.

An essential point it was indeed. As a

Above: Lower Manhattan Plan, 1966.

Below: Lower Manhattan Plan, impression
of the Hudson River waterfront.

successor to projects realized by Moses, who
had spent decades trying to dismantle the
nineteenth-century city, and to proposals
made by Jacobs, who had voiced opposition
to highways in an attempt to protect the
nineteenth-century city, this plan was the
first to demand that the development of new
highway structures and the revaluation of the
nineteenth-century city take place simultaneously.

Expectations for the new approach to
West Side Highway were highly optimistic;
the project was to fulfill an exemplary
function for all American cities confronted
with problems of this type.

Jonathan Barnett, the leading player in the
City Planning Department in the period
following Moses's supremacy, created a new

Political complexity of
the West Side Highway
project.

approach to urban design in New York and
used it, after 1969, to spearhead an intensive
operation to redesign the West Side Highway,
which was in a deplorable condition at that
time. Two matters previously considered
irreconcilable were to be united here in one
plan: the renewal of the highway, to improve
interlocal traffic conditions, and the reorganization of the waterside into a public zone
directly interconnected with the street
network of the grid.

Experiments included various designs,
among which were combinations of highway and waterfront parks at ground level,
and tunnel constructions for the highway.
Barnett called it a 'project of extraordinary
complexity,' referring less to the technical
and functional problems waiting to be solved
than to local social circumstances: the West
Side Highway's 6-kilometer-long route bordered on various communities, each with its
own community board. Barnett added this
telling comment: 'The right-of-way passes
through some of the best-organized and
most articulate communities in the city,
including the West Village, home territory
of Jane Jacobs.'[76]

Barnett was also forced to wrestle with
the problem posed by various official and
political institutions, all of which wanted to
have a finger in the West-Side-Highway pie.
Following the departure of Moses, a power
vacuum in the area of urban planning soon
led to the paralysis of projects like the West
Side Highway. The leading differences of
opinion existed between municipal departments (City Planning and the Parks Council)
and state institutions (the New York State
Urban Development Corporation and the
Battery Park City Authority), not to mention
institutions such as the Port Authority of
New York and New Jersey, which managed to
operate autonomously and to remain relatively uninfluenced by the city.

Earlier Moses, who had held positions of
power on both city and state levels, had had

constant success in achieving his goals. This
fact clearly illustrates the changed position
that American urban planning found itself in
in the 1960s, having experienced the 'broker
state,' in which a powerful man like Moses
could lobby his way through the realization
of large-scale projects, and now being part
of the 'consensus state,' in which support
for such big interventions, once considered
natural, had vanished to make way for an
obligatory consensus among those potentially
interested in each individual project.

This new situation made it nearly impossible, by definition, for anyone in New York
to realize large-scale public works bearing a
single design signature. In 1976 an attempt
in that direction was made anyway, when
Robert Venturi and Denise Scott Brown
were asked to design a project for New York.
Venturi and Scott Brown were known for
their study *Learning From Las Vegas*.[77] In the
world of architecture and urban planning,
Las Vegas exemplified all that was bad and
undesirable. This opinion was shared by both
functionalists and those critical of functionalism, such as Jane Jacobs, who did argue,
after all, not only for a revaluation of the
principle of the nineteenth-century city, but
also for a reassessment of the shape of the city.

Venturi and Scott Brown were the first to
see a new manifestation of modern urbanism
in the Las Vegas strip, which had risen with
barely a thought for urban design or urban
planning: an archetype of twentieth-century
public urban space, a replica of Broadway
adapted to the scale of modern motorized
traffic. Instead of regarding Las Vegas with
disapproval and ridicule, the authors looked
at it as a phenomenon that offered a chance
to learn what sort of guise new urban facilities
assume and what kind of relationship they
enter into with public space when they have
unlimited freedom. In Las Vegas the authors
observed a strong degree of autonomy in the
way in which programs for building, architec-

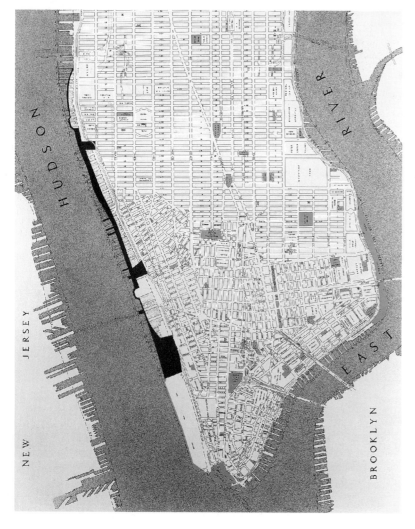

A map showing the
location (shaded black)
of Westway Park.

Hudson, they applied what they had learned in Las Vegas to New York. They used their knowledge of modern urban phenomena to develop these same phenomena and to adapt them to the shape and structure of the threatened grid city. The elongated shoreline area, most of which was to be created by filling in parts of the Hudson River, was to offer space for a park, while most of the highway would be contained in a tunnel. Land covered by the existing West Side Highway was to be made available for distribution.

Venturi's design may be seen as an important statement that presents a renewal strategy for the existing city. The emphasis lies on designing the infrastructure of public areas – both city park and highway – as one autonomous element that lends shape to the city as a whole. The entire park area covers a length of about 4 kilometers and displays a constant profile along the full length: an esplanade running directly next to the shoreline is sunken in relation to the green park strip. The park itself accommodates a promenade and a bikeway. A wall separates the park from the adjacent street and its buildings. With the accent on the continuity of this profile and on its plastic aspects (esplanade quay, difference in height between esplanade and park, verdure, and boundary wall), the park as a whole becomes an architectonic element that adds even more emphasis to the large scale of the Hudson River as a shape-determining element.

Besides the austerity and morphological continuity of this city park, the designers argued for virtually unrestricted freedom for the buildings involved. In presenting the plan, they used collages to stress the contrast between the continuity of public space, represented by Westway Park, and the potential diversity of nearby development; behind the uniform organization of the park, the collages show buildings rising in a cacophony of types, styles, and shapes.

tonic design, and the organization of public space relate to one another. Architecture here consists of nothing but 'decorated sheds,' which function as eye-catchers and have absolutely no relationship with the architectonic organization of the building behind the façade. The organization of the public domain is so generic and neutral that every conceivable program and 'decorated shed' can be coupled to it.

Although this knowledge could be used to cultivate the new manifestation, Venturi and Scott Brown recommended that it be developed and used to redesign the existing city, which was heading for disaster.

In their design for the east bank of the

In fact, Venturi's proposal was an expansion, as well as a detailed differentiation, of the concept behind the Henry Hudson Parkway: a blend of ideas borrowed from Olmsted and Moses. Examples include the way in which the park strip is linked directly to the street network of the grid; and the division of the park, in its entirety, into a series of smaller and larger parks, each of which contributes to the specific character of the district bordering it, while remaining part of the overall park system. The principle draws its inspiration directly from the park system in Boston. And the organization of the individual parks refers to Olmsted's repertoire; consider Central Park and Prospect Park, for example, which also display a combination of formal and informal elements, as well as the use of comparable ornamentation and street furniture.

Although the presence of Moses's parkways and highways divided the riverbank area into a *socialized* domain (parkways and highways) and a strictly functional, technocratic domain (harbor routes *under* the highways), Venturi and Scott Brown's intention was to redesign this area as a *public* domain. In the past, the construction of city parkways and highways had been based largely on a political consensus of the federal government that supported the need to 'socialize' the American population. But when this consensus ceased to exist, the federal financing of large-scale public works in urban areas ended as well. Previously, the central government could be counted on to provide 90 percent of the building and operating costs required for interstate highways passing through cities. A 1978 decision to divest city routes of their 'interstate highway' status brought the federal funding of such facilities to a screeching halt. Hence the West Side Highway continued its existence as the Westway.

Admittedly, the objectives of the Venturi-Scott Brown plan were quite the opposite of those in plans realized by Moses; all, however,

relied on the same sort of funding to finance the planning and implementation processes involved. To begin with, the plan could not be realized without a huge preinvestment from the public sector, and only when public works (park and underground Westway) had been completed could new building sites be issued to private parties. Profits from the sale of this property, along with anticipated property taxes, would be used to help finance the operating costs of the entire project.[78]

Financially, however, the city was in dire straits and thus unable to provide the enormous preinvestment required for this project. As countless businesses and many higher-income residents began leaving the city in the 1960s, New York saw its own income shrinking fast. By the mid-1970s, the city was able to stave off impending bankruptcy only by firing thousands of city employees, drastically reducing municipal services, and eliminating the maintenance of municipal facilities (the subway system, as well as gas, water, and electric networks).

Without federal funding, the whole concept behind the Venturi- Scott Brown plan was financially infeasible.

*West Coast cities:*
*San Francisco and Seattle*
The Venturi plan for New York was not an isolated incident. Before continuing the story of New York City, let us turn our attention to two other cities for which similar waterfront concepts were developed: concepts that focused on orienting the city toward the water and on using the waterfront as public space. Being in a better financial position, with a public sector that still enjoyed a little elbow room, certain cities were able to convert such concepts into concrete plans. This may be said of West Coast cities like San Francisco and Seattle, in particular, where the economic situation in the '70s was not as bad as it was in New York.

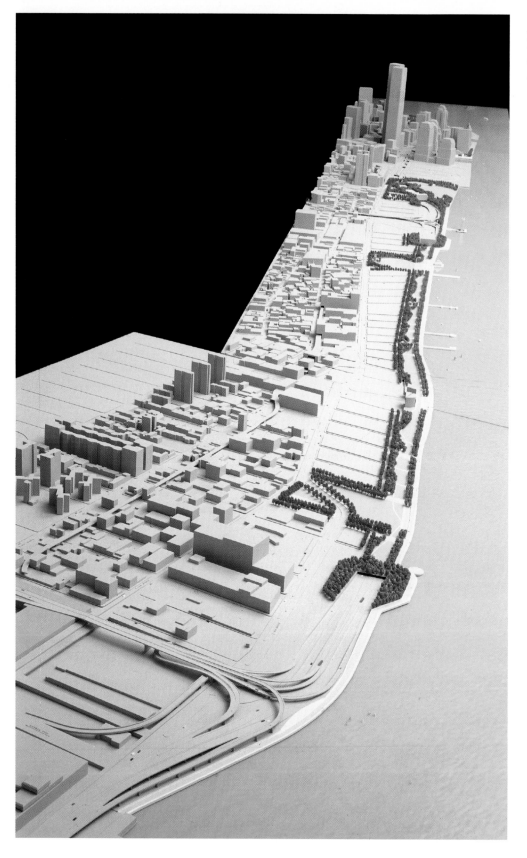

The Hudson River
shoreline, as designed
by Venturi, Scott Brown
and Associates. The West
Side Highway as part of
the interstate highway
network (above); the
composition of street
pattern and land parcels
as part of Manhattan's
grid (center); and
Westway Park as part of
the riverscape (below).

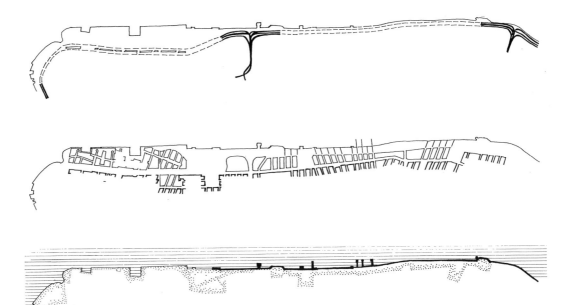

Westway Park as an
element reinforcing
the image of spatial
continuity and
uniformity projected
by the riverbank, against
the multiform façade of
Manhattan's buildings.

NEW YORK

Interestingly, in San Francisco and Seattle the informal and public atmosphere of the whole waterfront zone, a quality that also characterized harbor areas in New York prior to the 1930s, has never disappeared. Various factors are responsible for this phenomenon.

The first is the topographic situation. Both cities are located on relatively small peninsulas and surrounded by an abundance of scenic beauty. And steep hills offer an uninterrupted view, throughout both cities, of this natural panorama of water and mountainous terrain.

The scenic qualities and limited dimensions of these cities prevented a large-scale exodus of residents and businesses, an exodus experienced by nearly every American city in the '50s and '60s. As the United States gradually increased trade relations with Asia, to the detriment of its economic ties with Europe, West Coast cities profited financially from this shift as well.

During the same period local and regional authorities on the West Coast became aware of the vital importance of managing scenic features and natural resources as well as possible. Besides offering gorgeous views and recreational opportunities, the natural environment of both cities has a significant economic function, especially for the fishing industry.

*San Francisco*
Thanks to a combination of California legislation targeting San Francisco Bay and a new urban-design strategy conceived by the City Planning Department, San Francisco boasts the most sophisticated form of urban design in America.

This strategy was sparked by a rapid increase in large building volumes, which took place in the 1960s, and by plans for

building a coastal highway along the bay that would link the Golden Gate Bridge directly to the highway junction at the foot of the San Francisco Bay Bridge. Large structures included office buildings in the vicinity of Market Street, as well as a number of sizeable waterfront facilities designed as public attractions.

San Francisco's waterfront has been characterized, ever since the early 1900s, by a mixture of fishing and harbor activities, including facilities for entertainment and outdoor recreation. The city's north shore, featuring Fisherman's Wharf – San Francisco's original fishing harbor and fish market – is the oldest example of this type of mixed development. In the 1960s, an increase in scale was represented by the conversion of two abandoned factory complexes into centers for 'fun shopping': The Cannery and Ghirardelli Square. A similar facility, Pier 39, was realized on a former harbor pier. The problem inherent in these new centers, especially the Cannery and Pier 39, was their totally isolated nature, reinforced by using the public street mainly as a parking lot for cars and buses. The waterfront, so highly appreciated for its open, public character, was in danger of being transformed into a zone of closed boxes accommodating a concentration of city life, while public space was reduced to the status of a parking lot. Fears were that the situation would become worse, and culminate in an even greater devaluation of the waterfront, if plans for the projected highway were to be realized.

A 1968 plan for developing Embarcadero Center, a pioneer example of large-scale urban projects initiated by American real-estate developers, proved to be the last straw. Embarcadero Center, with its five building blocks, was to occupy a hypersensitive location in downtown San Francisco: a waterfront site at one end of Market Street, a main urban artery. Architect and developer

The Bay Conservation
and Development
Commission's plan for
San Francisco Bay, 1969.

made top priority. A coastal strip measuring
1,000 feet (about 300 meters) in width and
running along the entire length of the bay
was to remain, or to be made, available for
public use. This zone, declared the property
of the state of California, was to be managed
by the Bay Conservation & Development
Commission (BCDC). Municipalities,
businesses, and developers with plans for
projects in this coastal zone were to present
their proposals to the BCDC. Those who
failed to meet the conditions of the BCDC
risked having the state, acting as landlord
of the site in question, refuse their proposal.
This power of veto gave the state absolute
control over the quality of the environment
and over public accessibility to the entire
bay area.[80]

In 1971 the City Planning Department
presented the new *Comprehensive Urban
Design Plan*,[81] thus creating a formal
framework for dealing successfully with
matters such as the Embarcadero Center
incident. The plan consisted of an elaborate
series of zoning regulations and design
guidelines. The position of the city within
its scenic context is the focal point of the
plan, which features three aspects:
*a.* Scenic elements in the city are to form
San Francisco's primary morphological
structure: these include public parks, as
well as the entire waterfront.
*b.* The transparency of the cityscape is to
be maintained and reinforced.

This applies to the panorama offered to
one standing in the city and looking toward
the water, a view that takes advantage of
differences in height and the geometric
street pattern to present the surrounding
countryside from every spot in the city: a
cityscape that is to be safeguarded against
visual blockades formed by buildings. This
transparency also applies to the cityscape as
seen from the surrounding countryside and
from the water. Building regulations cover
both shape and color: high-rise buildings

John Portman – a specialist in the design
and development of large, autonomous,
self-supporting instant cities – initially
designed Embarcadero Center as a closed
complex, with a wholly inward orientation.
Not only did it visually sever Market Street
from the waterfront; it also harbored the
potential to absorb urban life at this spot.

Legend has it that Alan Jacobs, director
of City Planning in 1968, had to use the sum
total of his verbal might, not to mention a
good deal of political lobbying, to force Portman to adapt his design to its surroundings
and thus create a link, both visually and
functionally, with the public street.[79]

In 1969 San Francisco's waterfront
entered a new phase. This was the year in
which the state of California passed strict
laws to protect San Francisco Bay: urbanization and industrialization along the
shoreline was no longer permitted, and
public accessibility to this coastal area was

Detail drawing of Westway Park: design by VSBA.

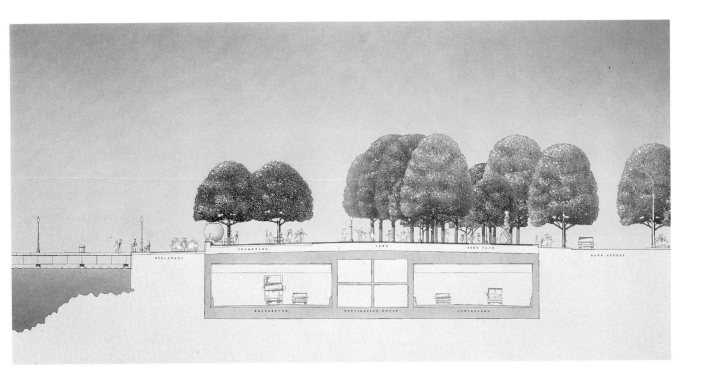

Section of Westway Park, including the Westway: design by VSBA.

Detail drawing of Westway Park: design by VSBA.

Embarcadero Center, with the Ferry Terminal in the foreground.

to the existing spatial framework of the nineteenth-century city.

In 1987 the Comprehensive Urban Design Plan was updated and retitled the Master Plan of the City and County of San Francisco, a scheme that 'froze' the touristic area around Fisherman's Wharf while placing great emphasis on reserving the northeastern section of the waterfront exclusively for public facilities: parks, promenades, plazas, and fishing piers. Existing harbor activities were encouraged to continue, as part of a policy that gave precedence to public transportation over water rather than to cars.

### Seattle

The old port at Seattle also consists of a 'classic' American harbor front, in the form of several piers standing side by side and, right along the water, downtown Seattle. Here, too, a mixture of functions has existed ever since the early 1900s, when the Port Authority began renting unused recreational piers to restaurant owners. As time went on, the Port Authority made a virtue of necessity, having realized that the steady stream of Seattle residents visiting these piers, who obviously considered the port an attraction, needed to be taken seriously. Since then, the warm welcome extended to visitors has become an important part of Seattle's waterfront policy.

Harbor Island, a large artificial land mass realized across the water from the old harbor front in the 1960s, now accommodates a concentration of modern port activities. As a result of this shift in function, piers belonging to the old harbor front were made available to proprietors of restaurants, souvenir shops, and a covered aquarium. Free access to the piers is offered along the sides and at the far ends.

The old harbor front still supports certain port activities. Ferries leaving Seattle

must be located in the immediate vicinity of Market Street and must be light in color.
*c.* Coastal areas, of both bay and ocean, are to be reserved for public use.

Extending the highway along the waterfront was no longer permitted. Connections to and between interstate highways crossing the city were geared to the existing nineteenth-century street network.

The new urban design was actually nothing but a number of rules and regulations aimed at protecting the spatial and structural qualities of the nineteenth-century city. Although new developments in the areas of traffic, transportation, and large-scale building projects were not prohibited, they were required to adapt

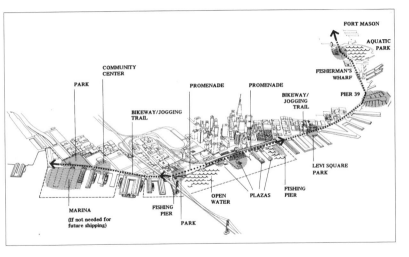

Master Plan of the City and County of San Francisco, 1987.

Above: Transformation of the waterfront into public space.

Center: Reorganization of public space surrounding Embarcadero Center and the Ferry Terminal.

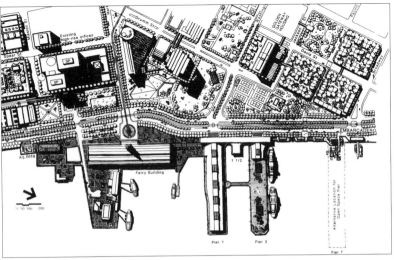

Market Street, with the Ferry Terminal tower in the distance.

for towns on the opposite side of Puget Sound, as well as for Vancouver (Canada) and Alaska, operate on an extremely frequent schedule. As these ferries still moor along the old harbor front, the (dis)embarking of passengers remains an integrated activity of the old port area.

Various resources have been used to create a new relationship between Harbor Island's busy, modern port and the city. For example, the unmistakable presence of Harbor Island as part of the archipelagic waterscape was emphasized by providing the old harbor front with large periscopes that offer a view of operations on Harbor Island. At the same time, the modern port has been interwoven with newly expanded areas of the urban public-space network: parks and fishing jetties lie between and next to grain elevators and container yards.

An essential condition for public acceptance of the port as part of the cityscape is the preservation of the unique ecological significance of Elliott Bay, which is the venue for commercial and recreational fishing, as well as for other water-related activities. The state of Washington and the Port Authority apply strict environmental standards to port-related industry. And as the port is both visible from the city and interwoven with urban public space, Seattle's population is able to exercise

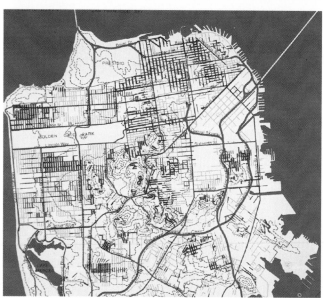

Above: San Francisco and San Francisco Bay, as seen from the southeast.

Below: San Francisco Comprehensive Urban Design Plan, 1971. Streets that offer panoramic views are outlined in blue.

San Francisco Comprehensive Urban Design Plan, 1971. Regulations for the color of buildings taller than the standard height of structures composing the cityscape. High-rise buildings are to be light- (above) rather than dark-colored (below).

San Francisco Comprehensive Urban Design Plan, 1971. Regulations for building height: high-rise construction is limited to Market Street and vicinity.

permanent control over those required to comply with these standards.

Seattle's inner city is located on the old harbor front, between two 'poles.' One is Pioneers Place, the original city center, which unlike many American city centers has remained largely intact, thanks in part to a complete renovation and restoration project that took place in the early 1980s. This historical center is located south of the downtown area, adjacent to the ferry piers. To the north lies the other pole, Pike Place Market, a covered facility run by the municipality, where farmers, fishermen, and manufacturers sell their wares without the intervention of wholesalers. A seat in one of the market's coffee shops or restaurants offers a breathtaking view of both port and bay.[82]

The modern section of downtown Seattle is found between Pioneers Place and Pike Place Market. In the 1950s, a double-decked highway was realized above the harbor front. To span the difference in height between the north and south sides of the waterfront, the viaduct was built so high that it does not form the sort of barrier between city and port that similar structures in other American cities tend to form.

This accumulation of various functions along the old harbor front makes Seattle a unique example of a seaport whose modern, active harbor has not vanished from, but still composes an integral part of, the cityscape. The waterfront is urban public space that supports various public functions in a newly combined way, and an area whose functions enjoy a broad versatility of use. This zone, between city and water, is used by (dis)embarking ferry passengers, dock-workers taking a break, shoppers, tourists, idlers on the dole, recreational fishers, business people out to lunch, and motorists driving by.

Both San Francisco and Seattle exemplify the city with a waterfront designed and filled in for the purpose of creating an essential structural element of urban public space. In both cases, this development was enabled by the absence of problems posed by interstate highways in many other cities, highways that exerted less pressure on the reorganization of these West Coast waterfronts. In San Francisco the realization of such a highway was superseded, in fact, by the revaluation of the significance of the waterfront for the cityscape and for the quality of the public domain.

Redesigning the waterfront highway in Seattle was less necessary, thanks to the height of the viaduct.

Furthermore, the limitations that accompany a less advanced highway system are compensated in these cities by the fact that waterfronts here function as vital links – as mooring places for ferries – within another important traffic system.

THE WATERFRONT AS EXCLUSIVE ENCLAVE: RECONSTRUCTION OF THE NINETEENTH-CENTURY CITY

In cities occupying a less favorable position, Venturi's concepts and the kind of city plans realized on the West Coast no longer stood a chance. Particularly in trouble were East Coast cities, which were far more seriously affected by economic stagnation and sub-urbanization than their western counter-parts.

In New York the development of Battery Park City was increasingly looked to as the way to save the city. Not only was a remedy needed to stave off bankruptcy; something also had to be done to put the city back in the black. Developing a model project like Battery Park City along the shoreline of New York City, which found itself in dire financial straits, was to play a

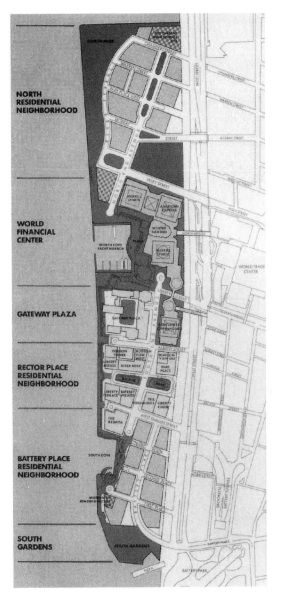

Urban plan for Battery Park City: design by Cooper & Ekstut.

ever, interpreted this concept in its own way.

The concept introduced in the area of plan development at this time was 'urban project.' The reference was to clearly defined projects of a limited size, which were realized, whenever possible, as architectonic-urban planning ensembles within a relatively short time; and which were considered strategically important to the redevelopment of larger urban areas.

In New York the urban-project concept was introduced by Jonathan Barnett, who looked for much of his inspiration to John Portman, with whom he had close ties and about whom he had published a monograph.[83] Architect and real-estate developer Portman was known for more than San Francisco's Embarcadero Center; he had realized major projects in Detroit (Renaissance Center) and Atlanta (Peachtree Center) as well. Portman was one of the first to accomplish *in the city* what developers such as Merrick, Fisher, and Disney had previously achieved outside the city proper: the realization of an urban world in the form of an architectonic megaproject. Portman's projects, which incorporate a complete arsenal of urban programs – department stores, supermarkets, hotels, restaurants, congress accommodations, apartments, parking facilities, and urban areas – are more or less oblivious to their surroundings. This is quite evident in the case of Peachtree Center in Atlanta, a project adjacent to a barren wasteland of temporary parking lots and partially or totally demolished building blocks. Peachtree Center gave downtown Atlanta renewed significance on the scale of the metropolitan region, but created no fresh stimuli for the immediate surroundings.

When attention shifted to the urban project, the approach taken by planners and designers experienced two essential changes. First, the ambition to develop integral plans

key role in achieving these goals.

Urgent issues pertaining to the redevelopment of sizeable urban areas, such as waterfronts, were: how to create *new financial frameworks* and, even more important, how to develop *new types of plans* to be used in reorganizing large-scale areas like Manhattan's waterfront.

In the case of financial frameworks and social consensus, the concept of 'civic culture' once more took center stage in the United States of the 1970s; each city, how-

The waterfront of Seattle.

Seattle's waterfront:
1 = Pike Place Market
2 = Central business district
3 = Pioneers Place
4 = Alaskan Way Viaduct
5 = Harbor Island

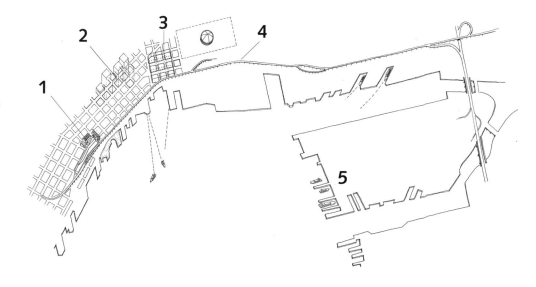

Pike Place Public Market, a vital element of the waterfront in its function as a public domain.

Seattle: symbiosis of dockside grain elevators and city park.

Ferry terminal on Seattle's old harbor front.

for the waterfront as a whole changed to a pragmatic approach aimed at sites of a limited size. Second, emphasis on the *open* and *public* quality of the waterfront changed to an accent on the realization of projects capable of generating fast profits from the sale of land and of creating a new, distinctive cityscape, regardless of the limited size of the site.

Barnett was a strong advocate of the potential of urban projects to provide *the* strategy needed for urban renewal.

The failure of Venturi's plan for Westway and the proclamation of the urban project as the basis for a new strategy naturally led to the question of coherence among individual projects. One important answer to this question was found in theories such as those developed at Cornell University under the leadership of Colin Rowe. Rowe came up with the 'collage city' concept after rejecting utopian urban planning concepts and their claim to authority. He was convinced that the paradox inherent in modern society (permanent conflicts between freedom and justice and between private profit and political equality) could not be solved in utopian models, but had to be accepted and made visible, not only in politics and culture, but also in urban planning. As a means of making this conflict visible, he promoted the collage technique: 'a strategy which can allow utopia to be dealt with as an image, to be dealt with *in fragments* without having to accept it *in toto*.'[84]

Of special note are proposals, in the 1970s, for two ways to achieve coherence in urban planning. One is Venturi and Scott Brown's proposal for Westway, with its accent on *public space* as the domain in which to introduce spatial relationships among neighborhoods, projects, and districts. The other is Rowe's theory, with its emphasis on the *morphology of buildings*, in which a carefully composed collage of fragments from urban planning utopias was supposed to lead to spatial coherence.

### Battery Park City: paradox of coherence and isolation

An important laboratory used to test the new urban-project strategy was Battery Park City. After the underground West Side Highway project was cancelled, a new urban design was needed for this 'landfill,' a design that was to incorporate the Westway and thus to take a completely different point of departure than that assumed by planners in 1969.

For that matter, Battery Park City Authority – established in 1966 by the city and state of New York as a nonprofit, cooperative organization – had failed throughout the years to arouse even a modicum of interest among developers and investors. Even the Rockefeller group, once so enthusiastic about the development of Rockefeller Center, was not willing to take the lead.

This situation changed in the late '70s, when a new federal law made it possible for private investments to be rewarded with bonuses provided by public funds. This law laid the foundation for public-private partnerships.

In 1979 Alexander Cooper and Stanton Eckstut, previously employed by Jonathan Barnett's Urban Design Group, were commissioned to create a new urban planning design for Battery Park City. These men advocated 'urban design as public policy,' a slogan promoted by the city's urban planning department; commissioning them was a way of exhibiting the intrinsic merit of this slogan at one of the most challenging sites in the city.

Cooper and Eckstut's design had to meet two conflicting requirements. To begin with, New York City wanted a design that would stress the relationship between the new district and the rest of Manhattan. On

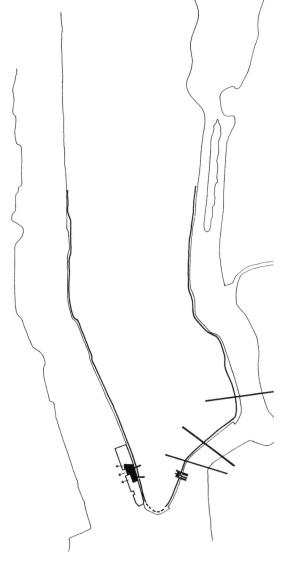

Battery Park City and South Street Seaport: two waterfront enclaves on Manhattan Island.

was to become a district that represented the best that New York had to offer: it would display the city's most characteristic and finest qualities.

Their plan included a number of 'visual corridors' that connected public areas in Battery Park City to the street network of Lower Manhattan. Based on the premise of a Battery Park City capable of representing the *crème de la crème* of New York, a detailed study was made of the full repertoire of public space in Manhattan, with special attention paid to monumental nineteenth-century squares and parks, such as Gramercy Park and Beekman Place, not to mention the Brooklyn Heights Esplanade. The design of public space featured a network of individual streets, avenues, esplanades, squares, and parks, almost all of which were derived from the monumental idiom of the nineteenth and twentieth centuries. Meticulous 'design guidelines' were established to regulate building lines and heights, as well as the use of materials, cornices, and monumental aspects, such as axes of symmetry.

Cooper and Eckstut's design entered the realization stage soon after it was presented, thanks to unexpected interest shown by Canadian real-estate developers Olympia & York, who agreed to take on the development of Battery Park City's office accommodations: approximately 700,000 square meters of office space contained in one complex, the World Financial Center.

Architect Cesar Pelli designed the entire WFC complex on his own, thus ensuring Olympia & York of a unequivocal architectonic image. The complex consists of four towers, ranging from thirty-three to fifty stories each. The space surrounding the towers at ground level accommodates a series of shopping areas that cover a total surface of 20,000 square meters. Although an element of public space, a large winter garden at the center of the plan was realized

the other hand, however, were demands issued by the Battery Park City Authority, which saw a greater degree of exclusivity as a major objective. Plunz points out that in the late '70s, the value of real estate began to rely more heavily than ever on factors such as security and exclusivity. Battery Park City's chances to survive and to be a profitable project depended entirely on the promise of a concentrated, exclusive housing environment, and not on visual appeal.[85]

Cooper and Eckstut's concept focused primarily on coherence. Battery Park City

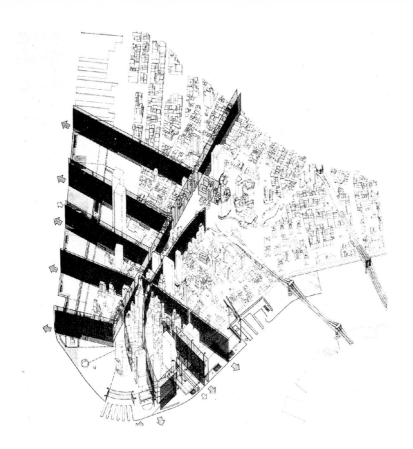

Design of visual corridors for Battery Park City.

so to speak, on the city. The most important pedestrian connection between Lower Manhattan and Battery Park City consists of two 'skywalks' between the World Trade Center and the World Financial Center.

Here lies the most essential difference between this plan and that of Venturi and Scott Brown, whose design was also based on creating a broad strip of land by means of an artificial fill. The strip itself was to become a new park, the design of which was to incorporate the Westway. New buildings, to be realized on property that formed the existing route of the Westway, would be both visually and physically connected to the street network of bordering Manhattan neighborhoods. The cancellation of this plan and, therefore, the preservation of the Westway route, produced a fundamentally different situation.

Today's Westway forms a wide barrier between Lower Manhattan and Battery Park City, which accentuates the exclusive character of the new model city and confines the interest of investors, entrepreneurs, residents, and consumers to the area covered by Battery Park City. The exterior side of Battery Park City – the side facing the city – is an iron-hard edge that accommodates no facilities. All facilities in the project are oriented inward, toward the waterside.

Even more important, however, is the guarantee provided by this barrier that undesirable aspects of city life in Manhattan will not spread in the direction of Battery Park City. Attempts have been made to reinforce this isolation using every resource imaginable. Both the Battery Park City Authority and Olympia & York have tried to prevent the construction of a subway station in Battery Park City. They have also supported a concentrated effort to keep the World Financial Center's winter garden (realized on public property) closed to the public.[87]

In short, in the case of Battery Park City

by Olympia & York; here office workers can sit beneath the palms and enjoy free lunchtime concerts, fully protected by a glass dome.

Seeing the amount of interest showed by Olympia & York, other developers followed suit, and construction soon began on the first residential complexes; a total of twelve thousand apartments had been planned for Battery Park City, most of which were intended for people in higher income categories.[86]

Thus while efforts were being made in the form of visual corridors and design guidelines created to guarantee both the visual continuity of Manhattan and an uninterrupted urban design repertoire, conditions for a maximum degree of isolation were being met as well: not one dollar was to be invested in the reorganization of the Westway, and Battery Park City itself was to turn its back,

the legacy left by Robert Moses appears
to function as, of all things, an essential
condition rather than as a disturbing
factor.

This quality of insulation, along with the
unique position of the water and the proximity of the city, lends a great deal of
'added value' to real estate at this location,
as compared with real estate in Manhattan
proper. The typologies of buildings, public
space, and residential floor plans are not
markedly dissimilar from typologies previously realized elsewhere in New York, a
situation totally in keeping with the aims
of Cooper and Eckstut. This combination
of a unique location and an air of isolation
was exactly what determined the commer-

cial success of the project. Or, as one real-
estate agent described it: 'Most people
buying apartments now come to Battery
Park City, at least to look, because of safety,
but also because they love the outdoor
space and the cleanliness. Most of all,
though, they talk about the similarity
to the suburbs.'[88]

Battery Park City plunged New York into
a paradoxical situation. On the one hand,
it may be called a success, and the project
has helped to stave off municipal bankruptcy. Investments made by the city and state
of New York – over 600 million dollars –
prompted private investors to come up with
nearly seven times that amount (4 billion
dollars). Extra income from tax proceeds

goes to public housing projects elsewhere in the city. Developers are quick to point out the added value of such revenues for the city. In an advertisement paid for by Donald Trump, who has also developed a plan for the east bank of the Hudson – 'Trump City,' which will boast the largest shopping mall in the United States – he estimates that extra tax proceeds from this project will allow New York City to hire twenty-five hundred new police officers.[89]

Battery Park City created thirty thousand jobs, and the construction of twelve thousand apartments made a slight breach in Lower Manhattan's 'office monoculture.'

The opposite side of the coin is the city council's initiation, support, and partial financing of a process that has encouraged the creation of relatively insulated enclaves with programs based on, strangely enough, the lack of a spatial relationship with the city and the absence of investments in elements meant to structuralize public space. Furthermore, these new enclaves are not *in* the city, but *next to* the city.

Although prior to the 1960s urban planning in New York was dominated by ambitions to transform the existing city itself, with the use of large-scale public works, this ambition has faded into the background. The existing city is no longer being transformed internally by means of public works; it is being expanded externally by means of private projects. And as long as such projects generate enough revenue to maintain existing urban facilities, the city council could not be happier.

## THE WATERFRONT AS STRATEGIC PAWN: THE SEARCH FOR NEW SPATIAL AND STRATEGIC CONCEPTS

Although Battery Park City has provided the municipality of New York with extra income, it has drawn extra criticism as well. On the other side of Lower Manhattan, along the East River near Fulton Fish Market, was another site designated as a large-scale expansion area in the 1969 Plan for New York City. Here, however, instead of creating an artificial fill next to the city, authorities took a different approach by initiating a process meant to produce a concentration of both public and private investments in the existing city.

This project, to be realized along the city's celebrated South Street, took New York's oldest waterfront neighborhood – home of Fulton Fish Market – as the point of departure for an approach that had previously proved successful in both Baltimore and Boston.

The man called on to help realize South Street Seaport was the same real-estate developer who had played a key role in the Baltimore and Boston projects: James Rouse, head of the Rouse Company. Rouse's significance lies in his active promotion of 'urban renaissance' in the United States; he uses his strategically chosen projects, moreover, as convincing evidence to support his arguments.

*James Rouse and the Rouse Company*
James Rouse, head of the Rouse Company, is one of the main exponents of the structural role played by private developers in postwar American politics, and specifically in the area of urban development. At first glance, his ideas seem strongly related to what became known in Europe, after World War II, as 'community development' (in England) or

'the neighborhood idea' (in the Netherlands). Rouse, however, does not implement his ideas with local or national planning in mind, but from the standpoint of the businessman. His message is that prosperity produces an active spending pattern and thus a favorable climate for private enterprise. His ideal is the construction of a city geared to man and market, which contributes to the prosperity of the general population and to profit for entrepreneurs.[90]

In the 1950s, before putting his ideas into practice, he established the basis for a judicial and political framework within which he would be able to function, at a later date, as a developer of housing projects.

When the Eisenhower administration appointed Rouse to design the new Housing Act in 1956, he described his point of departure by saying: 'Our cities grow haphazardly, according to the whims of the developer or of government institutions. This irrational process produces communities torn out of context, regions without ambiance or appeal. I believe that the great challenge facing our civilization lies in whether or not a contribution is made to the growth and advancement of human well-being. This demands an optimum human environment, both physically and sociopsychologically.'[91]

In 1957 Rouse founded the Rouse Company, the name under which he went on to realize a great many shopping malls and housing projects – often entire residential districts – throughout the country.

These are merely fragments, however. In the early 1960s he decided to build a completely new city, the design of which was based solely on his concept of the ideal urban community. This city, named Columbia, arose between Washington, D.C. and Baltimore in the late '60s.

The concept that led to Columbia greatly resembles that of the neighborhood idea, which provided a foundation for the development of postwar residential districts in Rotterdam. Rouse was assisted with the planning involved in such projects by an Advisory Board, a rather scientifically oriented committee of experts in the areas of sociology, industrial sociology, economics, transportation technology, and human relations.

Rouse's community ideal focused on integrating various ethnic population groups. Each of the city's neighborhoods was provided with a range of housing in diverse price categories. Rouse sees enormous ghettos in big cities as the worst product of the modern American city. His formula is to make inner cities attractive to whites again, and open up the suburbs to the blacks. Columbia is a model city in the sense of spatial organization, but even more in the sense of social composition.

After completing Columbia, Rouse dedicated himself to realizing his program within existing cities. Baltimore, his own hometown, became one of his most important areas of activity.

*Baltimore's role as pioneer*
As a resident of Baltimore, a member of the Greater Baltimore Committee and, later, as the developer of the city's 'festival marketplace,' Rouse played a leading role in the revitalization process experienced by Baltimore's city center.

By American standards and from a spatial point of view, as a seaport Baltimore deviates from the norm. Baltimore is not a peninsula surrounded by a harbor front, but just the opposite: a city wrapped around an estuary that empties into Chesapeake Bay. Here at the mouth of the Patapsco River lies the historic Inner Harbor. In the 1960s and '70s the limited dimensions of this harbor, along with the historic significance of the location, functioned as a fundamental rationale for

Map of Baltimore, 1950.

Baltimore: Master Plan of Charles Center and the Inner Harbor, 1965.

concentrating urban renewal within a relatively small area.

A second important spatial 'deviation' was the decision not to go ahead with plans for a waterfront highway – a decision that immediately brings to light another factor highly significant to development in Baltimore: namely, conflicting opinions held by both city council members and business people in Baltimore during this period.

In 1955 James Rouse was one of the driving forces behind a group of business people who believed that the city's right to exist lay in its ability to attract new economic functions. Together with the city council, they established the Greater Baltimore Committee, which dedicated its efforts to renewing downtown Baltimore, efforts that ultimately took the form of a master plan.[92]

The most important feature of this master plan was a clearly defined inner-city area only 13 hectares in size: Charles Center, a location that offered substantial tax advantages – applicable to this area only – meant to attract companies dealing in commercial services and communication, as well as department stores and hotels.

In less than ten years this measure yielded a handsome return: a new business center on a compact piece of land in the heart of Baltimore's inner city. The tall office buildings forming this close-knit entity rose in unison within this tightly framed territory, forming a new piece of the urban fabric.

When it became clear that Charles Center was headed for success, a decision was made in 1964 to expand the previously planned area to include the Inner Harbor. To achieve this goal, the realization of both projects was consolidated within one organization: Charles Center-Inner Harbor Management Incorporated (CC-IH), established in 1965. This private nonprofit

Above: Baltimore's Inner Harbor, as seen from the east, 1967. Harbor Park, in the center, functioned primarily as a festival site.

Below: aerial view of Baltimore's Inner Harbor, as seen from the northwest, ca. 1985. The two low-rise buildings in the foreground, which form a broken V in the 'corner' of the harbor, accommodate the festival market known as Harbor Place.

organization assumed responsibility for planning and implementing the new projects, while the city council and various municipal departments remained in charge of matters relating to function, land-price policy, and urban planning design.

A great deal of attention was paid to the architectonic quality of projects in the CC-IH area. A special Architectural Review Board was set up to guarantee standards of good taste.

The overall development of Charles Center, in combination with that of the Inner Harbor, occurred in five phases. After Charles Center had been completed (phase one), the redevelopment of the port area began with the realization of a venue for festivals and the creation of a festival organization, which invited and encouraged every ethnic and cultural group in the city to hold their festivals on the newly built site. Thus within a period of several years, an old, abandoned harbor area was transformed into a well-known spot: the focal point of Baltimore's social and cultural activities.[93]

When this process (phase two) was going strong, the third phase was launched: the construction of a festival marketplace next

Harbor Place, Baltimore's festival marketplace.

which made the project a bigger public attraction than Disney World.[94]

The brilliant success of Harbor Place was followed by two more developmental phases in this area: the realization of Inner Harbor I, on the south and east sides of Charles Center (phase four), and then Inner Harbor West, on the west side (phase five). The most crucial role in this phased planning operation was reserved for the festival marketplace, Harbor Place.

Harbor Place, designed by Benjamin Thompson (who was responsible for most of the Rouse Company's festival markets), consists of two pavilions with a total area of 16,000 square meters, distributed among an extreme diversity of about 140 cafés, shops, stalls, stands, and restaurants – which range from ultra-cheap to ultra-chic. Occupants pay rent based on turnover, a system that allows beginning entrepreneurs with little capital to try their luck at Harbor Place.

The formula for offering a varied spectrum of wares in festival markets is rooted in both commercial and sociocultural principles. Rouse sees these projects as symbols of a peaceful coexistence that includes every possible ethnic group and culture found in the United States.

'Cities are fun' is Rouse's concept, as well as his motivation for making the city into a new bearer of cultural identity: 'In a high-tech, cellophane-wrapper society, people are hungry for the kind of warmth, informality, color, texture, and fragrance they can find at such festival marketplaces.'[95] The 'cities are fun' concept may be seen as a fully developed and realized version of the ideal pursued by Jane Jacobs: a balanced microcosm of the modern city which has, however, decidedly antimodern undertones: this is a completely sheltered, wholly safeguarded microcosm, from which every modern element experienced as threatening has been banished.

In Baltimore's Inner Harbor a new type

to the festival site itself. Festival markets, which were Rouse's trademark, were considered the ultimate key to the successful revitalization of waterfront areas. Indeed, the festival marketplace realized in 1980 – Rouse Company's Harbor Place – was the motor that propelled Baltimore's Inner Harbor into the limelight. From that moment on, the Inner Harbor hosted an increasingly greater influx of visitors; in the late '80s annual numbers topped 20 million, of 'culturalized' city has declared itself: the 'amusement-park city' par excellence. Special security forces and janitorial services provide visitors with a feeling of safety and prevent the annoyance caused by litter. In this amusement park, the visitor can imagine himself an astronaut, a deep-sea diver, or the captain of a ship. And, above all, an explorer discovering a multicultural world.

Although Rouse's projects are often compared to Disney World, the big difference between the two is that the fun city uses the city's genuine cultural and ethnic diversity as an attraction. The Rouse Company's fun cities take advantage of the fascination people have for the cosmopolitan and multifaceted character of big cities: visitors become acquainted with this colorful world and enjoy themselves at the same time. Visiting a fun city is a safe version of the nineteenth-century activity known as 'going slumming.'[96]

Admittedly, the main objective of the fun city is the same as that of Disney World: visitors are welcome to look around, but preferably not without spending money!


*The festival market as a panacea*
In the early '80s, the festival marketplace seemed to be the consummate strategy for a rapid revitalization of decaying and deserted city centers. Of the sixteen projects that the Rouse Company has realized so far, however, barely half are operating successfully.

Not only have various festival markets shown substantial financial losses rather than the anticipated gains (losses felt most sharply by local governments, which made pre-investments and acted as underwriters); many markets have also failed to produce the flourishing city centers initially pictured.

Baltimore's Harbor Place is part of a broad range of initiatives that gelled to form a critical mass – the final result, moreover, of many decades of preparation – but urban authorities in many other cities assumed that the marketplace itself would lead to new initiatives and investments in adjacent areas. The lack of the success anticipated has sent several festival markets into bankruptcy, while others have been sold to new owners and, in the process, have received new functions. As a result, the parties involved can now turn to specialists touting a new branch of medicine: marketplace doctors.[97]


*Private urban planning with a public effect*
Even though the combination of Baltimore's Charles Center and Inner Harbor was developed as a (semi)private project, it did have a considerable effect on the city as a whole.

As is the case in Battery Park City, the primary significance of Charles Center and the Inner Harbor for Baltimore lies in the sale of land to new businesses, in the taxes collected from these businesses, and in the organization of an elaborate system of 'linkage projects,' a term that refers to contractual conditions placed on investors, requiring them to provide jobs, housing, and public facilities for the local population.[98]

Rising revenues from the sale of land and from taxes eventually led to a program for revaluating the city as a place to live. In the early 1970s, Baltimore became the first American city to present the Urban Homesteading Program.[99]

Ultimately, Baltimore turned out to be one of the few cities (along with Boston and Atlanta) in which urban revitalization had a positive effect on the prosperity of the city and on the welfare of its residents, an assessment based on average incomes and unemployment percentages.[100] Baltimore used the development of Charles Center and the Inner Harbor to improve a number of inner-city facilities, and therein lies the difference between this and other projects, such as Battery Park City. These inner-city facilities included city-managed public markets, with stalls rented to small-scale manufacturers and retailers. The popularity of Lexington Market, a large facility at the edge of Charles Center, and of various smaller indoor markets elsewhere in the city definitely stimulated the success of Harbor Place, the new festival market. But the opposite is true as well: the revitalization of Charles Center and the Inner Harbor has been an essential factor in the ongoing success of Lexington Market.

The same applies to Fells Point, a waterfront neighborhood about 1.5 kilometers from the Inner Harbor, where a conglomeration of bars and eating houses had already been transformed into an urban entertainment center in the 1960s, initially without the use of a plan for reorganization. The development of the Inner Harbor and the realization of a streetcar line connecting Fells Point to the Inner Harbor provided this district with an added stimulus.[101]

The primary significance of Charles Center and Inner Harbor for Baltimore lies in their effect on the old city center, to which they have given, step by step, a renewed functional and spatial structure. The waterfront along the Inner Harbor forms one link in this structure, a link developed only during a later phase.

*Boston: completion of the park system*
Boston and Baltimore are often bracketed together as examples of cities with successful waterfront areas whose development relied heavily on the expertise of the Rouse Company. In Boston even more than in Baltimore, however, efforts were made to include the waterfront in a larger spatial context, to put it on the level of the city as a whole, and to build on Olmsted's nineteenth-century park system.

Boston's waterfront began to deteriorate even earlier than Baltimore's port area; a decline was already apparent in the early 1900s, when port industry and shipyards started relocating from the main peninsula to roomier waterfront areas in South and East Boston, which were also more easily accessible. The disappearance of harbor activities from central Boston seriously undermined the position of the historic downtown area as well. In the 1950s a helping hand was extended to the city center in the form of a new highway viaduct (Central Artery) which connected the downtown area to the interstate-highway network. The unfortunate result was an even more marginalized waterfront.

In 1959 the city's Chamber of Commerce initiated the establishment of the Boston Redevelopment Authority (BRA), an agency subsequently commissioned to study possibilities for redeveloping the city center in connection with the waterfront. One advisor was Kevin Lynch, author of a book published in 1960, *The Image of the City*. Lynch noted in this study that the position of the historic city center had degenerated so badly that it was nothing but a blank spot within 'the Boston that everyone knows.'[102] (See illustration on page 274.)

Boston's city center, largely ignored by the city's population at that time, lies between the waterfront and the area covered by Boston Common, the Public Garden, and the stately nineteenth-century district of Back Bay. This attitude reflected the fact that Olmstead's one-hundred-year-old park system, a spatial network that provided the city with meaning and coherence, stopped precisely where it had once begun: Boston Common. This conclusion became a leitmotif in the redevelopment of the city center.

The strategy focused on the development of a system of public facilities and areas which, being connected to the Common, would draw both city center and waterfront back into the urban network, a network still supported by the park system.

Plans were made to realize a series of

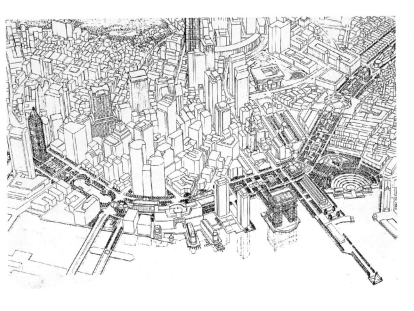

Boston: design for the reorganization of the Central Artery zone.

projects, from the Common to the waterfront, which together would form a 'walk to the sea.' This strategy was highly influenced by Lynch's ideas on 'designing the paths' and 'the sense of the whole.' Implementation of these ideas required design regulations for public space, as well as for buildings, that would create routes lined with visual and functional diversity while also radiating a sense of uniformity and coherence.

Furthermore, the 'walk to the sea' strategy was aimed at the long-term solution of problems surrounding the Central Artery. Unlike the situation in New York, the reconstruction of the walk to the sea began with new projects in the heart of downtown Boston and moved, step by step, toward the waterfront. (See page 275.)

The walk to the sea comprised four individual projects. The first, a civic center, was to be a new 'symbol of democratic government': a complex accommodating a new city hall, as well as various state and federal institutions. The other three projects were: a renovation of three old market halls at Faneuil Hall Marketplace, an underpass beneath the expressway, and a new Waterfront Park. Although all three (civic center, underpass, and park) were public facilities, the project actually

promoted as a public attraction – Faneuil Hall – was infeasible without private funds. Once more, the Rouse Company agreed to act as developer for this key project. Faneuil Hall was vital not only because it formed an essential link in the planners' carefully designed route, but also because it was one of the last surviving relics of Boston's nineteenth-century waterfront. Thanks to these three market halls (with old Quincy Hall at the center), Boston had been one of the few nineteenth-century American cities boasting a monumental waterfront. In later years, however, the use of artificial fills to expand the harbor area stripped these halls of their direct relationship with the water.

Faneuil Hall Marketplace was converted into a festival marketplace on the basis of the tried-and-true formula concocted by the Rouse Company. This complex is perhaps the only festival marketplace that is not on the water. It does function, however, as a *reference* to the waterfront; Faneuil Hall represents a historical testimony to the former harbor front, both in a spatial sense and as part of the walk to the sea.

Boston's festival-marketplace project and the role it plays in the walk to the sea serve the objective of drawing both waterfront *and* city center back into the network of public space.

Leaving the Rouse Company to supervise the development of Faneuil Hall, the Boston Redevelopment Authority turned its attention to two other projects: the Central Artery underpass and a new Waterfront Park. The revitalization of both sides of Waterfront Park, along with urban renewal on the 'inner flank' of the Central Artery, has been virtually completed since then: features include an aquarium and hotels, as well as apartment and office buildings.

The exceptional aspect of this development is the way in which the walk to the sea acted as a catalyst for this new period of economic recovery, while constantly

New York City's South Street Seaport, with Brooklyn in the background.

remaining the key to the accessibility and significance of the waterfront as public space.

The Rouse Company's activities here were directed, even more than in the firm's previous projects, toward using investments in public space to create a new, coherent network of public urban areas, of which Waterfront Park was the coping stone. The quality of this network has stimulated, in turn, new private investments in waterfront sites.

Today, new functions line nearly all of Boston's downtown waterfront. As was the case in Battery Park City, here, too, a primary focus was on visual corridors and design guidelines for both buildings and open space along the waterfront.

Finally, in 1986 preparations began on plans for providing the Central Artery with a tunnel and for converting the viaduct route into an elongated park zone with various public facilities.

As a result, two new structural 'public-space' lines have emerged in Boston: one that is a continuation of Olmsted's park system and one that runs parallel to the waterfront. The spot where they intersect, at Waterfront Park, has become a new urban focal point.

Thus Boston has replaced New York, with its West Side Highway, as the classic example of an approach to the waterfront based on the tandem development of projects to improve an interstate highway and to integrate the waterfront into the network of public urban space.

*New York City and South Street Seaport*
To what degree has New York been able to apply the experiences of Baltimore and Boston to its own situation?

The plan for South Street Seaport in New York was a source of controversy from the start, especially following the clearance of housing, studios, and businesses, an operation that violated one of Rouse's cardinal

South Street Seaport, New
York City.

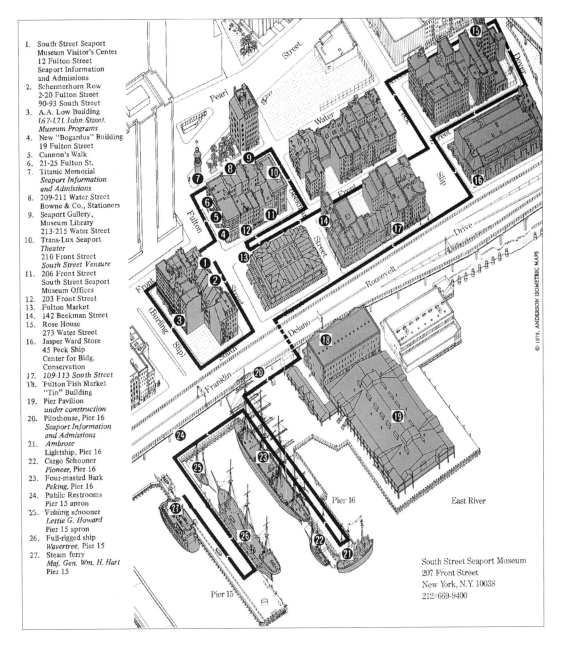

1.  South Street Seaport
    Museum Visitor's Center
    12 Fulton Street
    *Seaport Information
    and Admissions*
2.  Schermerhorn Row
    2-20 Fulton Street
    90-93 South Street
3.  A.A. Low Building
    167-171 John Street
    *Museum Programs*
4.  New "Bogardus" Building
    19 Fulton Street
5.  Cannon's Walk
6.  21-25 Fulton St.
7.  Titanic Memorial
    *Seaport Information
    and Admissions*
8.  209-211 Water Street
    Bowne & Co., Stationers
9.  Seaport Gallery,
    Museum Library
    213-215 Water Street
10. Trans-Lux Seaport
    *Theater*
    210 Front Street
    *South Street Venture*
11. 206 Front Street
    South Street Seaport
    Museum Offices
12. 203 Front Street
13. Fulton Market
14. 142 Beekman Street
15. Rose House
    273 Water Street
16. Jasper Ward Store
    45 Peck Ship
    Center for Bldg.
    Conservation
17. *109-113 South Street*
18. Fulton Fish Market
    "Tin" Building
19. Pier Pavilion
    *under construction*
20. Pilothouse, Pier 16
    *Seaport Information
    and Admissions*
21. *Ambrose*
    Lightship, Pier 16
22. Cargo Schooner
    *Pioneer*, Pier 16
23. Four-masted Bark
    *Peking*, Pier 16
24. Public Restrooms
    Pier 15 apron
25. Fishing schooner
    *Lettie G. Howard*
    Pier 15 apron
26. Full-rigged ship
    *Wavertree*, Pier 15
27. Steam ferry
    *Maj. Gen. Wm. H. Hart*
    Pier 15

© 1979. ANDERSON ISOMETRIC MAPS

South Street Seaport Museum
207 Front Street
New York, N.Y. 10038
212/669-9400

principles: to 'prevent displacement.' Prior to
the new plan, South Street – a commercial
center of the fishing industry – had been,
with its daily fish market and related activities, an area of special significance for nearby
residential districts in the Lower East Side
and Brooklyn. This significance would go up
in smoke when the new plan was realized.

Just as their Boston colleagues, planners
contemplating the shoreline of Lower Man-

hattan's East River were also forced to
contend with the presence of a highway
viaduct: Franklin D. Roosevelt Drive.

The phased strategy used in Baltimore
and Boston was repeated in the development
of South Street Seaport, which also included
a walk to the sea. Public interest in the waterside was roused at an early stage by organizing
maritime activities, but the actual development of the area had to wait until the final

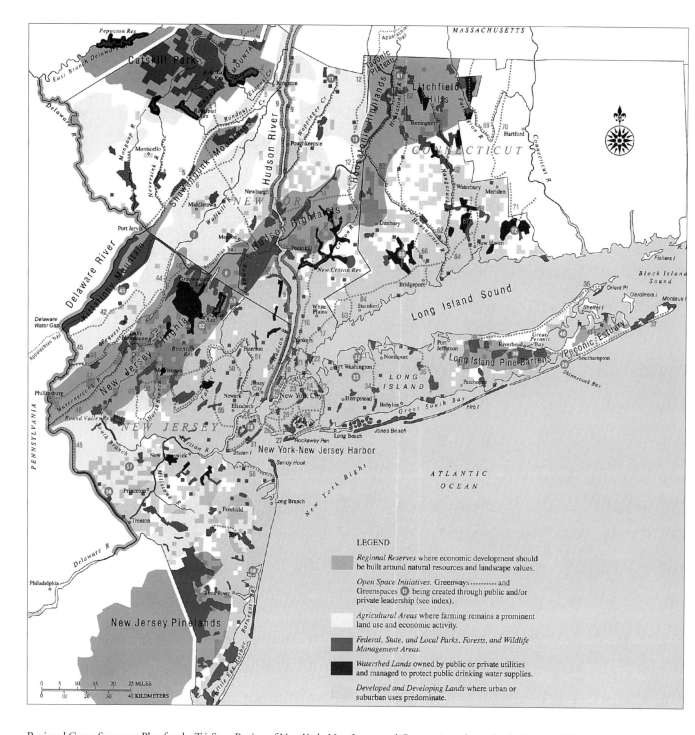

Regional Green Structure Plan for the Tri-State Region of New York, New Jersey, and Connecticut: design by the Regional Plan Association, 1993.

phase. Renovating Fulton Fish Market and opening it to the public was given top priority; only after this project was completed did authorities decide to 'take on' the barrier posed by Franklin D. Roosevelt Drive and, subsequently, to provide the riverside with a festival market on Pier 17 and an outdoor maritime museum on two adjacent piers.[103]

The entire area is open to pedestrians only, with the exception of South Street and Franklin D. Roosevelt Drive, which carries a roar of traffic above the small-scale, quasi-nineteenth-century pedestrian territory of South Street Seaport, apparently with little negative effect on the success of the new urban project.

Unlike the situation in Baltimore and Boston, where the Rouse Company was able to organize 'charisma' in a deliberate manner within the scope of a far broader strategy (for projects covering a much longer time span), plans for South Street included no strategy for the steady development of a new structural element for the city.

South Street Seaport has become an enclave, which may be a successful tourist attraction and a refreshing change for commuters who work in Manhattan's financial district, but in the context of contemporary New York it remains an isolated phenomenon and a rewarding target for sarcasm and irony: 'The seaport is a great success! Captain's Hook and Parrots, a fake nineteenth-century atmosphere of pirates and lawlessness in a cardboard setting. South Street isn't a dream the Dutch would have dreamt for themselves. It is the fabric of some interior city that has invaded New York, sat itself down in the metropolis like a merchandise market by the sea.'[104]

## IN SEARCH OF NEW SPATIAL AND FUNCTIONAL COHERENCE IN THE CITY

The incidental character of projects like South Street Seaport and Battery Park City, and the failure of these projects – despite substantial public investment in public space – to contribute to new urban spatial coherence led to the development of a new program in the 1980s aimed at the spatial and functional coherence of New York City as a whole. After Battery Park City had been completed, the desirability of filling in the entire east bank of the Hudson with similar projects, such as Trump City, was debated not only from the position of potentially lost public urban space, but also from the perspective of an increasing amount of pressure threatening Manhattan Island as an overfull central area, which would leave other parts of the city to fall even farther into marginality.

In 1987 the Commission on the Year 2000, a body created by the city council, published the report *New York Ascendant*, which presented a concept of the future development of several new centers in the other four boroughs: Brooklyn, Queens, Bronx, and Staten Island.[105] Manhattan's waterfront was to be used to strengthen the spatial coherence of these areas: 'a public waterfront, unifying the five boroughs.' Wagner and the commission argued that New York's waterfront areas were crucial to the future of New York because they still offered an abundance of inexpensive housing and commercial properties (the majority owned or managed by the city), as well as the promise of the creation of new public space. The commission saw both aspects as essential to the maintenance and reinforcement of New York as 'a city of opportunity.'

The development of a new concept of Manhattan's value in a regional context gained momentum in the late 1980s and early '90s,

**Priority Greenway Routes**

**Other Potential Greenway Routes**

..........

**Bourough Boundary**

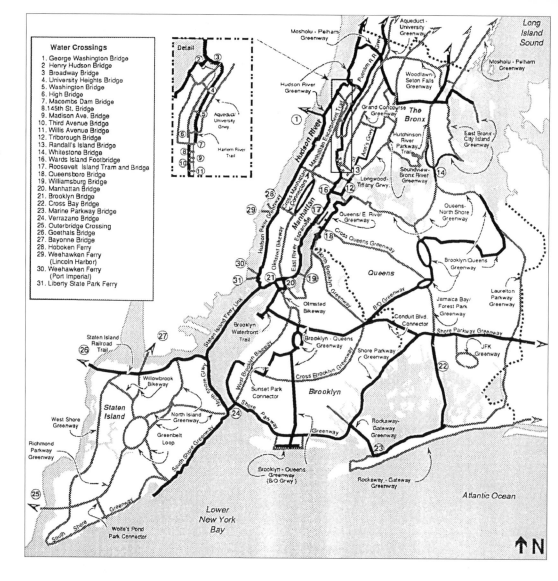

Water Crossings
1. George Washington Bridge
2. Henry Hudson Bridge
3. Broadway Bridge
4. University Heights Bridge
5. Washington Bridge
6. High Bridge
7. Macombs Dam Bridge
8. 145th St. Bridge
9. Madison Ave. Bridge
10. Third Avenue Bridge
11. Willis Avenue Bridge
12. Triborough Bridge
13. Randall's Island Bridge
14. Whitestone Bridge
15. Wards Island Footbridge
16. Roosevelt Island Tram and Bridge
17. Queensboro Bridge
18. Williamsburg Bridge
19. Manhattan Bridge
20. Brooklyn Bridge
21. Cross Bay Bridge
22. Marine Parkway Bridge
23. Verrazano Bridge
24. Outerbridge Crossing
25. Goethals Bridge
26. Bayonne Bridge
27. Hoboken Ferry
28. Weehawken Ferry (Lincoln Harbor)
29. Weehawken Ferry (Port Imperial)
30. Liberty State Park Ferry

thanks in particular to the involvement of the Regional Plan Association and its preparations for a new plan for the tri-state region (an area made up of parts of New York, New Jersey, and Connecticut).[106] This plan was based on the conclusion that New York's formerly concentric structure had changed into a structure resembling a flower. Suburbanization and the new economic significance of the region's so-called 'edge cities'[107] were responsible for the development of five sizeable, linear, urban corridors arranged in a fan-like structure comparable to the petals of a flower. Although this 'ROSEland' (ROSE =

Region's Outer Suburban Economy) no longer recognized Manhattan as the exclusive center of the region, the borough did make up part of each individual corridor and, as a binding and common element, was essential to the coherence of the region. As support for Manhattan's function as a binding element, the shoreline and the construction of new cross-river connections were granted an important role, which related to both the traffic network and topography of the region.

In the 1990s the City Planning Department began making concrete plans that would capitalize on Manhattan's new role.

The department's 1990 design for the east bank of the Hudson was a highly simplified, not to mention cheaper, version of Venturi and Scott Brown's plan for Westway Park.[108] The riverside route, which no longer bore the status of Interstate Highway, was now a regional connecting road. This change in status made it possible to design the road as an urban thoroughfare with a moderate speed limit and intersections at grade, provided with traffic lights; and it also allowed for a plan that would combine the road with a riverbank design geared to slow-moving traffic and a relaxed atmosphere. The design was remarkably similar to the plan for San Francisco's waterfront area. Several years later this concept became a basic principle in the development of New York's shorelines, as evidenced by the Greenway Plan for New York City.[109] Moses's parkways, realized in the 1930s, were the chief inspiration for this plan: routes designed in part as recreation areas, intended not only for motorized traffic, but also for cyclists and pedestrians. The New York City Planning Department wants to restore this multifaceted quality, especially along the waterfront. A network of greenways, combined with some thirty 'water crossings' – both bridges and ferries – is to lend new coherence to the urban archipelago.

Instead of focusing on the edges or 'frontiers' of the city, recent plans created by municipal departments and the Regional Plan Association highlight the importance of the water and the riverbank areas, elements capable of solidifying the region's urbanized landscape into a coherent entity.

# 5 Balance: Fragmentation or Coherence

In the nineteenth century the American urban waterfront became the arena of a battle involving various urban planning concepts, each with its own ideas on how to structuralize and design the city.

Initially and theoretically, the waterfront was part of a wholly neutral pattern formed by the urban street plan. But various influences affected this neutral pattern.

Tensions between economic and cultural considerations finally led to two major urban planning movements, one of which promoted public interests wherever possible and the other of which was based on private interests.

As early as the 1800s, champions of the first movement – 'public urban planning' – focused on reinforcing the collectivity of the urban population, a process whose success relied on structuralizing and designing the infrastructure of public space. Major players were Frederick Law Olmsted, in the decades following 1865, and Robert Moses, from 1920 to the mid-1960s. These periods, dominated by urban planning as a public affair, saw America's *scenic beauty* take center stage as the consummate element of collectivity.

Important trend-setters representing the other movement – 'urban planning as private enterprise' – were developers like Walt Disney, John Portman, and James Rouse, all of whom built complete cities. This movement emphasized an urban aesthetic based on a combination of the design of public areas (many of which, despite being called public areas, were not actually public) and the control, or at least guidance, of the design and programming of buildings. In fact, these men approached the city as an *architectonic megaproject*.

These two movements in American urban planning involve more than simply a controversy between public and private interests,

Boston, as seen from the northeast, 1975.

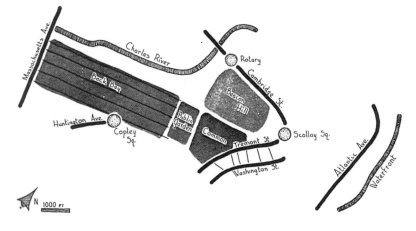

'The Boston that everyone knows': drawn by Kevin Lynch. The zone between the Common and the waterfront is Lynch's 'blank spot.'

Boston's Quincy Market.

Boston's Waterfront Park.

Boston's 'walk to the sea':
1 = Boston Common
2 = Civic Center
3 = Faneuil Hall, featuring
Quincy Market
4 = Waterfront Park
5 = Central Artery

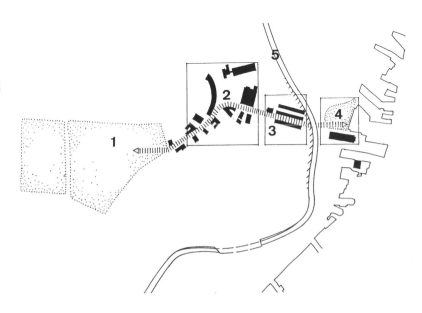

however. Public and private urban planning represent two different characteristics inherent in American culture. One is the neutrality of spatial networks: networks found not only in the city, with its neutral grid of streets, but throughout the entire country, with a highway network that functions as a large-scale grid. This neutrality creates a condition for the American way of life, an important part of which takes place on the road, and for the mobility needed to change one's place of residence with relative ease. The second characteristic, which is almost diametrically opposed to the first, concerns persistent efforts to identify with specific places by means of an emphasis on the spatial features of a certain spot, place, or region.

Current representatives of both movements are landscape architect John Brinckerhoff Jackson, and a group of architects and urban planners united under the name 'New Urbanism.'

In his book *A Sense of Place, a Sense of Time*[110] Jackson sings the praises of the neutrality of the American countryside and of American cities, and applauds the road as an essential component of the American countryside. He claims that American culture has never recognized 'a sense of place.' Europe may have its towns, cities, and neighborhoods, where people live in communities that look to public places and buildings – squares, monuments, city halls, and boulevards – for their identity. The tradition that has evolved in the United States, however, exhibits a much stronger division between the social domain and the politico-public domain. The social domain is determined largely by activities and rituals that give barely a thought to specific spatial phenomena. The rituals of social life have no trouble moving from one place to another: think of family reunions, which often change location from one occasion to the next, but which always take place in approximately the same kind of house, on the same kind of street, in the

same kind of town. Jackson believes that his assertions are substantiated by recent sociological studies, which have concluded that the social order of Americans is more temporal than spatial: the period of time and the frequence of activities are more important than the spatial characteristics of place.[111]

The only true politico-public domain recognized by Americans is the countryside, with the road as an essential component. In making such assertions, Jackson is following in the footsteps of Olmsted and Moses, for whom the realization of parkways and park systems represented a way in which to stimulate a collective sense of American identity that would work as an 'antidote' to the social fragmentation and segregation found in American society in the nineteenth and early twentieth centuries. Indeed Jackson sees the highway through the countryside as the heart of America's public domain – the space that proclaims free, republican citizenship – where Americans feel liberated of all social ties and where they realize, above all else, that they are free American citizens.

The New Urbanism movement, on the other hand, opposes the proposition that America has no tradition of a sense of place. In the space of only a few years this movement, created by a group of architects and urban planners, has become an established factor in the debate on urban development in the United States.[112]

In the 1980s Peter Calthorpe, Andres Duany, Elizabeth Plater-Zyberk, Stefanos Polyzoides, Elizabeth Moule, and several others launched a crusade for the restoration of the kind of urban planning willing to pay attention to diversity and to the *genius loci*. Their first experiments were based largely on the best conventions of design found in 'the traditional American town.' Basic urban planning elements – such as streets, avenues, squares, building lots, buildings, and building blocks – became subjects of design studies. A substantial number of these studies have been completed. Those that captured the most attention were projects that Duany and Plater-Zyberk carried out in Florida, where supportive developers allowed them to design model suburbs based entirely on their own ideas. The mini-city of Seaside, which is a particularly good example of the ambitions of New Urbanism, may also be seen as a recent gem studding the tradition of the architectonic megaproject.

Conflicts that surfaced in American port cities attempting to redevelop former harbor fronts included not only disagreements among various economic interests and between public and private parties, but also – and primarily – contention among various cultural concepts: one side supported the idea that the waterfront should be designed chiefly as an element combining a vast public landscape and the street network, while the other side promoted the concept of a waterfront capable of contributing to a sense of place. Ever since the 1970s both theories have fought for priority, with varying results, in cities featured in this book.

For the most part, plans described here fit into one of three categories.

*a. New autonomous enclaves: reconstruction and cultivation of the nineteenth-century city*

Exponents of this category are projects like New York's Battery Park City and South Street Seaport: precise reconstructions of typologies found in the public space and buildings of the nineteenth century.

More recent spatial phenomena of the twentieth-century city, such as highway systems, are omitted from the design of these reconstructions. These projects are, in fact, a continuation and expansion of the tradition of 'private urban planning' in the United States. Although this tradition originally evolved around the realization of autonomous enclaves, often built on undeveloped sites, today it is seen as a sovereign remedy to

be used within cities themselves.

Such projects strongly enforce the separation of various kinds of public space. This can be seen in the purely technical infrastructure of highways that function only as access routes to these projects, as well as in the type of public space within the enclave itself, which has a predominantly representational function: here the design of public space, which is geared to the design of architecture and to the program of buildings, serves chiefly to increase the value of real estate. The position of these highway networks within the urban topography is a deciding factor: running along the waterfront, such routes – in their present state – form enormous border vacuums between the urban network and the waterfront area.

When perfected nineteenth-century reconstructions and neglected highway systems are permitted to coexist, projects like Battery Park City and South Street Seaport function to an even higher degree as urban enclaves.

*b. New autonomous networks of multifaceted public areas*

Venturi and Scott Brown's design for Westway Park best exemplifies the plans in this category. As a contemporary version of the nineteenth-century park system, their design was aimed at realizing a new combination of large-scale networks, such as the interconnection of interstate highways and local urban networks. This approach injected a new stimulus into the tradition of public urban planning. Their design of public space was based largely on the integration or combination of various sorts of use, which applied to public space itself, and was highly autonomous with respect to buildings, which were subjected to only a few global regulations (building lines and heights).

The most drastic combination of the diverse functions fulfilled by public space in a port city is found in Seattle. Here the

Above: Battery Park City, 1990.

Above right: Battery Park City and the promenade along the Hudson River.

Battery Park City: design of the promenade.

New York City's South Street Seaport, featuring a renovated Fulton Fish Market.

South Street Seaport: a view of the East River waterfront.

Above: South Street Seaport, with Pier 17 in the foreground.

waterfront is both a public-space area that composes part of the urban network and an area that accommodates new large-scale networks of motorized traffic and ferryboats, while providing a view of modern port activities on Harbor Island. While such activities vanished from nearly every other port city in the United States a long time ago, in Seattle they remain a vital part of the cityscape.

*c.  Plans based on the strategic use of new typologies of public space and real-estate projects*

The main exponent of these plans, which are based on a combination of the first two categories, is Boston. Plan development within the urban planning tradition of Boston has been aimed at producing new typologies of public-space networks, within which an active role was set aside for private investors. Both the renovation of the Faneuil Hall-Quincy Market complex and the transformation of the Central Artery were part of an active urban planning strategy, the objective of which was to create a new symbiosis of historical spatial patterns and modern forms of urban life and infrastructure.

Differences in approach were due, to a great degree, to differences in financial situations, which related in turn to the amount of power held by municipal authorities. In the 1980s a virtually bankrupt New York City found itself in a much weaker position, when dealing with private investors, than the relatively rich cities of San Francisco and Seattle. Even so, this is not the only explanation for such differences. Boston was also in an awkward financial situation in the '80s.

The concept used in Boston strongly resembled that of New York's West Side Highway project: the position taken by the Central Artery within Boston's urban topography is comparable to the location of West Side Highway in New York, while the desire to develop a new spatial typology was present in both cities as well. The most important difference between the two projects, and also the reason for the success of Boston's highway and the failure of New York's scheme, lay in the planning strategy. In New York the transformation of the highway was a first step, a precondition for future developments. Boston's radical, not to mention costly, transformation was the final step in a long series – in terms of both space and time – of interventions, which began with projects geared to the main spatial structure of the nineteenth-century city and which used projects realized by private developers (like Quincy Market) as strategic pieces to complete the urban puzzle.

Chapter 5

*The Northwestern European Port City:*

# ROTTERDAM

*And the Dynamic of the Delta*

ROTTERDAM

# City, Port, and Dikes

I

Nothing characterizes port cities along the Northwestern European delta, with its core of Dutch seaports, like the constantly changing relation between land and water, between city and port.

A big part of the reason for this inconstancy is the multilayered significance of water in the region. Although water fulfills the role of transport infrastructure and remains a symbol of protection against foreign domination, it also poses a perpetual threat to the land.

The way in which planners have dealt with such factors has led to the design and development of diverse types of port cities, from the fortified seaport, built completely within the dikes, to the commercial port city, built outside the dikes. The location of dikes within the context of the city has been of overriding importance in this area.

The emergence of Dutch port cities, followed by their international hegemony in the seventeenth century, was a logical consequence of the maritime supremacy enjoyed by Mediterranean ports in the two preceding centuries.[1] Initially Antwerp played a leading role in this new hegemony, but the Spanish occupation of that city was to be a major factor in the subsequent prosperity of Dutch port cities to the north.[2] What the Low Countries experienced during this period was a concentration, an intensification, and a decrease in scale of the same principle that had once caused the Mediterranean region to flourish. Here in the

north an unprecedentedly dense network of cities evolved, interconnected by waterways and featuring the phenomenon of the barge.[3]

The geographical location of the network was unique: at the halfway point of the most important shipping route linking Northern Europe (Baltic Sea) and Southern Europe (Mediterranean Sea), and in the middle of Europe's greatest delta. Like Mediterranean ports, with the sea at their doorstep, Dutch cities were served by a wonderful infrastructure of rivers and polder canals: bodies of water that provided them with the same kind of protection against invaders from the hinterland that mountain ranges and deserts offered to areas surrounding the Mediterranean Sea. The inundation technique gave the Dutch an essential tool, which they put to good use in their war for independence against the feudal domination of the Spanish king.

Differences among various types of port cities were due chiefly to the position of dikes, a factor of vital importance to those shaping the relation between city and port: dikes enclosed an integrated system formed by these two entities and thus created a distinction between the inland port city, built within the dikes, and its less protected counterpart outside the dikes. The latter can be divided into subtypes: ports with highly indefinite, 'soft' waterfronts and

The Kop van Zuid, as seen from the southeast (inset, 1987; large photograph, 1996).

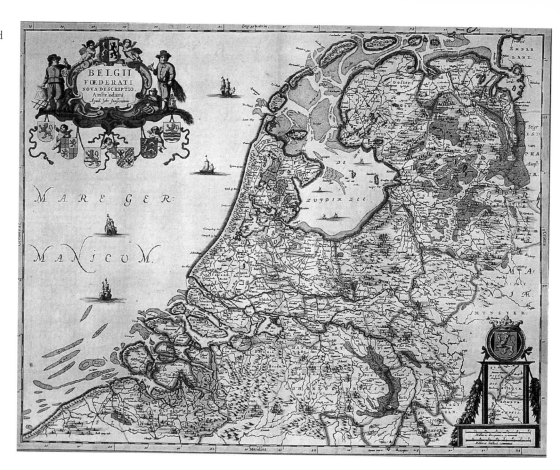

Map of the Seven United Provinces, published by Johannes Janssonius, Amsterdam, 1685.

Network of Dutch barge canals, 1665.

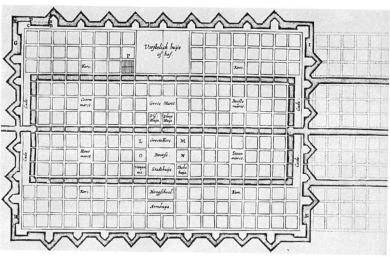

Simon Stevin, ca. 1600. Plan for the ideal city, as presented in *Vande oirdeningh der steden.*

Vlissingen in the
seventeenth century;
here the dike doubled
as a military rampart.

ports with definite, 'hard' waterfronts.

Most fortified port cities (Vlissingen, Hellevoetsluis, Den Briel, and Den Helder) were close to or on the coast, while commercial seaports (such as Amsterdam, Dordrecht, and Rotterdam) were located farther inland.

Of major importance in a strategic sense, fortified seaports also experienced a greater threat from the sea. They were forced, to a greater degree than others, to cope with problems that Simon Stevin believed he could solve with his ideal city, in which city and port were organized as an integrated system within the ramparts.[4] Vlissingen is a good example of a fortified city whose dike doubled as a rampart. Together, harbors and city formed an integrated system organized completely within the dikes. The entrance to the harbors was protected against both the

whims of the sea and enemy fleets by a system of locks. Thanks to these features the city assumed an important function in the early seventeenth century: as naval base of the United Provinces, Vlissingen was provided with a large dock and was developed into a complete war machine.

In the seventeenth century Dutch engineers exported the principle of the fortified seaport to cities across the continent, from the North Sea to the Baltic.[5] What remained a unique aspect of fortified ports in the Netherlands, however, were dikes that functioned simultaneously as ramparts. In the early 1800s, Napoleon went to Vlissingen to perfect the system.[6] But even after the city had lost its military significance, the interrelated quality of this port and city behind the dikes continued far into the twentieth century.

Anonymous, 1780. View of the river front of Rotterdam, as seen from the left bank of the Maas. In the foreground, the God of the Maas and the monograms of the East India Company and the West India Company.

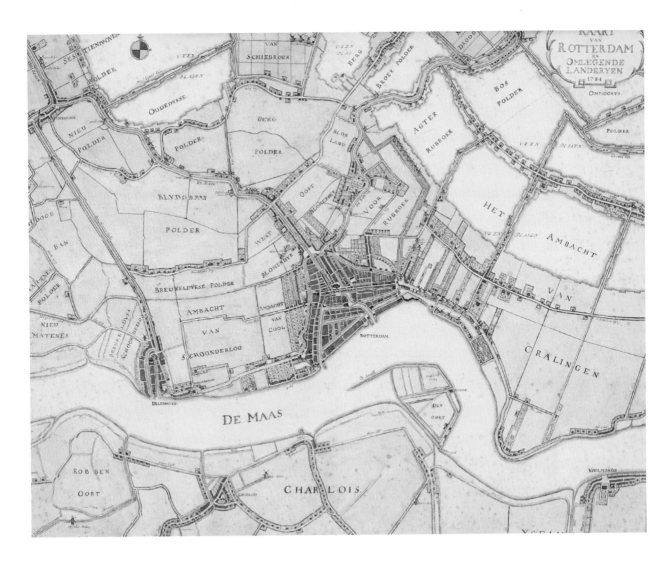

Map of Rotterdam and vicinity, ca. 1780.

The Boompjes, ca. 1700. Engraving by Petrus
Schenk.

For trade centers like Amsterdam and Rotterdam, enclosing the port behind a protective
system of dikes was less productive and,
moreover, unnecessary.

Amsterdam and Rotterdam evolved as
locations with similar geographical conditions: at the mouths of small marshland rivers
(the Amstel and the Rotte) within larger
bodies of water (the IJ and the Maas). Nonetheless, each has experienced a fundamentally
different form of development, especially in
terms of the relation between city and port.

In the seventeenth century, a 'soft,' indefinite harbor front began to emerge in Amsterdam, causing the city to grow away from the
water. The opposite occurred in Rotterdam,
however, where the 'hard,' well-defined
waterfront created during the same century
eventually caused city and port to merge.

Of importance to the development of
Amsterdam was the IJ, a marshy peat bog
with an open connection to the Zuider Zee,
in contrast to Rotterdam's Maas River. The
distance between Amsterdam and the open
sea, accompanied by an absence of currents
and a negligible difference between high and
low tides, made it possible to build a dike
directly on the IJ as early as the fourteenth
century. The 'front' of the city developed
along the mouth of the Amstel– the Damrak
– and additions to the dike system (a series of
raised mounds, for the most part) were
wrapped around the Damrak, so to speak.

The Damrak's central position, as a link
between city and port, remained fundamentally unchanged from the fourteenth to the
nineteenth century, while the significance of
this vital urban element continued to grow
throughout the years and was reemphasized
in the 1800s, with the construction of a new
city hall and an exchange. Although Prins
Hendrikkade also acquired a venerable status
in the eighteenth and early nineteenth

centuries, as more and more merchants built
their mansions along this street, it was, in
effect, an 'offshoot' of the Damrak.

A double row of palisades protected the
city from the rough waters of the IJ and from
enemy forces. Because the Damrak and the IJ
were not deep enough to allow large fifteenth-
century vessels to pass the palisades, ships
were loaded and unloaded on the open waters
of the IJ, where cargo was transshipped into
lighters that carried the goods to the exchange
on the Damrak or, along the canals, to the
city's warehouses and marketplaces. As the
years passed Amsterdam expanded, in the
form of man-made islands, toward the row of
palisades, but this growth occurred gradually.
During this process of expansion, a large zone
evolved between the 'real' harbor front of the
Damrak and the actual site at which transshipment activities were carried out on the IJ.
This zone– with its islands of varying sizes,
palisades, and the bustle of lighters and
rowboats coming and going– had an
extremely informal character.[7]

Amsterdam's seventeenth-century
expansion took place inland, where the ring of
canals, designed as a pleasant residential area
for well-to-do citizens, represented the city's
rejection, so to speak, of the marshy, mist-
filled world of the IJ.

In the second half of the 1800s, when a
modern shipping industry demanded ports
equipped with more advanced machinery and
trains entered the picture, the realization of
Amsterdam's Central Station radically
transformed the mouth of the harbor.
Although the station boosted the prominence
of the Damrak, it also provided the vast port-
related transition zone between the city and
the IJ with a distinct boundary line: the
formal façade of the station marked the area
on one side of this line, while the informal
area on the other side– to the rear of Central
Station, facing the IJ– was marked by an
expanse of water destined to accommodate a
new landscape of piers and ships.

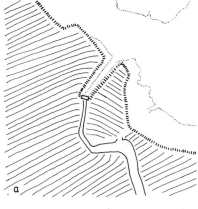

Amsterdam in the Middle Ages: the dam across the Amstel was part of the network of dikes.

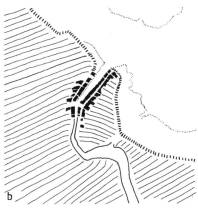

Initial development on opposite sides of the dike.

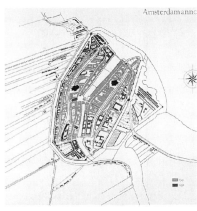

Amsterdam, 1544.

Amsterdam, 1795

## ROTTERDAM: 'LEAPS IN SCALE' MARK RELATION BETWEEN CITY AND PORT

The relation between city and port that began to evolve in Rotterdam in the sixteenth century was entirely different from that found in Amsterdam. Rotterdam's situation – 40 kilometers inland – was a safeguard against the direct rage of the sea, while the protective influence of fortified towns such as Willemstad and Hellevoetsluis, as well as the line of defense formed by the Dutch flood belt, shielded the city against enemy attacks by land.

Prior to the seventeenth century Rotterdam was situated entirely within its system of dikes. The city surrounded the mouths of two fenland rivers, the Rotte and the Schie, whose urban banks were lined with quays. Outside the dikes, where these rivers emptied into the Maas, salt marshes and flats formed an extension to the port: an area in which many ships remained anchored or moored to jetties along the banks. This landscape of marshes and flats formed a natural buffer between the city's dikes and the river, with its currents and alternating tides.

The development of a hard, well-defined harbor front in Rotterdam – a process already apparent in the sixteenth century – and the subsequent merging of city and port were due to several factors.

The first was related to geography: located on the banks of the Maas, Rotterdam offered deep berths to ships moored to its quays, an offer unavailable in Amsterdam. Furthermore, Rotterdam was a stopover on the Amsterdam-Antwerp route, and the river crossing from Katendrecht to Rotterdam was an especially important element of this traffic network. The panoramic view of the city from the left (south) bank of the Maas, as well as from ferries crossing the river, became a promotion point in the 1900s, as evidenced by lyrical descriptions found in travel guides and by paintings of the cityscape.

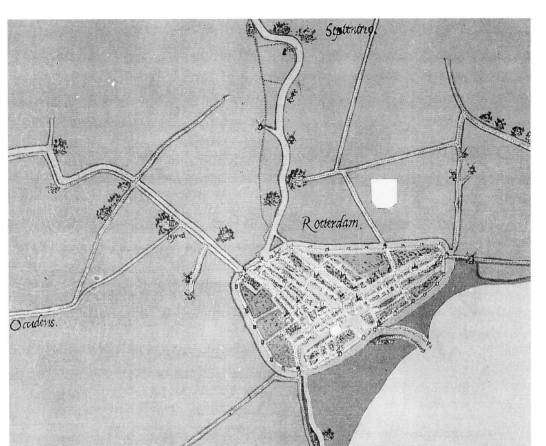

Map of Rotterdam drawn
by Jacob van Deventer,
1562.

The second factor was the erratic development of the port, a situation rooted in external political and economic causes. The first
developmental surge occurred in the sixteenth century, when the United Provinces
fought the Spanish throne in a war for independence. As a result of this war, Rotterdam's
importance as a seaport suddenly experienced
an enormous boost, since Amsterdam's original allegiance to the Spanish king left the
Provinces in need of a reliable port.[8] The
second surge took place in the nineteenth
century, when a boom in industrialization
propelled an ideally located Rotterdam to the
forefront of transshipment activities in the
Netherlands.

A third factor, cultural in nature, was the
way in which the city's bourgeoisie had made
the port into a fascinating urban spectacle, a
process that originated in the seventeenth

century. This factor was to be a leitmotif – far
into the twentieth century – in various urban
planning projects for the expansion and reorganization of both city and port.

From the sixteenth century on, Rotterdam
experienced constant change in the spatial
relationship between city and port, thanks to a
number of erratically occurring 'leaps in scale.'

The first of these leaps took place in the
late 1700s and early 1800s, when within a few
decades the entire city, previously surrounded
by dikes, transferred the heart of its economic
activities to the area beyond the dikes and, in
so doing, more than doubled its territory.

As a result of Rotterdam's abrupt promotion to the status of chief port of the United
Provinces, an extremely rapid and spectacular
expansion of the port transpired during this
period. This expansion was realized by raising

In Rotterdam, both city and port expanded toward the river and over the dikes. Top to bottom: the situation in 1400, 1500, 1600, and 1900.

Above right:
Dikes form an integral part of Rotterdam's urban landscape. The dike in the photograph is the Hilledijk, Rotterdam South, 1994.

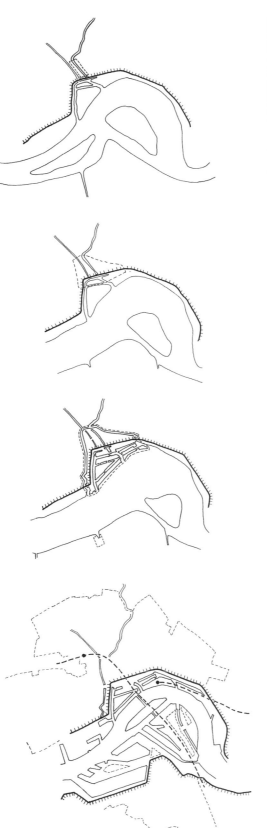

sand flats outside the dikes by a process of dredging and filling, after which the newly created territory became part of the existing city. This vast area of land and water, realized to accommodate future port-related functions, was larger than the area covered by the old city behind the dikes. The new area, however, was to remain outside the dikes, a situation that introduced a distinction between the historical *Landstad*, or *Polderstad* (both referring to the city within the dikes) and the new *Waterstad* (the part of the city outside the dikes).

Originally the distinction between Landstad and Waterstad went hand-in-hand with that between city and port: Waterstad, which represented the domain of the port, included new harbors and quays for loading and unloading ships; warehouses for storing goods; and sites to accommodate all sorts of port-related industry, such as shipyards, sailmakers' workshops, and ropewalks.

Largely because of its peripheral location, the outermost edge of Waterstad, along the river, was reserved initially for the industry that caused the most inconvenience: shipbuilding.

Although the riverbank played no role in the composition of the port, a row of palisades did protect it from enemy attack and from the negative effects of currents and backwash.

Nonetheless, in the course of the seventeenth century merchants and shipowners would also come to see Waterstad as a desirable location for both private residences and office accommodations. The more spaciously organized Waterstad, whose direct connection to the Maas provided its harbors with a constantly renewed flow of water, formed an attractive alternative to the crowded, malodorous Landstad. New occupants either put up with the inconvenience of cellars and ground floors occasionally flooded by overflowing riverbanks or contended with the matter by elevating ground floors to a higher level.

Moreover, the riverside quay also offered a wonderful view of ships moored in the harbors and, in the background, the scenic left bank of the Maas. Certain entrepreneurs managed to sidestep laws that prohibited functions unrelated to shipbuilding at this location by building their homes within the boundaries of their shipyards. The exclusive use of the riverside quay for shipyard activities came to a definite halt in the late 1600s, when the Rotterdam Chamber of the United East India Company decided to build its new headquarters on this quay. An agreement between this organization and the city council provided for the relocation of shipyards to other sites.

This agreement set the stage for a project that would transform the entire island, which lay between the river and Scheepmakershaven, into a distinguished urban façade: a location that would welcome, in the course of the eighteenth century, a long row of office buildings and stately mansions belonging to Rotterdam's most prominent shipping companies and merchant families. The situation on this

Rotterdam's Waterstad (the part of the city outside the dikes). Fragment of a map drawn by Johannes Vou, 1694.

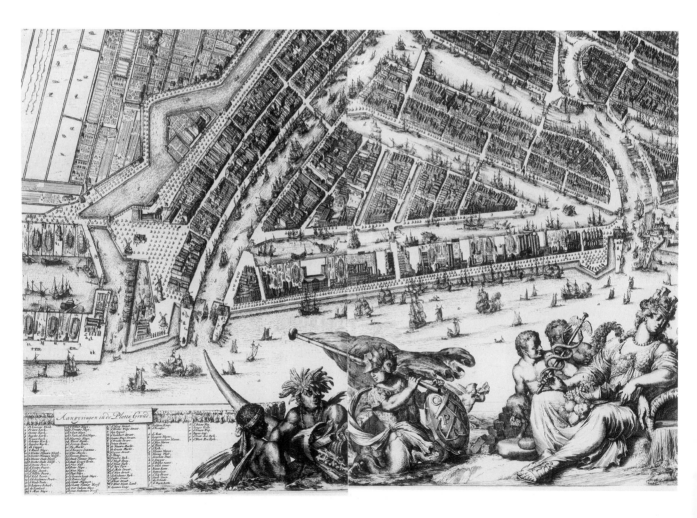

View of Rotterdam's river front, ca. 1800.

land parcel continued here as well.

The Boompjes became even more significant in the nineteenth century, when the military need for defensive palisades disappeared and the introduction of steamships, with their increasingly larger dimensions, called for the construction of new quays. Spacious, easily accessible quays were of particular importance to mailboats, which ran a regular service for both passengers and cargo, and which docked in many island towns in the provinces of Zeeland and South Holland, as well as in the riverside cities of Germany, England, and Northern France. Consequently, the Boompjes, redesigned with mailboats in mind, soon became *the* destination for these and other vessels. Rotterdam's main maritime station was the Boompjes.

The area's significance as 'city station' increased with the arrival of trains, which occasioned the construction of Maas Station on an island on the east side of the Boompjes, between Haringvliet and the river. With this new structure, the Boompjes entered its heyday as Rotterdam's central public area, an era in which it functioned as an attractive urban façade, an esplanade for the strolling public, and a hub of maritime and railroad traffic. In the nineteenth century, the Boompjes was a subject favored by writers and a place cherished as 'the pride and joy of Rotterdam.'[10]

This pride in the Boompjes, and the accompanying outrage at any disaster threatening this quayside area, was demonstrated when the partial collapse of a quay wall proved to be reason enough to have city architect Rose removed from office. Hydraulic engineering was developed in Rotterdam by subjecting the city's marshy, peaty soil to a trial-and-error approach. Quays regularly collapsed, either spontaneously or as a result of stress caused by moored ships or stored cargo. This phenomenon, which appeared all over Rotterdam, was part of the education of hydraulic engineers employed by the Department of Public Works. But when it

island typified the relation between city and port: here an urban waterfront, lined with prestigious residences and office buildings, represented the city, while the true essence of the port was found in the rear, along the quays of Scheepmakershaven, whose shipyards and warehouses had direct access, in most cases, to the mansions and offices 'out front.'

The relation between city and port was organized on the *scale of an individual land parcel*, with an imposing front side for the home or office, and a rear side for the warehouse or other port-related activity.

The quayside area was designed for a pleasant stroll and, owing to a double row of trees, came to be known as the 'Boompjes' (Dutch for 'little trees').[9] The shipyards moved to the newly excavated Zalmhaven on the west side of the city.

These developments represented the city's definitive 'leap' over the dikes. Waterstad was no longer a place reserved exclusively for port and industrial activities, but a blend of city and port that featured Rotterdam's most important public area, the Boompjes: the city now fronted the river. The combination of city and port, of housing and industry, on the scale of an individual

The Boompjes, ca. 1880.

The Boompjes, ca. 1880.

happened to the Boompjes, it was not tolerated: the collapse of a newly built quay in this area in 1854 was seen as an unacceptable blow to Rotterdam's reputation.[11]

The scenic quality of the view of both river *and* city was enhanced in the late 1700s when Rotterdam's first public park, the Oude Plantage, was realized at the curve of the river; visitors to this park were presented with a wonderful panorama that included both river and city.

## PUBLIC SPACE
### IN DUTCH PORT CITIES

If there is a single common denominator that characterized Dutch port cities in a spatial sense, it was the direct combination of port infrastructure and urban public space. The most important harbor quays were also a city's most important public areas, which accommodated a concentration of vital urban functions and the homes of prominent merchant families. Quays were the domain of

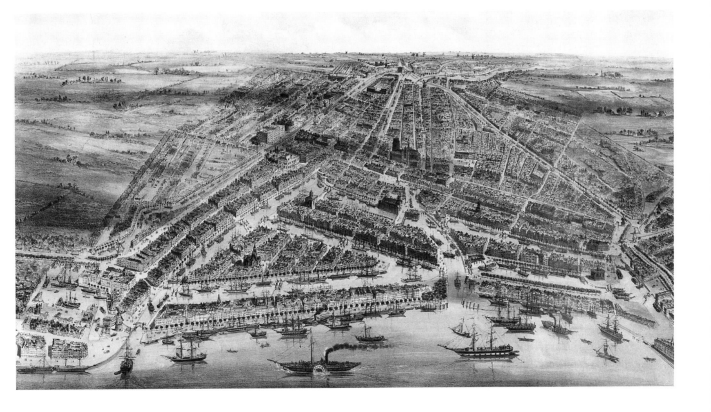

Canelle, 1855. Bird's-eye
view of Rotterdam.

trade, of loading and unloading, of markets,
but they were also an attractive spot for relaxation and enjoyment. This description applied
to the Boompjes in Rotterdam, the Damrak in
Amsterdam, and the Scheldekaaien ('Schelde
Quays') in Antwerp. The design and organization of these quay areas allowed them to fulfill
a dual function: they were broad enough for
storage, transshipment, and trading activities;
and they were lined with rows of trees – as well
as a pedestrian terrace in Antwerp – to accentuate their role as public space.

Admittedly, this combination of functional
and representative qualities was found in
many port cities, but nowhere was it developed more extensively and consistently than
in Dutch seaports. In Barcelona, for example,
the harbor front – renewed in the seventeenth
century – played a chiefly representative and
aesthetic role, and had no significance as a
quay prior to the mid-nineteenth century. In
the early 1900s London experienced a strict
differentiation of port functions along the

Thames, in the vicinity of the old City, and
the more pastoral riverbanks to the west,
promoted as areas of scenic beauty. The waterfronts of American port cities were dominated
almost exclusively by functional principles,
leaving little opportunity for aspects relating
to an attractive public environment.

Rotterdam was perhaps the most extreme
example of the tradition that combined
functional and representative qualities, thanks
to the leading role that the Boompjes played
for nearly two centuries in shaping both
cityscape and city plan.

Later, however, it became more and more
difficult to preserve and strengthen this
combination. In the course of the nineteenth
and twentieth centuries, the physical relationship between city and port has been confronted with an ongoing process of alienation, not
to mention an enormous increase in scale. At
the same time, continual efforts have been,
and are being, made to call attention to the
port and to incorporate it into the design of
the city.

# The Modern Transit Port:
# The Search for a New Symbiosis of Port and City

In seventeenth- and eighteenth-century Rotterdam, the shift that the city made toward the water was a modest overture when compared with events that were to take place in the following centuries. The second 'leap in scale,' which occurred in the 1800s, created a new relationship between city and port.

While the urban areas of Amsterdam and Antwerp began turning away from the water in the late nineteenth century, Rotterdam tried constantly, throughout the nineteenth and twentieth centuries, to orient the city toward river and port, in an attempt to continue the trend that began in the 1600s with the realization of the Boompjes.

The shift that took place in the relation between city and river after the Boompjes had been completed, however, was simply the first in a series of shifts that would continue to affect the way the two related in the centuries to come.

Nineteenth-century changes in technology and economics, as well as the dynamic manner in which Thorbecke's government created conditions for the realization of the Nieuwe Waterweg ('New Waterway'), propelled Rotterdam, in particular, into an unprecedentedly favorable position.

Northwestern Europe's port cities made a comeback, ending high on the list of world ports, but this success was not due to their prominent position as markets and depots linking Northern and Southern Europe with the colonies, but to their new role as ports for the transshipment of a flow of goods to and from developing industrial areas in England, North America, Germany, Northern France, and Wallonia. Rivers now functioned as more than simply protection and a route to the sea; of special value was their connection to the new hinterland.

The new status of these ports had little to do with the power and significance of the cities themselves, but with location: they were situated at crucial points along important new transportation networks, points at which goods had to be transshipped from one type of conveyance to another. The job of the modern transit port was fairly simple: incoming goods no longer had to be stored, processed, or traded, but transshipped as fast as possible and sent on their way.

It was as if a switch had been flicked in the relation between city and port. Although the two had been closely interwoven in Amsterdam, Rotterdam, and Antwerp – albeit differently in each case – the new transit port left no room for this sort of intimacy. In the best scenario, a ship stopped alongside the quay, barely 'grazing' the city, was loaded or unloaded, and quickly sailed on.

Modern nineteenth-century ports were geared totally to this new demand, which led to a brand-new relationship between city and port. This was to assume a different form in each of these cities, however. Once again, a crucial factor was the position of the dike system, but not as crucial as the position of another new phenomenon: the railroad station.

As previously explained, the construction of Amsterdam's Central Station – on the site of the former harbor mouth of the Damrak – was a highly significant intervention, which provided a new stimulus to the Damrak and, consequently, reinforced its central position within the city. At the same time, the construction of railroad lines on the banks of the IJ represented a definitive spatial separation of city and port. In the nineteenth century new harbors built on elongated artificial islands in the IJ – on opposite sides of the railroad

tracks – could not be seen from the city.

Even though the new station extended the fundamental structure of the city, the relationship with the port and the wide expanse of the IJ was broken. Referring to this spatial separation as definitive is hardly an exaggeration: for over a century not one effort of any importance was made to address the issue of the spatial relationship between the city and the IJ.

A different process was going on in Antwerp, where the main station on the east side of the city was built outside the former ramparts. This led to a development referred to as the 'toppling of the city.'[12] No longer were the Scheldekaaien seen as the central urban axis; this position was now held by the route from the Grote Markt, via Meir and De Keyserlei, to the station. A variety of important urban functions arose along this route, including department stores, banks, movie theaters, an opera house, snack bars, and *grand-cafés*.

A second facility, South Station, was built, together with a new dock, on the site of a former fortress. The result was a heavier flow of traffic between docks on the north side of the city and South Station; this traffic moved along new boulevards (the Leien) laid out to replace the old ramparts.

In the meantime, the Scheldekaaien had proved to be relatively unsuitable for modern transshipment activities. The Port of Antwerp dealt mainly with the transshipment of mixed cargo from ships to trains and other overland conveyances. An expansion of the system of docks on the north side of Antwerp and, consequently, the removal of port activities from the city seemed to be a better solution. The Scheldekaaien thus faded into the margin, with respect to both city and port.

One thing and another led to a shift in the spatial organization of Antwerp and to the city's alienation from both the river and the new harbors. In Antwerp, as in Amsterdam, more than one hundred years passed before a serious attempt was made to address the issue

Rose's concept of
Rotterdam: the urban
front faces the river, while
the port lies to the rear.

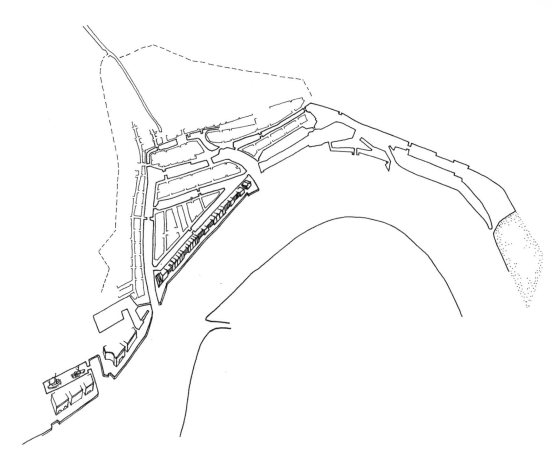

of the spatial relationship between the city
and the river.[13]

### THE ROTTERDAM DILEMMA:
### WEST OR SOUTH?

The extraordinary aspect of nineteenth- and
twentieth-century development in Rotterdam was the constantly changing structure of
both port and city, an aspect that included
one effort after another to orient the city
toward the river and the port. All these efforts
led to repeated shifts in the fundamental
structure of the city. Rotterdam can justifi-
ably speak of its dynamic relation between
city and port.

    The dynamics of this connection can be
divided into four stages.

    The first stage covered the late 1800s and

early 1900s, a period that began with an interwoven city and port – a relationship that
included the *representation* of the city on the
river – and ended with a far more self-
sufficient port and a city oriented toward the
water. The second stage occurred from the
1920s to the 1940s, a period featuring an
attempt to transform the city into an organic
entity. The postwar-reconstruction era represented the third stage, which centered
on the monumentality of the vast expanse
of the river. Perhaps the best description of
the fourth, or present, stage is the search for
something that will give the river new significance for the city.

    The question is: what direction should be
emphasized in planning the growth of the
city in relation to the growth of the port –
south or west? This issue has emerged as an
unavoidable dilemma in the design of nearly

every city plan presented in the nineteenth and twentieth centuries. Should city and port leap over the Maas, or should the two expand along the river in the direction of the sea? And what about the position of the city center with respect to these expansion areas – should it be oriented toward a westerly or a southerly expansion?

The repeated shifts in the main structure of the city are rooted in perpetual doubt and in changing opinions regarding this dilemma.

### DESIGNING THE STRUCTURE OF THE CITY

From the early 1800s on, Rotterdam became more and more constrained by its own urban boundaries. An increase in port activities led to a constant shortage of mooring space in Waterstad, as well as to a growing number of immigrants and the resulting crowded conditions. Between 1795 and 1840 the city's population rose from 53,000 to 78,000, and Polderstad (the part of the city within the dikes) recorded a density of one thousand inhabitants to a hectare.[14] This situation became extremely grave between 1832 and 1834, when a total of three cholera epidemics swept the city.

The biggest problem was the lack of water management in the city: watercourses in Polderstad were supervised by the Schieland Polder Board, which drained them only when water levels in the polder demanded it.

In 1839 W. N. Rose, 'First Lieutenant of the Engineering Corps and Professor of Civil Engineering at the Military Academy of Breda,' was appointed city architect and director of Public Works. Rose's contribution to the urban planning development of the city lay in two important proposals. The first called for the construction of a 5-kilometer-long ring of canals (and adjacent avenues) around the city, which would free Rotterdam from the authority of the Schieland Polder

Board and allow the city to regulate its own water management. And the second was an expansion plan that would allow the city to grow to the south as well as to the west, a scheme that offered relief to both growing population and thriving port activities.[15]

Rose's belt of canals introduced a new urban planning phenomenon into the city, which mixed necessity with pleasure. He took the prosaic function of these canals – designed as a drainage/sewage system – and combined it with a concept of canals as 'tasteful environs' lined with avenues for 'elegant strolls.' Of special note was Westersingel, which linked the zoological garden (Diergaarde) to the river; the design of this prominently positioned route was based on work by the Zochers, well-known garden and landscape architects. Land along the avenue was divided into large parcels intended for stately residences and villas.

Rose designated both Cool Polder, on the west side of the city, and Feijenoord, on the left bank of the Maas, as new urban expansion areas. These were to carry on the principle of the seventeenth-century Waterstad: a system of islands, intended for housing and other urban functions, surrounded by watercourses that could be used to expand the port.

Rose transcended the issue of whether to direct urban expansion toward the west or toward the south: the city was to grow in both directions, and both expansion areas were to continue the age-old principle of a fusion of city and port. In designing the area on the left bank, Rose tried quite literally to extend the seventeenth-century Waterstad. One of his designs depicted the island of Feijenoord transformed into a system of islands, directly linked to Waterstad, with the main watercourse of the river projected south of Feijenoord. (See illustration on page 307.)

With the expansion of Cool Polder in mind, the municipality of Rotterdam bought a piece of land from neighboring Delfshaven, which stipulated, however, that this land was not to be used for industrial purposes. Even though authorities hoped for a future withdrawal of this stipulation, they decided to use the land, in the meantime, to lay out a park. More than a century has passed, but the continuingly temporary character of this facility can still be heard in its generic name: 'The Park.' Thus mid-nineteenth-century Rotterdam had two riverside parks, on both sides of the city.

Rose's expansion plan for Cool Polder was based on his earlier, two-part plan, realized in the 1850s: the 'First New Work,' which consisted of two large building blocks on the south side of Zalmhaven; and the 'Second New Work' in little Muize Polder – just inside the municipal borders of Rotterdam – which included three large building blocks and two harbors, Veerhaven and Westerhaven, at right angles to each other.

Rose's designs were a formalization of the seventeenth- and eighteenth-century typology of an urban riverside waterfront, with port activities directly to the rear. An extensive system of building regulations prescribed a harmonious, monumental character for exterior walls facing the river and permitted the construction of warehouses only on adjacent rear lots with direct access to the quays of Westerhaven. These regulations applied not only to building lines and heights, but also to matters such as the articulation and color of exterior walls, and the color and pitch of tiled roofs.[16] These 'New Works' along the waterfront represented the continuation and perfection of a network of monumental public areas lining the Maas.

Thanks in part to Rose, a policy of public works gradually evolved that combined exigency and enjoyment. Canals and new expansion areas in the port were designed to fully serve the primary functions of these projects – drainage/sewage and port activities, respectively – but such functions did not dominate the cityscape. The city was enriched with a network of public areas that possessed qualities independent of their primary functions. Even if Westersingel were no longer to operate as a drainage canal, and if the New Works stopped functioning as transshipment quays, these areas would continue to enhance city life. For that matter, the New Works did lose their position as port facilities shortly after they were realized. The type of port city that Rose designed – a newer version of the seventeenth-century Waterstad – was not an adequate answer to problems presented by new shipping and transshipping technologies. Westerhaven and Veerhaven turned out to be too confining for large, nineteenth-century, ocean-going vessels; in less than twenty years, Westerhaven was ready to be filled in. (See page 306.) Despite the loss of this function, however, the monumental quays of Westerhaven and the area around Veerhaven remain essential to Rotterdam.

Two important principles formed the basis for achieving this kind of quality and autonomy in the design of public space: extra space and clear differentiation.

*Extra space* meant that designs were to provide the urban areas involved with dimensions larger than those strictly necessary for the primary function. This extra space created the conditions needed to assimilate the primary function, so to speak, into the design of a canal or harbor.

The *differentiation* and materialization of designs for new public areas pushed the primary function even farther into the background. Often a row of trees was used to draw a distinction between the shipping zone, for loading and unloading cargo, and the urban traffic zone. This row of trees also emphasized the spatial coherence of the quay as a whole, as well as its significance as a border separating the urban landscape from the waterfront. The best example of such an area is the Boompjes.

Extra space also meant added value in a literal sense, because spacious canal and quay

The new river front of
Rotterdam: view of
*Het Nieuwe Werk* ('The
New Work') from the
Katendrecht ferry
landing, ca. 1870.

in a southerly direction. Businessman and councilman Pincoffs, whose Rotterdam Trading Association had formed a kind of public-private partnership with the municipality for the purpose of developing the new port area, played a leading role in the realization of harbor works on the left bank. When the Rotterdam Trading Association went bankrupt in 1879, its demise was encouraging to those who supported the idea of a more autonomous municipal government prepared to take responsibility and show initiative in making future plans for the expansion of city and port.

The new director of Public Works, G.J. de Jongh, was the personification of this new policy.

areas provided a residential environment attractive to the city's upper classes. Profits from the sale of land were used to finance the construction of new public works. Rose's attempts to expand Cool Polder, however, ground to a halt after the realization of the New Works, partly because the new harbor basins were soon found to be unsuitable for modern ships, and partly because Rose's plans required the annexation of the neighboring municipality of Delfshaven, a step not favored by the city council.

The design for Feijenoord, on the other hand, was reintroduced in the 1860s, when a new railroad line between Rotterdam and Antwerp necessitated the reorganization of this island. Having been asked to design a plan for this area, Rose, now chief architect of the central government, produced a version of his plan for Cool Polder. The new plan for Feijenoord presented a district of mixed port and urban functions, which included monumental quays and squares along the river front. By means of a central axis and a main square (currently Stieltjes Square), Rose oriented the whole plan toward his conception of the city center: the St. Laurens Church.

Initially, for practical reasons, top priority was given to the growth of both city and port

## A NEW TYPE OF PORT CITY: ORIENTING THE CITY TOWARD THE NEW TRANSIT PORT

De Jongh believed it was his job to create a new infrastructure of public works, the nature of which was to be far more extensive than anything previously experienced in his department. The first item of note was a spectacular increase in scale in the design of new harbor basins and other sites intended for port activities. Port areas were no longer restricted to quayside strips accommodating warehouses; they now included entire piers and spits.

A second change greatly augmented the department's activities in the port area — work formerly limited, for the most part, to the design and organization of street plans and quays. In developing the new port area on the left bank of the Maas, the department expanded its activities considerably. After its civil engineers had designed and built an infrastructure consisting of harbors, quays, bridges, and roads, the Department of Public Works also took responsibility for the design, realization, and management of warehouses,

Expansion plan for Cool Polder, G.J. de Jongh, 1887.

entrepôts, harbor cranes, coaling stations, dry docks, ferries, and the like: in short, a complete arsenal of port facilities.[17]

Under the leadership of De Jongh, Rotterdam annexed Delfshaven, as well as Charlois and IJsselmonde on the left bank of the Maas, allowing city and port to expand both to the west and across the river.

Although the downfall of the Rotterdam Trading Association was largely the result of financial mismanagement attributed to Pincoffs, it was clear to De Jongh that part of the culpability also lay in the design of Rose's long, narrow harbor basins, which failed to meet the demands of modern transshipment activities.

De Jongh introduced an element of differentiation into designs for the south bank of the river and for the westerly urban

expansion area: large-scale development of the port would take place chiefly on the south bank, while the urban expansion area to the west was designated as the new residential and administrative center of the city.

The future of Rotterdam's port seemed to lie firmly in the transshipment of bulk goods: ore, coal, oil, and grain en route to the German hinterland. The most efficient transshipment method took place 'in midstream': cargo was unloaded from an incoming ship and loaded directly onto a barge while neither vessel was moored to the quay. With this operation in mind, De Jongh positioned his newly designed Rijnhaven and Maashaven parallel – rather than at right angles – to the river, with the entrance downstream to allow large ships to maneuver in and out with ease and to prevent the harbors from freezing over.

These harbors, which completed the transformation of an area now known as the 'Kop van Zuid,' produced an entirely new 'portscape': that of the transit-port city. Residential neighborhoods soon filled leftover pieces of land in this archipelago of piers, spits, and islands; in most cases, residents, shops, and businesses found in these neighborhoods had direct ties to modern harbor life.[18]

As De Jongh continued his development of Rotterdam as a residential city, he focused primarily on the expansion of Cool Polder. De Jongh believed that the heart of the city was shifting toward the west, and he envisioned Cool Polder as the new city center, with a new public- administration complex that included city hall and modern accommodations for the Department of Public Works.

De Jongh introduced a new kind of relation between city and port, an interconnection based not only on representative, monumental quays, but also on an orientation of main urban elements toward the river.

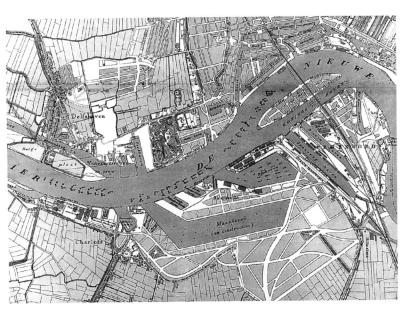

The new street plan that De Jongh designed for Cool Polder was based on two principal lines. The first, stately Heemraadssingel, a broadened version of Rose's canal-avenue design, was to be the main north-south connection and a beltway linking northern residential districts to the harbors. The second, elegant Mathenesserlaan, was designed as an exit route for traffic leaving the city in a westerly direction. The standard breadth of main avenues in this plan was 40 meters, which provided room for through-traffic lanes and service roads for local traffic, as well as space for a potential freight line, the type of function that De Jongh felt should never be ignored in a transport-oriented city like Rotterdam. As the city's new central boulevard, however, Heemraadssingel, which was to feature two prominent squares, would be twice as broad. A new central urban square (currently Heemraads Square), envisioned as the core around which a new city hall and other administrative buildings would rise, was projected at the intersection of Heemraadssingel and Mathenesserlaan. The other square was to be realized at the north end of Heemraadssingel. This square would bring

*Plan for urban expansion and new harbors on the left bank of the Maas, G.J. de Jongh, 1898.*

a fresh aesthetic quality to the city by accentuating the blend created by the residential character of this district and Rotterdam's function as port and transport-oriented city. This square, in the form of a gigantic viaduct over the railroad tracks, was to be the culmination of the public-space network. As De Jongh lyrically proclaimed in his explanatory notes: 'The panorama will be splendid from every angle … with the hustle and bustle of trains arriving and departing… In the south, one looks across Heemraadssingel, over 100 meters wide, to where the tops of ships' masts and smoke-stacks reveal the location of the Maas, bearer of Rotterdam's merchant fleet.'[19]

Ultimately, the heart of the city did not shift as De Jongh had anticipated. Although the city council did step in and take the initiative when plans were needed for developing the vast port area on the left bank of the Maas, acting as the authoritative body and implementing the compulsory purchase of private property on a large scale, that same city council was far more reluctant to take on the development of a residential area in Cool Polder. De Jongh's street plan was approved, but the municipality was unwilling to complete the project, which was left wholly to private developers. Thus Rotterdam West was developed one step at a time and haphazardly, according to the property lines of whatever site a particular developer may have acquired.[20] The street plan was also realized in bits and pieces, as streets were filled in where needed. Within the framework of this fragmentary development, a thrifty city council rejected both the radical relocation of administrative buildings and the raised square above the railroad, which was considered an unnecessary investment. The council also tightened the purse strings in the case of Heemraadssingel, only part of which was to boast the generous dimensions in De Jongh's original design.

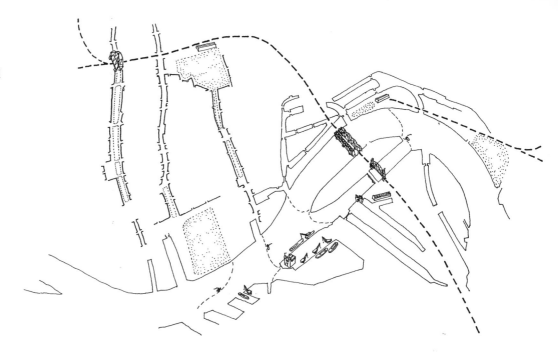

Rotterdam according to De Jongh: the port along the river and the city with its monumental boulevards oriented toward the river.

All things considered, however, the realization of Rotterdam West represented a major urban expansion project based on a new relationship between the city's residential and transport-related functions. This relationship found expression in the blend of housing and transportation incorporated in the main elements of the public-space network, and in the orientation of these elements toward new harbor complexes.

ECONOMY AND CULTURE —
COMBINING NECESSITY AND
PLEASURE

Designs for the new port area on the south bank and for the new residential quarter on the west side were rooted in De Jongh's desire to provide the modern port city with monumental allure.

De Jongh saw the emphasis on the design of a good infrastructure of public works not only as a technical necessity, but also as a matter of an aesthetic typical of Rotterdam, for 'an expansion of a trade center like Rotterdam calls for totally different things than that of a luxurious city like The Hague.'[21]

De Jongh also pursued a combination of necessity and pleasure in his design for the port area on the left bank of the Maas. He used the same principles as Rose had: excess and meticulous differentiation. He applied these principles to new urban boulevards, such as Mathenesserlaan and Heemraadssingel, the breadth of which allowed for a freight line to be added at a later date; but even without the presence of adjacent railroad tracks, these streets displayed well-balanced dimensions. The principles were applied to new expansion areas in the port as well. A good example is the plan for Rijnhaven and surroundings. For this area, realized to fulfill a basically utilitarian function, De Jongh's design included not only the shape of the harbor, the breadth of the quays, and building lines for architectural purposes, but also a system of footpaths and little parks created to lend access to the area and to make it attractive to those strolling by.

Ultimately, the new monumentality found in De Jongh's designs was not limited to public works. Developers involved in private building initiatives were eager to imitate this new monumentality, and the result was the emergence of a 'civic culture.'[22]

As early as the final decades of the nineteenth century, great concern was voiced by various groups alarmed about the adverse effects of the large-scale growth of Rotterdam on the city's cultural climate. A major consideration was the population boom, expressed by an average of ten thousand new inhabitants a year between 1890 and 1910. This great increase in population represented a genuine culture shock for the city, a phenomenon later described most aptly by Bouman and Bouman in *De groei van de grote werkstad* (The Growth of the Big Working City).[23] Studies such as this – as well as countless pamphlets, articles, and books written from the late 1800s on – related not only the poverty and social misery of a multitude of working-class people who had migrated to the harbors of Rotterdam to seek their fortunes, but also a great concern over the lack of a cultural environment. Newspaper columnist M. J. Brusse, one of the most prolific and well-known authors writing on this subject,[24] once commented ironically, 'And then I wonder: ARE there actually public figures in Rotterdam?'[25]

Besides being concerned about the sociocultural effects of new urban development, people were also worried about how the transformation of the city would influence the cityscape. Procrastination relating to the construction of a cross-river connection and a railroad line, and to the expansion of the port, was not for nothing. Every major intervention into the city was accompanied by heated discussions and countless publications issued by those for and against such projects, the subject of which invariably was an impaired cityscape and the implied cultural drain (the antis' argument) versus the economic necessity of such a project (the pros' argument). The construction of the cross-river connection (Willems Bridge), as well as of railroad bridges, was a highlight of these debates. Advocates of the new interventions were constantly forced to look for alternatives, since those out to preserve the proud waterfront of the Boompjes and the venerable Oude Haven were numerous and powerful.[26]

De Jongh added a new twist to this debate by suggesting that efforts to make Rotterdam into 'a luxurious city like The Hague' had little relevance. De Jongh was interested in neither economy nor culture, but in a combination of the two: in other words, the economy of Rotterdam *was* the culture of the city. In his eyes, necessity and pleasure were one and the same, a concept he stressed in the design of avenues that provided space for future railroad tracks, and in the creation of 'splendid panoramas' that included railroad yards and ships' masts.

The modern port and transportation were to form the core of a culture unique to Rotterdam. This was an idea that captured the fancy of Rotterdam entrepreneurs and which led a prominent group of businessmen, intellectuals, and other notables to get seriously involved in the vicissitudes of the city and to enter into a closely cooperative relationship with politicians and other official administrators. The 'civic culture' thus created was based mainly on an ideological consensus and on informal networks; throughout the period that this 'basis' existed – from the turn of the century until circa 1960 – civic culture refrained from assuming an institutionalized form.[27] The objective of the prominent group involved in the spatial evolution of Rotterdam was to mold the city's economic, social, and

Expansion plan for Cool
Polder and Feijenoord,
W.N. Rose, 1858.

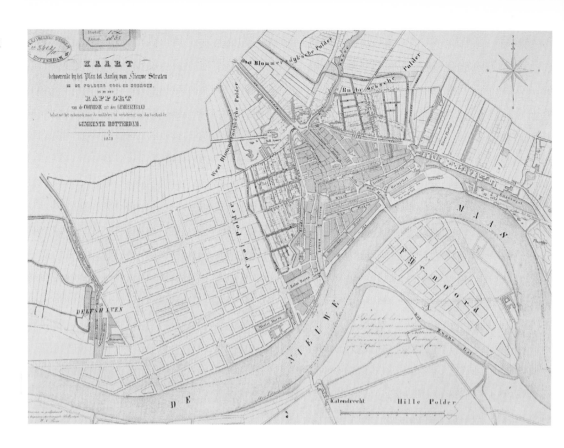

Harbor front of *Het
Nieuwe Werk* ('The New
Work'): Westkade, 1995.
Photomontage by
Piet Rook.

Alternative expansion plan for Feijenoord, W.N. Rose, 1864. By reorienting the riverbed toward the south, Rose gave the design the character of an expansion plan for the area known as Waterstad, on the right bank of the Maas.

Rotterdam in 1938: the old city center and, in the background, the new harbor landscape of the Kop van Zuid.

cultural developments into a harmonious, coherent entity.

Many members of this group would make names for themselves as initiators of new experiments in the area of working-class housing; as administrators of countless foundations aimed at improving the social and cultural aspects of urban life; and as founders, curators, and directors of museums, schools, hospitals, zoo, and the like.[28]

The city and the image it presented – the cityscape – were seen as the chief exponents of a harmonious coexistence of economic, cultural, and social developments.

A personage with close ties to the concept of civic culture was M. Mees, chairman of the board of the Holland America Line and, in 1900, the man who commissioned C. B. van der Tak to design new headquarters for the company on the Wilhelminapier. Van der Tak, the former director of Public Works (prior to De Jongh) was known best as the designer of the Willems Bridge.

Designing an 'image' for the new harbor landscape was a serious task, which lay in the hands of Rotterdam architects such as Brinkman, Van der Vlugt, Van den Broek, Bakema, and Maaskant.[29]

The system they and others designed included large harbor basins, piers, spits, quays, waterfront streets, and bridges, which together formed the framework of a new, monumental portscape to which individual buildings were to make their own contributions, even though neither the architectonic appearance nor programmatic realization of such buildings was established by the urban plan.

For a long time the core of the new urban landscape had been formed, to a great degree, by the area on the left bank of the

Maas, opposite the seventeenth-century Waterstad, together with bridges spanning the river. While Waterstad, with its Boompjes as the center of attraction, had been the hub of the seventeenth- and eighteenth-century commercial port city, in the transit-port city of the 1800s and early 1900s, this role was fulfilled by the Kop van Zuid.

The 'bridge' linking the two harbor areas – Waterstad and the Kop van Zuid – was more than simply a number of stationary cross-river connections; it also incorporated the construction of Rotterdam's first 'sky-scraper': the nine-story office building known as 'the White House.' Situated at the edge of Oude Haven, this tall building offered a view – from the roof garden – of the new urban landscape of the port city on the left bank of the Maas. The White House, product of a private initiative, was the culmination, both literally and figuratively, of the fusion of port and city, of public works and private enterprise.

# 3 Modernism in the Port City: A Dualistic Relationship Between City and Port

The duality of Rotterdam's city and port, a self-evident and culture-determining principle of urban development in the De Jongh era, became an increasingly important topic in the period following World War I, which eventually led to a new leap in scale in the city-port relationship.

Although civic culture strongly supported the duality of city and port, firm opposition to an overintense entanglement of the two still existed. Arguments involved in the debate focused on sociocultural, urban planning, and logistic issues. The sociocultural aspect pertained to a continuing concern about the influence of harbor life on urban culture. Many saw a uniquely cosmopolitan charm in the unconventional nature of life in harbor districts, in the comings and goings of seamen and dockers. But others were thoroughly convinced that activities on the waterfront would have a disorderly, subversive effect on the development of life in the city.[30]

Urban planning opposition to the entanglement of city and port was increasing as well. In his history of Rotterdam in the twentieth century, Van Ravesteyn – prominent notary, councilman, and historian, and thus a key figure in the city's civic culture – mentioned objections to large harbor basins penetrating deep into the land, and to railroad lines running straight through the city and thus spawning an incoherent series of residential neighborhoods.[31]

Another important argument pointed to the prediction, already voiced in the 1920s, that further expansion of the port in a westerly direction was inevitable. If the city unquestioningly followed the development of the port, Rotterdam would become a linear city, composed of a long row of harbor basins interspersed with fragmented housing districts.

The development of a coherent urban layout, which would require extra attention to be given to Rotterdam's residential function, was seen more and more as a separate task, demanding specialized knowledge. In 1926 a new division was added to Public Works, and in 1931 this division became an independent agency: the Department of Urban Development.

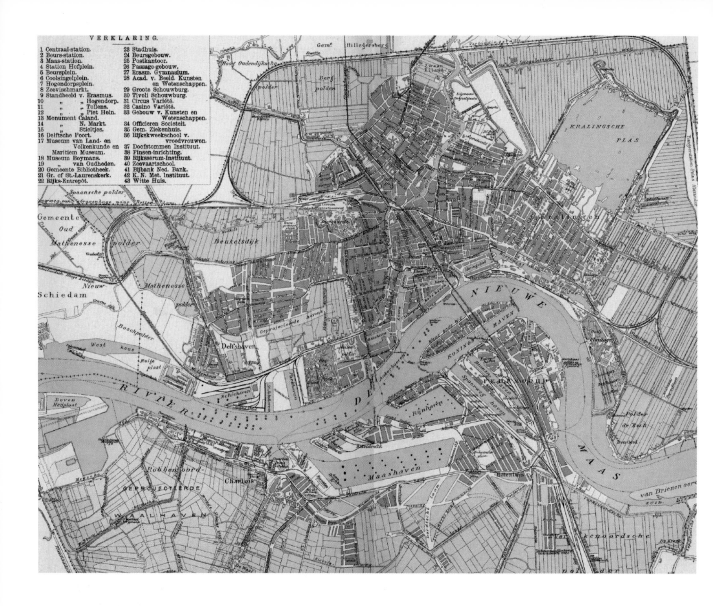

Above: De Jongh's Rotterdam. City map, ca.1910.

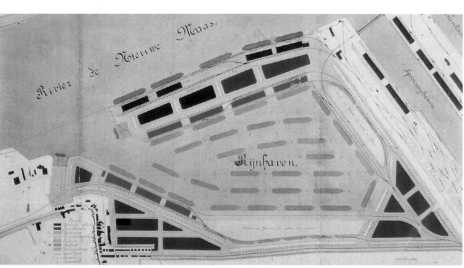

Plan for the construction of Rijnhaven, G.J. de Jongh, 1893.

Above: Bird's-eye view of
harbors on the left bank of
the Maas, as seen from the
south. Heliogravure by
E. Hesmert, 1904.

Headquarters of the
Holland America Line.
Architect: C.B. van der
Tak, 1901. Photograph by
Cas Oorthuys, 1959.

The 1920s also saw an increasing number of protests against the growing entanglement of city and port emerge from the world of port-related industry.

A major exponent of the call for a more autonomous development of the port and its commercial interests was a dissertation published by J.Ph. Backx in 1929.[32] At that time Backx was employed by Thomsen, Rotterdam's largest port-related organization and the company that would make him its director in the 1930s. After World War II Backx also became chairman of Shipping Association South (an interest group representing Rotterdam's shipping industry). He argued that developments in shipping, which included increasingly larger ships, and in transshipment technology were advancing so rapidly that the port should be renewed and expanded on a continual basis, a situation that made the development and management of the port too complex an issue to be left to the Department of Public Works, which had many other matters to deal with as well. Port-related industries were facing spatial problems caused by both a lack of attention to, and too little understanding of, the specific needs involved. Backx confirmed that the main transshipment activity in Rotterdam, measured in tonnage, was indeed the transshipment of bulk goods, but he also pointed out that, despite De Jongh's earlier hypothesis, the amount of mixed cargo transshipped had increased significantly and needed far more room on the quays, not to mention efficient road and rail connections.

In comparing the ports of Rotterdam, Antwerp, and Hamburg, Backx came to the conclusion that Rotterdam was the victim of 'an organizational error: just as in Hamburg and Antwerp, management of the port should be made independent and should be centralized.'[33]

Even more important was his observation that a one-sided orientation toward nothing but transit traffic provided Rotterdam's urban economy with a highly unstable basis. To begin with, transit traffic held little economic potential; any capital involved did not 'stick to the city.' Then, too, transit traffic relied too heavily on the hinterland. Backx argued for more emphasis on the development of a Rotterdam with its own trade center and its own industrial complex, perhaps with companies set up to process goods arriving in port for transshipment. Armed with its own trade center, Rotterdam – rising international hub of freight transport – would be capable of playing a more independent role.[34]

In the decades that followed, Backx's dissertation was to set the tone for Rotterdam's new policy on the port. Both the establishment of an autonomous Municipal Port Authority in 1932 and, in the postwar era, an accent on developing the petrochemical industry were results of a new way of thinking about the port, which Backx introduced in this study.

Although he made a case for *physical* distance between city and port, Backx believed that in a *mental* sense the urban community should become more involved in affairs surrounding the port. In the 1930s, '40s, and '50s, Backx was a pivotal figure in Rotterdam's civic culture, especially with respect to his efforts to solidify the spatial relationship between city and river.

This change in policy, which reflected a new approach to the relation between city and port, produced a new spatial orientation: city and port not only developed as separate spatial entities; they also turned away from harbor areas on the Kop van Zuid.

Both the Department of Urban Development and the Port Authority began shifting their activities to areas outside the Kop van Zuid. The Port Authority concentrated on new developments to the west: first the Vierhaven Area and Merwehaven on the right bank of the Maas, along with the enormous Waalhaven on the left bank, and later the vast postwar expansion project that included Botlek, Europoort, and the Maas Plain.

Urban Development, under the leadership of W. G. Witteveen (who headed the department, eventually as its director, from 1926 to 1944), focused on developing an 'organic city' that was to surround the historic city center, concentrically, on both sides of the river. Traffic and transportation were to continue to play leading roles, but specifically in harmony with park verdure and architecture. The main focus of urban planning operations shifted during this period from the monumentality of public works à la De Jongh to the development of a coherent cityscape of traffic infrastructure, mass-produced housing, and open space.

One of Witteveen's most significant manifestoes was an urban route, featuring tunnels, realized in the 1930s. The construction of a new, stationary, cross-river connection on the west side of the city was based on requests from port-related companies for a connection between the new Vierhaven Area on the right bank of the Maas and, across the river, Waalhaven. Witteveen combined their request with one that had been around even longer: the desire for a new, interlocal, overland connection between The Hague and Antwerp, via Rotterdam. In his plans for the route through the western part of the city, Witteveen was able to take advantage of De Jongh's spacious designs. Instead of lining the 40-meter-broad 's-Gravendijkwal with a railroad line for freight, Witteveen built a four-lane highway with tunneled intersections, and he used a tunnel for the cross-river connection as well.[35] Even after the four-lane highway for through traffic had been completed, the design provided space for rows of trees and service roads for local traffic. The whole route – including various overpass junctions, the Maas Tunnel, and two monumen-

tal ventilation buildings on opposite sides of the river – was designed and realized as one coherent architectonic structure.[36]

The significance of this route, which presented the Maas Tunnel as the symbol of a new Rotterdam, was fostered by the publication of *De Maastunnel*, a magazine that not only reported on the progress of building activities surrounding the tunnel, but also called attention to other new urban planning projects.

Witteveen drew much of his inspiration from examples of the park systems and parkways used to lend structure to modern American cities.[37] He proposed the development of a number of 'green wedges,' which were to allow the beauty of the countryside, combined with infrastructure for motorized traffic, to penetrate the center of the city, terminating only at the far end of Westersingel. Witteveen saw this spot, which accommodated the zoological garden and the Delftse Poort Station, as the new city center, but first the zoo had to be relocated to Blijdorp and Maas Station closed down, leaving Delftse Poort as the central station.

Witteveen's plans were a continuation of an earlier scheme, already in operation, to transform Coolsingel into a metropolitan boulevard lined with prominent administrative and commercial buildings, such as city hall, stock exchange, post office, banks, and department stores. The heart of downtown Rotterdam was to encompass the entire zone between 's-Gravendijkwal, the main interlocal highway, and Coolsingel, an urban boulevard bordered by administrative functions and featuring Rotterdam's central station, as well as a green wedge oriented toward the river, linking the city to the water. This area was earmarked specifically for the kinds of businesses that Backx had referred to in his arguments for a new, trade-based economy.

This concept shifted the city center toward the west, but not as far west as the center envisioned by De Jongh thirty years earlier.

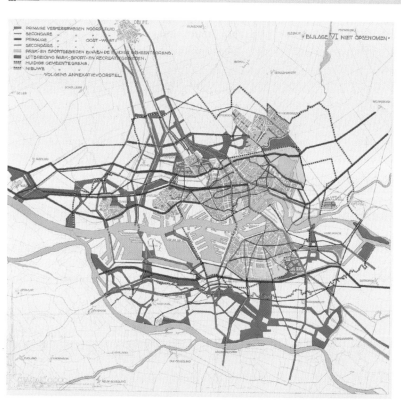

Expansion plan for
Dijkzigt, W.G. Witteveen,
1927.

Preliminary proposal for a system of parkways and green
wedges for Rotterdam and environs, W.G. Witteveen
and L.H.J. Angenot, 1928.

Rotterdam's inner city,
1945.

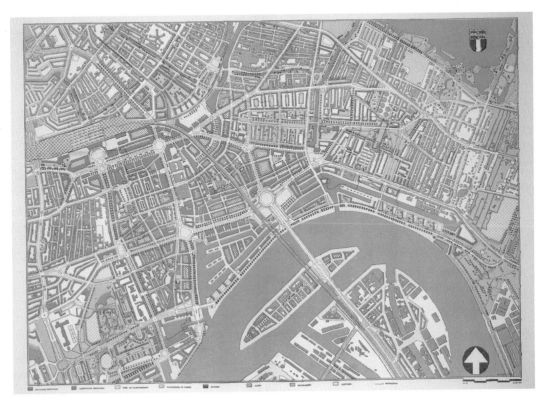

*Basisplan voor de Herbouw
van de Binnenstad*
('Basic Plan for the
Reconstruction of the
Inner City'), 1946.

Route featuring the Maas
Tunnel, Rotterdam West,
1995.

Besides symbolizing a new Rotterdam, the
realization of the Maas Tunnel also placed the
Vierhaven Area, in the west, in a favorable
position in relation to this brand-new interlocal highway, while the Kop van Zuid was
relegated to a more peripheral position with
respect to the main traffic infrastructure.

The Kop van Zuid no longer held an
important function in new urban plans or in
the development of the port. The area was
seen as a legacy of an obsolete concept of the
city *and* of an obsolete concept of the port.

Rotterdam's housing policy treated the
Kop van Zuid, and particularly the peninsula
of Katendrecht, as a dumping ground and an
area of concentration for groups of residents
and people passing through who were regarded as a bad influence on the social and cultural
well-being of the city's population. The area
accommodated emigrant hotels for Eastern
Europeans on their way to America and
dozens of boarding houses for foreign, mostly
Chinese, sailors; by the 1930s Katendrecht had
become Europe's largest Chinatown.[38]

Although the Kop van Zuid was only a few
decades old, planners of the '30s considered it
outmoded and of little significance to a port-
related economy or for purposes of urban
planning and public housing.

The realization of new concepts developed
for city and port in the 1930s gained
momentum after, and perhaps thanks
to, World War II; even the Kop van Zuid
experienced a brief moment of 'rehabilitation'
in the postwar era.

The destruction of Rotterdam's city
center by German bombs in May 1940 was
described, in retrospect, as a blessing in
disguise. 'Do you realize, Rotterdammer,
that many of your most cherished memories
of that which was lost during those days in
May adhere to the very things that were,
plainly seen, nothing but the inadequacies
of our old city?' The inadequacies referred to
in this 1946 brochure on the *Basisplan voor
de Herbouw van de Binnenstad* ('Basic Plan
for the Reconstruction of the Inner City')
included Polderstad's crowded and impoverished neighborhoods, which Rose had
deplored a century earlier, as well as a poor
urban planning structure, which affected
the whole central urban area – both Polderstad and Waterstad – and prevented the
inner city from rapidly evolving into a
modern trade center. Among various new
plans for the city center commissioned by
Witteveen before the war, the one that got
the most publicity was a design by J. Wils
for the reorganization of the zoological
garden site next to Delftse Poort Station.
The bombardment had removed the
problem posed by Polderstad in the blink of
an eye and thus facilitated the development
of a new city.

The devastation of the Boompjes, the
pride of Waterstad, was lamented by many,
but official propaganda underplayed this
loss, since it freed the way for an intervention proposed in the 1930s: the relocation
of the city's main dike, which ran from
Hoogstraat to Oostzeedijk, to a site be-

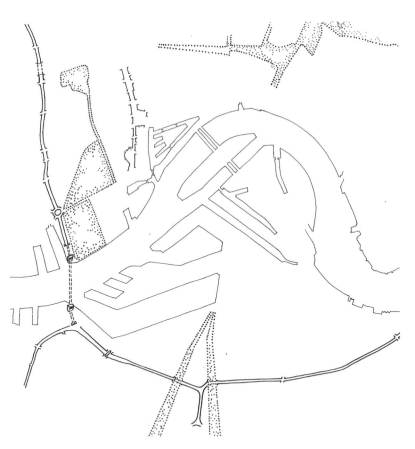

Rotterdam according to Witteveen: green wedges link the city to the (river) landscape, and the route featuring the Maas Tunnel is the main connection between the city center and the new interlocal network of highways.

tween the Boompjes and the Nieuwe Plantage. High water levels, followed by constant flooding in Waterstad, had prompted increasing demands for relocating the dike in the 1930s. Time after time, such demands had run into two objections: irreversible damage to the historic urban façade of the Boompjes, and railroad interests represented by Maas Station.

Aided by this prehistory, Witteveen was able to present a comprehensive reconstruction plan to the city council less than a month after the bombardment. The plan was founded on considerations that had already surfaced in prewar debates: a reorganized railroad network in the city could operate without Maas Station, allowing the main dike to be moved closer to the riverbank. Ultimately, this intervention would have far more serious consequences

for the relation between city and river than anyone could have imagined in the 1940s.

In his continued development of the plan, Witteveen emphasized the need to control the architectonic image presented by buildings lining the streets of the new city's chief structuralizing areas. This aspect of the plan had been the exact cause of Witteveen's earlier conflict with several 'captains of industry,' whose obstinate interference with the progress of the reconstruction plan during the war years[39] solidified when they formed a group known as the Inner Circle of the Rotterdam Club.[40]

Their criticism of Witteveen's plan was twofold; they felt that the plan aimed for too *much* coherence between urban planning and architecture, and for too *little* coherence in precisely the areas where it was most needed: the new residential districts. The group – and Backx in particular – also wanted a greater focus on the relation between city and water and, more specifically, between city and port. During the war years Backx published several reports, including two entitled *Rotterdam and Its Port* and *City and Port*, in which he argued for a closer association between people and port with even more conviction than for a spatial fusion of city and port.[41] In 1944 he established 'The Rotterdam Community,' which, claiming to represent the city's residents, concentrated primarily on publishing a series of booklets under the motto: 'How will we build Rotterdam?' One such book – written by H.M. Kraaijvanger and entitled *Hoe zal Rotterdam bouwen?* (How Will Rotterdam Build?) – paid close attention to 'Rotterdam on the river' and conveyed the author's concern about plans for the new dike on the Boompjes. Kraaijvanger believed that Rotterdam was in a position to develop a new relationship with the river, but went on to add: '… not only a grand boulevard along the river, but [a] road

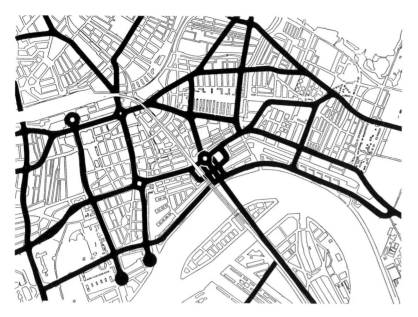

The name most closely associated with the definitive *Basisplan voor de Herbouw van de Binnenstad*, adopted by the city council in 1946, was C. van Traa, who succeeded Witteveen in 1944. The revised reconstruction plan was based on the mutual autonomy of urban design and architectonic design. Too many advance commitments related to the architecture of the new city were considered an impediment to future economic initiatives and, moreover, inconsistent with a free, democratic society. In the words of Van Traa's colleague, S. J. van Embden, the new Rotterdam should not be a city of 'imperious, dazzling, and compelling monumentality,' but a city of 'the freest possible development of the constituent parts without, however, sacrificing the unity of the whole.'[44]

The difference between Witteveen's postwar reconstruction plan and that of Van Traa lay, for the most part, in the position assumed by the urban plan with relation to the social field of influence. Witteveen's plan held an unambiguous position within this field of influence. To Witteveen, designing the city primarily meant designing structuralizing areas in the city: main thoroughfares and green wedges. The design of these elements involved the detailed planning and realization of public space itself, as well as the careful orchestration of the outward appearance of buildings. Good examples of this approach were the combination of 's-Gravendijkwal with the expansion plan for Blijdorp, and the combination of a new neighborhood in the Dijkzigt area with the green wedge to the river. The second aspect – controlling the image presented by buildings – conflicted with the interests of those who saw this careful supervision of architecture as a damper on the freedom

Main thoroughfares highlighted in the *Basisplan voor de Herbouw van de Binnenstad* ('Basic Plan for the Reconstruction of the Inner City'), 1946.

… linked clearly to the city in such a way that life in the inner city will expand until it reaches the river. Moreover, people in the city should be able to see and experience the river. Only then will Rotterdam be crowned the City on the Maas.'[42] Kraaijvanger mentioned Mediterranean cities like Lisbon (with its commercial square on the Tagus), Venice, and Marseilles as examples of cities closely related to the water. The danger that threatened to frustrate such efforts, Kraaijvanger warned, was the plan to move the dike to a location along the river: 'But does Rotterdam also realize what it would be giving up? The river will be barely visible from the city any more, for Rotterdam will be hidden behind a fence! This high dike will separate us from the river even more, and indeed, the question of whether or not to build this dike is a very urgent problem and one that requires a swift solution.'[43]

Areas outlined according
to general function in the
*Basisplan voor de Herbouw
van de Binnenstad*
('Basic Plan for the
Reconstruction of the
Inner City'), 1946.

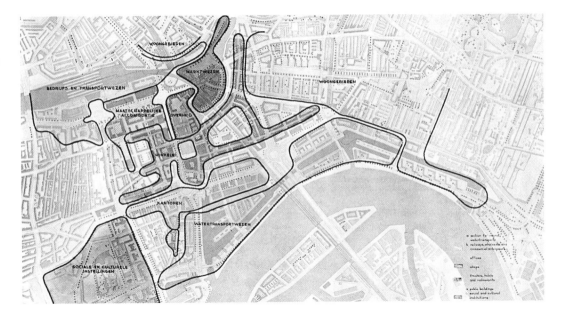

of private enterprise, economic growth, and expansion.

Van Traa's concept of the role of urban planning differed only slightly from that of Witteveen. As mentioned earlier,[45] Van Traa, Van Embden, and their co-workers also believed that the reconstruction of Rotterdam should lead to renewed social coherence and that a centrally organized orchestration of the cityscape was indispensable to this goal. Admittedly, the 'social issue' had been a source of constant concern before the war, but immediately afterward people feared that the war years had led to an even greater 'moral decline' and to the social disintegration of the population, while the efforts and involvement of the population were precisely the element considered vital to the success of the reconstruction.[46] Following in the footsteps of Witteveen, Van Traa adhered to a strict regime in dealing with the architecture of buildings within a cityscape designed to represent the new collective identity of the urban community.

Two main differences distinguished Witteveen's plan from that of Van Traa. The first was the *way in which* the architectonic

appearance of buildings was controlled. Officially, Van Traa's *Basisplan* bore the status of a completely neutral city plan, a position that engendered broad support for the design. Behind the scenes, however, the cityscape *was* carefully steered and orchestrated by means of an elaborate system of guidelines and the scrupulous supervision of building projects. Nonetheless, no official relationship existed between the *Basisplan*, as a planning document, and the practical orchestration of the cityscape.[47]

The only cityscape-related point that appeared in the official *Basisplan* was the structure of public space. And here lay the second difference between the two plans: Witteveen's urban design had devoted a great deal of thought to an architectonic approach to public space, but public space in the postwar era was a far more abstract concept. Even though the *Basisplan* paid serious attention to a hierarchical, rational organization of the system of public space, including the differentiation of various types, it failed to present a clear picture of the specific way in which each individual element was to be designed.

Maas Boulevard in Rotterdam, as seen from the southeast, 1995.

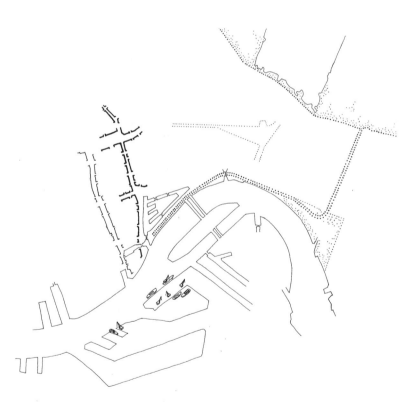

Rotterdam according to Van Traa: the 'Window to the River' starts in the inner city, and Maas Boulevard is portrayed as the new entrance to the city.

In referring to the most essential aspect of the new Rotterdam, Van Traa used the term 'openness,' by which he meant an overabundance of open space: for 'above all else, open space is social progress.'[48] And the river and its port-related activities - together, the main element of open space – deserved to be given a special position within the urban design.

The task of strengthening the relation between city and river was based on creating a collective identity, as well as a collective involvement in the vicissitudes of the port. In the design of the link connecting city and river, two things were revealed: the lack of clarity in the organization of public space and the phenomenon of 'openness' as a quality embraced by the public.

The desire to reinforce the relation between city and river had the strong support of two new elements in the city plan: the 'Window to the River' and Maas Boulevard.

Although Van Traa made an effort to satisfy the wishes of Backx and Kraaijvanger, he was unable to alter the plan for the dike along the river. Built largely along the quayside of the Boompjes and the former Maas Station railroad yard, the new dike was to function, first and foremost, as a 3-kilometer-long 'grand boulevard, high above the water; a lower quay is projected for the purpose of loading and unloading vessels. The result is an unobstructed view of the river, as well as the preservation of the inspiring contact with the image of work and, in particular, with that of work next to and on the water, which is so typical of Rotterdam.'[49] These words describe the origins of Maas Boulevard, a Dutch version of America's riverside parkways.

Maas Boulevard was not a product of the kind of careful design that had characterized the best examples of such parkways. The spatial quality of this boulevard, which

The 'Window to the
River,' photographed by
Cas Oorthuys, 1959.

prompted J. J. Vriend to call it the 'high
point of postwar reconstruction in Rotterdam,'[50] was due primarily to the route of
the boulevard along the curve of the river
and to the height of the dike, which lent
articulation to this enormous 80-meter-
broad urban element.

The 'Window to the River' and Maas
Boulevard underscored the relation between
motorized traffic and the river: both
elements were not only new open urban
areas, but also new routes within the city's
network of thoroughfares.

Emphasis on the relation between river

and motorized traffic was heightened
by plans for a new bridge, which was to
be a worthy counterpart of the Maas
Tunnel. Originally, planners studied
Witteveen's prewar proposal for a new
city bridge that would extend the Cool-
singel-Schiedamsedijk axis. They feared
that the design would lead to traffic jams
at the intersection of Coolsingel and
Blaak, however, and their apprehension
was compounded by the objections of
port-related interests to a bridge at this
location.[51]

In the end they decided to build a new

The Latenstein elevator complex. Architects: J.J.M. Vegter and A. Aronsohn, 1951/1964.

bridge on the east side of the railroad tracks, a plan that included a traffic circle at Oude Haven, now filled in, which would be directly linked, via Mariniersweg, to Hofplein and Coolsingel.

If Maas Boulevard was to offer 'the image of work' to traffic entering the city from the east, then the 'Window to the River' – right in the middle of the city – would show Rotterdam's significance as a hub of international transport. This view, which presented the ships of the Holland America Line (hal) moored to Wilhelminapier, was framed by 'the big window through which one experiences the river and sees the ships of the home fleet, where activity and industry are realities that represent Rotterdam.'[52]

In addition to the home fleet, the

'Window to the River' also framed an ensemble of highly diverse port structures. New exponents of Rotterdam modernism emerged among nineteenth-century warehouses lining the partially destroyed quays of Wilhelminapier and Rijnhaven; companies such as HAL and Latenstein bv, both of which had showed interest in becoming part of Rotterdam's architectonic culture even earlier, became the proud owners of splendid new complexes. An extremely varied spectrum of buildings soon provided Rijnhaven with a new skyline: for emigrants leaving Wilhelminapier for the shores of America, this was a preview of the panorama they would see a week later as their ship sailed into New York harbor. 'Manhattan on the Maas' existed long before the term coined to describe it.

## TWO DUALISMS IN THE RELATION BETWEEN CITY AND RIVER

The new relation between city and river, which was the goal of those involved in the postwar reconstruction of Rotterdam, was based on two dualisms.

The first, which pertained to the position of the port within the cityscape, was personified by J. Ph. Backx. On the one hand, the separation of the authentic, operational port located outside the city increased during the reconstruction era, when large port areas such as Botlek and, later, Europoort were laid out exactly as Backx had proposed in 1929. (See illustrations on pages 338 and 339.) At the same time, planners were trying to tie 'the image of work' and 'ships of the home fleet' to the cityscape for the purpose of getting people more involved in port-related developments. The game was lost, however, before it even started.

Wrestling with the contradictions represented by a new dike and the introduction of a 'Window to the River,' perhaps Van Traa hoped that Kraaijvanger's 'fence' along the waterfront would not be as bad as it sounded. Bad it was, however: in 1953, while Maas Boulevard was under construction, the Netherlands experienced a disastrous flood that led to the adoption of the Delta Act, a law that prescribed a new 'minimum safe height' for the country's main dikes. Rather than the initially planned 4 meters, the new law required Maas Boulevard to be 5.45 meters above Normal Amsterdam Level, a turn of events that closed the shutters to the 'Window.'

At the same time, 'the image of work' disappeared as well. Shipping activities, which were to have been framed by the Window, relocated to new harbors in Botlek and Europoort, far from any view provided by the city center. In 1971 the *Nieuw Amsterdam*, bound for New York, sailed away from Wilhelminapier for the last time.

The second dualism concerned the location of the city center itself and, more specifically, the main activities and functions of the city center, as they related to the river. Before the war, the Boompjes and its riverside zone accommodated a series of inner-city functions: Schiedamsedijk, as seamen's quarter and the heart of urban night life; Maas Station, as a busy hub for travelers on the go; and the Boompjes itself, as the façade of Waterstad, the part of the city that offered a blend of urban and port-related activities.

After the bombardment, all remaining traces of this functional orientation of the city toward the river were destroyed during postwar reconstruction: buildings surrounding Oude Haven, the only complete urban planning ensemble to survive the war virtually intact, were demolished to make place for a traffic circle designed to link the new cross-river connection to Maas Boulevard.

While the riverbank was reserved primarily for motorized traffic, the heart of the city center shifted toward the northwest. Prewar Rotterdam's city center had been located within the historical urban *triangle*. The new Rotterdam, however, had a new city center, whose borders were marked by Blaak, Binnenrotte, Westersingel, and Weena: the *orthogonal* area enclosed would be referred to later as the *centrumruit*.

The accent on this area had a highly practical, strategic basis: initially, there was nothing to indicate that retailers would want to relocate to the barren wasteland of the city center. During and after the war, the majority of retail businesses had found accommodations in temporary shopping centers set up at the edge of the devastated heart of town. These provisional centers had become so successful that no one felt the need to pioneer a move to the new city center. The Departments of Urban Devel-

The inner city of
Rotterdam in 1955 with,
in the foreground, the
virtually undeveloped
Waterstad. (See, too, the
photograph at the top of
page 342.)

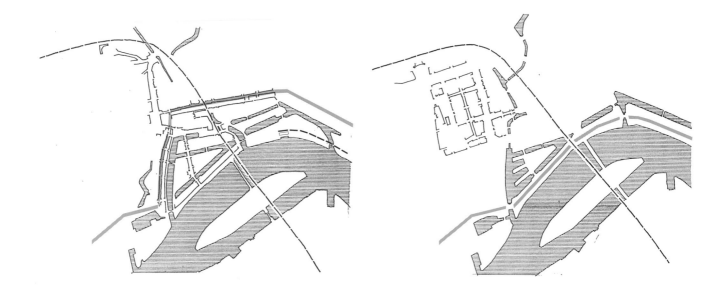

The shifting of the city center: (left) the inner city's main streets before (left) and after (right) 1940. On the right, the main dike (▬▬) has been relocated to a position along the riverbank.

opment and Postwar Reconstruction interpreted this reluctance as a sign that a new shopping area could get started only if it (a) was so compact that a 'critical mass' could be created quickly; (b) provided a connection to existing shopping streets in nineteenth-century districts; and (c) formed one continuous entity, uninterrupted by physical barriers, such as reservoirs and railroad viaducts. The section in question satisfied these requirements. Within this section, Coolsingel stood out – even more than it had before the war – as a central urban boulevard and the backbone of an important shopping area: Hoogstraat on the east side and, to the west, the new Lijnbaan complex. In 1950 and 1951 the first two chain (department) stores appeared on strategic corners of the *centrumruit*: Vroom & Dreesman and Ter Meulen.[53]

Although the strategy used to reconstruct the central shopping area was highly effective, the approach to the Waterstad area was far less successful. To be sure, the intention of the *Basisplan* was to restore urban life to Schiedamsedijk and Waterstad. The plan designated the former area of Schiedamsedijk and Witte de Withstraat as a 'seamen's quarter.' Later documents and explanatory remarks mentioned a 'Centre Maritime' and an 'entertainment quarter.' The policy on this area, however, was continually marked by indecision and varying opinions on the manageability of marginal phenomena associated with urban night life, such as prostitution. Planners, police officials, and council members found it impossible to agree. On the one hand, the area seemed ideal as an entertainment center, certainly after the completion of West-Blaak, the new traffic breakthrough that was to create a buffer between the new city center and the entertainment quarter, which was to enjoy a 'lenient enforcement of public-morality laws.'[54] On the other hand, as time went by the police, in particular,

showed an increasing preference for concentrating prostitution and the accompanying night life on the peninsula of Katendrecht, which had become a principal center for sailors and entertainment, especially following the disappearance of the old Schiedamsedijk in 1940.[55]

Hence a number of bars and dance halls did appear on Witte de Withstraat, but not a trace of night life was to be found along the relocated Schiedamsedijk, between Coolsingel and the river.

The Waterstad area, and particularly the island between Scheepmakershaven and Wijnhaven, was designated partly as an 'inland-navigation center' and partly as a location for office buildings. It would no longer connect the shopping and entertainment area centered around Coolsingel, Hoogstraat, and Lijnbaan to the river. The development of new building projects on the riverbanks themselves was impeded, moreover, by operations in the '50s and '60s to raise the dikes.

The entire area between Blaak, 'conceived' as the southern border of the new city center, and the river was little more than an inner-city periphery and, in certain spots (such as Oude Haven and vicinity), a veritable wasteland.

The renewed Schiedamsedijk, the Boompjes, and Maas Boulevard were to function chiefly as thoroughfares. Here a blend of traffic and other urban functions belonged to the past. And like the approach to the 'seamen's quarter,' Waterstad, and the area around Oude Haven, plans for these areas lacked a clear concept, not to mention an urban planning strategy that would lend concrete substance to the relation between city and river.

One result of these decisions was disregard for the Kop van Zuid, which was receding into an increasingly marginal position with respect to both port and city. The heart of the port

Rotterdam as a dynamic port city, photographed by Cas Oorthuys, 1959.

was moving west, farther and farther away from the city, and the new traffic infrastructure – in the form of a metro line (and, later, a railroad line) – bypassed the Kop van Zuid or tunneled its way to the other side. By the end of the '60s, the Kop van Zuid had become a largely peripheral urban enclave with quays no longer maintained by the Port Authority, and streets no longer paved by Public Works.

### THE MYTH OF THE PORT AS PART OF THE CITYSCAPE

The significance of a cityscape that included the port was a highly promoted subject even before the war; in the postwar era, however, it threatened to enter the realm of mythology. As the harbor area closest to the city – right across the river from the city center – the Kop van Zuid played a particularly important role in creating and cultivating this myth.

From the late nineteenth century to the 1960s, this area was a source of fascination and euphoria expressed in a voluminous series of pictorial, literary, photographic,

and cinematic impressions: paintings and drawings by Paul Signac, photographs by Cas Oorthuys, Joris Ivens's renowned film about the Hefbrug ('lift bridge'), and C.B. Vaandrager's book on the same subject are but a few highlights of this creative profusion.

This role in the conceptualization of the city was played not only by the Kop van Zuid itself, but primarily by the river and cross-river connections. The bridges and ferries not only offered a view of the river as the most important artery within all this new vitality; they also represented the link between the old city and the new. Those struck by the fascination of the view from the bridges were able to identify fully with the idea that Rotterdam was the center of a world charged with vitality, movement, and change. This image could be found in countless paintings, photographs, films, and literary accounts, such as A. M. de Jong's book *In de draaikolk* (In the Whirlpool), in which Merijntje, a ten-year-old boy from a working-class family originally from Brabant, returns on Saturday evening from a visit to the exhilarating seaport world of the Kop van Zuid: 'But at

View from the Euromast, photographed by Frits Rotgans, 1960.

the Maas bridges he suddenly woke up. Because the charm of the enchanting river was more powerful than all his exhaustion and drowsiness. He could never get enough of the thousands of lights hanging in the air on both sides of the bridge, above the black, incandescent waters; the green and red and yellow winks from all those ships; all the magical, floating houses where people lived and that sailed from place to place, over and over again … And then the streaming water swirled around the piers, and gurgled and splashed, and a little tugboat chug-chugged below, and somewhere in the night the heavy, melancholy voice of an ocean-going vessel wailed … And a train, all lit up, thundered over the rails, whistling with a shriek, and he saw the rosy glow of the fire, flung open and blazing against a white wisp of smoke … He woke right up at the sight of it all and turned his head from left to right, not knowing where the prettiest lights might be bursting open in the darkness… And Merijntje fell asleep almost before he got undressed, feeling lucky to have experienced such things, while the boys back in the village could never even imagine that things like that

existed … poor country bumpkins …'[56]

In the late 1950s, cultivating the myth of the port seemed to have reached a high point. Cas Oorthuys's 1959 book of photographs, *Rotterdam dynamische stad* (Rotterdam Dynamic City), illustrated these mythical overtones. The book – an homage to Rotterdam against a Neo-Realistic backdrop – presented the city as a place filled with diversity: a port and city of workers, with an urban landscape of harbors and cranes; a city of lights, with innovative features such as the Business Center and its illuminated advertising; and a verdant garden city of postwar residential districts. These photographic images showed more of the Kop van Zuid than a spatial typology of water surfaces and warehouse ensembles lined with quays and streets: also visible – and almost audible and smellable – are characteristic elements of the area such as heavy plumes of smoke, dust from coal and grain, sweat and blood, rattling trains and screaming steam whistles.

The book *Rotterdam dynamische stad* was, in fact, a final outpouring of a positive, almost romantic, interpretation of what the port meant to the city. It portrayed what Van Traa had in mind when he envisioned the 'Window to the River' and Maas Boulevard, which were to make 'the image of work' part of the cityscape. But the disappearance of this image left nothing but emptiness.

The realization of the Euromast – built in 1960 for the Floriade, an event held in The Park – represented a final effort to create a visual link between city and port. The Euromast rose at the farthest point of the area still considered part of the city center: the south ernmost tip of Witteveen's green wedge, close to the intersection of Westzeedijk and 's-Gravendijkwal as it approaches the Maas Tunnel– the two main thoroughfares that run straight across town. Looking through a telescope atop the Euromast – an urban crow's nest with the port in its sights – one can see the new harbors of Botlek and Europoort.

The Euromast symbolizes an attempt to stand in downtown Rotterdam – on tiptoe, squinting impatiently at the horizon – and to catch one last glimpse of the operational port.

# 4　After Modernism:
# The Search for New Fundamentals of Design

Until the mid-1960s, the message being circulated confirmed that the reconstruction of the city center was proceeding as planned. In 1965 R. Blijstra published his monumental ode to postwar reconstruction efforts – *Rotterdam, stad in beweging* (Rotterdam, City in Motion) – in which he concluded that 'Rotterdam's inner city will be able to offer so much variety that everybody can find what they are looking for.'[57]

Barely three years later R. Wentholt questioned this statement in his book *De binnenstadsbeleving en Rotterdam* (The Inner City Experience and Rotterdam).[58] Wentholt pointed to the population's increasing dissatisfaction with an inner city that failed to provide a good answer to the need for 'a vibrant, varied, convivial, pleasant, intimate city';[59] and he warned that the situation would worsen as existing plans for traffic routes were implemented.[60] He cited the demolition of buildings around Oude Haven, a preparatory step in the realization of a traffic circle for a new cross-river connection, as an example of his thesis: 'Unconditional surrender to the omnivorous expansion of road building, without giving the matter a second thought, would spell disaster for urban planning.'[61]

Essential to Wentholt's argument was his criticism of the way in which reconstruction plans dealt with the remains of the old, prewar city. Thoughts long present in the minds of many were now expressed in words, and these words were in a book published by the Vroom & Dreesman department store!

Wentholt, harshly critical of the onesided modernism of reconstruction activities, argued for the preservation of existing structures for the sake of 'a reason unique to Rotterdam': namely, 'the important function that relics have begun to fulfill in the visual and psychological perception of the city.'[62]

Wentholt's plea did not lead to an immediate reversal of municipal policy.

Two plans that appeared around 1970– *Plan 2000+* and *Structuurnota* ('Regional Plan') *1972* – proposed an extrapolation of the concept of urban growth and an expanding city, an idea that had formed the basis of urban development in Rotterdam ever since the postwar reconstruction era.

In 1969 three municipal services – Urban Development, Public Works, and Port Authority – presented *Plan 2000+*, which covered the entire delta and all its islands (belonging to both Zeeland and South Holland), and which outlined the future development of the port of Rotterdam as it related to the port of Antwerp and to a central open area. The plan called for the urban and industrial areas of both cities to expand substantially along opposite sides of the delta, leaving the Oosterschelde in the middle, as the core of a communal open area. (See page 338.)

Presented three years later, *Structuurnota 1972* focused on a developmental model for Rotterdam itself. Proposed spatial development was to border a number of radial traffic routes and public-transportation lines that ran from the inner city to outer areas. This plan was based on earlier plans, which were at an advanced stage in 1972, for the construction of new approach roads into the city from the north (via a to-be-filled-in Rotte River) as well as the south (through the district of Feijenoord and across the new Willems Bridge). The realization of these routes would have resulted in enormous demolition operations in the districts of Oude Noorden, Crooswijk, Rubroek, and Feijenoord.

The future of Rotterdam's old nineteenth- and early-twentieth-century housing districts had been the topic of studies and debates ever since the first reconstruction plans were being designed; all this research and discussion, however, rarely led to practical results. Concepts proposed by the city council and municipal departments alternated between 'redevelopment' (which usually meant totally demolishing these districts and replacing housing with new functions) and 'rehabilitation' (which usually meant totally demolishing these districts and building new housing),[63] options that combined physical reorganization with *social* reorganization. Old districts were seen and treated as concentrations of antisociality, an unwanted stain on the blazon of a modern urban community.[64]

While most of the many plans designed for these districts in the 1950s and '60s remained unimplemented, their main effect was that both private owners and public agencies stopped making serious investments in such districts, which then fell victim to neglect.

In the late '60s, the proposals for the demolition of these old housing projects – once a self-evident solution – became a topic surrounded by doubt and opposition. The theme of antisociality had faded into the background, and assertive neighborhood organizations, which demanded the preservation and restoration of their housing environment, were evolving into an increasingly important factor within urban political relations.

*Structuurnota 1972* was the last straw; it set the stage not only for mass demonstrations organized by residents in the old districts and for a change of power in city council, but also for a period in which the Department of Urban Planning was forced to relinquish its prominent position.

URBAN RENEWAL: HIGH POINT OF SOCIAL-DEMOCRATIC CONSENSUS

In 1974 a changing of the guard within Social Democracy led, in Rotterdam, to a completely renewed city council composed of leftist parties.[65] At the heart of the council's program was a new policy for urban development and public housing: a policy that radically opposed the urban planning concepts of the reconstruction era. The position taken on this issue was the principal common denominator uniting the new city council.

The 'expanding city' model, featuring a city center reserved exclusively for commercial services, made way for the concept of the compact city, in which the urban housing function took precedence over everything else, even in the city center.[66] The new council's greatest concern was the disappearance of the city as the physical prerequisite for, and the breeding ground and generator of, modern civilization.[67] Looking at the city as a civilizing agent, council members distinguished economic, cultural, and social components. The great majority were prepared to call a halt to a prolonged, one-sided emphasis on Rotterdam's economic situation, at the expense of cultural and social interests, and to make an about-face: cultural and social factors were to be accentuated in the new urban development policy, to the detriment of the economic interests so greatly favored in the preceding decades. The '70s image of the economic component – another term for the port sector – was that of an undesirable element, a source of annoyance and pollution, which did not belong in the city.

After a quarter century of plans to demolish and dismantle old districts, from 1974 on urban renewal was declared 'political priority number one'; and after a quarter century of emphasis on the city center as 'Central Business District,' from 1974 on the focus shifted largely to housing and entertainment functions for the inner city.

Based on these objectives, a policy was launched that called for a *reparation of the city*. Full of holes, the city was in danger of imminent collapse and badly in need of a large-scale repair job. This reparation meant an overhaul of the physical, architectural, and urban planning characteristics of the city, as well as of its sociocultural structures.

Although urban renewal was viewed as a necessity, its social and cultural elements were not automatically in line with each other. A movement within the country's refurbished Social Democracy stressed social renewal, while others put cultural interests first. These conflicts were solved by dividing the city into territories: the city center was earmarked for cultural renewal, and nineteenth-century districts became the focus of social renewal.

The municipality was in a relatively comfortable position with respect to implementing its policy on urban renewal. Politically speaking, a solid consensus backed this policy: thanks to a majority of leftist parties in the council, the return of Social Democracy to the national government, and an active core of neighborhood organizations, the policy enjoyed unprecedentedly broad political and social support. From a financial perspective, Rotterdam was anticipating proceeds from the Municipal Port Authority, part of which would be diverted to a purchasing policy needed in urban-renewal districts. As for commissioning architects and hiring others required for the realization of renewal projects, a consensus also existed between the city council and those organizations directly involved in urban-renewal districts: housing corporations. In the field of local politics the '70s were, without a doubt, the high point of postwar Social Democratic consensus.

This politico-social consensus was not accompanied by new urban planning concepts, however. Although Wentholt's argument for 'integration of old and new' became a slogan of renewed city politics after 1974, there was no consensus with respect to the question of *how* to achieve this integration. Although functionalist urban planning had lost its prominent position, no clear alternative appeared to take its place. In the late '70s the ideal cityscape was the subject of a complete spectrum of standpoints and theories that found their way into policy documents, but not into new urban planning concepts.

In the 1970s and early '80s, three themes determined the political debate in Rotterdam: the ideal of the culturally vital city, the ideal of the socially balanced city, and the ideal of the economically sound city.

### The ideal of the culturally vital city

The reparation policy was marked in every sense by a reaction to postwar reconstruction modernism, and particularly to the loss of a link between city center and river. 'Giving the river back to the city' was the watchword of the councilman for physical planning, H. Mentink, who was responsible for the renewal of the city center and who made a name for himself by pronouncing the Shell Building on Hofplein 'the final erection of big business.' All plans for similar buildings in the inner city – and certainly along the river – were to be rejected.

The first two projects developed to exemplify this new aim also represented a radical break with the previous policy and its support of motorized traffic and office buildings: the Leuvehaven Project and the Oude Haven Project. The former was a housing complex to be realized on the quays of Leuvehaven, a site that had been the recent (1973) subject of an agreement in principle – concerning the construction of a World Trade Center – between the municipality and the Dutch Employees' Pension Scheme. The new housing complex was part of a larger operation, the 'Water Connection,' designed by architect J. Hoogstad in collaboration with the Department of Urban Development for the purpose of creating a 'walk to the river,' which was to incorporate the last remnants of open water in the inner city.

The new Leuvehaven Project was one of the most obvious examples of a new policy that discouraged the construction of office buildings in the inner city, while promoting housing and cultural renewal. But even more spectacular was a new building project planned for Oude Haven. Oude Haven had assumed the martyr's role in criticism of reconstruction modernism: the remaining survivor of the old city center, it had been demolished in the '60s to make place for a new traffic route from Rotterdam South to the inner city.

Although it was too late for city council to cancel plans for the new bridge itself, it did discontinue plans for the thorough-traffic route and a traffic circle on the site of Oude Haven. As a result, access to the new Willems Bridge, completed in 1980, was adapted to conform to the existing traffic network, producing a veritable fun house of curves, meanders, and inclines.

Cancellation of the traffic circle cleared the way for the reconstruction of Oude Haven to be used as a model to demonstrate the municipality's concept of the compact city. This building project represented the restoration of the city: the restoration of the inner-city housing function and its melting pot of social categories; the restoration of the inner-city entertainment function and its wide range of hotel-restaurant- and bar-related facilities; and the restoration of prewar images and functions, including the designation of this harbor as the mooring place for historic sailing vessels.

New accommodations for another important urban function, the Central Library, were built close to Oude Haven, next to the marketplace on Gedempte Binnenrotte. The new chain of urban functions – market-library-Oude Haven – was underlined by incorporating an elevated pedestrian section, including shops, and 'cube houses' into the design for Oude Haven.

The Oude Haven Project also demonstrated renewed interest in a harmonious cityscape, and especially in its architectonic appearance. The city council extended its influence on the final result by choosing the architect (Piet Blom) and negotiating with him directly. This approach produced a finely tuned coherence of the various elements composing the ensemble, as well as a sense of compatibility between the

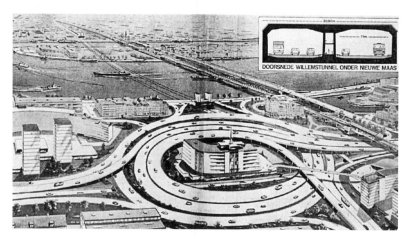

DOORSNEDE WILLEMSTUNNEL ONDER NIEUWE MAAS

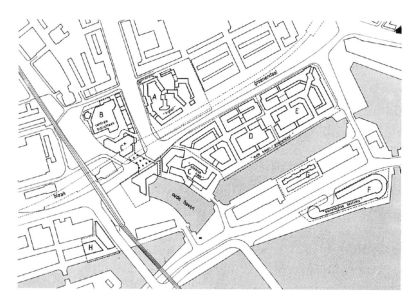

Three of the many plans for Oude Haven.
Above: Design for traffic circle and bridge, Emmen, 1941.
Center: Willems Tunnel traffic circle, 1964.
Below: Urban design for Oude Haven and Groenendaal, 1981.

architecture of the buildings and the organization of public space.

Plans developed for the Boompjes, the main connection between Oude Haven and Leuvehaven, also included a number of apartment buildings that were to lend shape to a new river front.

Although an attempt was made to place the new projects for Oude Haven and Leuvehaven in a larger context, in most respects they remained isolated incidents within a greater whole. Despite its desire to be more influential, the city council failed to determine much more than the level of scale to be used in designing an isolated urban ensemble. The 'context' in which both projects were to play a role was made up largely of pedestrian routes which, being neither spatially nor functionally of any great relevance to the structure of the city, hardly functioned as a context.

Furthermore, the new policy to stop potentially undesired developments was not supported by a broad consensus. This clearly emerged in the case of a project that was to have been the apotheosis of the new river front; the location, at the approach to the old Willems Bridge, was the spot at which the Boompjes meets Oude Haven. This historically charged site was to feature a new stimulus for the renewed cityscape: a multifunctional, transparent building designed by Rem Koolhaas, combined with a vertically positioned segment of the old, demolished Willems Bridge.

These plans were shelved, however, and the site became the home of new accommodations for Nedlloyd, the largest shipping company in the Netherlands and one of the largest in the world. Nedlloyd's board of directors had pressured the city council into allowing the company to build its new headquarters at this location. The building, designed by W. Quist, rose as a monolithic wall, 100 by 100 meters, which exceeded the building lines to such an extent that the

Oude Haven in 1990, as seen from the south.

The Boompjes, as depicted by OMA: a proposal for two buildings along the Boompjes. Design by OMA (Rem Koolhaas and Kees Christiaanse), 1981.

design for the ground-level area permitted no more than minimal sidewalks and meandering bikeways.[68]

The realization of this design clearly marked the end of a one-sided emphasis on the cultural renewal of the inner city, a renewal defined by the bumpy progression from one isolated incident to another.

*The ideal of the socially balanced city*
The municipal policy on nineteenth-century districts surrounding the inner city was aimed at stopping a 'unilateral composition' of the urban population, the disappearance of traditional neighborhoods, and problems of assimilation suffered by newcomers to the city. These themes formed the core of the city council's policy documents and of nearly every policy plan for urban-renewal areas in

the 1970s.[69] The way in which such goals were achieved differed from neighborhood to neighborhood, however; decisions were often left to the discretion of individual neighborhood organizations, the architects involved, and housing corporations.

This course of action led in the first instance to a high degree of 'introversion' and to a complete lack of spatial and functional coherence on the level of the city as a whole.[70]

The new inner-city policy designated the seventeenth-century Waterstad as an important development area, while the urban-renewal policy earmarked nineteenth-century harbor areas as a *deus ex machina*. The two main tasks given to these harbor areas, which bordered the urban-renewal districts, were to prevent these districts from disintegrating and to compensate for the loss of housing caused by demolition and consoli-

dation operations associated with urban renewal. Once again, economic interests were forced to take a back seat.

Converting harbor areas into housing sites was remarkable in a city whose politics had been determined, since time immemorial, by the primacy of a growing port and a growing commercial sector. Besides raiding the coffers of the Municipal Port Authority for urban-renewal projects, the city council also attacked the hegemony of a municipal policy based on a port-related economy by using harbor sites to build housing.[71]

A direct link between the reorganization of old harbor areas and the urban-renewal process was most evident on the left bank of the Maas.[72] A total of 7,500 dwellings were planned for old harbor sites along this riverbank. Some 5,000 would rise on the Kop van Zuid, on waterfront and switchyard areas

Former harbor areas eligible for housing according to a government report entitled Reorganization of Old Harbors and to the Rotterdam 'Within the *Ruit*' Structure Plan, 1977.

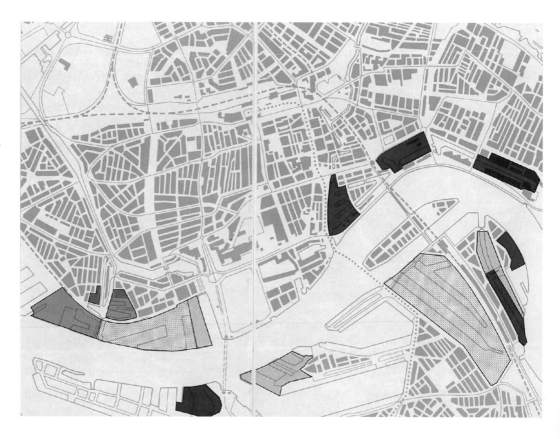

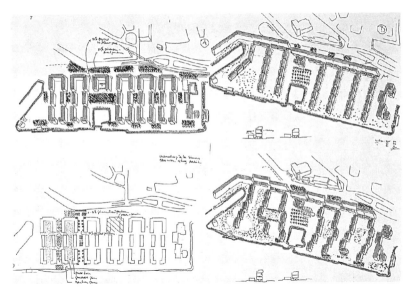

The first generation of housing plans for old harbor areas consisted of reproductions of housing typologies already existing in the city. For example, the typology and the pattern of land division found in Feijenoord's 'Simonsterrein' were also used in suburban expansion projects realized during the same period; and Delfshaven Buitendijks was based on the Warande, one of the first postwar reconstruction housing projects. As time went on, this arbitrary use of land division models drew growing criticism from those who saw them as examples of the lack of a clear and coherent urban planning basis for transforming old harbor areas.

Sketches for a Detailed Urban Plan (DUP or, in Dutch, GESP) for housing in the Delfshaven Buitendijks area. Design by Gijs Snoek in collaboration with Carel Weeber, 1980.

of Binnenhaven and Spoorweghaven, and on the Wilhelminapier.

The early 1980s saw the realization of plans for smaller harbor areas in the districts of Feijenoord, Katendrecht, and Charlois. The main advantage of these locations was their relatively small size and the ease with which they could be linked directly to the urban structure of existing residential areas in these districts – certainly in the case of harbors in Feijenoord and Katendrecht.

Finding a way in which to increase the municipality's influence on the architectonic appearance of the urban ensemble – a strategy applied earlier in Oude Haven – was also considered a worthwhile effort in the approach to projects planned for urban-renewal districts. A so-called Detailed Urban Plan (DUP or, in Dutch, GeSP) was to be made for each large building site in these districts; such plans would focus on the external appearance of buildings, which would be regulated precisely by means of drawings featuring axonometric projections of the various plans.[73]

In 1980 the DUP procedure was applied to urban plans for several old harbor sites, including the area of Delfshaven Buitendijks and Dokhaven on the left bank of the Maas.

*The ideal of the economically sound city: old harbors as high-quality business environments*

Although the dominance of a Social Democratic consensus made itself felt well into the 1980s, the first cracks in this consensus were soon to appear. Social and cultural arguments had monopolized the official political and public debate for a long time, but gradually urban planning, plagued by a lack of lucid concepts, was called to account for its inadequacies. In the offices of the Port Authority, Erasmus University, and Shipping Association South – and, gradually, in the '80s in those of the Department of Physical Planning and Urban Development – a need emerged for new ideas for an efficient economic and spatial development of the city.

As two matters of essence demanded more and more of the city's attention, this need edged its way forward. The most obvious of the two, which first became apparent in the late '70s, was a rapid decrease in jobs, which quickly led to a high percentage of unemployment.[74] Less obvious, but equally alarming, was the development of international economic networks, which threatened to undermine Rotterdam's leading position as a transit port, unless the city was quick to take

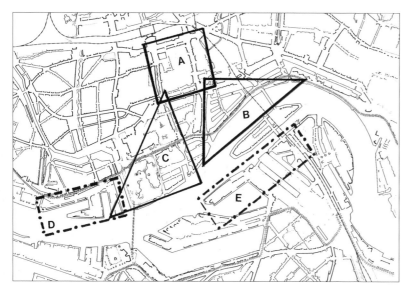

Sub-areas of Rotterdam's city center, as depicted in the *Binnenstadsplan* ('Inner-City Plan') of 1985: (a) the city quadrant, (b) Waterstad, and (c) the park triangle. In addition, two potential expansion areas for the city center: (d) Mullerpier and the Schiehaven area, and (e) the Kop van Zuid.

a wide range of urban phenomena – the service-sector policy, education and the sciences, small and medium-sized businesses, the employment policy and, last but not least, the policy on new businesses and new residents – would have to be adapted to fit the framework of this new goal.

The group most closely associated with this idea was known as Rotterdam Tomorrow, a circle composed of people from Erasmus University and its affiliate, the Dutch Economic Institute, as well as from the Chamber of Commerce.[77]

### A new coalition between cultural and economic policies

While a need to strengthen cultural functions had risen from protests against one-sided economic interests, the Nedlloyd affair had revealed the limitations of a municipal policy aimed solely at cultural renewal and based on incidental interventions. Clearly economic and cultural interests were interdependent, and the result was a mutual attempt to restore the spatial relationship between city and port. For the time being, such efforts led to nothing more than a greater focus on the completion of the inner city. Only later was the port to enter the picture.

A new integral plan for the entire inner city was presented in 1985, the first to appear since the *Basisplan voor de Herbouw van de Binnenstad* was introduced in 1946.[78] This *Binnenstadsplan* ('Inner-City Plan'), which set the stage for the creation of an integral framework for individual urban planning 'incidents' realized between 1975 and 1985, brought back two important ideas conceived in prewar Rotterdam.

The first was to provide Waterstad, as depicted in the new plan, with 'a totally new function: an expansion area of the inner city. In addition to many dwellings and offices, Waterstad will be given an important recreational function.'[79] The second idea

drastic measures to renew port-related infrastructure and to revive the local economic climate in general.

Prior to this time, Rotterdam had functioned primarily as a transit port, a transshipment station serving a single route to and from Germany's industrial area. In the early '80s, the Port Authority put forward an idea to transform the area into Europe's *mainport*: the hub that would tie Europe to intercontinental transport networks and that would organize the distribution of goods throughout Europe.[75]

A case was made for converting port activities 'from large-scale transshipment to a logistic conception,' which required the metamorphosis of the seaport 'from working city to logistic hub.'[76]

This metamorphosis demanded economic *revitalization* in a number of areas. Not only would industries directly related to the port have to acquire advanced information systems for tracing the movement of goods all over the world; the city itself needed to be transformed into an attractive business environment for organizations dealing in advanced areas of trade, transportation, and distribution. The need to create such an environment sent a vital message to the city:

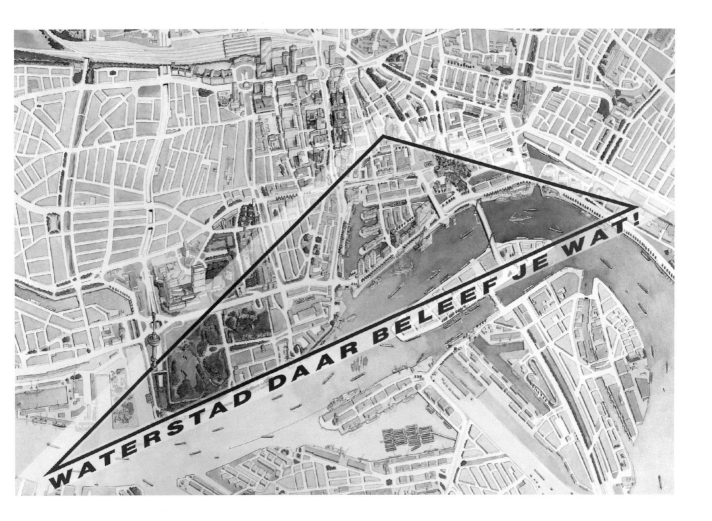

was to breathe new life into the concept of
Witteveen's green wedge by designing a 'park
triangle,' with an accent on cultural functions
(museums) and a coherently planned park
structure. A third important development
area, adjacent to Waterstad, was the route
followed by the railroad viaduct, a zone that
would become available upon completion of
the new railroad tunnel. For the time being,
there appeared to be no lack of 'expansion
areas for the inner city.'

The Waterstad Plan seemed to provide a
good basis for a new collaboration between
the municipality and major commercial
interests represented by Rotterdam Tomorrow. This group envisioned a port area that
resembled Baltimore's renewed Inner Harbor;
after Rotterdam Tomorrow promoted the

idea, Rotterdam and Baltimore became 'sister
cities.'[80] Interest in Baltimore was based
primarily on what the Inner Harbor's cultural
and touristic facilities had done for the local
economy and for employment opportunities
in that city.

Presented in 1986 by the municipality and
Rotterdam Tomorrow, the Waterstad Plan,
which built on the development of Oude
Haven, was a first attempt to translate ideas
inspired by Baltimore into a new policy. This
project offered fresh support to the housing
function in all areas of seventeenth-century
Waterstad, expanded museological functions,
introduced various touristic and recreational
facilities, and transformed the cityscape by
adding a number of tall apartment and office
buildings to the Boompjes.

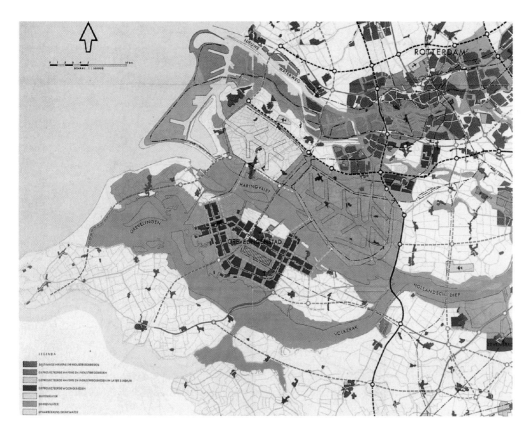

Plan 2000+

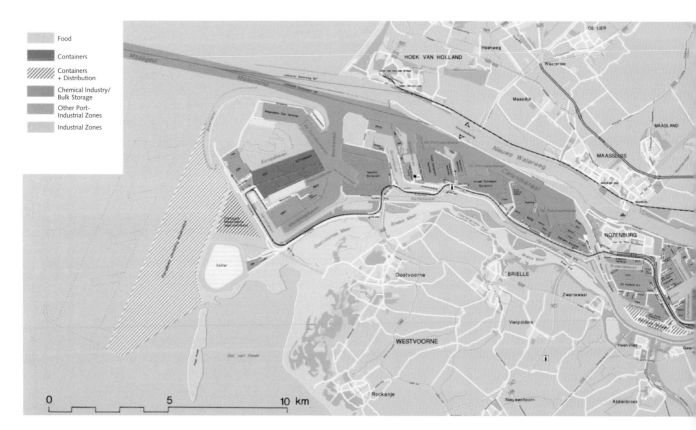

Botlek, the first harbor complex built after World War II. Rotterdam's inner city is visible in the background (above left), 1990.

Map of the Port of Rotterdam, 1996.

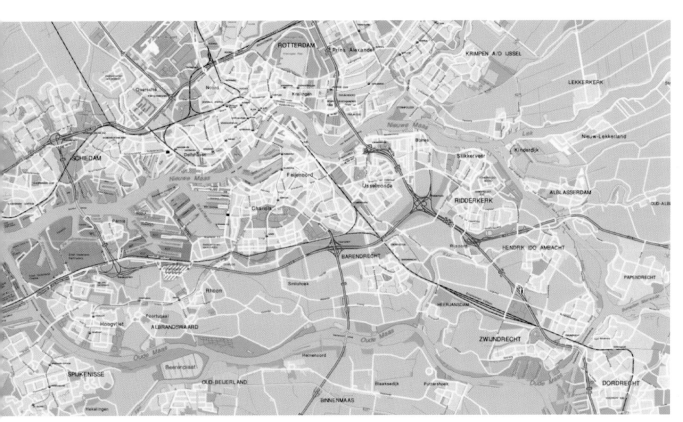

But while the tabula rasa on which plans for Leuvehaven and Oude Haven were realized had produced bits and pieces of an ideal city, most of Waterstad had already been developed by 1986. Converting Waterstad into an 'expansion area for the inner city' meant radically transforming the area already developed.

Only the borders of the plan area were suitable for rapid development, as this peripheral zone had been more or less ignored since the reconstruction era. A new Maritime Museum, an Imax Theater, and a hotel went up along Schiedamsedijk; and a Sunday market at this address was meant to encourage the public to 'lay claim' to this area.

Although a renewed relationship between inner city and river *was* taking shape, one step at a time, the result was not solid enough to support Coolsingel on its journey to the river.

Obviously, the realization of an ideal cityscape for an economically sound city required more than simply plans and building sites. Both Rotterdam Tomorrow and the city council were becoming more and more convinced that two conditions were essential to the creation of a new cityscape: an area that offered urbanists and developers a tabula rasa, and a tightly orchestrated urban planning approach. These conditions generated renewed interest in two old harbor areas close to the city center: Mullerpier, on the west side of the inner city; and the Kop van Zuid, directly across the river. This dual interest marked the return of a hoary dilemma: in which direction should the inner city expand? Should new development be oriented toward the west and thus build on the legacy of De Jongh's monumental canals and avenues in this part of the city, and on the heritage of Witteveen's green wedge and tunnel route? Or should the accent lie on the other side of the river, where development could pick

up the thread of Rose's ideas for expanding Waterstad and of Van Traa's 'Window to the River'?

THE PROFESSIONAL DEBATE:
SEARCHING FOR NEW CONCEPTS
OF SPATIAL COHERENCE

Apart from the cultural, social, and economic motives that dominated the urban political debate, urban planners and architects concentrated on independently redefining their position and on creating new principles for plan development. The profession was engaged in a struggle to regain its footing. Leading this struggle was the Rotterdam Arts Council (Rotterdamse Kunststichting, RKS). The RKS, founded in the early years of reconstruction to foster cultural life in Rotterdam, decided in 1974 – a pivotal year – to establish a special architecture division. From 1979 to 1982, this division organized a series of events promoted as 'Architecture International Rotterdam' (AIR), the purpose of which was to use the gist of the Dutch debate on architecture to forge a link with theories being developed in Europe at that time. Among those developing architectural theory in the '70s, Italian architects and architecture historians were seen as leading figures, certainly by the Dutch. A few Italians – including Francesco Dal Co, Giorgio Grassi, and Aldo Rossi – played a major role in AIR activities.[81]

The final event was an invitational competition for which four foreign designers (Josef Paul Kleihues, Aldo Rossi, Oswald Mathias Ungers, and Derek Walker) created urban designs for the Kop van Zuid: a splendid laboratory in which to experiment with new design concepts and strategies. Two men essential to the inception of AIR, Carel Weeber and Jacques Nycolaas,[82] took the lead with their initiative for the 'Peperklip.' Weeber's design for this public-

The Peperklip, the first
housing complex realized
on the Kop van Zuid.
Architect: Carel Weeber,
1981.

housing complex was a provocation thrown
in the face of existing urban-renewal concepts. Both design and scale were references
to the port and to shipping, and thus
emphasized the independent status of
harbor areas outside the dikes rather than
establishing a connection to the morphology of the bordering district of Feijenoord.
The project was an initial indication that
architects and urban planners were ready to
experiment, to make contributions unique
to urban planning and less dependent on
prevailing procedures and concepts applied
to the organization of urban renewal in
Rotterdam.

In addition, AIR was set up specifically
as an *intervention* into the practice of urban
planning and architecture in Rotterdam,[83]
most of which dealt with urban-renewal
projects at that time; apart from this, however, the RKS itself chose to survey the development of the cityscape from a neutral point
of view.[84]

Weeber had advocated a clearer division
of tasks between architecture and urban
planning even earlier, when he suggested
that rather than determining the degree of
multiformity suitable for buildings, urban
planning should direct its efforts at defining
public space.[85]

Nevertheless, urban plans featured by AIR
still focused on creating an urban *image* in the
form of a specific architectonic manifestation
of the buildings involved. The time had not
yet arrived in which urban planners would
approach the design of public space as an
independent task.[86]

AIR and its activities did mobilize, however, a wide range of concepts and approaches
pertaining to urban design, some of the
most prominent of which tried to define
the relation between architecture and urban
planning, and the link between history and
design. The former relation deals with the
question of how much influence urban plans
should have on the external appearance of
buildings; and the latter concerns the issue of
the extent to which historical research and
historical data can play a productive role in
the design of urban plans.

*The study of urban form: how to remold*
*structure and shape into a coherent entity*
Around this time, the Department of
Architecture at the University of Technology
in Delft added a new stimulus to the debate
on the relation between history and design. A
leading player in this turn of events was Rein
Geurtsen, who had introduced the subject of
urban form and urban design to this school in
the late '70s, after which he and his students
went on to complete a substantial number of
studies in this field.[87]

The 'discovery' of concepts of history
developed at Fernand Braudel's French
Annales School and of even earlier experiments, which had been part of the study of
urban form in Mediterranean countries,
particularly Italy, led to a new approach to
the design of urban plans, which the Dutch
called *stadsontwerp* ('urban design') in order
to stress the difference between this new
approach and the design of 'traditional' urban
plans.[88]

In the 1980s Rotterdam became a vast

Waterstad in 1994. (See, too, the photograph on page 324.)

Reorganization of the Boompjes, 1992. Design by OMA (Kees Christiaanse).

The park triangle in 1995, as seen from the southwest. The large green area in the foreground is The Park, featuring the Euromast.

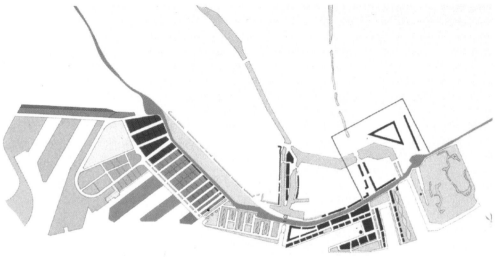

Proposal for a park lane in Rotterdam West. Design by the Department of Urban Development (Roy Bijhouwer et al.), 1987.

experimental area for (former) Delft students interested in urban form. Frits Palmboom, an exponent of the new Delft generation who had been hired by the Department of Urban Development, published an analysis of the city in 1987: *Rotterdam, verstedelijkt landschap* (Rotterdam, Urbanized Landscape). The Rotterdam described in this analysis is the result of various production processes experienced by the urban landscape.[89] The book is an indirect criticism of postwar functionalist design and of the way in which urban planning had affected the urban-renewal strategy of the 1970s. Both Van Traa's attempt to provide Rotterdam with an orthogonal grid and the introverted spatial concepts applied to urban renewal not only interfered with the continuity of long lines formed by old polder roads and ribbon development, but also provided no solutions to congested junctions.

Palmboom's book is a plea for an approach to the kind of urban design that combines an unequivocal, systematic treatment of coherent structures with specific solutions for junctions found within such structures, as a 'condition for the continuation of the dynamic interplay between intervention and geomorphological subsoil.'

The book lays an operational link between historical research and urban design; here the term 'historical research' refers primarily to the history of morphological development.

Palmboom advocates a revaluation of the significance of structuralizing urban elements: 'long lines,' most of which were created by an evolving combination of territorial characteristics (such as ribbon development and dikes) and essential infrastructural components of public space. Using this approach, urban planners would pay more attention to the design of structuralizing urban elements, without being unduly influenced by a policy on the functional organization of the city. The structuralizing urban elements that appear in *Rotterdam, verstedelijkt landschap* seem to be relatively impervious to specific kinds of use and have seen, in the course of time, a number of functions come and go.

In the 1980s this approach to the study of urban form assumed a major role in projects realized by the Department of Urban Development[90] and led to renewed emphasis on the dual significance of *the river* within the cityscape: first, as a line that structuralizes the city as a whole – a line to be regarded more as a common element uniting the two parts of the city on opposite sides of the river rather than as a divisional body; and second, as an element closely interwoven with the entire area outside the dikes and physically characterized by the space it provides for large-scale construction and infrastructure vital to a transport-based economy, a function in stark contrast to the one it performs in the densely developed, small-scale area within the dikes.

*The history of architectonic and urban planning images and types*

Of the four designs for the Kop van Zuid presented within the framework of AIR, Rossi's plan most successfully targeted the issues involved. First, with respect to the relation between history and design, Rossi introduced the historical-analogy method. The analogy he drew was not between the Kop van Zuid and the specific morphology of adjacent residential districts but – in an attempt to create a repertoire of architectonic forms and images for the area – an analogy between the Kop van Zuid and other port cities, such as Venice and New York. His analogies referred to cities in which a specific architectonic instrument essentially transformed and determined the urban image: for example, Palladian villas in Venice that

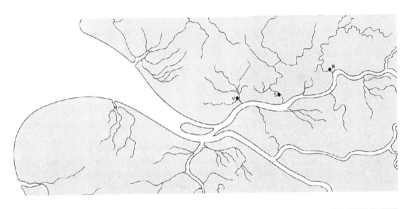

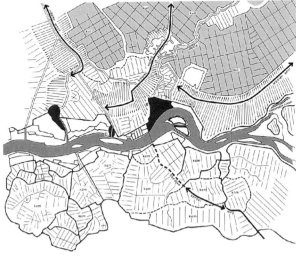

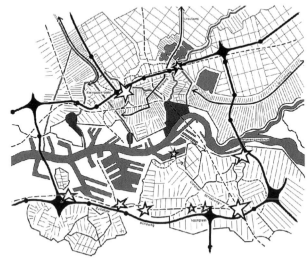

Rotterdam according to Frits Palmboom. The fundamentals of the physical structure of the city: (above) the natural river landscape, (center) the man-made landscape of dikes and other water-management systems, and (below) the traffic machine.

Pages 346 and 347: Map of Rotterdam (1990) on a scale of 1:25,000.

project into the Canal Grande and the Giudecca and, in New York, the skyscrapers of Manhattan. Although Rossi used both visual types in his design for the Kop van Zuid, it was not the history of the area that he wanted to accentuate, but the history of visual architectonic production in waterfront cities. His proposal was the most far-reaching and explicit in its rendering of what the Kop van Zuid means to the image of the city as a whole. Rossi wanted his design to show that the transformation of the Kop van Zuid could transcend any importance related to the location itself; here was an opportunity to effect a potential change in the comprehensive cityscape of Rotterdam. A series of tall buildings on the left bank of the Maas, from Wilhelminapier to Dokhaven, would provide the southern part of the city with a waterfront 'façade' and, consequently, a position rivaling that of the right bank of the Maas.

To begin with, the Department of Urban Development carefully embroidered on the evolution of a new visual typology of high-rise towers on the left bank by concentrating on an urban plan for a residential area for the harbors of Katendrecht.

Several years later the idea of a 'Manhattan on the Maas' would become an apotheosis, both on the level of using buildings to create an architectonic image and on the level of intensified programs, public space, and traffic connections.

*The history of urban planning concepts*
An important contribution to the debate was that of Italian architect Giorgio Grassi, who argued for viewing the city as a 'spectrum' of deliberate morphological choices and for organizing a historical study of 'the city as it has been marked over time, the conceived and imagined city.'[91]

In the Netherlands this approach and, more specifically, an approach that centers on

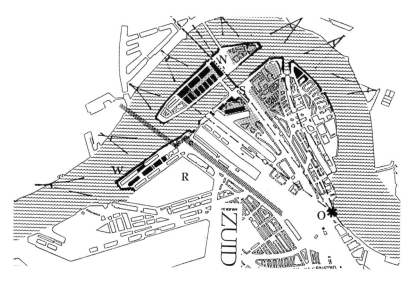

with Stieltjes Square as focal point, and the urban planning structure of Noorder Island); and second, five large buildings on the Wilhelminapier, which together helped to determine urban planning structure as well as the characteristic urban space that had evolved between these buildings.

To complement the historical-morphological study, Van Voorden implemented, in particular, the historical study of the deliberate, culturally determined, adaptations and changes of this morphological structure, in the form of urban and civil-engineering designs, to facilitate the new urban design.

*Map depicting sites and objects of cultural-historical value on the Kop van Zuid, F. van Voorden, 1991.*

analyzing the conceived city and drawing conclusions relevant to contemporary design took root, for the most part, in the sector devoted to preserving monuments and other historic structures. Owing partly to economic considerations and partly to efforts to emulate innovations in urban planning, not to mention an increasing emphasis on urban design, this sector entered a period of transition: the traditional focus on individual buildings shifted as more attention was paid to historical urban planning structures and to the legacies of urban design concepts from the past.[92] The term 'historical structural analysis' began to play a key role in the policy on the preservation of historic structures.

Later the municipality would ask Frits van Voorden, a member of the Historic Buildings Council and professor of restoration at the University of Technology in Delft, to make a 'cultural-historical structural analysis' of the Kop van Zuid as a basis for deciding what was worth preserving from a cultural-historical perspective.[93] Van Voorden's map depicting structures of cultural value stressed two things: first, the important legacy of Rose's 1860 plan and the structural parts of this plan that were still recognizable (particularly its orientation toward the St. Laurens Church,

*Collective memory versus history*

One of the most problematic aspects in the debate on the relation between history and design is the chronicle of the cultural connotations of urban structures, shapes, and images.

As a result of the construction of a railroad tunnel, which eliminated the need for the railroad viaduct through the city – including the bridge over the river and the lift bridge (the 'Hef') over Koningshaven – Willem Frijhoff, professor of social history in Rotterdam, introduced the term 'collective memory' as an indispensable aspect of the day-to-day use of the city by its inhabitants.[94] Frijhoff explicitly placed memory next to, or opposite, history: memory is not an 'objective' reconstruction of historical facts, but the result 'of a complex interaction between the historical, material structure and infrastructure of the city and the diversity of social activities practiced by its residents.' Memory is a reorganization, an adaptation of history based on reference points taken from history. Where one finds a common recognition of such reference points, one finds 'collective memory.'

Frijhoff described three kinds of reference points: material objects, social rituals, and 'testimonies' such as literature, music, the visual arts, and film. After World War II the past became the subject of nostalgia in Rotterdam, a city with a lack of reference points.[95]

The Hef was a striking illustration of Frijhoff's argument. This bridge fit into all three categories defined as 'reference points for the collective memory': a material object with a highly ritualistic significance, the Hef appeared in countless literary, cinematic, and photographic testimonies, from Joris Ivens's film *De Hef* to C.B. Vaandrager's book of the same name, which opens with the now immortal line: 'The Hef is filled with a mobility that I covet.'[96] It is possibly the only bridge in the Netherlands to which a entire biography has been devoted[97] and which has been used as a commercial trademark and as a logo for the advertisement of certain events. The city council's 1994 resolution to preserve the Hef was a sensation, because for the first time, certainly in the history of Rotterdam, an obsolete infrastructural element was marked for preservation – and granted several hundred thousand guilders annually for maintenance – on the basis of its associative, emotional, or mental significance, without first having been given 'official' recognition as an object of cultural or historic value.[98]

The other side of this success story, however, was the absence of a clearly operational means with which to continue charting the 'collective memory.' While other approaches to the relation between history and design included the development of techniques for the creation of this association (such as morphological analyses and the reconstruction of cartographic images, aside from one or two experimental efforts[99] arguments for a collective memory never got much farther than a declaration of intent.

*Historical motives as a weapon against functionalism*

The various approaches that emerged from the professional debate on new principles for urban plan development were not always strictly at odds with one another; although these approaches stressed different points, they often overlapped as well. The main characteristic shared by all was an underlying desire for an urban design practice that was not based primarily on functional considerations. Together they formed a bombardment of motives and arguments meant to persuade Rotterdam planners to make a definitive break with the kind of urban planning practiced in the postwar era, with its highly functionalist tendencies.

The revaluation of historical components found in urban design was, in fact, a revaluation of urban planning as a public affair. In each of the four designs for the Kop van Zuid, the focus on historical components was motivated by a particular interest in the historical components of 'ordinary' public urban life. Historical continuity – or at least the deliberate adaptation of elements from the past – was used by various designers who saw it as a factor capable of liberating urban design, to a great degree, from specific functional requirements and to prepare it to cope with unforeseen functional changes in the city.

After *the river*, in particular, and its harbors had been 'discovered' as elements crucial to the shape of the city, as bearers of a history of urban planning concepts, and as part of a collective memory, the question remaining was to what extent new urban planning strategies, which dealt with the position and significance of the river, would truly be able to escape the hold of functionalist tradition.

The transformation of the Kop van Zuid in full swing, 1995.
Above right: Wilheminahof under construction. Nineteenth-century warehouses along
Rijnhaven have just been demolished in preparation for the construction of the road
along the water. Photomontage by Piet Rook.

## THE IDEAL OF THE COMPLETE CITY: THE KOP VAN ZUID AS THE EPITOME OF A NEW CONSENSUS

An extremely complicated situation emerged in the course of the 1980s. Cultural and social premises supporting the Social-Democratic consensus were undermined by the appearance of new arguments in the areas of economy and urban planning.

Even though a diversity of opinions and positions existed within each of these standpoints, all of them – backed by their own spokespersons and supporters – wished to exert the greatest influence on the urban-development policy and, specifically, on plan development for the Kop van Zuid.

The Kop van Zuid was threatening to become a battlefield for various groups with various claims.

### 1987: A magical year

The year 1987, in which the situation changed completely, was a magical year for Rotterdam.

First, the desire for innovation expressed in all three standpoints reached a climax in 1987 when, among other things, a number of publications soon to be widely discussed were presented.[100] The titles of government reports, books, and conferences often included the adjective 'new': *The New Rotterdam, Renewal of Rotterdam*, and so on.

Second, this was the year that saw the rise of a plea for the integration of various ideals and arguments, a plea for consensus. The new Rotterdam was to be 'a job for all Rotterdammers.'[101]

The changes advocated were considered feasible only in the presence of a broad consensus – across all levels of Rotterdam society – on the necessity for change. The desire for an ideological consensus and for the restoration of civic culture à la the 1950s could be heard quite clearly in the various reports, which even included the statements

of prominent entrepreneurs, such as K.P. van der Mandele.[102]

The most important of these documents was a report published by the city council: *Renewal of Rotterdam*. This report introduced the concept of the *complete city*: an urban entity that combined the aforementioned arguments into a single comprehensive standpoint. The concept of the complete city was presented as a hexagon; in addition to the complete city itself, its objectives were referred to as: *economic renewal, attractive residential city, beautiful cityscape, broad social basis*, and *enterprising city council*.[103]

And third, a new urban plan for the Kop van Zuid completed in 1987 was presented as the consummate exponent of 'The New Rotterdam'; this plan combined innovations in the economic, cultural, social, and spatial development of the city.

The initiative for this plan dated from the previous year, when Riek Bakker became director of the Department of Urban Development. Under her leadership, an inventory was made of various plans for individual districts, after which those considered essential – the so-called 'spearhead plans' – were highlighted on a map of Rotterdam. This map was the first tangible planning document to translate 'urban renewal' – a slogan that had been around for years – into concrete projects distributed throughout the city.[104]

Two areas assumed prominent positions on this map. As areas of importance to a new symbiosis of city and port, both were eligible for renewal: Delfshaven Buitendijks, in the western part of the city, and the Kop van Zuid. Once more urban planners were confronted with the dilemma of 'orientation' in Rotterdam's urban development: should the city elect to grow in a southerly or in a westerly direction?

Proposals for Delfshaven Buitendijks were based partly on plans initiated by the Municipal Port Authority to transform old

Map of Spearhead Plans. Design by the Department of Urban Development, 1987.

harbors in this part of the city into a large, integrated port terminal for fruit and fruit juices; partly on ideas put forward by the Rotterdam Tomorrow group to use Muller-pier for city-center functions; and partly on the concept of the park triangle, which appeared on the 'spearhead map' as a large area covering both Mullerpier and Lloydspier.

The Department of Urban Development suggested converting the switchyard running along these harbors into a 'park lane.' This park lane was to combine a city park, which would serve as a facility for the bordering district, and an urban thoroughfare, which would connect the city center to Highway A13 and the airport. Port-related companies could build new headquarters in the park, with their entrances facing the thoroughfare. These plans were augmented with other proposals presented by the Department of Urban Development, in collaboration with French architects Nouvel and Alba, for

Lloydspier at Schiehaven. The latter were for a new urban area, featuring a multimedia center, on the spit.

The idea behind these plans was to create a new and very direct symbiosis between a renewed city and a modernized port. A combination of city park, park lane, fruit terminals, and a new expansion area with modern urban functions was to have given shape to this symbiosis. (See illustration on page 343.)

The heart of these plans for Delfshaven Buitendijks lay in a spectacular treatment of public space: an elongated city park and, at Lloydspier, an elongated 'row of dunes' meant to function, among other things, as a main dike.

The development of both projects – Delfshaven Buitendijks and the Kop van Zuid – would have been too much for a medium-sized city like Rotterdam. Developing the plans for Delfshaven Buitendijks seemed to be the most obvious choice. It would have meant an important and long-awaited expansion of public space in that district, and from a directional perspective these plans corresponded to the way in which the city was expanding 'naturally.' If a new symbiosis of city and port was to be created, this was the most logical location: both De Jongh and Witteveen had anticipated such development, and the Euromast referred to it as well.

Nevertheless, the Kop van Zuid – and not Delfshaven Buitendijks – was the area ultimately launched as the paradigm of the *complete city.*

*The Kop van Zuid as a 'collage city'*
The big breakthrough that accompanied the presentation of a new plan for the Kop van Zuid by Teun Koolhaas Associates in 1987 lay in the creation of a new synthesis of the individual standpoints. The design for the Kop van Zuid introduced two new

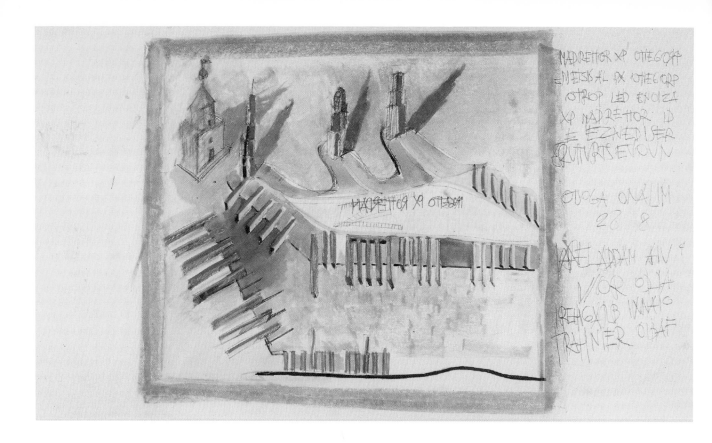

Fragment, depicting Katendrecht, of Aldo Rossi's sketch for the Kop van Zuid, 1982.

Maquette of the urban plan for the Kop van Zuid, Teun Koolhaas, 1987.

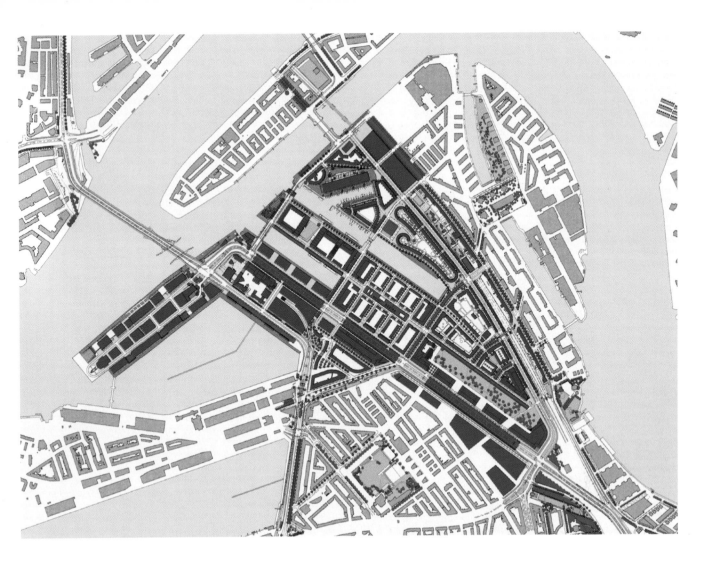

Map featured in the master plan for the Kop van Zuid, 1996.

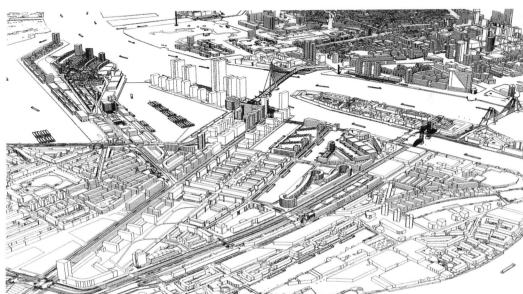

Bird's-eye view from the master plan for the Kop van Zuid, 1996.

Aerial photo of the Kop van Zuid, as seen from the southeast, 1986.

approaches. To begin with, the design paid heed to the professional debate by focusing closely on the special significance that this area has for the relation between city and river. Teun Koolhaas and Hubert De Boer interpreted the area as a central component of the city's river landscape outside the dikes. Wilhelminapier – earmarked for highly dense development, with sizable high-rise buildings – was to carry forth the tradition of large-scale development in the area outside the dikes and, at the same time, to accentuate the importance of the centrality of the river landscape to Rotterdam's urban image. Secondly, the design took advantage of the need to restore and intensify the relation between city and port. According to this plan, the Wilhelminapier area, in particular, was a suitable location for businesses with direct or indirect ties to the port, and especially for

companies interested in a 'high-quality business environment.'

The development of Waterstad, then in its initial stage – which included the establishment of the first, extremely fragile, ties between city center and river – now found itself totally eclipsed by the new plan for the Kop van Zuid. The role of future *expansion area for the inner city* was to be given not to Waterstad, whose Wijnhaven Island had already been developed, but to the Kop van Zuid. Restoring relations between the city center and the river was not envisioned as a step-by-step strategy to be carried out in Waterstad, but as a spectacular leap over the river or, in other words, as a leap over both Waterstad and the river.

The main strength of the plan for the Kop van Zuid was its capacity to function as the

A 1986 series of photo-
graphs taken on the Kop
van Zuid.

creator of a consensus in Rotterdam politics and in a cultural context. The various seemingly irreconcilable standpoints that had emerged throughout the 1980s were united here in one plan. The urban design was not so much the *expression* of a social consensus, which may be said of postwar reconstruction plans; no, the design for the Kop van Zuid had become, in and of itself, a means for reaching a new consensus among a diversity of groups and interests.

In a programmatic sense, the design rendered a translation of the need, formulated in the economy-based argument, for attractive business locations for high-tech companies and for pleasant residential environments in or close to the city center. The plan's generous office program provided for 278,000 – later increased to 400,000 – square meters of office space. Although this program was presented, time and again, as an essential expansion of the city center, it was based on highly pragmatic principles as well. In the course of the '80s, the whole financial system underlying public housing in the Netherlands was seriously threatened. A 1980 plan for 8,000 dwellings on old harbor sites may have had no problem receiving a substantial government contribution, but in 1987 state subsidies could no longer be taken for granted. Larger government funds were made available for projects aimed at the economic revitalization of big cities. New infrastructural elements, such as cross-river connections and a metro station, also required a land-grant policy that would result in a higher yield than that expected for housing projects alone.

To ease the (many) minds of those who doubted the feasibility of the large office program,[105] the *Rotterdam City Plan*, published in 1992, tried to present a picture of the city's position in a regional, a national, and an international context. In line with the national government's so-called A-, B-, and C-Locational Policy,[106] the Kop van Zuid,

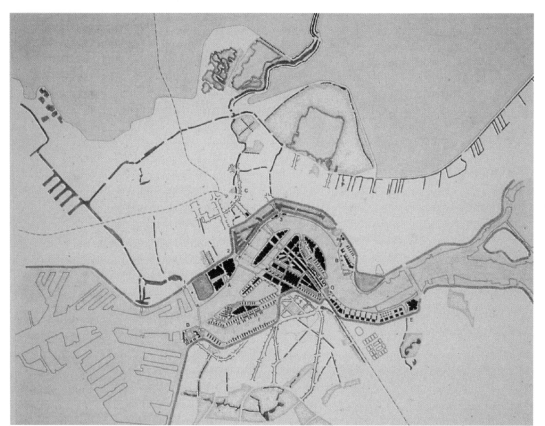

The river, with the urban landscape outside the dikes depicted as Rotterdam's city center, as pictured in the book *Kop van Zuid Kwaliteitsboek Buitenruimte*. Design by Paul Achterberg, Jaap van den Bout, and Stefan Gall, 1990.

Panorama, as seen from the west: in terms of size, the pylon of the Erasmus Bridge and the new building complex on the Kop van Zuid are on a par with the river, the harbors, and the elevator complexes.

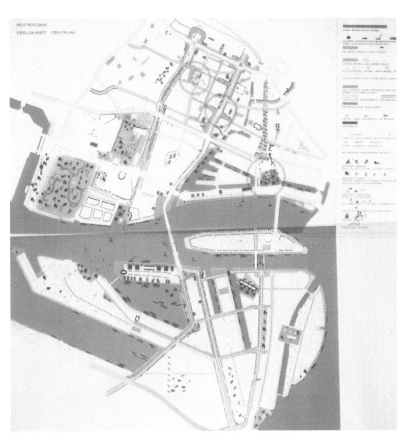

Policy plan for public open space on the Kop van Zuid, Frank Josselin de Jong, 1993.

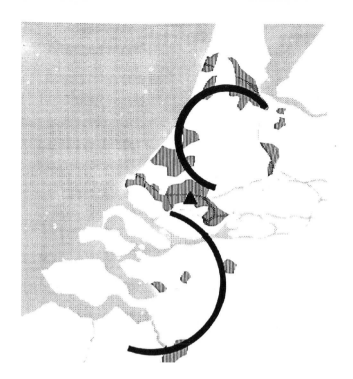

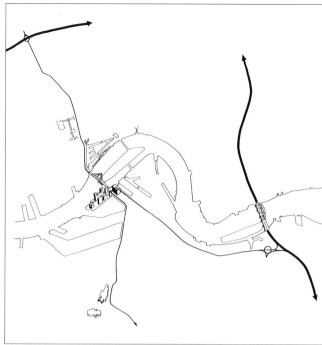

together with the city center on the right bank of the Maas, received A-Location status.

This status was based on a portrayal of Rotterdam as the link between two important, although dissimilar, spatial-economic zones: the zone featuring a ring of service-sector activities that line the highways of the Randstad, and the zone of port and industrial activities between Rijnmond and Antwerp. The essential link that ties these two zones together is Rotterdam and, more specifically, the Kop van Zuid. In its function as link, the Kop van Zuid looked like *the* location, bar none, for establishing businesses operating on the 'double track' of port industry and the service sector: 'on the cutting edge of wet and dry economies, which can be located, almost literally, on the Wilhelminapier … the "desk" of the port, the logistic nerve center of the Netherlands.'[107]

In any case, the port itself was represented in the plan by a new training center for nautical personnel, new headquarters for the Port Authority (not yet realized), berths for barges in Rijnhaven, and a terminal for cruise ships.

In a social sense, the plan was presented as a link essential to the establishment of equality between the two parts of the city on opposite banks of the river. The new cross-river connection between north and south, and the development of the Wilhelminapier into a part of the city center, were motivated by the proposition that Rotterdam South would finally be freed of its subordinate position as the stigmatized 'farmers' side' of town: 'a psychological gesture of prime importance, a symbol of the undivided city, of a Rotterdam united.'[108]

At the same time, the development of the project would also go hand-in-hand with an employment program of particular benefit to neighboring districts saddled with Rotterdam's highest unemployment percentages. This program was based largely on the creation of a special body responsible for securing a 'social return' on the project, an idea inspired by American experiences with 'linkage': the organization of the concrete

effects that new urban planning projects can have on the existing city, in the form of contractual conditions placed on investors, requiring them to provide jobs, housing, and public facilities for the local population.[109]

The design for the Kop van Zuid may also be interpreted as a 'collage city' composed of two images: one resembling New York, a paradigm of the successful, economically vital city, where the concept of private enterprise without restrictions is expressed by an accumulation of skyscrapers; and a second, resembling the garden city, a paradigm of social progress – the successful, well-controlled, equitable, harmonious city.[110]

A sharp dividing line, which was to separate these two images while also forming the bond that would connect both of them to the city as a whole and to the Randstad's network of highways, was the route of a new city boulevard also designed as a new cross-river connection.

The plan used Rotterdam's *water* – river and harbors – as a vast, binding, collective factor, which was to unite not only the individual fragments of the plan, but also the Kop van Zuid and the city center, the left and right banks of the Maas. The new Erasmus Bridge would be the totem accentuating the significance of the river and making it a

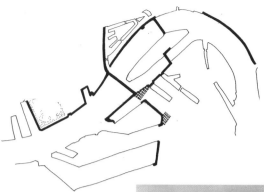

Above: Harbor and river
quays with an urban
character.

Right: Erasmus Bridge,
the public square at the
foot of the bridge, and
Wilhelminakade, 1996.

The city boulevard along
Rijnhaven: an urban quay
in the making, 1996.

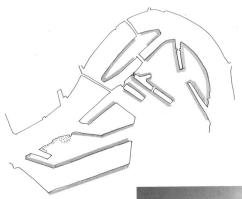

Above: Residential quays along harbors and river.

Right: Binnenhaven, a domain of residential quays, 1996.

The city boulevard on the right bank of the Maas, as it approaches Erasmus Bridge and the Kop van Zuid, with Leuvehaven to the left.

visible part of nearly every facet of the cityscape. The Maas was seen as more than simply a binding factor; it was to act as the bearer of a 'collective identity,' as a force that would reduce a broad range of concepts and ideals to a single common denominator.

Later the plan was modified for the purpose of shifting the focal point in the structure of public space. The significance of the Kop van Zuid as a link between the northern and southern parts of the city, and of the role of water as a unifying element, was reinforced by redesigning the city boulevard to allow a major section to run directly along the east side of Rijnhaven. The new design lent the whole course – from city center to Zuidplein – the character of a theatricalized route on the border of water and land, a route that would include a 3-kilometer-long stretch lined with a series of distinctive bodies of water: Leuvehaven, followed by the Nieuwe Maas, Koningshaven, Rijnhaven, and Maashaven.

In this context, the south-bank approach to the bridge would fulfill the special function of central entrance to Rotterdam South. The square at the foot of the bridge was envisioned as the core of newly organized traffic patterns, buildings, and urban programs directly on the water: the square was linked not only to the approach to the bridge, but also to the new metro station, courthouse, theater, and shops, bars, and restaurants surrounding it.

By repositioning the route and by elevating this square to the status of a public facility for the entire city, urban planners also injected the debate on the bridge with new meaning. Instead of selecting the bridge designed by the Department of Public Works – a neutral, civil-engineering-based structure – the city council chose Ben van Berkel's design for a bridge intended as a monumental, architectonic work of art.[111] Together, this bridge design and a city boulevard whose main route had been moved to follow the banks of Rijnhaven, definitely placed the accent on the bridge's significance as a 'psychological gesture,' as an element emphasizing the unified city and the close ties between city and river, leaving little remaining of the original proposal for a component to

Transparent rendition of
Wilhelminahof.

A plan for the organization
of the public square at the
foot of Erasmus Bridge,
Kop van Zuid.

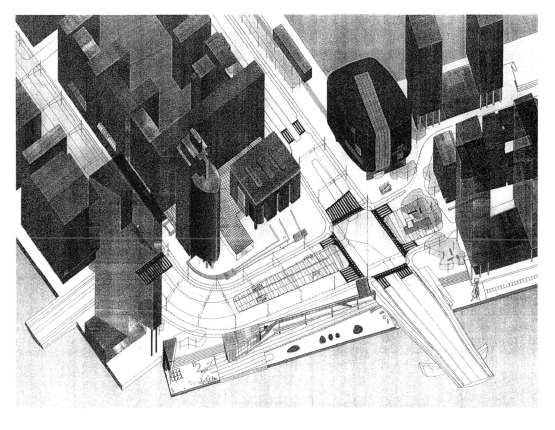

'Confrontations' between city and port. Entry, submitted by Han Meyer and Arnold Reijndorp, to a 1986 competition organized by the Eo Wijers Foundation: 'Netherlands-Land of Rivers.'

Europoort as a recreational area. Watercolor by Jenneke ter Herst

Rijnhaven as a recreational area. Watercolor by Loes Verhaart.

Proposal for a World Port Center to be located on the Maasvlakte ('Maas Plain'), Jean Nouvel, 1989.

The port as an integral part of the urban landscape of the
Rijnmond area. Design by the Bureau for Urbanism
DBSV (Roel Bakker), 1995.

Right: the Kop van Zuid
and its connections to the
local network of adjacent
urban districts.

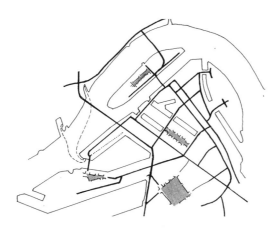

Below: Hotel New York
(hotel and restaurant),
formerly the headquarters
of the Holland America
Line, Kop van Zuid, 1996.

begin with, this concept served as a handle
for the programmatic infilling of the three
'entrances' to the Kop van Zuid: the former
headquarters of the Holland America Line
was earmarked as a café-restaurant; in keeping with the entertainment function of Oude
Haven, the Entrepôt Building would be converted into a 'festival market'; and a building
complex that included a courthouse and
offices for tax authorities was planned, as an
extension of Coolsingel, for the area at the
foot of the bridge. In addition to a programmatic aspect, the concept of three routes had
a strategic side as well: the three entrances
were to be the initial projects, those that
would set the tone for developing the whole
area.

*The paradox of designing urban complexity*
How successful was plan development for the
Kop van Zuid in creating a new relationship
between the structuralization of the city and
the design of individual urban ensembles?
The postwar reconstruction era had seen the
emergence of a striking division between the
two, and as a result the significance of structuralizing elements found in public areas –
such as Maas Boulevard and the 'Window,'
both of which were originally important
components of public space – decreased
sharply.

Within the system of planning guidelines
for the Kop van Zuid, much attention was
given to public space, building typology, and
the programmatic substance of buildings,
all matters for which 'quality books' were
published.[113] These books were the municipality's declaration of intent, a pledge to implement the urban plan according to high
standards, and had no official status as planning documents. They did provide criteria,
however, to be used by a special 'Quality
Team,' which was established as a separate
branch of the Committee for Architecture
and Monuments to ensure that all standards

augment the Randstad's highway network.[112]

Besides introducing a new city boulevard
and its bridge, the project to link the Kop van
Zuid area to the city center was able to build
on two existing initiatives, the first of which
was Westersingel in its new role as a 'cultural
boulevard' spanning the river and reaching
the other side at one end of the Wilhelminapier. The second initiative involved the debate on the significance of the Hef; although
no longer a working railroad bridge, the Hef
could form at least a visual, if not a functional, connection between the two banks of the
Maas. What followed was the concept of
three different routes between the city center
and the Kop van Zuid: a 'cultural route,' the
city boulevard, and a 'marketplace route.' To

Right: 'Programmatic routes' designed to link the Kop van Zuid to the right bank of the Maas.

Right: 'Programmatic routes' designed to link the Kop van Zuid to the right bank of the Maas.

Below: the former Vrij Entrepôt, which has been converted into the 'Exotic Festival Market.'

point was a varied program that provided a range of public facilities in an 'urban plinth' at ground-floor level.
– The level of public space: this level included a combination of public, semipublic, and private areas.

The Department of Urban Planning focused on the third aspect, in particular – a combination of public open space with areas that were, in fact, private open space – as a means of maintaining a grip on the overall design and infilling of both Wilhelminapier and Wilhelminahof. As the first big office project to be developed, Wilheminahof would put this strategy to the test.[114]

This office complex, with a new metro station as part of the project, was to be a hub of public transportation, while urban plinths accommodating 20,000 square meters of shopping facilities were planned at ground level.

The developer, however, presented a plan in which the ground floor was dominated by a parking garage. An urban plinth with a public function was not considered lucrative. Ultimately, the municipality and the developer compromised: most of the parking accommodations were relocated underground, while the exterior wall facing Rijnhaven was designed to allow for the long-term realization of public facilities.

Instead of a building complex with an urban plinth on all sides, this 'dead' street façade at ground level was earmarked for Rijnhaven, of all places, the side along which the city boulevard was projected; and instead of a combination of metro station and public facilities, people leaving the station would enter an atrium offering nothing but office functions.

The desire to design urban complexity was even greater in the case of the Wilhelminapier. The entire pier was to be designed as 'an architectonic entity,' with a complex and diffuse network of public, semipublic, and

of quality would be satisfied.

The initial aim was to create a high degree of reciprocity among the three categories. This aim applied particularly to the two parts of the plan meant to express, above all else, the complex urban nature found in a bustling, vital city center: the ensemble surrounding the square at the foot of the bridge (Wilhelminahof) and that of the adjacent Wilhelminapier.

The complexity of these two ensembles was defined on each of three levels:
– The level of spatial composition: the accent here was on a great deal of variety in the typology and architectonic appearance of individual components within the ensemble.
– The level of the program: here the focal

Three renditions of Wilhelminapier.

Above: As it was in 1955.

Center: Wilhelminapier as a 'cruise ship' in *De Kop van Zuid, kwaliteit en beeldvorming*, 1990.

Below: Maquette of the master plan for Wilhelminapier, 1993. Design by the Department of Urban Planning and Public Housing (Jaap van den Bout) and Norman Foster.

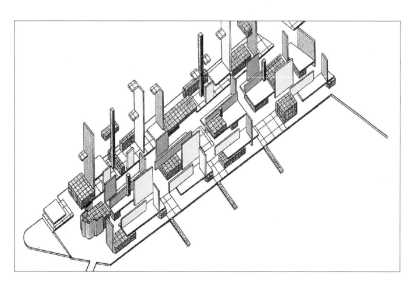

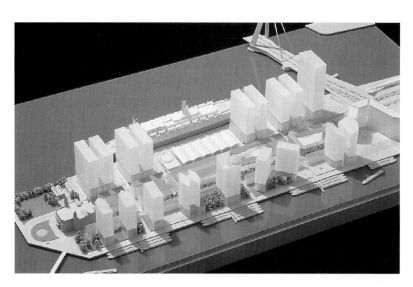

private areas. The metaphor for this project was a cruise ship, 'where social and dynamic activities take place on a number of "decks," in lounges, restaurants, ballrooms, cabins, captain's quarters, engine rooms, which together create the conditions for a pleasant voyage': in short, a complex entity for which 'classic urban planning resources are insufficient.'[115]

Eventually, the plan for the Wilhelminapier was greatly simplified, however: the 'experience' gained in planning Wilhelminahof clearly showed that such a complex blend held too much uncertainty and risk, for both authorities and private parties. Together with Sir Norman Foster, who was hired as an urban planning consultant by the Wilhelminapier development consortium, the Department of Urban Planning designed a new master plan, which introduced a lucid, 'classic' distinction between public space and land-grant property, and which made use of traditional planning resources: explicit building lines, maximum heights, zoning regulations for both building volumes and programs, and clear guidelines for providing access to buildings and for linking them to public space. This more relaxed, classical approach also allowed those buildings in the central zone, which had been selected for

preservation as historically valuable structures, to be incorporated into the urban plan
with relative ease.

The quality book on public space was
the only one developed extensively enough
to serve as a basis for a 'policy plan for open
space.' This plan provided the whole network
of public space with finely detailed differentiation and with a hierarchy, which included
a clear distinction between (a) the Kop van
Zuid's main structural elements – routes,
quays, and squares – which were to anchor
the area to the urban context, and (b) public
space in the form of internal, 'social' areas
found in residential neighborhoods and office
complexes. Every type of public space was
governed by strict regulations for organization, materialization, and verdure.

Owing to the greater emphasis on structuralizing and designing public space, the
development of the plan for the Kop van
Zuid has become less dependent on the realization of a specific program for the use of
buildings. Ultimately, the creation of a great
deal of office space on the Wilhelminapier
will be of particular importance to the
profitability of the plan: the enormous
financial resources that the municipality has
invested in infrastructure and public space
must be recovered in the form of maximal
land prices, which can be realized only if the
office program is completed as planned. Thus
in many ways the development of the Kop
van Zuid finds itself competing with the
development of other potential expansion
areas for the city center, such as Waterstad,
whose future development is, in fact, essential
to a coherent relationship between the city
center and the Kop van Zuid.

NEW CONNECTIONS BETWEEN
CITY AND PORT

The plan for the Kop van Zuid was one
example of a renewed search for a mutual

relationship uniting city, river, and port. It
represented an attempt to reawaken the city's
awareness of the river and the port. Other
examples of this renewed pursuit were new
plans for Botlek, Europoort, and Maas Plain:
the modern, working area of the port. In the
mid-'80s a topic of discussion emerged that
focused on the other side of the coin: the
presence of the city in the port.

The go-ahead for developing this subject
was given by an independent organization,
the Eo Wijers Foundation, which organized a
competition in 1985 that included the entire
'delta region' of the Netherlands. Certain
competition entries for the Rijnmond area
were based on the concept that many harbor
sites are suitable for urban functions, such
as recreation and housing.[116] Some of the
proposals contained in these plans can be
found in *Masterplan Wereldhaven*, published
by the Municipal Port Authority in 1989,
which presented the port area as a 'challenge
to tourism and recreation.' The heart of this
master plan lay in the development of an
'International Port Center' on Maas Plain,
which was to provide congress and office
facilities, as well as touristic and recreational
functions. This center was to be the initial
impetus for weaving urban functions into
the fabric of the port area. (See page 366.)

Although the plan was never realized, it
drew attention to an important change in
the way people thought about the relation
between city and port. Since the 1960s both
phenomena – city and port – had been
treated to an increasing degree as incompatible quantities and had been developed sepa-
rately from each other, but now even the port
sector was beginning to see the advantages in
a renewed kinship between city and port. The
port had become too much of a terra incognita, and as a result the port sector found
itself in an isolated position, both politically
and socially. The *Masterplan Wereldhaven* was
aimed largely at the reinforcement of political
and social support for Rotterdam's port.

Six years later, in 1995, a retrospective of fifty years of reconstruction activities provided a framework for building on these ideas and, simultaneously, set the stage for an event dedicated to 'the next fifty years.'[117] As part of this event, the municipality invited a number of designers to submit proposals for locations that referred directly to the relation between urban development and port development. Besides presenting the Delfshaven Buitendijks area as a development site, Rem Koolhaas also proposed a concept for development in the vicinity of the 'A4 corridor,' which forms the western part of the beltway around Rotterdam; and landscape architect Roel Bakker introduced his study of potential development in Rotterdam's modern, postwar port area. The proposals made by Koolhaas and Bakker, in particular, indicated the feasibility of entirely new spatial and programmatic developments that would shift the focal point of the relation between city and port much farther west, in the direction of the modern, working port. (See page 367.)

Koolhaas showed that an improved connection between Highway A4 and the national highway network was vital to a new symbiosis of highway infrastructure and port infrastructure and, consequently, to the creation of new economic activities and new urban programs. Transportation and distribution organizations directly related to the port, as well as less directly related businesses, would be able to locate their operations along this highway corridor.

Roel Bakker's proposal was based on the assumption that the relation between city and port can no longer be relegated to a single location. In his design, a nearly 40-kilometer-long area between the Kop van Zuid and the coast was to accommodate all sorts of mutual relationships between city and port, each of which would be based on the specific conditions provided by its location. Bakker suggested an intensive blend of urban functions and port activities for the Waalhaven area and

situated an exclusive urban enclave with the air of a monastery amid container terminals on Maas Plain. In essence, however, the plan presented none of these specific proposals as sustainable solutions. Hence top priority was given to a 'scenic parkway,' which was to form a central element in the harbor landscape and to introduce a new type of multifunctional public space. Its primary role was as main access route to port-related industry, but it was given the nature of an urban attraction as well, of a pleasant road between city and coast, along which new urban programs *could* be established. But even without these programs, this parkway was designed as an important urban facility.

Although this concept did lend concrete shape to a new relation between city and port, it did not relegate this association to one location. The relation between city and port emerged, for the most part, from a new sort of network of public areas. The space-time continuum is formed by this new public space or, in other words, by the parkway itself.

AMSTERDAM: CONTINUOUS ALIENATION BETWEEN THE CITY AND THE IJ

The temptation to return to the discussion of the Netherlands' other large waterfront project – the banks of the IJ – is too great to resist.

Although plan development for the banks of the IJ in Amsterdam is based on a number of principles that differ in many ways from those used in Rotterdam, striking similarities between the two plans exist as well.

Differences pertain to traditions in urban planning, the current social context, and design concepts.

While Rotterdam has an urban planning tradition based on a ceaseless search for another, and yet another, new relationship with the water, Amsterdam has displayed a tradition of ironclad consistency marked by the city's continuous alienation from the IJ. Ever since the creation of the ring of canals, designed as a comfortable residential area for an affluent bourgeoisie, the city has turned its back on the boggy, mist-filled world of the IJ. The canal system gave the relation between city and water the sort of structure that characterizes a *rhizome*, to use a rather fancy word.

Since that time, this separation of the city and the IJ has only intensified. The realization of the station, which represented a logical step in this development, was a guarantee, furthermore, that the Damrak would maintain its central position within the spatial and functional organization of the city.

The city's alienation from the IJ continued on into the twentieth century. Viewed in the context of the city as a whole, the development of Amsterdam North remained an incident, nor did it lead to a reorientation of the city toward the IJ. For that matter, even the garden-city communities in Amsterdam North were interwoven with the polder landscape rather than being directly oriented toward the IJ. The IJ was simply something to be crossed.

What strikes one most about urban planning in Amsterdam is the rigid consistency with which planning concepts have been implemented. An undeniable fact about the urban planning culture of Amsterdam is: whatever they do, they do consistently. This applies to the creation of the ring of canals; to Berlage's realization of Amsterdam South; and to postwar development in which, even today, the concept of Van Eesteren and Van Lohuizen's 1934 General Expansion Plan (GEP or, in Dutch, AUP) asserts its presence. The AUP was another plan that failed to grant a meaningful role to the IJ. Although the concept of a lobate structure, which allowed the city to grow in both westerly and southerly directions, was adapted and expanded

down through the years, it never experienced any fundamental change. This stability formed the main basis for the relatively successful development of the Eastern Harbor Area and set the stage for the realization of a new lobe, which extends in an easterly direction, via IJ Island, and includes the area now known as IJburg. Another stabilizing element was a program for the Eastern Harbor Area that was an established fact (virtually 100 percent housing) at an early stage, not to mention that there was no lack of interested clients.

In Rotterdam the plan for the Kop van Zuid required a completely new structural concept for the city as a whole, and the municipal government had little grip on the ambitious program projected (particularly in the case of the office program). In Amsterdam's Eastern Harbor Area, on the other hand, urban planners could build on a structural concept that had been used for over half a century, and the program involved was familiar to all. These relatively stable conditions provided ample opportunity for experimentation in the search for a new relationship between the coherence of the whole and the degree of autonomy in smaller parts. As these individual parts of the project were realized, such experiments led, little by little, to a definitive new concept for the Eastern Harbor Area as a whole.[118]

Initially, the chief point of departure was the preservation of the area's existing island structure. From the very beginning the water, with its various harbor basins and quays lined with buildings, was designated as the main structuralizing component, which was to provide the area with spatial coherence. In the course of the planning process a second component was highlighted as well: the essential structure of public space, which was to lend access to the individual islands and, as an area of parks and recreation, to provide the project with extra quality. Finally, when plan development began for the last two islands in the project, Borneo and Sporenburg, a third

Above: within the lobate structure of Amsterdam, the Eastern Harbor Area and IJburg are a new lobe that projects into the water.

Below: composition of the Eastern Harbor Area. From bottom to top: the water as a structuralizing component; the islands as individual ensembles; the system of sculptural building blocks; and the network of public areas.

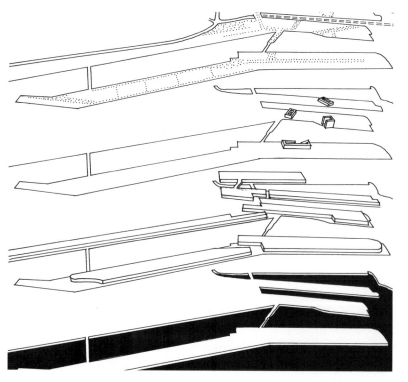

component was introduced in the form of a series of 'sculptural building blocks.'

What originally started as a pragmatic in-filling of individual islands ultimately grew into an urban planning structure, in which three separate components created a coherent entity that offered an opportunity to those involved – clients, architects, and supervisors – to fill in each of these islands according to their own views and wishes, with relative freedom and autonomy. Then, too, as the development of new islands in Lake IJ (IJburg) progressed, planners based their activities on the principle of determining urban design primarily by focusing on the spatial characteristics of the watery land-scape, the infrastructure, and sculptural volumes.

On the other hand, the development of the banks of the IJ cannot boast of a trouble-free adaptation to traditions established by the General Expansion Plan; in fact, it did not fit in at all. These banks remain a blank page in the legacy of the AUP.

The concept of the 'IJ axis' was based largely on a fear that the city center would fall into decline as a result of urbanization along the 'south axis' (the southern section of the beltway) and around the 'mainport' of Schiphol. The Amsterdam Waterfront Finance Company (AWF) hoped to prevent this with a substantial program that included 500,000 square meters of office space and 100,000 square meters of facilities.

The design studio for the IJ project, run by Rem Koolhaas and colleagues, was a laboratory of inventors looking for totally new building typologies, which were to exemplify new developments in the areas of industrial planning, housing culture, and entertainment culture. No reference was made to familiar images; on the contrary, the plan was an appeal to a fascination for the new, the unexpected, the unknown. These designers turned the world upside down: quite literally, in the case of the topsy-turvy station roof. The plan presented the banks of

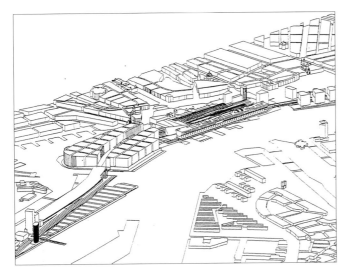

the IJ as a new, autonomous world facing a
vast expanse of open water, a world meant to
create – without relying on the traditional
Amsterdam – a foundation for new forms of
urban life, a world able to distinguish itself
from the existing city precisely because of
its open relationship with the IJ. The open
expanse of water was used to accentuate the
exclusivity of the location.

The concept behind the IJ project built on
the development of the Eastern Harbor Area:
one island at a time. The banks of the IJ also
form a series of islands, which could be largely developed, theoretically, on an independent basis. What these banks lacked, however,
was a clear distinction between main and
autonomous elements, a distinction plainly
visible in the Eastern Harbor Area. In developing the banks of the IJ, a project with an
extremely ambitious but indefinite program,
such a distinction should have been all the
more obvious.

Instead, a plan was presented which
seemed to have nothing but main elements
and which implied a desire to allow the
development of the entire plan area to be
managed by one central director. With
intentions such as this, the Amsterdam
Waterfront Finance Company went considerably farther than anyone had gone in

planning the Kop van Zuid. The realization
of the concept for the banks of the IJ, in
which any 'traditionally' implemented
element may have detracted from the plan's
innovational élan, demanded a meticulous
orchestration. The AWF, which was in fact
a private organization, claimed the right to
develop and manage the entire IJ project,
including public space.[119] This meant not
only an infringement of the public character
of such space, but also the absence of any
real surprises or unexpected deviations in
the project.

In addition to the Amsterdammers' strong
anarchistic aversion to a central direction of
this sort, the withdrawal of investors from the
AWF was a definite sign that no support
existed for these incongruous plans for urban
development in Amsterdam. After the experiments of the AWF, the municipality of Amsterdam appears to have regained its senses.
The focus has shifted from developing ultra-
revolutionary types of office buildings to
fitting IJ Boulevard efficiently into the plan –
the main project – and to creating an attractive recreational environment, while further-
ing the area's central role in the city's public-
transportation network. The pivot around
which everything revolves is 'Stations Island,'
which is to be converted into a unique and

fascinating traffic and transportation hub on the water.

Thus the chief similarity between the banks of the IJ and the Kop van Zuid is a shared 'rediscovery' of public space as an important object within the process of urban planning, while both projects have also faced difficulties in pursuing a consistent development of the new prime elements of public space, owing to departments of urban planning with too many goals to achieve. As a result, in both cities the most structural elements of public space, which are essential to the desired relation between city and open water, continue to be the most uncertain: in Rotterdam, the development of the entire route of the city boulevard; and in Amsterdam, Stations Island.

## 5    Balance: Restless Relations Between City and River

The urban planning culture of Rotterdam is characterized by unrelenting efforts to tie the city to the river. Particularly in the twentieth century, each generation of urban planners seems eager to develop another new concept, but they often lack the perseverance necessary to turn these concepts into realized projects. The city is littered, so to speak, with a variety of design concepts.

A notable reason for this inconstancy lies in the changeability of the port and in its ongoing increase in scale. Prior to the nineteenth century, the port was a clearly localizable phenomenon, the position and size of which had changed very little throughout the course of three centuries. After the mid-1800s, this clarity came to an abrupt halt. Not only did the port grow; the heart of the port began a seemingly unending journey, as it shifted farther and farther away from the original site. While urban planners tried to use the orientation toward the port as a solid, sustainable basis for the city plan, the port slithered like a slippery eel, constantly changing its position and continuing to grow.

The paradox of the growing independence of the port, as it relates to the city, and the contradictory nature of continuing attempts to unite city and port was epitomized — many years ago, in the prewar era — by Backx. Since then, the capriciousness of both phenomena has only intensified. The speed of techno-logical developments and economic processes makes it virtually impossible to predict how the modern distribution port will function ten years from now, what role the city of Rotterdam will play in port activities, and what type of industry will prefer one location or another at that moment. In short, a desire to steer economic activity in a given direction may be high on a city's list of priorities, but it is becoming increasingly risky to separate the success of an urban plan from the realization of specific programs.

In the various design concepts of the past century and a half, the association between the urban plan and specific programs has been defined in a number of ways, with associations sketched in the first generation of designs being notably different from those found in later generations. Certain nineteenth-century interventions implemented by Rose and De Jongh have proved strong enough to stand the test of time. Over one hundred years later, most of these nineteenth-century works are still meaningful urban elements, even though they no longer orient the city toward the port, as originally intended, and even though many buildings have experienced marked changes in both function and architectonic appearance. While the life span of any structure built in this 'dynamic city' is completely unforeseeable — even the postwar city is being subjected to major demolition operations – the better elements of public space seem to be functioning as structures of the *longue durée*, of historical continuity. The various orientations have remained relatively stable, but they are joined constantly by new orientations.

The secret of these nineteenth-century structuralizing elements lies in a high capacity for varied use, made possible by designers who carefully fashioned these elements as important areas of public space. From one end to the other, Westersingel, Westerkade, and Heemraadssingel were beautifully designed as a combination of broad urban thoroughfares and canals. The design of these public areas did not refer directly to the primary functions for which they had been realized: they were not created simply as drainage canals or as routes for through traffic; the quays were to function as more than just zones for loading and unloading vessels. Secondary motives, which played a major role in these designs, produced a combination of functions suitable for open space. These became vital components of the city's traffic and transportation infrastructure, functioning as new centers of public urban life and serving Rotterdam as important areas of distinction. The way in which the primary functions of these quays and canals were put into perspective has allowed them to continue playing a leading role as structuralizing elements for their own particular localities, even though they are no longer essential in an infrastructural sense, or as connecting routes between city and port.

The precision with which public space was designed and prepared for multiple functions was not matched by a detailed regulation of architectural development. Nineteenth-century city architects were not eager to direct and orchestrate the appearance and use of buildings in any far-reaching manner; they relied on a number of building regulations for the control of such matters.

It is precisely because such elements have had so little to do with the specific functional infilling necessary to their realization that they have continued to be so important to the city.

In the twentieth century, however, urban planning has been dominated to an increasing degree by the desire for a city whose architecture and functions are meticulously orchestrated according to an urban plan.

In the postwar reconstruction era, urban planning was influenced strongly by efforts to shape program and architectonic appearance into a coherent entity on the scale of the ensemble. Ultimately, this exaggerated accent on the scale of the urban ensemble led to a greater fragmentation of the city. The nineteenth-century city's highly structuralizing elements are no longer present in the twentieth-century city, with a few noted exceptions such as Witteveen's Maas Tunnel route, Maas Boulevard, and Coolsingel.

Other postwar plans for public areas that were to serve as structuralizing urban elements often failed to meet their goals, the most notable example being the 'Window to the River.'

After the dikes were reinforced and the ships of the Holland America Line vanished from the scene, stripping the 'Window to the River' of its literal significance as an urban porthole, nothing of substance remained to lend meaning to Schiedamsedijk.

Various recent plans may be seen as attempts to pick up the thread of nineteenth-century urban planning. Proposals for a park lane in Rotterdam West, for a 'scenic parkway' in the Europoort area, and for the A4 corridor are efforts to create new types of public space, which can be added to the existing network of public areas that link city and port. The primary goal of these new types is to establish conditions for new urban activity and industry. But no one knows exactly how, or to what degree, these new additions to the network will lead to the development of urban activity. Hence the design of these new elements is conceived as a task that includes providing them with spatial autonomy, creating strong links that do not have to rely on the whims of urban and port-related programs.

The Kop van Zuid's city boulevard is another new addition to the network of public areas. After all, a vital aspect of the Kop van Zuid project is the new system of public areas that this plan is adding to the city, of which the city boulevard is the pivot. This new thoroughfare and its accompanying bridge could prove to be the first new structuralizing element in Rotterdam's postwar history that has significance on various levels of scale: as a connection to the highway network, as a local connection between the two halves of the city, and as a common element uniting bordering urban neighborhoods. Designing this new system as a sustainable network of public areas is the main task facing those developing the Kop van Zuid, and the results of their work will be the basis upon which this half of the city will be judged twenty, fifty, or a hundred years from now. Although the realization of a vast program of 'high-quality activity' is surely one of the most important reasons for developing the project, it is also one of the most uncertain factors. The unstable nature of the development of the port and the changing relations between city and port are precisely why the quality of a project like this should not have to rely on the success or failure of an ambitious program for buildings on the Kop van Zuid. And if and when such a program is completed, its realization offers no guarantee of how the situation and the use of the buildings will appear several decades from now.

Theoretically, the new city boulevard is backed by enough starting points to become an element vital to the structuralization of the city: an element that not only connects a series of important urban functions, but also serves as a clearly defined route that makes the city intelligible and easy to comprehend – a thoroughfare that expresses Rotterdam's intrinsic nature as a delta city as it passes a series of harbor basins and the river. The development of the east side of Rijnhaven and Maashaven is of particular importance. Here the water and the roadway, as well as the dike and the viaduct (at Maashaven), form the basic ingredients for a city boulevard designed to become a central urban public area. The development and emphasis of this quality should produce a city boulevard that is a sustainable element over the long term, so that fifty or a hundred years from now, when many a building will have assumed a new function or a different form, and the 'logistic nerve center' will have relocated or become consumed by networks of 'virtual companies,' the city boulevard will still be just as significant as Rotterdam's nineteenth-century public works are today.

# Chapter 6

*Urbanizing Infrastructure: An Urban Design Project*

This analysis of the development of four port cities clearly shows that from an urban planning perspective the twentieth century has been characterized by difficulties in situating large-scale infrastructure networks (not only harbors, but also highways, railroads, and airports) with respect to urban settlements. In most cases, large infrastructural elements are conceived as a paradoxical combination of ballast and necessity: they are seen as barriers, as a source of inconvenience, but the city cannot do without them.

The situation was not always so. Each of the four cities discussed here has its own urban planning tradition with regard to the design of infrastructure as an integral part of the urban landscape. And each city has experienced the loss of this tradition, followed by recent attempts to pick up the thread of its urban planning legacy. These attempts combine a search for new functions for obsolete infrastructural elements (old harbor areas) with the realization of new elements – roads and highways, for the most part, as well as railroad facilities and airports (London).

At the same time that the importance of an integral approach to public space and infrastructure is gradually being 'rediscovered' as an urban design project, we are being confronted with urban planning's long 'absence' from these areas, which has resulted in the fragmentation of complex infrastructural issues into a variety of subdisciplines.

CONFRONTATIONS AND RELATIONS AMONG VARIOUS LEVELS OF SCALE

'Large-scale infrastructure' has two main characteristics: the first pertains to physical-spatial networks vital to the coherence of large areas, networks whose importance transcends the scale of an individual city. The second characteristic refers to the physical-spatial shape and size of such infrastructures, which demand a relatively large amount of space in both a two-dimensional and three-dimensional respect.

This duality of magnitude is also an urban planning problem. As interlocal or international networks, large-scale infrastructures are of great importance to the city. They open up the city, are essential to its relevance in a broader regional or international context, provide fresh economic and social vitality, and function as locations from which a city's established groups and institutions can present themselves to the 'outside world.'

The immensity of infrastructural elements, however, forms an impediment to linking or adapting them to the existing city. Owing to the dimensions of ships, trucks, and airplanes; to increasing speeds; and, more recently, to the rise of air and noise pollution, large-scale infrastructure networks are subjected to special regulations and conditions, which differ from the norms and standards applied to ordinary urban street networks.

This problem, like any problem, may be viewed as a *project*, the objective of which is to solve the problem or at least to find an acceptable response. Such a project can be worded as follows: *'Design large-scale infrastructure in such a way that the local situation thus created leaves the function of the infrastructure itself intact and, at the same time, lends added value to the immediate urban context.'*

In most of the cities discussed here, efforts to provide the local context of large-scale infrastructure with multiple functions was a more or less self-evident aspect of urban plans prior to the early 1900s. As far back as the nineteenth century London exhibited a clear-cut division between large-scale infrastructure serving Docklands, on the one hand, and the residential city, on the other. Planners in other cities appearing in this book, however, developed a design practice which continued well into the twentieth century and which based the relationship between infrastructure and urban context on four important principles:

1. The infrastructural elements involved (harbor quay, drainage system, highway) were always considered part of the overall network of public urban space. These were *public works*, and even though they were of an order and a scale previously unknown, the task was to combine and connect the new and the enormous with the traditional, existing network of public space. This principle is quite apparent from the drafts and planning maps themselves, on which recently built public works often fulfilled a new, structuralizing role within the greater entity known as public space. The way in which they were designed brought a new logic, a new readability, to the urban network. This logic applied not only to nineteenth-century harbor quays, but also to the new system of highways in Barcelona, to American parkways, and to canal-lined avenues in Rotterdam.

2. Each of these new public works was marked by a *differentiation in scale*, allowing it to play a role in large-scale networks as well as in the local urban network. In most cases, this differentiation in scale was created by means of the section, sometimes with a subtle and relatively simple design, such as a row of trees along a quay to differentiate between harbor zone and urban zone; and sometimes with a more radical plan, such as the sunken roadway in Rotterdam's Maas Tunnel route.

3.  Urban design *authorship* allowed new public works to be designed as coherent urban areas, despite the differentiation in scale. All aspects – including the project's linkup to various networks, the creation of distinctive features, materialization, greenery, and technical construction – were integrated into one coherent design. The row of trees along the quay not only lent spatial articulation and functional differentiation to the design, but also gave the quay a unified appearance. The designer was able to create this row of trees, however, only as part of the design for the construction of the quay itself, which in Dutch port cities, for example, included a complex system of tie rods and osier mats. Fitting quays, water and park systems, and sunken roadways into the urban context was made possible through close cooperation between civil engineers and urban planners. Civil-engineering designs and urban plans were inextricably entwined.

4.  In most cases, the primary function of these public works did not dominate the design: an apt description would be the *'defunctionalization'* of the urban plan. The design of new public works was not a direct result of the primary functions for which they were planned: Rotterdam's canals and adjacent avenues were not created exclusively as a drainage/sewage system lined with thoroughfares, Olmsted's park systems were more than simply networks linking one part of the city with another, and the quays of Barcelona and Rotterdam were not designed purely as zones for loading and unloading cargo. Secondary motives – a major part of each design – produced a combination of public-space functions and thus allowed these works to develop a deeper significance within the everyday life of the urban population.

FOUR DIFFERENT APPROACHES TO THE DESIGN OF INFRASTRUCTURE

Renewed interest in the design of public space and infrastructure, now seen as the domain of urban planners, emerged in the 1980s. Of the various approaches developed in that decade and the next, four are easily distinguishable:

1.  *A clear division between city and infrastructure for the sake of harmony and coherence between public space and architecture.*
    The urban planning paradigm found in this category is that of the urban ensemble as *Gesamtkunstwerk*, in which architecture, the design of public space, and function are interrelated. Inherent to this approach is a distinct separation of different types of public areas with varying functions and implications: on the one hand, 'real' public space, in which the urbanite can relax and recreate and, on the other hand, the infrastructure – an autonomous technical system separated from this public space to the greatest extent possible. Prototypical examples are urban enclaves

developed in London's Docklands and in various 'rousified' harbor areas in North America.

Within the evolution of the current generation of 'stable, definitive-image plans,' organizations based on public-private cooperation (PPC) have assumed the role of plan developer, a key position formerly held by local authorities. This evolution may be viewed in the context of two simultaneous processes. The first is the 'regionalization' of the city, which implies an increase in the scale of urbanization at the regional level; and the second is the lack of a clear political and social consensus at this same level. As part of these contexts, PPC organizations take recourse in well-defined subareas, which are expected to fulfill strategic positions as hubs of new networks as the urban region develops. Within the boundaries of these subareas lies an opportunity for the various partners involved to come to a new sort of consensus: within these boundaries, a fluctuating market and any number of unstable political relationships are inactivated, so to speak. The parties in this arrangement see public space primarily as a component of the ensemble, a factor that adds value to the whole.

In the majority of these projects 'cultural quality' is characterized as a state of coherence present in the overall image, a state to be created by blending architecture, the design of public space, and the function of both. This interpretation of cultural quality is largely a legacy of the period marked by a Social Democratic consensus. A more detailed definition, as well as the regulation and control of this state of coherence, was once seen as an obvious task of the government – and in many of these projects, as the task of municipal urban planning departments. When the Social Democratic consensus ceased to exist, people began losing faith in the government. Instead of seeing the government as an institution superior to the political parties composing it, they increasingly view the government itself as a party. At the same time, the definition of 'cultural quality' has changed very little during this period. The job of regulating and controlling the coherent image projected by architecture, public space, and function is assigned to others considered 'superior to political parties': experts given the special status of supervisors or appointed to serve on 'Quality Teams.'

All areas, in both the public and private domains, have to pass muster: precise guidelines exist for the design of public space, for architecture, and for function.

Each project exhibits clearly defined distinctions between public-space networks on various levels of scale, distinctions expressed in the design of outdoor areas carefully geared to the architecture of adjacent buildings and in the application of a purely 'technical' infrastructure for through traffic. In the first place, PPC organizations are often faced with the practicalities associated with financing, implementing, and managing infrastructure projects. But even more important are the intrinsic motives of clients, who see a high degree of accessibility to the project as a threat to its exclusivity; an example is residential squares in London's West End, which were surrounded by fences in the nineteenth century to protect them from the outside world.

Heightened interest in the integral design of *urban projects* is accompanied by a lack of attention to the design of connecting routes between hubs. Although the projects themselves are subjected to criteria like 'cultural identity' and 'spatial quality,' such criteria are rarely applied to the infrastructure of new routes that link one project to the other. The new infrastructure composed of highways and railroad connections is evaluated only on its technical merits as a link between individual hubs and not on its capacity to interrelate with intermediary parts of the urban landscape. Thus the urban landscape becomes even more fragmented and, as a result, a great deal of the city is excluded from these networks. The situation is, in fact, a continuation and a reinforcement of the resulting separation between the socialized and the technocratized public domains. This approach perpetuates the ideological and political vacuum surrounding the significance of public space.

2. *The relationship between city and infrastructure as a fashionable design project.*

Noise and odor nuisance, which is associated in particular with highways that border residential urban neighborhoods, has led to an enormous increase in acoustical walls along these routes. Following criticism of the unattractive nature of the first generation of acoustical walls, the '90s approach to the fashionable design of these barriers has been based on presenting the highway as an aesthetically acceptable element. 'Design' is the key word, however: such additions are subject to changing trends and fashions, and although they do influence the spatial image, they do nothing – either negative or positive – to change the relationship between highway and city. This relationship can even be damaged by the addition of acoustical walls, and often is. At various spots along metropolitan beltways, new economic activities have emerged as a result of how well a company can be seen from the highway. Acoustical walls thwart these developments.

3. *The relationship between city and infrastructure as an architectonic project.*

Another movement actually propagates and cultivates a new relationship between city and infrastructure. Building on the great paradigms of the modernists, such as Le Corbusier's Obus Plan, supporters of this approach wish to express this new relationship in an architectonic design for a project that combines infrastructure, buildings, and public urban space into an inextricable entity. The movement's most important built design is the Euralille project, designed and supervised by Rem Koolhaas. Euralille is based on an obsessive desire to encompass a new social complexity within a single project. The larger question at the heart of this complexity – at present a designed, constructed complexity – is whether or not it can provide the space needed for social complexity, especially in the long term. Infrastructure, public space, and buildings are interwoven into one project to such an extent that an eventual modification of any one of these components will surely cause tremendous problems.

In fact, this category is another version of the first approach, that of the *Gesamtkunstwerk*. Although here the main objective is not harmony but the desire to design contrasts, one cannot deny that both categories are based on the idea of architecture and urban planning as an entity and on the need to have full control of the final image.

4.  *The relationship between city and infrastructure as an urban design project.*

Meanwhile, experiments have also proved that the design of new relationships between city and infrastructure can be interpreted and developed as an urban planning project.

In this approach 'culture' is a dynamic concept subject to constant change, in terms of content, and to the influence of interaction among various networks. In recent decades all four cities discussed here have made urban development on a regional scale an important project for urban planning and design. Infrastructural elements that can lend coherence to the region as a whole and, at the same time, can link the region to large-scale, international networks are becoming extremely important. In the search for resources capable of providing a region with spatial coherence, the reinforcement and exploitation of structural elements found in nature have been 'rediscovered.' Together with marked contrasts in height, large areas of water and the boundary between land and water are the most obvious examples of natural structural elements. The realization of strong spatial coherence between main components of the traffic infrastructure and natural structural elements, such as bodies of water and their shorelines, is a vital part of new spatial strategies developed in Barcelona, New York, and Rotterdam. The design of this combination of traffic infrastructure and natural structural elements demands an approach that 'includes a wide range of scale': elements that lend coherence to the region as a whole are important to the cityscape on a local level, as well as to the accessibility of boroughs, districts, neighborhoods, and fragments.

Noteworthy examples of the concept that an urban highway can be designed in combination with specific places that have a special significance for the city are the unrealized design for the Westway in New York, by Venturi Scott Brown Associates; the project for the Central Artery Zone in Boston, now under construction; and de Solà-Morales's realized harbor front in Barcelona. The importance of this last design lies not only in the combination of various networks, but also in the spatial effect produced by the treatment of the basal area, which provides the cityscape with an essential ingredient quite unrelated to the purely functional aspect of the design.

This new design for the Moll de la Fusta reemphasizes differences in height: once more the city rests on a 'plinth.' This aspect of the plan creates a clear differentiation in the section, thus allowing the expressway and the urban balcony overlooking the port to be integrated into one design.

In the Netherlands, the design for the Kop van Zuid – with the pregnant position of the city boulevard and the new Erasmus Bridge, and the contemporary significance of former harbor basins as spatial elements in the cityscape – has set an important innovative tone.

The flat Dutch landscape features dikes, watercourses, canals, and harbors, infrastructural elements whose three-dimensionality dominates the cityscape: dikes elevate the flat surface of the land, and harbors and canals make deep incisions in the landscape.

Of great import to the cityscape are major dike-construction projects like Rotterdam's Maas Boulevard and the seafront boulevard in Vlissingen. The significance that both of these projects hold for the cityscape was viewed as a positive urban planning quality and was a primary factor in the choice of materials and verdure.

A continuing increase in scale is making it more and more difficult to fit new dikes and harbors into the urban landscape. Recent developments in the reinforcement of river dikes, however, show that an increase in scale does not necessarily mean the end of inventive design solutions. Since the late 1980s various initiatives have led to studies of how, and to what degree, a technical improvement of dike systems – in both riverside cities and the open countryside – can be linked to the preservation or adaptation of cultural-historical and natural structures of value to society.[1]

These recent examples of the relationship between city and infrastructure as an *urban planning* project are all based on the same principles found in previously discussed projects from the nineteenth and early twentieth centuries: (a) infrastructure is seen and treated as an *essential part of the public domain*; (b) *differentiation in scale* can be used to combine large-scale infrastructural elements with local networks within one integral design; (c) important parts of the infrastructure can be assigned to one designer – a concept known as *authorship*; and (d) the primary function of the project need not be the primary theme of the design – in other words, *defunctionalization* of the urban plan.

These principles provide a new foundation for the *urbanization of the infrastructure*.

STEERING THE PROGRAM: AN OBSOLETE TASK

If this analysis of four port cities has clarified anything at all, it is that the idea of making the urban plan subservient to the realization of specific, desired programs is outmoded. The urban plan may be used to create conditions for specific programs but should also offer space, certainly from a long-term perspective, for changes in programmatic infilling.

Such changes put even more demands on the spatial quality of the urban plan or, in other words, on the quality of the composition of the city. This composition should be so well-grounded that even long-term social processes and programmatic changes can occur without affecting the city plan.

In the short term, the realization of certain programs is important in the area of land development. This applies in particular to expensive infrastructure projects, which force local authorities to 'earn back' part of their investments by means of a land-price policy.

When infrastructure and new urban ensembles are carefully designed to create a coherent entity, the new ensembles can be geared to relate to the existing city and to existing centers, thus allowing them to become part of the city and to give it added value. This is a quality that extends much deeper, and which is far more essential, than the often trend-influenced programmatic infilling of such ensembles.

Urban planning, therefore, must have the wherewithal to realize this quality. Planners should pay more attention to the possibility of designing spatial compositions that function on more than one scale and, in keeping with this idea, should take a greater interest in the (civil) engineering principles of the discipline, which will benefit the realization – material, form, and construction – of these compositions.


THE CURRENT PROJECT: DEVELOPING PROFESSIONAL
SKILL IN URBAN PLANNING

All this is putting demands on professional skill in urban planning.

The first thing required is *technical* expertise: the ability to design urban planning structures for public space– structures that will lend shape to new links – and to establish building regulations that will enable buildings to contribute to the intended character of a given link. This demands the knowledge and skill needed to design new forms of multifunctional public space and to adapt them to specific characteristics of the territory in question. The design of new intermediary public areas also requires a great deal of integration within various fields of design. Instead of the current process, in which traffic design, civil engineering, and landscape architecture are going their separate ways, what urban planning needs is strongly integrated coordination among these disciplines. Especially imperative at present is the return of civil engineering to the urban planning educational curriculum, a subject that has virtually vanished from urban planning courses offered in recent decades.

The second requirement that has emerged from new links between networks and fragments is a high degree of *cultural* consciousness and insight, which will invest the design with the capacity to anticipate specific cultural conditions within the city, and to recognize and react on the appearance and meaning of the various domains – public, social, and private – in a specific situation.

*The* cultural quality does not exist, and certainly not with reference to public space, which is, after all, space that welcomes many groups of users, each with its own cultural values and assumptions. The designer, of course, has to find a way to lend shape to this space and, in so doing, to create a plan that includes various forms of use and offers various interpretations of cultural quality.

# Notes

A cross-reference system has been used in the following notes. Authors' names indicated here refer to publications found in the bibliography, which begins on page 408.

CHAPTER 1

1 Important international waterfront organizations are:
– 'Citta d'Acqua,' located in Venice, which organizes international congresses and publishes the periodical *Aquapolis*.
– 'Villes et Ports,' located in Le Havre, which organizes international congresses.
– 'The Waterfront Center,' located in Washington D.C., which organizes an annual international congress and publishes the periodical *On the Waterfront*.
2 Initially, such disaster struck projects in certain areas of London Docklands, as well as various waterfront projects in North America. For examples in London, see Chapter 2, Section 4; for examples in North America, see Chapter 4, Section 4.
3 This description applies to the redevelopment of the banks of the IJ in Amsterdam, as well as to that of the *kaaien* ('quays') and *Het Eilandje* ('The Little Island') in Antwerp. For Amsterdam, see Chapter 5, Section 4; for Antwerp, see Van Reusel and Uyttenhove.
4 I use the terms *'functionalism'* and *'modernism'* interchangeably.
5 Influential Americans in particular, such as urbanist Edmund Bacon and geographer Lewis Mumford, devoted many words of praise in the 1950s and '60s to Rotterdam, an ideal example of the modern city.
In his *Design of Cities*, Bacon wrote: 'The bombing during World War II was so extensive in the center of Rotterdam that the opportunity was provided here to demonstrate what a new city core could be if it was built afresh. The splendid system of space organization designed around the Lijnbaan, the central pedestrian mall ... the design influence of the Lijnbaan extends outward into the fabric of the city, successfully overlies and counterpoints the web of arterial streets, and connects with the old city, the cathedral, and the port ... in the vast planning made necessary by the extent of the damage to the city, the needs of human sensibilities were taken into account.' Of note is that this ode to Rotterdam was left out of a later edition of the book, published in 1974. Apparently by that time Bacon had been 'cured' of his unconditional admiration for Rotterdam's postwar reconstruction project.
6 An important signal indicating the end of the functionalist dream was given in R. Wentholt's book (1968), written *nota bene* for Vroom & Dreesman on the occasion of the firm's seventy-fifth anniversary. Wentholt pointed to a growing discontent among Rotterdam's professionals, residents, and business people with regard to the new city center. Contrary to international expressions of praise, local criticism was aimed at, of all things, the *lack* of sufficient attention to 'human sensibilities.'
Parallel to this criticism, from the end of the 1960s on, protests from people living in old districts surrounding the city center grew in vehemence; according to postwar plans that culminated in the *Structure Plan* of 1972, these districts were earmarked for eventual 'elimination.' See also Chapter 5, Section 4.
7 The term *stadsontwerp*, 'coined' by Rein Geurtsen, was first used in a lecture entitled 'Rotterdam and the *Stadsontwerp*,' which was presented in 1979 at the request of the Rotterdam Arts Council.
In the 1970s and '80s Geurtsen, a leading innovator in his field, created design courses in urban planning for the Department of Architecture (Delft University of Technology), in which he paid particular attention to the introduction of historical-morphological studies as a foundation for urban plans. See, among others, various versions of the synopsis of Geurtsen's textbook: *De stad, object van bewerking*, 1980-1988. See also Chapter 5, Section 4.
8 Braudel, 1979.
9 Harvey.
10 Raban, 1974.
11 Ibid., p. 10.
12 Calvino.
13 In the Netherlands, many urban plans designed by Kuiper Compagnons – a firm headed by Ashok Bhalotra – were accompanied in the 1980s and '90s by jargon and quotations from Calvino's Invisible Cities.
14 As the book progresses, the terms 'postmodern' and 'postmodernism' will be used very little. I am not interested in deciding whether projects and plans can or cannot be categorized as 'postmodern.' Furthermore, usage of the term 'postmodernism' in general, and especially in the area of urban planning, is questionable in itself.
15 See the government report entitled *Nota Architectuurbeleid*, issued in 1990 by the Ministry of Welfare, Education, and Culture, in which 'architectonic (and urban planning) quality' is defined in terms of practical value, future value, and cultural value.
For more on the cultural quality of urban design see, in Hans van Dijk et al., the contribution by Maurits de Hoog: 'De vorm van de stad: object van onderzoek en ontwerp.'
16 The most tragic and absurd example of the (mis)use of the concept of identity in this manner was the civil war that took place in the former Yugoslavia.

17 Paz. My thanks to K. Michiel, who mentioned this poem in the column he writes for the magazine *Krisis, tijdschrift voor filosophie* (No. 60, September 1995).

18 See, for example, the introduction in Davids et al. (eds.).

19 Frijhoff, 1992.

20 Van der Staay.

21 Taeke de Jong, 1995.

22 Quotation taken from a leading Dutch encyclopedia (and translated into English): *Nieuwe Winkler Prins Encyclopedie*, 7th ed., 1962.

23 Van der Woud describes the beginning of this process in the Netherlands. See Van der Woud, 1987 [I].

24 See Hanappe and Savy; see also Van der Knaap and Van der Laan, p. 18.

25 See Burke.

26 The analytical division of urban planning into four main tasks was devised by Jan Heeling: the discipline of urban planning directs the spatial-functional organization of the city, designs the city map, lays down building regulations, and provides for the design and realization of public space. See Heeling, 1991; see also Krop.

27 Oosterman.

28 See, among others, Boomkens, 1993 and 1994; and Benjamin, 1979 and 1992. See also various issues of *Krisis, tijdschrift voor filosofie*, such as Nos. 35 and 41.

29 Boomkens, 1994, p. 39. Boomkens points in turn to Richard Sennett, who elaborates on the theme of the emergence of the new sphere of privacy in the nineteenth century – a 'safe haven' – in his book *The Fall of Public Man*.

30 'The reality of the public realm relies on the simultaneous presence of innumerable perspectives and aspects in which the common world presents itself and for which no common measurement or denominator can ever be devised. For though the common world is the common meeting ground of all, those who are present have different locations on it, and the location of one can no more coincide with the location of another than the location of two objects … The end of the common world has come when it is seen only under one aspect and is permitted to present itself in only one perspective.' Arendt, pp. 57-58.

31 Berman.

32 Sennett, 1991. Of particular interest is Chapter 5, 'Exposure – An Exile's Knowledge: The Stranger's Knowledge.'

33 With regard to a 'modern savoir-vivre,' Marshall Berman shares a personal experience involving the demolition of the neighborhood in which he grew up to make way for an expressway. Berman, p. 295. See also Chapter 4, Section 3.

Sennett summarizes this 'savoir-vivre' as follows: 'What it's really about is the absence of identity, the uprooting, the fact that as a modern city-dweller, you can no longer call on norms from the past for life in the present. These are "radical" aspects of modern life, and you have to look at every meaningful political practice as a continuation of these aspects.' Richard Sennett, in an interview with Irene Klaver and René Boomkens, 'Stilte is een vorm van openbaar leven geworden – Richard Sennett en de voordelen van eenzaamheid in de grote stad: een interview,' *Krisis, tijdschrift voor filosofie*, No. 31.

34 See Berman; see also Sennett, 1977.

35 See Croutier.

36 Corbin, p. 231 ff.

37 Corbin.

38 This does not imply that Baudelaire was unfamiliar with harbor life. In *Paris Spleen* he writes: 'The port is a charming haven for a soul who is weary of the battle of life. The expanse of the firmament, the mobile architecture of the clouds, the alternating colors of the sea, and the gleam of the lighthouses form a prism exceptionally suited to diverting the eye while never causing fatigue. The slender patterns of the ships, complexly rigged and undulating in harmony with the swell of the waves, provide the soul with a love of rhythm and beauty. Moreover, for one lying atop the watchtower or propped against the jetty on his elbows, no longer curious and drained of ambition, it is above all a mysterious and aristocratic kind of pleasure to observe all this activity – the movements of those arriving and departing, of those still possessing the strength to desire, to long for travel or for the chance to improve themselves.'

39 Pons.

40 Genet. See also Choukri and Bowles.

41 Tangier repeatedly appears in Bowles's novels as the scene of the action, such as in *Réveillon à Tanger* and *Let It Come Down*. See, too, another book by Bowles, *Tanger, Vues Choisies*.

42 Slauerhoff, 1992.

43 Arendt, p. 38 ff. See also Tijmes.

44 See Van Engelsdorp-Gastelaars.

45 The two most prominent schools of architecture were the so-called Delft School, associated mainly with the Roman Catholic segment, and functionalist architects of the Nieuwe Zakelijkheid (who formed the Amsterdam group 'de 8' and the Rotterdam group 'De Opbouw'), known for their association with the Social-Democratic segment.

46 See Note 30 (Chapter 1).

47 The process, as it relates to the United States, is described by, among others, Boyer, 1994, pp. 7-11.

48 See, among others, Van Vught; and De Liagre Böhl et al.

49 Gunn.

50 A study of postwar cultural and educational policy now seen as a classic is the dissertation by Smiers.

51 Meyer et al., 1980; Meyer et al., 1981; De Klerk and Moscoviter (eds.); Reijndorp and Van der Ven (eds.).

52 In the case of Rotterdam, this is described by Wagenaar.

53 For the 'parkway' concept, see Note 45 (Chapter 4).

54 Meyer et al., 1991.

55 See, among others, Hoekveld; Deben et al.; Sassen; and Castells.

56 Gottmann says that the renewed marketplace function is based on three characteristics:

– The *principe de communication*: the city as meeting place. Here the accent is on the city's internal function as a sociocultural center and source of new ideas and conceptions.

– The *principe de circulation*: the city as distribution center of goods, services, and conceptions about its environment.

– The *principe de carrefour*: the city as hub within a network of cities on various spatial levels of scale.

57 Webber.

58 Ibid., p. 147.

59 In using the term 'technologization,' I am referring to the important role that motorized vehicles, air traffic, and telematics have assumed in the everyday life of much of the population.

60 See, among others, Virilio; see also Mitchell.

61 Mitchell.

62 Friedrichs et al.

63 Burgers (ed.). Information on 'postmodern lifestyles' and on 'the culturalization – or aestheticization – of urbanism' can be found in Mike Featherstone's contributions to books published in 1989 [I] and [II].

64 Oosterman.

65 Zijderveld; see also Boogaarts.

66 Knight describes the process as such: 'In order to keep their intellectual wells from running dry, industrial cities must upgrade their human and cultural resources and their built-up environment. In other words, they must build world-class, advanced, industrial cities – cities prepared to compete for talent worldwide. They should be able to offer future white-collar workers a good quality of life and stimulating working conditions on a par with those available in other metropolises.'

67 Castells; Sassen.

68 Sorkin, 1992 [II].

69 The first to classify city dwellers as 'stayers,' 'new urbanites,' and 'migrants' were Anderiessen and Reijndorp, but the Dutch words for these terms have become so much a part of the Dutch language that the *NRC Handelsblad* now uses them in articles on big-city issues. See, among others, an article entitled 'Atlas van het ongenoegen,' printed in the March 18, 1995, edition of this newspaper.

70 Castells.

71 See Davies.

72 Davies, p. 155.

73 Sorkin, 1992 [II].

74 See, among others, TNO; Ministerie van Verkeer en Waterstaat; Drewe and Jansen; and Drewe.

75 Since the late 1980s, the Dutch government has been trying to develop a new, coherent policy on infrastructure based on a concept known as 'Mainport Holland.' The mutually coherent entity to be created by this policy – an entity composed of the (presently) strong position of Rotterdam's port and Schiphol Airport, combined with better highways and, even more important, railroads (High-Speed Train and Betuwe Line) – would make Randstad Holland into Europe's prime logistic hub. Drewe and Jansen; Drewe.

76 Not only did the acquisition of a central position as 'electronic port' become a *conditio sine qua non*; it was no longer even necessary to be located in the direct vicinity of the 'normal' flow of goods. When the developers of the Mainport Holland policy considered the relatively poor returns of transshipment and transit activities, they wondered if developing Holland as a logistic hub would not enable them to pursue a far more selective policy with regard to the 'real' flow of goods. Moving goods by means of a process that yields a relatively low return, while also placing a burden on both infrastructure and environment, could be orchestrated from locations abroad; on the other hand, a flow of goods linked to (environmentally friendly) processing or assembly industries in the Netherlands could well be directed within the country itself. See Roobeek.

77 In the 1980s the amount of air cargo handled in the Netherlands increased by 76 percent, while road transport grew by 11 percent and water transport by 6 percent. Beek et al.

78 Albeda; Wagner.

79 See Reijndorp, 1992.

80 Changing views on the relationship between the public domain and the private domain were also found in education and art (interaction with the business community, through sponsoring, and increasing pressure to think and act in a market-oriented way); the health-care sector (the reduction and privatization of various types of national insurance); politics and law enforcement; the media policy; and so forth.

As this book reaches completion, in the spring of 1996, three related topics dominate the headlines of Dutch newspapers: the results of a parliamentary inquiry into investigation methods used by the judiciary and police (in the form of a report issued by the 'Van Traa Committee'), the repeal of the Dutch Health Law, and the decision of the Royal Dutch Soccer League to sell the rights to future matches to a commercial television station rather than to allow them to be broadcast by the stated-owned network.

Possibly the most distressing case is the debate on investigation methods in law enforcement. The parliamentary inquiry into this subject is the result of increasing differences of opinion on what now prevails in today's Dutch constitutional state: the police as *representative* of this state, which guarantees primarily the public nature and security of the public domain; or the police as a *business*, which is supposed to provide a *product* of impeccable quality, which can be expressed in the number of arrests. The latter interpretation inevitably implies a decline of the principles of the democratic constitutional state. As Martin van Amerongen observed in *De Groene Amsterdammer* (April 29, 1995), within a span of three cabinet periods government policy has changed from the former interpretation to the latter.

81 For example, consider the situation in Breda where a site accommodating the former Chassé Barracks was to be reorganized. In 1994 the city council of Breda invited five designers, together with five developers, to present proposals for an urban plan. A committee of experts was appointed to evaluate the designs. The design chosen by this committee, which judged the entries purely on their intrinsic value, was a proposal presented by OMA. Implementing this plan would have cost the municipality about ten million guilders. Another plan, designed by Kuiper Compagnons, was presented as a scheme that would generate that same amount in revenues for the municipality. For this reason and no other, the city council vetoed the committee's decision and awarded the commission to Kuiper Compagnons (*de Volkskrant*, August 16, 1995).

82 In 1993 J. van Rijs, director of the Amsterdam Waterfront Finance Company (AWF), argued that the design, realization, and management of public space on the banks of the IJ should be the responsibility of the AWF. See Gall et al., pp. 132-133.

83 Sorkin, 1992 [II].

84 Boyer, 1994.

85 Wetenschappelijke Raad voor het Regeringsbeleid ('Scientific Council for Government Policy') (WRR).

86 Frijhoff, 1993.

87 The concept of an 'unhurried' or an 'accelerated' city is taken from Van Teeffelen et al. (eds.).

88 The increase of leisure time, both voluntary and involuntary, in the lives of many people, and the claim that this development lays on the use of the city has been the subject, for some time now, of a so-called leisure-time sociology. For more on the subject, see Braham; Mommaas; and Featherstone, 1989 [I] and [II].

89 Wetenschappelijke Raad voor het Regeringsbeleid ('Scientific Council for Government Policy') (WRR), p. 31.
This argument for a 'civic culture' is based on traditional examples in various American and British cities, where public-private partnerships have created a new culture of shared responsibility for the city. These partnerships differ from the sort of 'public-private cooperation' found in the Netherlands, which consists mainly of incidental ad hoc collaboration between local authorities and investment and development companies, and which is aimed purely at the development (in other words, the economic success) of urban projects. Anglo-Saxon examples are characterized by a far broader basis of cooperation, involving various social groups, and by a much larger sphere of action; such partnerships focus not only on directly discernible economic results, but also on social, cultural, and ecological consequences, which are hard to measure in many cases.

90 Various sources. Since population statistics for the year 1850 are often estimates (or are given as averages of censuses taken in 1840 and 1860, over which more detailed data exist in certain cases), all figures have been rounded off to the nearest 10,000.

91 Sources: annual reports issued by the Port of London, the Port de Barcelona, the Port of New York and New Jersey, and Havenbedrijf ('Port Authority') Rotterdam.

CHAPTER 2 – LONDON

1 The typology of the English home is described in detail in, among others, Rasmussen, p. 292 ff.; and Olsen, p. 89 ff.

2 In 1898 Howard (1850-1928) published his book *To-Morrow: a Peaceful Path to Real Reform*, in which he introduced the concept of the garden city. A revised edition of this book, published in 1902, was entitled *Garden Cities of To-Morrow*.

3 Unwin collaborated with Barry Parker to design the first garden cities based on Howard's concept: Letchworth in 1904 and Hampstead Garden Suburb in 1909.

4 Rasmussen.

5 The ideological foundation underlying the concepts of garden cities and regional planning is described in, among others, Hall, 1988; and Smit, Part I: 'Het pad naar de tuinstad.'

6 Canetti, p. 191.

7 Barker.

8 In the mid-nineteenth century, 82 percent of the world's tonnage was built in England, and most of it came from the London area. Mingay, p. 81. See also Hostettler.

9 Disraeli.

10 Eldridge.

11 Chambers. See also Mingay, Chapter 4: 'Workshop of the world.'

12 Himmelfarb, p. 307 ff.

13 Himmelfarb, p. 312; Canning (ed.).

14 Himmelfarb, p. 350.

15 Epstein Nord.

16 See, for example, Dicken's *Oliver Twist*, in which over half the chapters begin with a description of the outdoors as a damp, murky, gloomy, twilit place.

17 Olsen, p. 23.

18 Dickens, 1860.

19 Dickens, 1863.

20 Rasmussen, p. 271 ff.

21 See Cole; Hostettler; and various publications issued by The Island History Project, London 1980-1987.

22 The form assumed by the trade-union actions in Docklands played a major role in the way in which trade unions throughout England were organized (relatively independently of industrial groups with their own 'shop stewards'), as well as in England's policy on incomes and even in international politics. One of the most successful actions, during which Docklands acquired legendary status as a bulwark of socialist internationalism, occurred in 1919, when a boycott of Polish freighters that were to be loaded with weapons for the battle against the Bolsheviks in Russia resulted in the end of England's official support of the Belorussian resistance. Lord Howie, 'Dock Labour History,' in Carr, 1986.

23 Mingay, p. 167.

24 Rasmussen, p. 426

25 Ibid., p. 427 ff.

26 *County of London Plan.*

27 For the 'parkway' concept, see Note 45 (Chapter 4).

28 Hall, 1995, p. 229.

29 Ash.

30 Ibid., p. 21. Ash notes that of the total housing production realized in the period between world wars, only 17 percent consisted of multistory dwellings.

31 Rasmussen, p. 386. He added an extra chapter to the revised edition of 1982: 'A new and more happy ending but no end.'

32 Hall, 1995, p. 232.

33 Greater London Plan, p. 101.

34 Greater London Development Plan.

35 Ibid., p. 653.

36 Docklands. Redevelopment Proposals for East London.

37 London Docklands Strategic Plan.

38 Bianchini.

39 Three organizations carried out preliminary studies and collaborated on the development of this program: the Docklands Joint Committee, the London Historical Museum, and the North East London Polytechnic; in addition, various community associations organized their own 'history workshops.'

40 Catchpole, 1988.

41 Cooke, 1988 [II].

42 A series of articles on the rivalry between London and Paris, written by a number of prominent French planners and politicians, were published in *Le Monde* on March 29, April 26, June 14, and July 28, 1988.

43 This budget set aside 399 million pounds for infrastructure and acquisitions, and 302 million pounds for subsidies, including those

granted to private investors and developers. Source: *The Economist*, February 13, 1988 (information provided by the Dockland Consultative Committee, 1988).

44 According to Peter Buchanan, the fundamental problem lay in the central government's lack of political will, which made it impossible to develop a coherent and convincing concept for a feasible and desirable infilling of the area. Buchanan.

45 Gosling and Maitland, p. 147 ff.

46 The first category to set up business in Docklands was the printing industry. The newspaper branch, led by the *Daily Telegraph*, set the ball rolling: since 1981, in a veritable mass migration, one organization after the other has made the move from London's distinguished Fleet Street to Docklands. Rather than a simple act of relocation, however, this development represented a radical reorganization of the newspaper industry for the dual purpose of job reduction and the commercialization of news services. In the case of the *Daily Telegraph* alone, 1,500 of the paper's 5,500 employees lost their jobs when the organization relocated to Docklands. The editorial staffs of several newspapers have found these developments disturbing. A good example is Robert Chesshyre, who commented in *The New Statesman*: 'Strangely enough the diaspora of newspaper buildings is accompanied by a rapidly increasing centralization of "the news." The result is "safe" homogenized newspapers, largely run by yuppies. The diaspora is harmful not only to the journalist, but also to the reader.'
   The second largest category was the retail sector, including wholesale trade, the distribution industry, supermarkets (ASDA), hotels, and catering services. This sector was described as being relatively 'footloose,' a term used to define businesses that are not tied to a certain location in the city but need only a place in or near the urban context. A direct link to the city center or to large residential districts has become less important than possibilities for expansion, a chance for unrestricted growth if needed, and the proximity of a transportation network connected to the national and international infrastructure.
   The third category was made up of financial organizations such as banks and insurance companies. Although this category is the most vital when it comes to anticipating international developments, a great deal of uncertainty surrounds the manner in which its presence will evolve in Docklands. See Church.

47 Figures published by the LDDC show that 8,000 new jobs were created in Docklands in the period 1981-1987. Of these, according to The London Planning Advisory Committee, 5,000 were positions within organizations that had moved from the City of London to this mecca of free enterprise. Besides the companies that relocated, a number of new businesses provided the Docklands area with an additional 3,000 jobs.
   On the other hand, having reorganized the area, the LDCC was responsible for the elimination of as many as 7,000 jobs, most of which had been filled by local residents.
   Thus the net result was the loss of thousands of jobs. Qualitatively speaking, the newly created jobs were in a completely different category than the ones that had been eliminated: the jobs lost, most of which had belonged to semi- and unskilled workers, were 'compensated for' by creating better-paying jobs at higher levels.

Unemployment figures in small working-class neighborhoods throughout Docklands have risen sharply in the past eight years: approximately 20 percent of the working population in the late '80s was unemployed.
   Admittedly, the LDDC has collaborated with several established businesses to set up an extra-training and occupational-resettlement program known as Skillnet, which is intended to give East Enders a chance to join one of the area's new companies. So far, however, this program has resulted in only fifty jobs for local residents. The brevity of the courses offered severely limits the potential of such a training program; furthermore, Skillnet has had to contend with a dropout rate of about 50 percent. Docklands Consultative Committee, 1985 and 1988.

48 Of the 17,000 new dwellings, 2,000 were built by local governments (boroughs) and housing associations: the final legacy of the policy pursued by the Greater London Council prior to 1981. The other 15,000 were dwellings for sale to private parties on the open market.

49 In 1985 the LDDC began requiring every housing project built on its property to offer 40 percent of the dwellings involved to local residents, for a maximum price of 40,000 pounds, during a six-week period immediately following the completion of the project.
   In that same year Dockland inhabitants initiated a build-it-yourself project composed of ninety-four single-family dwellings: the largest of its kind in the world. Each unit cost 38,500 pounds, including 6,000 pounds for the land. During the realization of these dwellings in 1988, the land price of adjoining properties skyrocketed to more than ten times its original worth, while the market value of the dwellings increased sixfold. Hence the initially planned follow-up to this project was cancelled owing to market-related developments.

50 Docklands Consultative Committee, 1988.

51 Although the LDDC has hesitatingly begun to develop a 'heritage' policy, up to now this policy amounts to nothing more than a proposal to conserve a few individual buildings found here and there throughout the area. See Lyders and Harrison (eds.).

52 Certain complexes in a dangerous state of disrepair had been vacated even earlier. Consequently, the original residents were literally forced out on the street: the number of registered homeless households in Docklands rose from 1,600 in 1981 to 4,400 in 1987.

53 In 1987 Catchpole made a detailed study of the effects of Canary Wharf on London's cityscape.

CHAPTER 3 – BARCELONA

1 Braudel, 1966.
2 Calabi.
3 Burke.
4 Poleggi, 1988.
5 Florêncio.
6 Ibid.
7 Links.
8 Poleggi, 1982.
9 Braudel, p. 145.
10 For further information, see, among others, Vila; see also Duran i Sanpere.

11 Hughes, p. 128.

12 Braudel, p. 145.

13 Hughes, p. 104.

14 Busquets, p. 43. Busquets describes the Santa Maria del Mar as a 'paradigm of Catalan Gothic.'

15 Today 'Ramblas' is used as a plural noun, since the boulevard has been divided into five different sections, each of which has its own name: Rambla de Canalettes, Rambla del Estudios, and so forth. In general, I have used the Catalan spelling of topographic names (such as streets and squares) in this chapter.

16 Busquets, p. 58.

17 Braudel describes the second half of the fifteenth century as a period of decline for autonomous city states and as a time in which territorial giants emerged to rule the roost in the Mediterranean region. Braudel, p. 338.

18 Hughes, p. 173.

19 A detailed explanation of the origins and development of La Barceloneta can be found in Tatjer, 1973. See also Tatjer, 1988.

20 See, among others, Oliveiras Samitier.

21 In addition to publications by Tatjer (see Note 19 of this chapter), for in-depth information on the development of La Barceloneta see de Solà-Morales et al.; de Solà-Morales, 1985 [II]; Fabre and Huertas; and Sabatar.

22 La Barceloneta remains the city's conscience, even today: not only as the district that descendants of the Barrio Ribera – those most closely tied to the sea – call home, but also as the most republican district of Barcelona.
La Barceloneta is still reputed to be Barcelona's most republican neighborhood. In 1873 La Barceloneta was the stage of a revolutionary uprising. In 1911 the 'Casino Republica de la Barceloneta' ascertained that the district had the highest percentage of Barcelona's republican votes. During the civil war (1936-1939), Trotskyite and trade-union militias encamped in the district, a situation that George Orwell described in his *Homage to Catalonia*.

23 Hughes, p. 214.

24 McCully.

25 Rohrer.

26 See Roca.

27 Hughes, p. 235.

28 Background information on the design and development of the Ensanche can be found in, among others, Magrinyà i Salvador Tarragó (ed.). See also Ajuntament de Barcelona, 1983 [II] and de Solà-Morales, 1985 [I].

29 The theory and method behind Cerdà's urban plan are discussed in detail in Magrinyà i Salvador Tarragó (ed.).

30 See Meyer et al., 1991, for a more elaborate explanation of how urban structure and urban shape are treated as separate entities in many modernist urban plans.

31 Tatjer, 1988, p. 268.

32 See, among others, the text by Barcelona's mayor, Maragall, in *Ajuntament de Barcelona, Barcelona Spaces and Sculptures*, 1987.

33 See Bohigas's detailed 'manifesto.' Bohigas, 1983.

34 Van der Schans.

35 Vegara-Carrio.

36 Busquets, p. 311.

37 *Lotus International*, No. 23.

38 De Solà Morales, 1979.

39 For an account of the polemic significance of plans designed by Muratori and Quaroni for the Barene de San Giuliano competition, see Taverne, 1993. For a more detailed description of Quaroni's design for San Giuliano, see Terranova.

40 In the Netherlands, too – and, more specifically, at the Architecture Department of the Delft University of Technology – an approach to design based on typological research would rise to a dominant position in the 1970s and '80s. For additional information, see, among others, Leupen et al. (eds.), p. 179 ff.

41 One publication that wholeheartedly praised the inspiration that many have drawn from Quaroni's work was the Laboratorio d'Urbanismo's official magazine, *Urbanismo Revista*, which devoted a special issue to Quaroni nearly twenty years after his participation in the competition for La Barceloneta. See *Urbanismo Revista* and, in particular, the long interview that de Solà-Morales had with Quaroni shortly before he died. In this interview, Quaroni described himself as someone who was more a part of the modern tradition than an opponent of it.

42 De Solà-Morales, 1987.

43 The 'rehabilitation' of these representatives of the other modern tradition was reemphasized when the magazine *Urbanismo Revista* (of which de Solà-Morales was editor in chief) published in-depth monographs of Martin (No. 5, 1987), Quaroni (No. 7, 1989), and Van Eesteren (No. 8, 1989).

44 De Solà-Morales, 1986. In the original Catalan edition of this article, de Solà-Morales discussed 'La construcció de la ciutat és parcel.lació + urbanització + edificació.' Published in de Solà-Morales, 1993.

45 Bohigas, 1983.

46 Ibid.

47 Acebillo.

48 Àrees de nova Centralitat.

49 Meyer, 1989 [II].

50 The Enterprise Development Corporation had its roots in the Rouse Company. For more on the Rouse Company, see Chapter 4.

51 De Solà-Morales, 1992.

52 See Martorell et al.

53 See, among others, Ajuntament de Barcelona, 1983 [II]; see also Barjau et al.

54 These terms are attributed to Hannah Arendt, who makes a distinction, when discussing the public domain, between a political domain and a social domain. This is explained in greater detail in Chapter 1.

55 See also Muntaner.

56 At an early stage MBM already had an agreement with SA-HOLSA, the municipal development company set up especially for this project, to order large consignments of bricks from brickyards all over Spain. Architects and real-estate developers were required to make use of this stock in their projects.

57 Converted to US dollars, a three-room apartment cost $175,000 in 1992.

58 This situation is also highly characteristic of Venice's Canal Grande, which derives its meandering course from its origins as one of the streams flowing from the Po.

59 Hughes, p. 28 ff.

1 Huizenga.

2 Raban, 1990.

3 Clark and Remini.

4 Morton and Lucia White.

5 See Marx.

6 See Bender, 1975.

7 See Draper.

8 See Schuyler, p. 20.

9 See, among others, Smith; see also Garreau.

10 Buttenwieser, p. 64 ff.

11 Langdon.

12 Taken from Cohn.

13 Schuyler, p. 19.

14 Ibid., p. 6 ff.

15 Quoted in Schuyler, p. 66.

16 Boyer, 1985, p. 15 ff.

17 Schuyler, p. 76.

18 Ibid., p. 77.

19 Barlow.

20 Buttenwieser.

21 Draper.

22 See Manieri.

23 See Hall, 1988, p. 182; see also Boyer, 1985, p. 289.

24 See, among others, Barlow; Fabos et al.; Schuyler; Olmsted Jr. and Kimball (eds.); Fein (ed.), 1967; and Fein, 1972.

25 Van Leeuwen; Weiss.

26 Van Leeuwen.

27 Warner.

28 While searching for the true identity of his city, New York writer Jerome Charyn visited places that had been his parents' and grandparents' introduction to the New World: Ellis Island and the Lower East Side. Charyn discovered the trials and tribulations that awaited the millions of destitute travelers arriving at the Ellis Island immigration station, beginning in the late 1800s. He concluded that these immigrants, having first survived a long and exhausting voyage only to be confronted with the humiliating experience in store for them at the hands of immigration authorities on Ellis Island, must have had incredible faith in the future, not to mention a powerful fighting spirit. Charyn.

29 Dasnoy, p. 137 ff.

30 See, for example, *World's Fair*, a novel by E.L. Doctorow.

31 See also Plunz, 1993.

32 Much of the information in this chapter is based on works by the following four authors: Caro, Cutler, Goddard, and Schwarz.

33 Goddard, p. 86.

34 In late 1957, the length of all the railroad tracks in the United States was only half of what it had been in 1916. Goddard.

35 'The intersectional misunderstanding which gave rise to it could not have reached the critical stage of war had it been possible as it is now for the Southern planter to spend his summer in Maine and the New England businessman to journey southward in his own car for golf at Pinehurst and a winter vacation in Florida.' MacDonald, as quoted in Goddard, p. 103.

36 Van der Woud, 1987 [11].

37 The onset of New York's skyscraper boom was accompanied by growing criticism of the amorphous character of this artificial 'mountain range,' a situation that was to have far-reaching consequences for the initial neutrality of the city's grid of streets. From the very beginning, New York had been a pioneer in establishing regulations for the design and use of big and tall buildings.

Two arguments played an important role in efforts by local authorities to prevent the unbridled growth of skyscrapers: a desire to protect the quality of the public street and the intention to create a more attractive cityscape.

The fact that the grid imposed restrictions on the horizontal plane (by means of building lines) but not on the vertical plane meant that high-rise buildings in certain parts of the city virtually eliminated sunlight from both the streets they lined and adjacent buildings. Moreover, this upsurge of building activity led to an explosion of street life, which some interest groups considered detrimental to the exclusivity of streets like Fifth Avenue.

In 1916 the municipality of New York became the first city to establish a zoning law, which included regulations for maximum heights to be imposed on various types of buildings. The first category included buildings that covered the entire building site and that rose straight up: these were not permitted to be taller than two to two and a half times the width of the street. The second category included buildings designed with setbacks: although these were allowed to be taller, building-height regulations applied to this category varied from district to district. No restrictions were imposed on the heights of buildings in the third category, which included structures covering less than 25 percent of the building site. These new regulations formed a strong incentive for a new architectonic style that featured two main themes: the setback and a sense of autonomy with respect to the public street. According to Bender, New York architects designing the first generation of skyscrapers continued to stress the horizontal structure of their buildings. This horizontality emphasized the way in which the building related to the public street. The public street – the 'ordinary' street found in the grid – had been seen as the public domain, a domain meant to accommodate the city's most important buildings. The Zoning Law of 1916 brought a halt to this idea. The architecture of skyscrapers built in the 1920s and, in particular, the '30s focused increasingly on the verticality of the building, thus demonstrating the structure's independence from the bordering street.

As the first zoning law was being developed and implemented, a debate was taking place in New York on the influence of a forest of skyscrapers on the cityscape in general. The Zoning Law of 1916 applied only to private enterprise and thus affected the volume and architecture of urban development. The shape assumed by the public domain, as an autonomous grid of streets and avenues, remained unaffected.

See, among others, Weiss; Tafuri; and Bender, 1987.

38 Van Vught, p. 22 ff.

39 Schwarz, p. 217 ff.

40 The realization of the program for greenbelt towns was divided into

NOTES

two sub-programs: a program for building the new towns themselves, which was the responsibility of the Resettlement Administration, headed by Tugwell; and a program for infrastructural elements – in the form of public-transportation systems, including railroads and new highways – which were to connect the new greenbelt towns to large city centers. A newly established Public Works Administration assumed responsibility for the latter sub-program. G. Wright, p. 220 ff.

41 F.L. Wright.

42 Greenbelt, near Washington, D.C.; Greendale, near Milwaukee, Wisconsin; and Greenhills, near Cincinnati, Ohio. See G. Wright, p. 222.

43 Cutler, p. 11.

44 Cutler.

45 In the United States, distinctions made between parkways, expressways, and highways are sometimes unclear. Generally speaking, the term 'parkway' refers to a road within a (park-like) spatial context. 'Expressway' usually refers to a road that runs straight through an intensively developed urban area. In most cases, a 'highway' is part of the nation's Interstate Highway network. Hence a highway can pass through both urban and park-like areas.

46 The total length of these parkways and expressways was 75 miles. See Cutler, p. 52.

47 Although Moses is usually portrayed as an urbanist, an architect, or a planner, he began as a political scientist. He saw his work on the physical structure of the city as a logical consequence of his views on the need for a reorganization of society.
Moses studied political science at New York's Columbia University, where he drew attention to himself in 1914 by writing a thesis in which he argued for a drastic reform of the machinery of government in America.
In 1918 the newly elected governor of New York, Alfred E. Smith, asked Moses to serve on the New York State Reconstruction Commission. Moses virtually had carte blanche in his efforts to reorganize the fragmented state machinery, consisting of 1,887 departments, into a compact entity of 16 departments. He was especially interested in the 18 departments that developed and managed state parks: each park had its own department. Moses combined them into a single State Council of Parks, of which he was president, a function he was to hold until 1963. He provided himself with wide powers and a generous budget, enough to realize an unprecedentedly ambitious program of parks and parkways.
He set down much of this program in a brochure published in 1922, *A State Park Plan for New York*, in which three developments were interrelated: the explosive growth of New York City, an increasing amount of free time and the consequent need for outdoor recreation, and a rapidly growing number of car owners.
During this period, New York City welcomed 100,000 new residents every year. While Moses was still at school, Bronx, Queens, and most of Brooklyn were covered by woods and farmland, but in 1922 he saw nothing but an endless ocean of housing in these boroughs. Manhattan residents who wanted to spend a day or a weekend 'out of town' faced hours of driving through the streets of Brooklyn or Queens, or an even longer trip on the car ferry, before arriving at one of the few public or privately operated parks and

beaches in the vicinity. In the 1920s, the free Saturday afternoon had already become part of working-class life in America, as had the automobile: the United States boasted 23 million cars in 1923. Moses's task was, literally, to break open the city and the state and to adapt them to these new developments, a job that created the consummate opportunity for developing a new, collective sense of identity in America.
With this new, collective sense of identity in mind – a communal spirit that was to eliminate the borders between groups, races, and cultures, as well as between cities and states – Moses was able to get right down to work when his friend La Guardia was elected mayor of New York City in 1933. La Guardia immediately appointed Moses to do the same thing for the city that he had done for the state: consolidate various park departments into one department, with Moses himself as City Park Commissioner, a position he held until 1966.
Thus Moses filled a unique combination of self-created key functions in the state and city of New York. In addition, he knew as no other the ins and outs of power relations in both city and state; after all, his was the brain behind the reorganization of many government departments. Owing to his numerous functions, Moses remained the most powerful man in New York for a long time. His nickname – 'Power Broker' – later became the title of Robert Caro's extensive biography of Moses. See Caro; see also Rosen, p. 2.

48 Rosenblum et al.

49 Caro, p. 318.

50 The way in which Moses operated in New York was characteristic of his behavior as a 'power broker': officially, as the new City Park Commissioner, his authority did not go beyond the initiation of plans, which subsequently were to be developed and implemented by the Civil Works Administration. Moses put the CWA out of action by selecting and hiring (at twice the salary they would have received working for the CWA) six hundred architects on his own initiative. Moses also proclaimed himself 'City Construction Coordinator,' a title that gave him the authority to realize his projects without the interference of the CWA. Caro.

51 Buttenwieser.

52 Quotation taken from Caro, p. 343.

53 As Giedion declared, with regret: 'It may be pointed out that, standing amid the chaos of midtown New York, it is not surrounded by greenery but instead is confined by the limitations of street and traffic.' Giedion, p. 579.

54 Tafuri.

55 Caro.

56 Ibid., p. 318.

57 Berman, p. 136.

58 *Fortune.*

59 Ibid.

60 Fitzgerald; see also Marx.

61 Talese.

62 Giedion, p. 579.

63 Goddard, p. 208.

64 Ibid., p. 194.

65 Berman, p. 295.

66 See Hatton; and Allman.

67 Goddard, p. 60.

68 Dunhill.

69 The first two aspects are supported by a design that is and has been centrally directed from the word go: programming, development and, following the completion of the project, management. This applies to Disney World in its entirety (over 100 square kilometers), only 40 hectares of which accommodate the actual amusement park (Magic Kingdom). This situation was created in 1967, when the state of Florida passed a law that called for a special administrative structure to be established for the territory of Disney World. This structure, the Reedy Creek Improvement District (RCID), has its own system of building and zoning regulations, and is also responsible for the transportation, energy, and water facilities that make up the infrastructure of Disney World. Sorkin, 1992 [11].

70 Webber; see also Chapter 1, Section 3

71 Jacobs.

72 See Jacobs, pp. 181, 386, and 439, among others.

73 Rockefeller and Butt.

74 In 1966 Governor Nelson Rockefeller addressed the public in a letter in which he described Battery Park City as 'an opportunity unique for Manhattan: the creation, literally from the ground up, of a large-scale, imaginatively planned community comprising residential, business, light industry, and recreational facilities. Not one family would be displaced and yet new homes would be provided for 13,982 families. Battery Park City would also represent a new departure in urban renewal. Private enterprise would be supported by public cooperation rather than by public funds.' See Tafuri.

75 Plan for New York City.

76 Barnett, p. 144.

77 Venturi et al.

78 Various models were developed in the 1970s for the underground section of the highway as well as for new construction. Costs related to the highway models varied from 200 to 360 million dollars. The profits from the sale of land for new construction would cover 30 to 40 percent of the operating costs, depending on which model was chosen. See Barnett, pp. 148-149.

79 Adams.

80 See Gilliam; see also Batts.

81 The Urban Design Plan for the Comprehensive Plan of San Francisco.

82 Although such public markets could be found in nearly every American city prior to the 1950s, they were to disappear from the urban scene soon afterward. In Seattle, too, diverse attempts were made by private developers to purchase the market site in order to convert it into a contemporary shopping mall, but the city always managed to prevent this from happening. The market's importance as a public facility was greater than the extra income that a modern mall might mean for the municipal treasury.
In 1988 the city was confronted with a proposal made by the Rouse Company for a festival market on the waterfront. Thanks in part to a referendum, this proposal was turned down; the city's rejection contained a reference to Pike Place Market, a public facility that was considered far more valuable to the city than a new waterfront festival market. The Rouse Company was allocated a site in the city center; the waterfront was to remain, at least theoretically, a public area.

83 Portman and Barnett.

84 Rowe and Koetner, p. 149.

85 Plunz, 1993.

86 One- and two-room apartments cost between $150,000 and $250,000; four-room apartments go for about $1,000,000.

87 The conflict between the city of New York and Olympia & York concerned the opening hours of the winter garden. O & Y were willing to open the garden to the public only during office hours. Because the garden, together with a skywalk, formed one of the few access routes to the riverbank, the city demanded that it be open to the public twenty-four hours a day.

88 The West Side Spirit, October 3, 1988, p. 14.

89 Ibid., p. 20.

90 Rouse.

91 Quotation taken from Dorenbos.

92 For a more detailed history of the planning process in Baltimore, see Goldberg.

93 Festival markets have become an unavoidable instrument in American (and, more recently, Dutch) strategies for urban revitalization. See Boogaarts.

94 A study of visitors to a number of festival marketplaces on new waterfronts in American cities shows that 69 percent of all the visitors to Harbor Place are from Baltimore and vicinity, while in comparable projects – such as Boston's Quincy Market and San Francisco's Pier 39 – only 38 and 40 percent, respectively, of all the visitors are local residents.
Nonetheless, the Baltimoreans who visit Harbor Place plan most of these outings for special occasions: weekend excursions or family celebrations – the same reasons that prompt people to visit Disney World, for example. The main difference is that Inner Harbor is closer to home and less expensive. Martin and Jones.

95 Rose.

96 See, in this book, Waterfront slums (Chapter 4, Section 2, p. 203).

97 In 1989 the municipality of Flint (Michigan) sold the festival market it had spent $22,000,000 to build in 1985 for $50,000 to the university, for use as a center for student activities.
In other cases, cities are still trying to save festival markets with a program of special promotions and events, as well as with active recruitment campaigns set up to make investors and developers more aware of the areas immediately surrounding such markets. Walters.

98 The American tax system allows the municipalities themselves to collect a considerable share of the taxes paid by residents and businesses. Thus a large percentage of the property and sales taxes paid by new businesses operating in the Inner Harbor area goes directly into the municipal treasury. Consequently, tax revenues in the city of Baltimore rose by 66 percent in the period 1978-1988. A great deal of this extra income goes into a fund established in 1983 known as Neighborhood Progress Administration (NPA), in which both the municipality and neighborhood organizations are represented. The NPA is responsible for developing and implementing housing, employment, and occupational-resettlement programs for the residents of Baltimore's poorer neighborhoods.
One example of linkage is a pledge made to the municipality by companies located in or close to the Inner Harbor that they will hire

a minimum number of unemployed persons and that a certain number of positions will created for trainees.

The municipality has also mediated in arrangements between local high schools and new businesses in the Inner Harbor and in Charles Center that guarantee jobs to a minimum number of graduates from each school. These arrangements have fueled competition at the schools themselves (only the best students can count on jobs provided by this system of guarantees), which has resulted in considerably higher grade averages and in an increased respect for the schools involved.

Even though the Inner Harbor has experienced the disappearance of traditional port activities and related industry and, consequently, of thousands of jobs, the same Inner Harbor has once more become a significant factor in the local job market. Harbor Place alone provides jobs for 2,300 people, a third of which were unemployed before going to work here. Together, Charles Center and the Inner Harbor have provided a total of 25,000 jobs.

Keep in mind, however, that the character of the job market has undergone a drastic change. Most functions in the 'old' job market were in industry and were filled by skilled laborers backed by strong unions, which in the course of time had managed to command good working conditions and benefits for their members. Today's jobs are usually part-time positions with poor working conditions, few or no benefits and, in many cases, only seasonal contracts.

99  This program allowed residents in certain areas to buy dwellings for one dollar each, provided that he or she agreed to invest $20,000 to $30,000 within a period of three to five years in renovation activities for the dwelling purchased. As a result of this program, thousands of dwellings were completely refurbished. See, among others, G. Wright.

100  Wolman et al.

101  One of the most visible stimuli in Fells Point is Brown's Wharf, a nineteenth-century warehouse complex whose restoration was completed in 1989; this complex now accommodates a facility quite similar to a festival market: 14,000 square meters of restaurants, shops, and so forth. See Breen and Rigby, p. 75.

102  Lynch.

103  The present plan is to add two adjacent building blocks on the north side, which now house tradespeople who work in the fish market, to the South Street Seaport complex.

104  Charyn, p. 270.

105  Wagner. According to this report, New York was in a period of strong economic recovery, as evidenced by a high concentration of economic activity in Manhattan and a simultaneous decline in boroughs such as Brooklyn and Queens. Wagner believed that these developments needed to be directed. In the 1980s – at a time when the spectacular growth of established economic powers was suffocating Manhattan and driving away small-scale businesses and artists – Wagner argued that Manhattan should consider the importance of preserving conditions for the development of new economic and cultural initiatives, which in their early stages are always dependent on inexpensive accommodations. He also proposed that the enormous economic pressure on Manhattan be shifted to 'Regional Centers' in the other boroughs, allowing them to profit from the economic revival to a greater degree.

106  Beginning in 1989, the Regional Plan Association issued a series of preparatory publications. One bulletin published regularly was *The New Century – Forecasts for the Tri-State Region*, New York, 1989-1995; another brochure was called *The Region That Works*, New York, 1993. The definitive Regional Plan is expected in late 1996.

107  Garreau.

108  West Side Waterfront Panel.

109  *A Greenway Plan for New York City.*

110  Jackson.

111  Jackson (p. 160) is referring to Zerubavel.

112  See Calthorpe; Katz (ed.); and Ferguson (ed.).

## CHAPTER 5 – ROTTERDAM

1  A detailed and well-documented publication on the development of Dutch port cities from 1500 to 1800 is Sigmond's *Nederlandse zeehavens tussen 1500 en 1800.*

2  Between 1585 and 1591, 34,000 of Antwerp's residents left their city in the southern part of the Netherlands for the northern provinces. Most of these people were merchants and artisans with many international contacts, as well as a great deal of knowledge and experience. Sigmond, p. 68.

3  De Vries; Maczak. According to Maczak, many seventeenth-century visitors to the Netherlands greatly admired the system of barge canals and declared this country – of all the nations in Europe – to be the one with the most efficient and comfortable transportation network.

4  Taverne, 1978, p. 35.

5  Geurtsen and Bos, pp. 14-51.

6  With the construction of yet another broad moat and a ring of ramparts around the city, Napoleon made the port of Vlissingen into a virtually unassailable naval base. In the late 1700s and early 1800s, every important Northwestern European seaport ruled by the French was provided with large navel docks inside the city ramparts. Cherbourg, Calais, Dunkirk, Antwerp, and Vlissingen were all transformed into veritable war machines, which together functioned as a 'pistol aimed at the breast' of England.

The conversion of Northern French ports into war machines is covered in depth in Demangeon and Fortier, as well as in Fortier (see, in particular, the chapter entitled 'La paix des citadelles,' pp. 35-60).

7  Mak, p. 106: 'A watery landscape with a structure entirely its own, and it even included, as if lost among the ships, a number of wooden buildings on piles: little shipping offices, an island with two strange wooden cranes, sentry boxes, dredges, the "boom bell" that rang every evening when from the water's edge the city was closed off with a "boom," and a substantial wooden building – the "City Inn" – for lonely foreigners no longer permitted to enter the city.'

8  Grimm (ed.), p. 9.

9  For a detailed and well-documented history of the Boompjes see Meeldijk and Roelofsz (eds.).

10  Van Ravesteyn, 1974, p. 52.

11  Nieuwenhuis, p. 50.

12  Van Reusel.

13 Lombaerde.

14 Van Ravesteyn, 1974, p. 10.

15 For further information on Rose's plans see, in addition to Van Ravesteyn (1974), De Graaf et al.

16 See Smook; see also De Graaf.

17 See, among others, Nieuwenhuis.

18 See also Meyer, 1983.

19 De Jongh's explanatory notes for his 1909 plan, as quoted in Brouwer.

20 Van Ravesteyn, 1974; Wattjes and Ten Bosch, p. 47.

21 Quotation taken from Nieuwenhuis, p. 106.

22 According to Jan Nieuwenhuis, in his history of Rotterdam's Department of Public Works, De Jongh 'found himself on equal footing with the most prominent members of Rotterdam's business community.' And his position was based not only on his authoritative personality but also, and particularly, on his conception of the city, in which he combined the necessity of developing an infrastructure for the growing transit port with the creation of attractive, perhaps cultural, urban facilities. Nieuwenhuis, p. 94.

23 Bouman and Bouman.

24 Compilations of M.J. Brusse's columns, written for the Dutch newspaper *NRC Handelsblad*, can be found in Brusse, 1899; Brusse, 1920; Brusse, 1921; and Brusse, 1924 [1]. He also wrote a famous Dutch novel, *Boefje*, which tells of the life of a Rotterdam street urchin.

25 Brusse, 1921, p. 18.

26 Van Ravesteyn, 1974, p. 47 ff.

27 Entrepreneurs such as M. Mees, H. Muller, J. Dutilh and, later, K.P. van der Mandele (from the 1920s until long after World War II) were to be trend-setting players within this civic culture. Ideas like this also appealed to prominent union leaders and, as time went on, to municipal authorities, categories exemplified by H. Spiekman and J. Brautigam. See, among others, De Klerk and Moscoviter (eds.), 1992; De Goey; Teychiné van Stakenburg; De Ruyter-de Zeeuw; and Brautigam.

28 Networks of port-related entrepreneurs involved in social and cultural institutions have been charted by De Goey.

29 An exhaustive inventory of architecture in the port area has been published by De Winter (ed.).

30 An incident that illustrates the latter view occurred in 1917, when the new city hall first opened its doors to the public. Marius Richter's murals for the council chamber, which depicted the daily activities of hard-working dockworkers, were considered undecorous by many and hence were removed from the chamber, on orders from the city council, immediately following the dedication ceremonies. Not until sixty years had passed – at a time when these paintings had become part of history and the cultivation of Rotterdam as a bustling port city devoted to hard work was a topic imbued with a great deal of nostalgia – did the murals return to the spot for which they were originally intended.

31 Van Ravesteyn, 1948, p. 233.

32 Backx.

33 Ibid., p. 253.

34 Ibid., pp. 260-263.

35 Vreugdenhil.

36 See also Wattjes and Ten Bosch, p. 164 ff.

37 See also Wagenaar, p. 66 ff.

38 See Meyer, 1983.

39 For more on this subject, see the comprehensive description in Wagenaar, p. 215 ff.

40 The key figure in this group was the director of the Van Nelle factory, C.H. van der Leeuw. Other prominent members were the chairman of the Chamber of Commerce, K.P. van der Mandele; the aforementioned shipping entrepreneur, J.Ph. Backx; and the director of the Holland America Line, W.H. de Monchy.

41 Roelofsz, p. 138.

42 Kraaijvanger, p. 32.

43 Ibid., p. 34.

44 Van Embden.

45 Tijhuis.

46 See Meyer et al., 1980.

47 Tijhuis.

48 Van Traa.

49 *Het nieuwe hart van Rotterdam*, p. 16.

50 *De Groene Amsterdammer* (November, 1946).

51 Blijstra, p. 81.

52 Van Traa, 1953.

53 See Rutgers.

54 *Rapport over een zeemanskwartier*, undated memo (initials P/Bc) from the files of the Department of Urban Development, which pertained to a meeting attended by representatives of the business community (including Backx and Van der Leeuw), the police department, and the Department of Urban Development; the topic discussed was the developmental potential of an entertainment quarter in the district north of Zalmhaven.

55 Meyer, 1983.

56 De Jong.

57 Blijstra, p. 163.

58 Wentholt. See also Note 6 (Chapter 1).

59 Wentholt, p. 80.

60 In writing about the new traffic route that was to link the city center to Rotterdam South, Wentholt noted (p. 91): 'This calls for the demolition of one of Rotterdam's most attractive spots; the continuity with the eastern part of the city will be severed completely, and an element vital to the urban silhouette [the White House and vicinity] will disappear.'

61 Wentholt, p. 92.

62 Ibid., pp. 146-147.

63 See Lucas.

64 Habets et al. in Barbieri, Bijhouwer et al., 1981; Meyer et al., 1980; Meyer, 1983.

65 This process is described in greater detail in Meyer et al., 1980.

66 The concept of the compact city was not, in fact, a spatial concept. The focus was on the existing urban area – the territory within municipal boundaries – and the objective was to stop the decline in population that had begun in the 1960s (731,000 inhabitants in 1965 and only 600,000 in 1975). The departure of higher-income and middle-class groups, along with the serious neglect of older residential districts, caused three fundamental social problems: the

growing impoverishment of the urban population as a whole, a rising social unrest in the older districts, and an increasingly insufficient number of urban facilities.

Both aspects of the new policy – an urban-renewal program for the old districts and the reinforcement of the residential function in the inner city – were dominated by sociocultural ideals especially popular among Social Democrats at that time. See Meyer et al., 1980, and, more specifically, Section 4.2, p. 120 ff.: 'De stad als woonplaats.'

67 'What use are big cities anyway? What makes them worth preserving?' Having asked these questions, Jan van der Ploeg, alderman for urban renewal, went on to answer them himself: 'The big city is … the consummate place for giving social renewal an optimal chance … Cities are typical centers of cultural and dynamic creativity. Cities offer space, literally and figuratively, to multi-formity and to emancipation movements in any number of areas. These advantages make the city worthy of preservation.' Van der Ploeg.

68 The municipality found itself in an extremely sticky position. For although the city council was very eager to implement the Koolhaas design, at the same time they could not afford to antagonize Nedlloyd. At virtually the same moment that the municipality had become aware of how essential to the port it was for an information infrastructure serving the transport-based economy to be present in the city, one of the world's major transportation companies was threatening to leave town if it failed to get its own way. Needless to say, Nedlloyd got what it wanted.

69 See the following municipal reports: *Leegloop en toeloop*, 1979; and *Leegloop en toeloop*, 1980. For more on this subject, see De Klerk (ed.), 1982.

Efforts to create a harmonious composition of the population were aimed at realizing a 'balance' between higher and lower incomes, as well as a 'balance' between autochthonous and allochthonous residents, or at least a balanced distribution of the latter throughout the city.

70 De Ruiter et al. (eds.). See also De Kleijn.

71 In 1974, its first year on the job, the new city council adopted the 'Den Dunnen motion,' which stated that 'granting new functions to old harbor sites is not a matter to be decided exclusively by the business community and by the Municipal Port Authority, but is rather the concern of the municipal government, which is responsible for physical planning and urban renewal,' and that 'preparations for development plans for old harbor sites to be used for housing are permitted to commence before existing port-related activities have actually been suspended.'

In 1976 the council published *Nota Herstructuring oude havens*, a report on the reorganization of old harbor sites with a remarkably global approach. It sketched in broad lines those harbor areas that qualified for reorganization or, where appropriate, for housing projects; and in the same broad terms it designated where operational port-related companies could be reaccommodated. It also provided an outline for a financial framework. Plans for each urban sector were to be developed, in greater detail,  on an individual basis. The report served primarily as a foundation for negotiating with the central government for a contribution to the overall operation.

In 1980 municipality and central government reached an agreement based on a housing program in the old harbor areas that was to include 8,000 dwellings, 60 percent of which would be public housing. Most of this public housing was planned for old harbor sites adjacent to urban-renewal districts – sites that could, as such, function as 'overspill areas': locations meant to compensate for housing demolished during urban-renewal operations in the city's older districts.

The majority of the 'private-sector' housing was planned for sites bordering the city center: quayside areas situated in the former seventeenth-century Waterstad.

72 Most of the old harbors on the right bank of the Maas were part of the inner-city district. On the west side of the city, Delfshaven Buitendijks functioned as an overspill area. Furthermore, large building sites – such as former industrial sites and space once used as a cattle market – were available in the urban-renewal areas themselves.

On the left bank of the Maas, however, similar building sites were not available; here a whole series of nineteenth-century harbors had been designated as overspill areas for urban-renewal districts.

73 For a description of the first GeSPs, see Van Hattum et al. For a comprehensive history of the development of the GeSP phenomenon, see Lambert.

74 In the period 1977-1985 the number of jobs in the city decreased by more than 30,000 (based on a total of nearly 294,000 in 1977), and the number of unemployed people increased to about 50,000 (out of a total work force of about 230,000). See Seinpost.

75 One of the first studies to indicate a change in this situation was carried out in 1983 by economists Poeth and Van Dongen for three organizations: the Municipal Port Authority, the Rijnmond Public Corporation, and the Transport and Seaport Companies Cooperative. Poeth and Van Dongen pointed to the rapidly decreasing significance of traditional industrial centers and to the emergence of new and smaller centers, which were spread throughout Europe. The worldwide distribution of consumer goods was gaining in importance as well. If Rotterdam wished to maintain its position as Europe's biggest port city, then the port could no longer be geared exclusively to transit and transshipment activities aimed at a single hinterland area, but would have to be converted into a central hub serving Europe's entire distribution network. Rotterdam had to be developed into a European *mainport*.

Three things were considered essential to the pursuit of this goal: an expanded transportation infrastructure, special distribution centers, and a well-developed information infrastructure.

Poeth and Van Dongen saw the creation of a superior information infrastructure as the main condition for the development of the distribution function. A first-rate mainport would require not only a Port Authority with a sophisticated information system capable of moving a multifarious flow of goods to every corner of the globe, but also a city capable of evolving into an attractive business location for high-tech organizations in the areas of trade, transport, and distribution. This aspect held the most important message to the city. For while the other two aspects (expanded infrastructure and new distribution centers) would have relatively little effect on the city, the development of an information infrastructure inevitably called for a drastic improvement of the kind of business and housing climate found in the city, and a radical renewal of Rotterdam's image as a place to live and work. Poeth and Van Dongen.

76 *Nieuw Rotterdam.* The phrases enclosed in quotation marks are the (translated) titles of two chapters – Chapter 2 and Chapter 1, respectively – in this publication.

77 A thesis written by one of these advisers, Leo van de Berg, may be seen as the group's manifesto. In his thesis, Van de Berg argued for an improved climate for companies settling in Rotterdam; he suggested that the city provide an attractive housing market for skilled employees working for high-tech organizations. Van de Berg emphasized that this meant that Rotterdam had to stop focusing on building public housing at locations preeminently suitable for the creation of attractive housing environments for highly qualified members of the work force. Van de Berg.

See also arguments presented by C.A. van Lammeren, director of Rodamco, at a 1986 congress held in Rotterdam: 'The City, Engine of Economic Recovery.' Van Lammeren cited three principal criteria that international corporations keep in mind when making investments: political and social stability, an abundance of available land, and an economically and culturally diverse environment. Van Lammeren noted that points two and three were areas in which Rotterdam failed to command the respect of the business world. He concluded that Rotterdam had to do everything in its power to create a greater supply of land, as well as an environment characterized by economic and cultural variation.

78 *Binnenstadsplan Rotterdam 1985.* A 'public version' of this plan for the inner city was published under the title *Leven in de stad. Rotterdam op weg naar het jaar 2000*, Rotterdam, 1987.

79 *Binnenstadsplan Rotterdam 1985*, p. 31.

80 On October 8, 1986, the municipality of Rotterdam and the Chamber of Commerce organized an official conference – 'City Revitalization' – at which representatives of Baltimore and Rotterdam exchanged ideas on urban and economic renewal. See also Vader, 1988 [I and II]. Jan Willem Vader headed the inner-city-district section of Rotterdam's Department of Urban Development.

81 Francesco Dal Co was involved in the 'evaluation project' that the RKS organized in 1978-1979 and was one of the speakers at the 'Designer and History, Historian and Design' symposium in 1980, which was the first event on the AIR program and which presented various standpoints on the relation between history and design. Giorgio Grassi also spoke at this symposium, and Aldo Rossi was invited to design a plan for the Kop van Zuid.

For the texts of Dal Co's and Grassi's lectures, see *Plan*, 1981, No. 9, which contains most of the contributions to this symposium. For more on Rossi's plan, see Barbieri and Van Meggelen (eds.).

82 Carel Weeber, Rotterdam architect and professor of architectonic design in Delft, chaired a study group called 'Design' organized by the RKS's architecture division.

Jacques Nycolaas, from Delft, worked for the Department of Urban Development as the 'district head' responsible for Rotterdam South. In 1987 he was named professor of urban design at the Delft University of Technology, a position he held only briefly until his unexpected death in 1988.

83 Barbieri and Van Meggelen (eds.), p. 16. The introduction to this book gave the following reasons for selecting the Kop van Zuid as a design location: 'to provide an alternative to the spatial-political practice that has been "imposed upon" the residents of South prior to this time' and 'to set out new lines of development that harbor the potential for dynamism (opening) within the scope of public housing and urban-renewal practices.'

84 'We asked for nothing. Neither for the beautiful Rotterdam of the future, which has so far refused to appear, nor for attention to be given to the collective nostalgia for prewar Rotterdam, with the "bombardment border" as wailing wall.' From Weeber's introduction in Barbieri and Van Meggelen (eds.), 1982.

85 Weeber, 1979.

86 Besides hosting a debate on the image and form of the city, the RKS also focused on the role of the city as a center of facilities for art and culture. According to the RKS, this role meant more than simply fulfilling an accommodational position; the city itself was to be seen and used as a *stage*. This was the main theme behind the RKS's 1988 initiative to proclaim Westersingel a 'cultural axis' and to provide this route – from station square to Wilhelmina Pier – with a series of artworks; Westersingel was one of a number of projects and activities organized in recognition of *The City – a Stage*. Aldo Rossi's two lighthouses represented the 'leap over the river' to the Wilhelmina-pier, where the Holland America Line's former departure hall had been converted to an exhibition hall. This project was the first to make the Kop van Zuid, and particularly Wilhelminapier, a functional as well as a visual component of the city center: a part of the actively cultural city.

87 Morphological studies of Amsterdam, Rotterdam, Groningen, Kopenhagen, and Barcelona can be found in the various editions of Geurtsen's *De stad als object van bewerking*. See also Geurtsen et al., 1980-1987.

88 The term *stadsontwerp* was introduced by Rein Geurtsen in a lecture given at the request of the RKS in 1979. The title of the lecture was telling: 'Rotterdam and the *Stadsontwerp*; discipline at its nadir and a plea for revaluation.' (Published in *Wonen/TABK*, No. 22, 1979.) Geurtsen pointed out the total absence of spatial design in urban planning and vehemently criticized the continued espousal of the *Basisplan voor de Wederopbouw*, which he saw as the consummate model for 'the failure of the discipline.' Geurtsen characterized the Basisplan as a completely artificial plan as far as the spatial design of the city was concerned: he claimed that all planning objectives in the area of spatial design were totally fictitious, that they existed only as verbal and conceptual notions, and that they were backed by no tools to convert them into spatial forms. Within the debate on the renewal of the profession, Geurtsen's argument was a noteworthy example of the new significance being placed on the myth of a Basisplan with no visual value. While this myth – which portrayed a Basisplan devoid of a three-dimensional cityscape – had been created and cultivated by the makers of the Basisplan itself, and had fulfilled the postwar role of keeping alive the suggestion of a democratic and flexible type of urban planning, some twenty-five years later the same myth functioned as an introduction to an urban planning policy bent on controlling the design of the cityscape.

89 Palmboom identified three types of developmental processes, each

of which created its own 'layer' and, in so doing, became a determining factor in the structure and form of the city:
– The dynamic of the delta, which provided the geomorphological foundation.
– The processes of dike construction, polder creation, reclamation, and urbanization, which together produced our man-made landscape.
– The transportation-based economy, which in Rotterdam, city of transportation, resulted in a relatively autonomous 'traffic machine' that runs straight through and over existing structures.
This stratification produced a city in which Palmboom recognized two types of spatial features:
– Elements or long lines whose spatial structure was characterized by a fairly unambiguous coherence.
– Junctions at which various layers or areas collided with one another.
An unequivocal, systematic approach was to be applied to the coherent structures, lines, and elements; while the junctions were to be viewed as specific design projects, each of which required individual treatment. Palmboom.

90 The Department of Urban Development issued a number of 'district policy plans' in 1987, which were based largely on Palmboom's analysis and arguments. One of these, *Beleidsplan District Zuid*, presented a detailed morphological analysis of Rotterdam South, which featured a discussion of the stubborn presence of former polder structures, as well as of the distinction between urban areas inside and outside the dikes.

91 Grassi.

92 For more on this change in orientation within the Historic Buildings Council, see Van Voorden.

93 This analysis, depicted on a so-called map of cultural values, distinguished between three different kinds of elements with cultural value:
– Individual buildings, as representatives of a specific type of/style of architecture.
– Groups of buildings, which together form characteristic urban planning ensembles and urban areas.
– Structural legacies of urban planning concepts, as 'cultural-historical chassis.'
Although traditionally the Historic Buildings Council had always concentrated on the first category, the analysis of the Kop van Zuid brought with it many recommendations pertaining to the second and third categories. Van Voorden.

94 Frijhoff, 1989.

95 Nostalgia in Rotterdam, according to Frijhoff, was due to distorted recollections and to a past that had not yet been put to rest: 'Rotterdammers carry the prewar city with them, in body and soul … and are searching for a lost city.'
Frijhoff appealed to those dealing with the development of urban plans to keep in mind structures, images, and objects throughout the city that are of essence to the collective memory: 'If one wants to work with his city, he can better decipher its memory than its history, which is, after all, nothing more than a consciously composed part of that memory. The memory is richer and fuller than history and, frankly, less inhibited by shared values or taboos.'
Frijhoff, 1989.

96 Vaandrager.

97 De Boode and Van Oudheusden.

98 Moscoviter, 1994.

99 Katalyn Szanto made an interesting attempt to map the collective memory of the Kop van Zuid.

100 Three such publications are Palmboom's book and two government reports: Rotterdam City Council, *Vernieuwing van Rotterdam*; and the Advisory Committee for the Sociocultural Renewal of Rotterdam, *Nieuw Rotterdam – Een Opdracht voor alle Rotterdammers*.

101 Advisory Committee for the Sociocultural Renewal of Rotterdam.

102 Ibid.

103 Rotterdam City Council, p. 37.

104 The so-called '30 point map' was published in *Werkprogramma Stadsontwikkeling 1987* and later reappeared in a somewhat revised version in the government report Vernieuwing van Rotterdam, which the city council presented in that same year. See Rotterdam City Council. The latter publication was considered the foundation – the bible – of urban renewal in Rotterdam.

105 The presentation of the plan by Teun Koolhaas Associates occurred at the same time that urban plans were being developed for the northern part of the city center, in the vicinity of the Weena; as well as at the same time that a reorganization project was taking place on Rotterdam's *Noordrand* ('Northern Edge'), around the to-be-relocated airport. Both plans also included a great deal of office space, and office development was still experiencing a rapid increase on Rotterdam's east side as well.
When the municipality of Rotterdam asked Erasmus University to make a more detailed study of a tendency among international organizations to set up shop on the Kop van Zuid, the results indicated indecision. Only the national office market showed an interest in the Kop van Zuid. In the years that followed, the municipality grew increasingly doubtful, even with regard to a national interest, and expressed the fear of an 'internal relocation of businesses': a situation in which only companies that already had offices in Rotterdam and vicinity would be attracted to the Kop van Zuid. In fact, the municipality and the central government set the tone for this themselves when they moved courthouse buildings, tax offices, and the Municipal Port Authority from the right bank of the Maas to the Kop van Zuid. See Mik (ed.). See also the Report of the Brainstorming Session for the Kop van Zuid Project (attended also by outside consultants), the subject of which was the *Bestemmingsplan ('Zoning Plan') De Kop van Zuid*: June 23, 1993 (unpublished).

106 The A-, B-, and C-Locational Policy, which was introduced in a report by the central government - *Vierde Nota Ruimtelijke Ordening* (The Hague, 1990) - was primarily meant to curb the 'automobility' of commuter and other business-related traffic.
A-Locations, which lay in central urban areas close to public-transportation junctions, were to accommodate office buildings of a superlocal (national, international) nature, with many employees.
B-Locations were on the urban periphery, close to public-transportation junctions and expressway exits.
In the case of C-Locations, the emphasis was on companies dealing in the transport of goods. The proximity of the highway was the

main consideration; public transportation was less important.

107 *Kop van Zuid, Programmascenario*, p. 20.

108 *De Kop van Zuid, een stedebouwkundig ontwerp*, p. 7.

109 Although the plan for the Kop van Zuid was drawn up in close collaboration with residents' organizations (particularly groups from Feijenoord) and although it always emphasized the socioeconomic spinoff that the project would have for the bordering districts, uncertainty about this aspect entered the picture time and time again. If anything was clear in the 1980s, it was that a growing economy was no guarantee of an increase in job opportunities, and most definitely not in the case of semi- and unskilled workers, many of whom lived in districts adjacent to the Kop van Zuid. Implementation of the plan for the Kop van Zuid was accompanied by a special 'mutual benefits' organization, which set up training programs, tried to make sure that local construction workers were hired to realize the plan, and focused on creating jobs for the long-term unemployed by attempting to establish companies in the service sector. Ultimately, however, even members of this organization had to admit that such projects could succeed only in the presence of a general improvement in the job market. See Rotterdams Instituut Bewonersorganisaties, 1990 [I and II]; Seinpost; and Belderbos, p. 59.

110 Rowe and Koetner. For a more thorough description of the 'collage city' concept, see Chapter 4, p. 256.

111 A comprehensive history of the design for this bridge and of the debate that surrounded it is well-documented in Moscoviter, 1992.

112 This motive not only played an important role in the minds of residents and members of sub-municipal councils. Initially those on the city council – among whom the alderman for finances, in particular – had serious reservations about the plan, which were rooted in doubts concerning its added value for Rotterdam South. This was the theme of 'Three Aldermen for Physical Planning, 1974-1990,' a lecture given by J. Linthorst at a meeting organized by the Rotterdam Arts Council on June 17, 1995 (unpublished).

113 Titels of the three 'quality books' are: *De Kop van Zuid, kwaliteit en beeldvorming* (on the architectonic development of buildings in the area), *De Kop van Zuid, buitenruimte*, and *Kop van Zuid, Programmascenario*. See also Van den Bout.

114 Wilhelminahof accommodates a substantial part of the overall office program for the Kop van Zuid. The total surface area devoted to office space in Wilhelminahof is 128,000 square meters, 78,000 of which are for courthouse buildings, tax offices, and customs authorities; the remaining 50,000 are earmarked as rental space for private enterprise. In addition, an urban plinth directly linked to the public area outdoors was designed to accommodate a range of public facilities.

The spatial structure – a 'visual composition of large and small elements' – is symbolic of the 'ultimate leap in scale.' (The material enclosed in quotation marks is a translation of ideas found in *De Kop van Zuid, kwaliteit en beeldvorming*.)

The project as a whole was realized through the complex collaborative efforts of the municipality, the Government Building Agency, the Tax Department, and two real-estate developers.

115 *Kop van Zuid, kwaliteit en beeldvorming*.

116 Entries of note were *Konfrontaties* by Han Meyer and Arnold Reijndorp, in cooperation with Jenneke ter Horst, Loes Verhaart, and Johanna Vos; *Schei* by J. Meeuws; *Slib uit* by J. Jonkhof, F. Saris, and J. v.d.Berg; *MU* by K. Hoenjet and J. ten Hoeve; *Water-noden* by P. Terreehorst; and *Bazel 1013* by J. Freie, B. Harmelink, Th. Roersma, and M. de Vries.

117 Van Teeffelen et al. (eds.).

118 For an in-depth description and documentation of the development of the Eastern Harbor Area in Amsterdam, see Koster.

119 See the contribution by Van Rijs in Gall et al. (eds.).


CHAPTER 6

1 These studies relied greatly on the activities of the Technische Adviescommissie voor de Waterkeringen ('Technical Advisory Committee for Dikes'), as well as on private initiatives such as *Waterwerk* ('Water Work'). *Waterwerk* was an exhibition (with accompanying catalog) organized by the Fort Asperen Foundation in 1995 in response to floods in Limburg, Brabant, and Overijssel: the result of rivers that overflowed their banks in the winter of 1994-1995. It was feared that these floods would once more give the upper hand to those supporting the type of dike reinforcement that causes cultural and environmental damage. In an effort to prove the existence of many other methods for strengthening dikes, the Fort Asperen Foundation asked eight designers to submit studies on dike reinforcement.

# Acknowledgements

The research and preparatory work that went into this book falls into four categories: (a) visits to the cities and sites involved, (b) discussions with designers, planners, and critics, (c) a study of relevant planning documents, and (d) literary research.

Concerning category (a): visits to cities and sites

From 1986 to 1996 I made a number of trips to London, Barcelona, Amsterdam, and New York; I visited each of the other cities mentioned in the book one or more times during this period. Throughout these years I was a resident of Rotterdam, and up until 1990 I worked in and for Rotterdam as an employee of the Department of Physical Planning and Urban Renewal.

Concerning category (b): discussions with designers, planners, and critics

I owe a great deal of thanks to the following persons for their willing assistance.

London: Nicholas Falk (Urbed, London), John Popper (London Planning Advisory Committee), Tim Catchpole (London Research Centre), Ted Johns (Joined Dockland Action Group), Jenny Hazlewood (London Docklands Development Corporation), Keith Hearn (London Docklands Development Corporation), Bob Aspinall (Port of London Authority, Museum of Docklands), and Gavin Morgan (Museum of London). I gathered inspiration from Annemarie de Boom, whom I supervised in 1995-1996 as she worked on a plan for the Thames as part of her final university project.

Barcelona and the Mediterranean: Joan Busquets (architect, Serveis de Planejament), Manuel de Solà-Morales (architect, Laboratorio d'Urbanismo), Josep Acebillo (architect, Serveis de Projectes Urbanes), Josep Parcerisa (architect, Laboratorio d'Urbanismo), Olga Tarasso (Serveis de Planejament), Jordi Heinrich (Serveis de Planejament), J.A. Solans i Huguet (Generalitat de Catalunya), David MacKay (Martorell, Bohigas, MacKay & Puigdomènech), Mercedes Tatjer (human geographer, Barcelona), Jaime Salazar (Collegi d'Arquitectes de Barcelona), Josep Ribera (Port Autonom de Barcelona), Victoria Mora (Museo de Historia de la Ciudad de Barcelona), Ennio Polegi (University of Genoa), and Mario Caselli (Porto di Genova).

New York and North America: Barry Seymour (Department of City Planning, New York), Nicholas Quenell (Quenell Rothschild Associates, New York), Paul Buckhurst (BFHK, New York), Marshall Berman (Columbia University, New York), Virginia Dajani (Municipal Art Society, New York), Robert Geddes (architect, Princeton University, Princeton), James Rouse (Enterprise Development Corporation, Baltimore), Martin Millspaugh (Enterprise Development Corporation, Baltimore), Eva Liebermann (Department of City Planning, San Francisco), Joann Smith (Seattle Department of Community Development), Douglas Hotchkins (Port of Seattle), Elbert Waters (Department of City Planning of Miami), Lourdes Slazyk (Department of City Planning of Miami).

Rotterdam and the Lowlands: Naming those who have been important in providing me with information on Rotterdam and Amsterdam is quite a complicated affair. Not all of my information was gathered as a direct consequence of my work on this project; much of it was the result of the position I held from 1980 to 1990 as an employee of the Department of Physical Planning and Urban Renewal. Many people unknowingly played the role of 'informant.' In addition, I had discussions with a number of people who were guest lecturers at the Delft University of Technology. In any case, I want to thank Jaap van den Bout, Stefan Gall, Roy Bijhouwer, Paul Achterberg, Mariet Schoenmakers, Loes Verhaart, Jacques Nycolaas†, Jan van der Schans, Arjan Knoester, Gijs Snoek, Karen van Vliet, Frank Josselin de Jong, Jan van Teeffelen, and Piotr Ostojski Ostoja (all associated with the Department of Physical Planning and Urban Renewal of Rotterdam, which has been called the Department of Urban Planning and Public Housing since 1990); Annemie Devalder (Rotterdamse Kunststichting), Hubert de Boer (Teun Koolhaas Associates), Joost Kuhne (Feijenoord Residents Organization), Frits van Voorden (Delft University of Technology), Gert Uhrhan (Department of Physical Planning of Amsterdam, prior to 1990), and Bruno Huls (Amsterdam Council for Urban Development).

Concerning categories (c) and (d): literary research

Sources consulted are listed in the bibliography on the following pages.

# Bibliography

Planning documents are in chronological order; the rest of the literary material is in alphabetical order.

## GENERAL LITERATURE

Arendt, Hannah, *The Human Condition*, Chicago/London, 1958.

Bacon, Edmund, *Design of Cities*, London, 1967 (revised edition, 1974).

Baudelaire, Charles, *Le Spleen de Paris*, Paris, 1869; English translation by Varese, Louise, *Paris Spleen*, New York/London, 1988.

Beek, W.J., et al., (eds.), *Kijken over de eeuwgrens, 25 fascinerende trends*, The Hague, 1993.

Benjamin, Walter, *Charles Baudelaire: een dichter in het tijdperk van het hoog-capitalisme*, Amsterdam, 1979.

Benjamin, Walter, *Kleine filosofie van het flaneren*, Amsterdam, 1992.

Berman, Marshall, *All that is Solid Melts into Air*, New York/London, 1983.

Boomkens, René, 'Domweg gelukkig in mijn database,' in Boomkens, René (ed.), *Ontwerpen voor de Onmogelijke Stad*, Amsterdam, 1993.

Boomkens, René, *Kritische massa – over massa, moderne ervaring en popcultuur*, Amsterdam, 1994.

Bowles, Paul, *Let it Come Down*, New York, 1952.

Bowles, Paul, *Réveillon a Tanger*, Paris, 1981.

Bowles, Paul, *Tanger, Vues Choisies*, Paris, 1991.

Boyer, Christine, *The City of Collective Memory: Its Historical Imagery and Architectural Entertainments*, Cambridge, Mass., 1994.

Bramham, Peter (ed.), *Leisure and Urban Processes: Critical Studies of Leisure Policy in Western European Cities*, London/New York, 1989.

Braudel, Fernand, *Civilisation matérielle. Economie et capitalisme XVe-XVIIIe siècle*, Paris, 1979; English translation by Reynolds, S., *Civilization and Capitalism*, 3 vols., London/New York, 1981-1984.

Breen, Anne, and Dick Rigby, *Waterfronts: Cities Reclaim Their Edge*, New York, 1994.

Burgers, Jack (ed.), *De uitstad. Over stedelijk vermaak*, Utrecht, 1992.

Burke, Peter, *Venice and Amsterdam*, London, 1974.

'Metropoles portuaires en Europe,' *Les Cahiers de la recherche architecturale*, (special issue), Nos. 30/31, Paris, 1992.

Calvino, Italo, *Le Città Invisibili*, Turin, 1972; English translation: *Invisible Cities*, London, 1974.

Canetti, Elias, *Masse und Macht*, London, 1960.

Castells, Manuel, *The Informational City*, Oxford, 1989.

Choukri, Mohammed, and Paul Bowles, *Jean Genet in Tangier*, New York, 1973.

Corbin, Alain, *Le territoire du vide. L'Occident et le désir de rivage*, Paris, 1988.

Croutier, Alev Lytle, *Taking the Waters: Spirit, Art, Sensuality*, New York/London, 1992.

Davids, Karel, et al., (eds.), *De Republiek tussen zee en vaste land – Buitenlandse invloeden op cultuur, economie en politiek in Nederland 1580-1800*, Leuven/Apeldoorn, 1995.

Davies, Mike, 'Fortress Los Angeles: The Militarization of Urban Space,' in Sorkin, Michael (ed.), *Variations on a Theme Park: The New American City and the End of Public Space*, New York, 1992.

Deben, Leon, et al., *Capital Cities as Achievement, Essays*, Amsterdam, 1990.

De Jong, Taeke, *Kleine methodologie voor ontwerpend onderzoek*, Meppel/Amsterdam, 1992.

De Jong, Taeke, *Systematische transformaties in het getekende ontwerp en hun effect*, Delft, 1995.

De Liagre Böhl, Herman, et al. (eds.), *Nederland industrialiseert! – Politieke en ideologische strijd rondom het naoorlogse industrialisatiebeleid 1945-1955*, Nijmegen, 1981.

De Solà-Morales, Manuel, 'Openbare en collectieve ruimte – de verstedelijking van het privé-domein als nieuwe uitdaging,' *Oase*, No. 33, Delft/Nijmegen, 1992.

Drewe, Paul, *De Netwerk-stad VROM. Bijdrage van informatietechnologie aan nieuwe concepten van ruimtelijke planning*, Delft, 1996.

Drewe, Paul, and Ben Jansen, *What port for the future? From 'Mainports' to nodes of logistic networks*, Delft/Tilburg, 1995.

Featherstone, Mike, 'City Cultures and Postmodern Lifestyles,' in *Congresverslag van het 7e European Leisure and Recreational Association Congress*, Rotterdam, 1989 [I]. Featherstone, Mike, 'Postmodernism and the Aestheticization of Everyday Life,' in Friedman, J., and S. Lash (eds.), *Modernity and Identity*, London, 1989 [II].

Friedrichs, Jürgen, et al., *The Changing Downtown*, Berlin/New York, 1987.

Frijhoff, Willem, et al., *De Rotterdamse cultuur in elf spiegels*, Rotterdam, 1993.

Frijhoff, Willem, 'De stad en haar geheugen,' *Oase*, No. 24, Delft, 1989.

Gall, Stefan, et al. (eds.), *Stedebouw in beweging*, Rotterdam, 1993.

Genet, Jean, *Journal du voleur*, Paris, 1949.

Geurtsen, Rein, *De stad, object van bewerking*, 1980-1988, (lecture notes).

Geurtsen, Rein, 'Rotterdam en het stadsontwerp; dieptepunt discipline en pleidooi voor opwaardering,' *Wonen/TABK*, No. 22, Amsterdam, 1979.

Geurtsen, Rein, et al., *LAS-boek*, Delft, 1980-1987.

Geurtsen, Rein, and Luc Bos, 'Kopenhagen, dubbelstad. Een bewerkte reisindruk,' *Wonen/TABK*, Nos. 10/11/12, Amsterdam, 1982.

Geuze, Adriaan, 'Het vermeende succes' (Maaskant lecture), *de Architect* (Feb., 1996), The Hague.

Giedion, Sigfried, *Space, Time & Architecture: The Growth of a New Tradition*, Cambridge, Mass., 1941.

Gottmann, J., *Megalapolis: The Urbanised Northeastern Seaboard of the United States*, New York, 1961.

Hall, Peter, *Cities of Tomorrow*, London, 1988.

Hanappe, P., and M. Savy, 'Industrial Ports and the Kondratieff Cycle,' in Hoyle, B.S., and D.A. Pinder (eds.), *Cityport Industrialisation and Regional Development*, Oxford, 1981.

Harvey, David, *The Condition of Postmodernity: An Enquiry into the Origins of Cultural Change*, Cambridge, Mass., 1990.

Heeling, Jan, 'Historische continuïteit,' in *Architectuur in Bedrijf*, Dienst Ruimtelijke Ordening en Economische Zaken Gemeente Groningen, Groningen, 1990.

Heeling, Jan, *Stuurman op de wilde vaart* (inaugural speech accompanying Heeling's acceptance of a professorship in the department of urban design at Delft University of Technology), Delft, 1991.

Hoyle, B.S., and D.A. Pinder (eds.), *Cityport Industrialisation and Regional Development*, Oxford, 1981.

Hoekveld, G.A., 'Het wereldsysteem, terrein van onverhulde ideologie,' in Hoekveld, G.A., and L. van der Laan (eds.), *Regio's in wereldcontext*, Meppel, 1987.

Hugill, Stan, *Sailortown*, London, 1967.

Knight, Richard, *The Advanced Industrial Metropolis: A New Type of World City*, New York, 1985.

Koolhaas, Rem, *S. M. L. XL.*, Rotterdam, 1995.

Kostof, Spiro, *The City Assembled: The elements of urban form through history*, London, 1992.

Kostof, Spiro, *The City Shaped: Urban patterns and meanings through history*, London, 1991.

*Krisis, tijdschrift voor filosofie*, No. 31, *Republikeinse politiek* (special issue), Amsterdam, 1988.

*Krisis, tijdschrift voor filosofie*, No. 35, *Walter Benjamin, Richard Sennett* (special issue), Amsterdam, 1989.

*Krisis, tijdschrift voor filosofie*, No. 41, *Stad en roes* (special issue), Amsterdam, 1990.

Krop, Hans, 'Gewoon, stedebouw,' in Hermans, Willem, et al. (eds.), *Woorden beelden plannen - over het stedebouwkundig meesterwerk*, Delft, 1995.

Leupen, Bernard, et al. (ed.), *Ontwerp en analyse*, Rotterdam, 1993.

Meyer, Han, et al., *De beheerste stad - ontstaan en intenties van een sociaal-democratische stadspolitiek: een kritiek*, Rotterdam, 1980.

Meyer, Han, et al., 'Over sociaal-democratie en volkshuisvesting,' in Spiekerman van Weezelenburg, Sonja, and Stef van der Gaag (eds.), *Raderwerk, 10 jaar Projectraad Bouwkunde*, Delft, 1981.

Meyer, Han, et al., *Sleutelen aan de Bijlmer*, Delft, 1991.

Ministerie van Landbouw, Natuurbeheer en Visserij, *Visie stadslandschappen*, The Hague, 1995.

Ministerie van Verkeer en Waterstaat, *Sustainable Transport: Studying New Dimensions*, The Hague, 1993.

Ministerie van WVC, *Nota Architectuurbeleid,* The Hague, 1990.

Mitchell, William J., *City of Bits: Space, Place and the Infobahn*, Cambridge, Mass., 1995.

Mommaas, Hans, *Moderniteit, vrije tijd en de stad; sporen van maatschappelijke transformatie en continuïteit*, Utrecht, 1993.

Neutelings, J.W., 'De ringcultuur,' in *Vlees en beton*, Antwerp, 1989.

Olsen, Donald J., *The City as a Work of Art*, New Haven/London, 1986.

Oosterman, Jan, *Parade der passanten. De stad, het vertier en de terrassen*, Utrecht, 1993.

Paz, Octavio, *Nachtmuziek over San Ildefonso*, Amsterdam, 1993.

Pons, Dominique, *Les Riches Heures de Tanger*, Paris, 1990.

Prélorenzo, Claude (ed.), *Vivre et habiter la ville portuaire/Port-city lifestyles*, Paris, 1995-1996.

Raban, Jonathan, *Hunting Mr. Heartbreak*, London, 1990.

Raban, Jonathan, *Soft City*, London, 1974.

Reijndorp, Arnold, 'Afscheid van de Volkshuisvesting,' in De Klerk, Len, and Herman Moscoviter (eds.), *En dat al voor de arbeidende klasse, 75 jaar volkshuisvesting Rotterdam*, Rotterdam, 1992.

Reijndorp, Arnold, and Hanneke van der Ven (eds.), *Een reuze vooruitgang. Utopie en praktijk in de zuidelijke tuinsteden van Rotterdam*, Rotterdam, 1994.

Rudolph, Wolfgang, *Die Hafenstadt. Eine maritime Kulturgeschichte*, Oldenburg/Munich/Hamburg, 1980.

Sassen, Saskia, *The Global City*, Princeton, N.J., 1991.

Sennett, Richard, *The Conscience of the Eye: The Design and Social Life of Cities*, New York, 1991.

Sennett, Richard, *The Fall of Public Man*, London/Boston, 1977.

Simonis, J.B.D. (ed.), *De staat van de burger. Beschouwingen over hedendaags burgerschap*, Meppel/Amsterdam, 1991.

Slauerhoff, J., 'Tanger, Parel van het Oosten,' *De Groene Amsterdammer* (Sept. 22, 1934); included in the compilation *Alleen de havens zijn ons trouw*, Amsterdam, 1992.

Slauerhoff, J., *Verzamelde gedichten*, Amsterdam, 1995.

Smiers, Joost, *Cultuur in Nederland 1945-1955*, Nijmegen, 1977.

Sorkin, Michael, 'See you in Disneyworld,' in Sorkin, Michael (ed.), *Variations on a Theme Park*, New York, 1992 [I].

Sorkin, Michael (ed.), *Variations on a Theme Park: The New American City and the End of Public Space*, New York, 1992 [II].

Taverne, Ed, *Architectuur en geschiedenis, College-dictaat Historiografie, Geschiedenis van architectuur en stedebouw*, Rijksuniversiteit Groningen, 1993.

Tijmes, Pieter, 'De domeinen van Hannah Arendt,' *Krisis, Tijdschrift voor filosofie*, No. 56 (Sept., 1994), Amsterdam.

TNO, *Logistiek & Transport*, Delft, 1986.

Van der Knaap, G.A., and L. van der Laan, *Stedelijke vernieuwing: onderwerpen voor onderzoek. Analyse van de onderzoeksbehoefte ter voorbereiding van de Meerjarenvisie Ruimtelijk Onderzoek 1991-1996 van het Programmeringsoverleg Ruimtelijk Onderzoek*, The Hague, 1991.

Van der Staay, Adriaan, 'Gelukkig één stad zonder culturele identiteit,' in Frijhoff, Willem, et al., *De Rotterdamse cultuur in elf spiegels*, Rotterdam, 1993.

Van Dijk, Hans, et al. (eds.), *Architectonische kwaliteit als opdracht voor openbaar bestuur*, Rotterdam, 1991.

Van Engelsdorp-Gastelaars, R., 'De toekomst van de openbare ruimte' (round-table discussion), *De Blauwe Kamer*, No. 6, Wageningen, 1995.

Van Teeffelen, Jan, et al. (eds.), *Omzwervingen door het landschap van de* toekomst - Rotterdam 2045, visies op de toekomst van stad, haven en regio, Rotterdam, 1995.

Van Vught, Frans, *Sociale planning - Oorsprong en ontwikkeling van het Amerikaanse planningsdenken*, Assen, 1979.

Virilio, Paul, *l'Horizon Negatif*, Paris, 1981.

Webber, Melvin, 'The urban place and the nonplace urban realm,' in Webber, M., et al., *Explorations on Urban Structures*, Philadelphia, 1964.

Wetenschappelijke Raad voor het Regeringsbeleid (WRR), *Van de stad en de rand*, Rapport aan de regering nr. 37, The Hague, 1990.

Zijderveld, A.C., *Van stedelijkheid en stedelijke festivals*, Rotterdam, 1994.

THE ENGLISH PORT CITY:
LONDON AND THE WONDER OF DOCKLANDS

*Planning documents*

*County of London Plan*, London County Council (Abercrombie, P., and J.H. Forshaw), 1943.

*Greater London Plan*, Ministry of Town and Country Planning, His Majesty's Stationery Office (Abercrombie, P.), 1944.

*Administrative County of London Development Plan 1951*, London County Council, 1951.

*Greater London Development Plan*, Greater London Council, 1973.

*Docklands. Redevelopment Proposals for East London*, London Docklands Study Team, 1973.

*London Docklands Strategic Plan*, Dockland Joint Committee, 1976.

Gosling, David, et al., *Isle of Dogs: A Guide to Design and Development Opportunities*, 1982.

*Isle of Dogs Enterprise Zone: Scheme*, London Docklands Development Corporation, 1982.

*Isle of Dogs Urban Design Plan*, London Docklands Development Corporation Urban Design Team (Hollamby, E.), 1982.

*The Future of London's River: A Design Guide for Thames Side*, Greater London Council, 1986.

*London Docklands Building Agreement and Licence for Redevelopment of Land*, London Docklands Development Corporation, 1986.

*Policy Issues & Choices. The future of London in the 1990's*, London Planning Advisory Committee, 1988.

*Canary Wharf Masterplan*, Olympia & York, 1988.

*London Docklands Transport: The New Network*, London Docklands Development Corporation, 1993.

*The Isle of Dogs Development Framework*, London Docklands Development Corporation, 1994.

*Canary Wharf and Heron Quays Masterplan*, London Docklands Development Corporation, 1996.

*Literature*

Ackroyd, Peter, *Dickens' London*, London, 1987.

Ash, Maurice, *A Guide to the Structure of London*, Bath, 1972.

Bacon, Edmund, *Design of Cities*, London 1967 (revised edition, 1974).

Barker, Felix, and Peter Jackson, *The History of London in Maps*, London, 1990.

Barker, Theo, 'Dockland: Origins and Earlier History,' in *Dockland: An Illustrated Historical Survey of Life and Work in East-London*, London, 1986.

Beioly, Steve, et al., 'London Docklands – the leisure element,' in *Leisure Management*, London, 1988.

Bianchini, Franco, 'Cultural Policy and Urban Social Movements: The response of "New Left" in Rome (1976-1985) and London (1981-1986),' in Bramham, P., et al. (eds.), *Leisure and Urban Processes*, London/New York, 1989.

Bill, Peter (ed.), 'Canary Wharf: A Landmark in Construction,' *Building* (special issue), London, 1991.

Broodbank, Sir J.G., *History of the Port of London*, 2 vols., London, 1921.

Buchanan, Peter, 'What City? A Plea for Place in the Public Realm,' *Architectural Review*, No. 11, 1988.

Canetti, Elias, *Masse und Macht*, London, 1960.

Canning, John (ed.), *Mayhew's London: The classic account of London street life and characters in the time of Charles Dickens and Queen Victoria*, London, 1986.

Carr, R.J.M. (ed.), *Dockland. An Illustrated Historical Survey of Life and Work in East London*, London, 1986.

Catchpole, Tim, 'Control of the River Prospect on the Thames in London,' in *Watersite 2000: Proceedings of the International Congress on the Rejuvenation of Former Dockland and Island Waterways*, Bristol, 1988.

Catchpole, Tim, *London Skylines: A Study of High Buildings and Views*, London Research Centre, London, 1987.

Chambers, J.D., *The Workshop of the World: British Economic History 1820-1880*, Oxford, 1968.

Chesshyre, Robert, 'Journalistiek in de diaspora,' (Dutch translation of Chesshyre's 'Journalism in the Diaspora'), *NRC-Handelsblad*, Dec. 21, 1987.

Church, Andrew, 'Demand-led Planning, the Inner-city Crisis and the Labour Market: London Docklands Evaluated,' in Hoyle, B.S., and D.A. Pinder (eds.), *Cityport Industrialisation and Regional Development*, Oxford, 1981.

Clark, E.F., 'Transport East of London Bridge after 1825,' *East London Record* (October, 1987), London.

Cole, Thomas J., *Life and Labor in the Isle of Dogs: The Origins and Evolution of an East London Working-Class Community 1800-1980*, Oklahama City, 1984.

Collins, Philip, 'Dickens and the City,' in Sharp, William, and Leonard Wallock, *Visions of the Modern City*, New York, 1983.

Cooke, Phil, 'The changing city estate,' *New Society* (April, 1988), London [II].

Cooke, Phil, *Localities*, London, 1988 [I].

Cooke, Phil, and Richard Meegan, 'Urban Development Corporations,' in preliminary congress book, Vol. I, ELRA Congress *Cities of the Future*, The Hague, 1989.

Cox, Alan, *Docklands in the Making: The Redevelopment of the Isle of Dogs 1981-1995*, London, 1995.

Dickens, Charles, *A Tale of Two Cities*, London, 1860.

Dickens, Charles, *The Uncommercial Traveller*, London, 1863.

Disraeli, Benjamin, *Sybil, or the Two Nations*, London, 1845.

Docklands Consultative Committee, *Four years review of the LDDC*, London, 1985.

Docklands Consultative Committee, *Urban Development Corporations: Six Years in London's Docklands*, London, 1988.

Douglas Brown, R., *Port of London*, Lavenham, 1978.

*The Economist*, 'London Docklands, Where Derelict Land is a Greenfield Site' (February, 1988), London.

Edwards, Brian, *London Docklands: Urban Design in an Age of Deregulation*, Oxford, 1992.

Eldridge, C.C., *England's Mission: The Imperial Idea in the Age of Gladstone and Disraeli 1868-1880*, London, 1973.

Elmers, Chris, and Alex Werner, *Dockland Life: A pictorial history of London's Docks 1860-1970*, London, 1991.

Epstein Nord, Deborah, 'The Social Explorer as Anthropologist: Victorian Travellers among the Urban Poor,' in Sharp, William, and Leonard Wallock (eds.), *Visions of the Modern City*, New York, 1983.

Fox, Celina, *London World City 1800-1840*, New Haven/London, 1992.

Gosling, David, and Barry Maitland, *Concepts of Urban Design*, London, 1986.

Groak, Steven, 'London's Docklands – Neue Architektur ohne neue Ideeen,' *Architese*, 3-88, Berlin, 1988.

Hall, Peter, 'Bringing Abercrombie Back from the Shades,' *Town Planning Review*, Vol. 66, No. 3, Liverpool, 1995.

Hatton, Brian, 'The development of London's Docklands: The role of the Urban Development Corporation,' *Lotus International*, No. 67, Milan, 1990.

Hibbert, Christopher, *London: The Biography of a City*, London, 1980.

Himmelfarb, Gertrude, *The Idea of Poverty: England in the Early Industrial Age*, New York, 1983.

Hollamby, Ted, and Paul da Luz, 'Londres ouvre ses docklands a l'investissement privé,' *Urbanisme* (July, 1988), Paris.

Howard, Ebenezer, *To-Morrow: a Peaceful Path to Real Reform*, London, 1898; revised edition is entitled *Garden Cities of To-Morrow*, London, 1902.

London Docklands Development Corporation, *Annual Review 1987-1988*, London, 1988.

London Docklands Development Corporation, *Annual Review and Financial Statements for the Year Ended 31 March 1996*, London, 1996 [I].

London Docklands Development Corporation, *Attitudes to London Docklands 1994: A Survey of Local Business*, London, 1994.

London Docklands Development Corporation, *Key Facts & Figures*, London, 1996 [II].

Lyders, Carol, and Averill Harrison (eds.), *Docklands Heritage: Conservation and Regeneration in London Docklands*, London, 1987.

Middleton, Michael, *Cities in Transition: The Regeneration of Britain's Inner Cities*, London, 1991.

Mingay, G.E., *The Transformation of Britain 1830-1939*, London/Boston, 1986.

Naib, S.K.A. (ed.), *Dockland: An illustrated historical survey of life and work in East London*, London, 1986.

Phillips, Tony, *A London Dockland Guide: A gazetteer to points of historical and architectural interest*, London, 1986.

Port of London Authority, *Port of London Handbook*, London, 1980-1995.

John Pudney, *London Docks*, London, 1975.

Rasmussen, Steen Eiler, *London the Unique City*, London, 1934 (revised edition, 1982).

Reid, George, *River Thames in the late Twenties & early Thirties*, London, 1987.

Ritchie-Noakes, Nancy, *Jesse Hartley: Dock Engineer to the Port of Liverpool 1824-1860*, Liverpool, 1980.

Rose, M., *The East End of London*, London, 1951.

Royal Commission of the Historical Monuments of England, *Survey of London*, Vols. XLIII/XLIV, *Poplar, Blackwall and The Isle of Dogs*, London, 1994.

Smit, Frank, *De droom van Howard. Het verleden en de toekomst van de tuindorpen*, Amsterdam, 1990.

Thomas, Ben, *Ben's Limehouse*, London, 1987.

Trease, Geoffrey, *London, a concise history*, London, 1975.

Weightman, Gavin, *London River: The Thames Story*, London, 1990.

Weightman, Gavin, and Steve Humphries, *The Making of Modern London 1914-1939*, 3 vols., London, 1983.

THE MEDITERRANEAN PORT CITY:
BARCELONA AND THE OTHER MODERN TRADITION

*Planning documents*

*Plan General Metropolitan*, Ajuntament de Barcelona, 1976.

*Pla Especial de Reforma interior de la Barceloneta*, Ajuntament de Barcelona (De Solà-Morales, Manuel), 1980-1981.

*Projecte d'urbanització del Moll de la Fusta*, Ajuntament de Barcelona & Port Autònom de Barcelona (De Solà-Morales, Manuel), 1982.

*Esquema de Vies Bàsiques*, Ajuntament de Barcelona, Serveis de Planejament, 1983.

*Pla de Vies de Barcelona*, Ajuntament de Barcelona, Serveis de Planejament, 1984.

*Pla Especiàl d'Ordenació Urbana de la Façana al Mar de Barcelona, al sector del Passeig de Carles I i de l'Avinguda d'Icaria*, Ajuntament de Barcelona (Martorell et al.), 1986.

*Àrees de Nova Centralitat*, Ajuntament de Barcelona, Serveis de Planejament, 1987.

*Pla Especiàl d'adequació de l'area recidencial i la Vila Olímpica i de la zona d'equipaments costaners als ajustos esdevinguts necessaris al Pla Especiàl de 1986*, Villa Olímpica S.A. (Martorell et al.), 1989.

*Proyecto de reordenacion del Paseo Nacional, Muelle de la Barceloneta y Muelle del Reloj*, Ajuntament de Barcelona, Serveis de Projectes i Obres (Tarassó, Olga, and Jordi Henrich), 1991.

*Proyecto de reordenacion de la Zona del Mar de la Barceloneta*, Ajuntament de Barcelona, Serveis de Projectes i Obres (Tarassó, Olga, and Jordi Henrich), 1992.

*Literature*

Acebillo, Josep, 'Structure and Significance of the Urban Space,' in *Barcelona Spaces and Sculptures 1982-1986*, Barcelona, 1987.

Ajuntament de Barcelona, *Barcelona – Espacio Publico*, Barcelona, 1993.

Ajuntament de Barcelona (Arriola, A., and Carme Fiol, eds.), *Barcelona Spaces and Sculptures (1982-1986)*, Barcelona, 1987.

Ajuntament de Barcelona (Torres M., ed.), *Inicis de la Urbanística*

*Municipal de Barcelona*, Barcelona, 1985.

Ajuntament de Barcelona (Bohigas, O., ed.), *Plans i Projectes per a Barcelona 1981-1982*, Barcelona, 1983 [II].

Ajuntament de Barcelona, Àrea d'Urbanisme (Busquets, J., and J.L. Gómez Ordóñez, eds.), *Estudi de L'Eixample*, Barcelona, 1983 [I].

Ajuntament de Barcelona, Centre de Cultura Contemparània (Garcia Espuche, A., and Teresa Navas, eds.), *Retrat de Barcelona*, Vols. I/II, Barcelona, 1995.

Ajuntament de Barcelona, Museu d'Història de la Ciutat (Caballé, F., and M. Tatjer, eds.), *La Barceloneta. Origen i trasformació d'un barri, 1753-1994*, Barcelona, 1994.

Ajuntament de Barcelona, Planejament Urbanístic, Àrea d'Urbanisme i Obres Públiques (Barnada, J., ed.), *Urbanisme a Barcelona. Plans cap al 92*, Barcelona, 1986.

Barjau, Santi, et al., *La Formació de l'Eixample de Barcelona*, Barcelona, 1990.

Bet, Els, 'Het stedelijk speelveld,' in Bekkering, Juliette, and Paul van Ark (eds.), *Beschreven leegte*, Rotterdam, 1993.

Bohigas, Oriol, 'Per una altra urbanitat' (English translation: 'Barcelona: Programme for the City's Reconstruction. Towards a New Civic Style'), in *Plans i Projectes per a Barcelona 1981-1982*, Barcelona, 1983.

Bohigas, Oriol, et al., *Barcelona City and Architecture 1980-1992*, Barcelona, 1991.

Braudel, Fernand, *La Méditerranée et le monde méditerranéen à l'époque de Philippe II*, Paris, 1966; English translation: *The Mediterranean and the Mediterranean World in the Age of Philip II*, London/New York, 1972.

Busquets, Joan, *Barcelona – Evolución urbanística de una capital compacta*, Madrid, 1992.

Byrne, E Conçalo, 'Rebuilding the city: Pombal's Lissabon,' *Lotus International*, No. 51, Milan, 1986.

Calabi, Donatella, 'Images of a City "in the Middle" of Salt Water,' in Salzano, Eduardo, *An Atlas of Venice*, Venice, 1989.

'Catalonia, territory, architecture,' *Lotus International* (special issue), No. 23, Milan, 1979/II.

Colebrander, Bernard, *Chiado Lissabon. Alvaro Siza en de strategie van het geheugen*, Rotterdam, 1990.

De Solà-Morales, Manuel, 'Barcelona: Ancho es el Ensanche,' *Arquitecturas Bis* (March, 1985), Barcelona.

De Solà-Morales, Manuel, 'Barcelona, la ciudad y el puerto: la historia continúa,' *Arquitecturas Bis* (June, 1985), Barcelona.

De Solà-Morales, Manuel, 'The Identity of the Territory,' *Lotus International*, No. 23, Milan, 1979.

De Solà-Morales, Manuel, 'La segunda historia del proyecto urbano – otra tradición moderna: The Second Story of the Urban Project – Another Modern Tradition,' *Urbanismo Revista*, No. 5, Barcelona, 1987. This article was also published under the title 'Another Modern Tradition – From the Break of 1930 to the Modern Urban Project,' *Lotus International*, No. 64, Milan 1989 [I].

De Solà-Morales, Manuel, *Les Formes de creixement urbà*, Barcelona, 1993.

De Solà-Morales, Manuel, 'Ludivico Quaroni,' *Urbanismo Revista* (special issue), No. 7, Barcelona, 1989 [II].

De Solà-Morales, Manuel, 'Openbare en collectieve ruimte – de verstedelijking van het privé-domein als nieuwe uitdaging,' *Oase*, No. 33, Delft/Nijmegen, 1992.

De Solà-Morales, Manuel, 'Space, time and the city,' *Lotus International*, No. 51, Milan 1986.

De Solà-Morales, Manuel, et al., 'Revivir La Barceloneta,' *CAU* (May, 1982), Barcelona.

Duran i Sanpere, Agusti, *Barcelona i la seva història*, Barcelona, 1972.

Fabre, J., and J.M. Huertas, *Tots els Barris de Barcelona: La Barceloneta*, Barcelona, 1976.

Florêncio, Augusto Rentes, 'Over catastrofe en nieuwe vormen, de aardbeving van Lissabon en de hervormingen van Pombal,' in Lankers, Anne-Marie, et al. (eds.), *Fascinaties*, Vlaardingen, 1986.

Geurtsen, Rein, 'Om de waardigheid van het stedelijk landschap. Barcelona 1979-1992: Public Design op vele fronten en schaalniveaus,' *de Architect* (March, 1988), The Hague.

Hughes, Robert, *Barcelona*, New York, 1991. Dutch translation: *Het epos van Barcelona - koningin der steden*, Amsterdam, 1991. (page numbers in notes refer to Dutch translation)

Links, J.G., *Canaletto*, Oxford, 1982.

Magrinyà i Salvador Tarragó, Fransesc (ed.), *Cerda. Ciudad y Territorio*, Barcelona, 1994.

Martorell et al., *La Villa Olímpica. Barcelona 1992. Arquitectura. Parques. Puerto deportivo*, Barcelona, 1991.

McCully, Marilyn, 'Introduction,' in McCully, Marilyn (ed.), *Homage to Barcelona: The City and its Art 1888-1936*, London, 1986.

Meyer, Han, 'Barcelona, stad aan het water,' *Archis*, 5-86, Amsterdam, 1986.

Meyer, Han, 'Barcelona, stad der wonderen,' *Archis*, 6-92, Amsterdam, 1992.

Meyer, Han, 'Inspirerende experimenten in Barcelona. Werken aan de openbaarheid van de stad,' *Stedebouw & Volkshuisvesting* 6-88, Alphen aan den Rijn, 1988.

Meyer, Han, 'Moderne stedelijke complexiteit in Barcelona,' *de Architect*, The Hague, 1989 [I].

Meyer, Han, 'Regisseurs van het moderne stadsleven,' an interview (translated into Dutch) with Joan Busquets and Manuel de Solà-Morales, *de Architect* (October, 1989), The Hague, [II].

Ministerio de Obras Públicas y Transportes (Climent Soto, L., et al., eds.), *10 years of town planning in Spain*, Madrid, 1991.

Molas, Isidre, 'Barcelona, a European City,' in McCully, Marilyn (ed.), Homage to Barcelona: The City and its Art 1888-1936, London, 1986.

Muntaner, Josep Maria, 'The Idea of the Olympic Village in Barcelona,' *Lotus International*, No. 67, Milan, 1990.

Oliveras, Jordi, 'Nuevas Poblaciones en la España de la illustration,' *Urbanismo Revista* no. 2 (May, 1983), Barcelona.

Oliveras, Jordi, 'Nuevas Poblaciones en la Espana de la Ilustración,' *Urbanismo Revista*, No. 2, Barcelona, 1985.

Orwell, George, *Homage to Catalonia*, London, 1938.

Palà, Marina, and Olga Subirós (eds.), *1856-1999 Contemporary Barcelona*, Barcelona, 1996.

Poleggi, Ennio (ed.), *Città portuali del Mediterraneo. Storia e archeologia*, Genoa, 1989.

Poleggi, Ennio, 'The historical evolution of the historic centre and the old port,' in *Genova Towards 1992*, Genoa, 1988.

Poleggi, Ennio, *Paesaggio e Imagine di Genova*, Genoa, 1982.

Quaderns [1] = *Barcelona, A Virtual Geography*, Barcelona, 1993.

Quaderns [2] = *Barcelona 1993*, Barcelona, 1993.

Quaderns [3] = *Guia d'Arquitectura Contemporània Barcelona i la seva àrea territorial, 1928-1990*, Barcelona, 1993.

Quaderns 1993 = *Linked Images*, Barcelona, 1993.

Roca, Francesco, 'From Montjuich to the world,' in McCully, Marilyn (ed.), *Homage to Barcelona: The City and its Art 1888-1936*, London, 1986.

Rohrer, Judith, 'The Universal Exhibition of 1988,' in McCully, Marilyn (ed.), *Homage to Barcelona: The City and its Art 1888-1936*, London, 1986.

Sabatar, L.B., *Barceloneta, dedicado a los niños con motivo del II centinario (1753-1953)*, Barcelona, 1953.

Sagarra, Ferran, et al., *La Formació de l'Eixample de Barcelona – Aproximacios a un fenomen urbà*, Barcelona, 1990.

Tatjer, Mercedes, *Burgueses, Inquilinos y Rentistas – Mercado inmobiliario, propiedad y morfología en el centro histórico de Barcelona: La Barceloneta 1753-1982*, Madrid, 1988.

Tatjer, Mercedes, *La Barceloneta – Del Siglo XVIII al Plan de la Ribera*, Barcelona, 1973.

Taverne, Ed, *Architectuur en geschiedenis, College-dictaat Historiografie, Geschiedenis van architectuur en stedebouw*, Rijksuniversiteit Groningen, 1993.

Terranova, Antonio, 'The Design of the City,' *Urbanismo Revista*, No. 7 (special issue on Quaroni), Barcelona, 1989.

*Urbanismo Revista*, No. 7, 'Ludovico Quaroni – de cerca,' Barcelona, 1989.

Van der Schans, Jan, *Verslag excursie projectgroep Kop van Zuid naar Barcelona*, Rotterdam, 1986 (unpublished report).

Van der Ven, Cornelis, *Bouwen in Barcelona*, Amsterdam, 1980.

Vegara-Carrio, Joseph, *The City of Barcelona: Facts and Figures*, paper for congress, 'The City, engine behind economic recovery,' Rotterdam, 1986.

Vila, Pau, *Barcelona i el seu pla*, Barcelona, 1981.

THE NORTH AMERICAN PORT CITY:
NEW YORK, A BOUNDLESS URBAN LANDSCAPE

*Planning documents*

NEW YORK

*Lower Manhattan Recommended Land Use Redevelopment Areas and Traffic Improvements*, Downtown Lower Manhattan Association, 1958.

*Lower Manhattan Plan*, Department of City Planning of New York City, 1966.

*Plan for New York City*, Department of City Planning of New York City, 1969.

*Masterplan for the West Side Highway and renewal of the Hudson River waterfront in Manhattan, New York City*, Venturi, Rauch & Scott Brown, 1978-1985.

*Masterplan Battery Park City*, Battery Park City Authority (Cooper & Eckstud), 1979.

*South Street Seaport Redevelopment Plan*, Rouse Company/ Department of City Planning of New York City, 1980.

*The Future of the Piers. Planning and Design criteria for Brooklyn Piers 1-6*, Brooklyn Heights Association (Buckhurst Fish Hutton Katz), 1987.

*A Vision for the Hudson River Waterfront Park*, West Side Waterfront Panel, New York, 1990.

*A Greenway Plan for New York City*, Department of City Planning of New York City, 1993.

SEATTLE

*Harborfront Public Improvement Plan*, Department of Community Development of the City of Seattle, 1987.

BALTIMORE

*Masterplan Inner Harbor & City Hall Plaza*, Greater Baltimore Committee and the Committee for Downtown Inc., (David Wallace and Thomas Todd), 1965.

*Baltimore's Inner Harbor Redevelopment Program*, Charles Center-Inner Harbor Management Inc., 1986.

BOSTON

*Downtown Waterfront Faneuil Hall Urban Renewal Plan*, Boston Redevelopment Authority, 1964.

*Harborpark: Interim design standards for the Inner Harbor*, Boston Redevelopment Authority, 1984.

*Harborwalk: Design guidelines for Phase One*, Boston Redevelopment Authority, 1987.

*Planning Study for Central Artery Corridor*, City Planning Department of Boston (Chan Krieger & Associates), 1991.

SAN FRANCISCO

*The Urban Design Plan for the Comprehensive Plan of San Francisco*, Department of City Planning, San Francisco, 1971.

*Master Plan of the City and County of San Francisco*, Department of City Planning, San Francisco, 1987.

*Literature*

Adams, Gerald, 'Two Chiefs,' *Planning*, Vol. 46, No. 3 (March, 1980).

Allman, T.D., *Miami City of the Future*, New York, 1987.

Barlow, Elizabeth, *Frederick Law Olmsted's New York*, New York/Washington/London, 1972.

Barnett, Jonathan, *Urban Design as Public Policy: Practical Methods for Improving Cities*, New York, 1974.

Batts, Charles, 'San Francisco Bay: An Estuary in Change,' *Water Environment & Technology* (Sept., 1989), Washington.

Becker, Ulrich, and Annalie Schoen (eds.), *Die Janusgesichter des Booms. Strukturwandel der Stadtregionen New York und Boston*, Hamburg, 1989.

Bender, Thomas, 'New York as a Center of "Difference": How America's Metropolis Counters American Myth,' *Dissent (Autumn, 1987)*, New York.

Bender, Thomas, *Toward an Urban Vision, Ideas and Institutions in Nineteenth Century America*, Lexington, Ky., 1975.

Berman, Marshall, *All that is Solid Melts into Air*, New York/London, 1983.

Boogaarts, Inez, 'Food, Fun and Festivals,' in Burgers, Jack (ed.), *De uitstad. Over stedelijk vermaak*, Utrecht, 1992.

'Boston Design,' *Process*, No. 97, Tokyo, 1991.

Boston Society of Architects, *Boston Architecture*, Cambridge, Mass., 1970.

Boyer, Christine, *The City of Collective Memory: Its Historical Imagery and Architectural Entertainments*, Cambridge, Mass., 1994.

Boyer, Christine, *Manhattan Manners: Architecture and Style, 1850-1900*, New York, 1985.

Brooklyn Museum, *The Great East River Bridge 1883-1983*, New York, 1983.

Butterwieser, Ann L., *Manhattan Water-Bound: Planning and Developing Manhattan's Waterfront from the Seventeenth Century to the Present*, New York, 1987.

Calthorpe, Peter, *The Next American Metropolis: Ecology, Community and the American Dream*, Princeton Architectural Press, 1993.

Cameron, Robert, and Herb Caen, *Above San Francisco: A New Collection of Nostalgic and Contemporary Aerial Photographs of the Bay Area*, San Francisco, 1986.

Caro, Robert, *The Power Broker: Robert Moses and the Fall of New York*, New York, 1974.

Charyn, Jerome, *Metropolis: New York as Myth, Marketplace and Magical Land*, New York, 1986.

City of New York Parks & Recreation, *Three Hundred Years of Parks: A Timeline of New York City Park History*, New York, 1987.

Ciucci, Giorgio, et al., *The American City*, Cambridge, Mass., 1979.

Clark, James I., and Robert V. Remini, *We the People: A History of the United States*, Beverly Hills, 1975.

Cohen, Barbara, et al., *New York Observed. Artists and Writers Look at the City, 1650 to the Present*, New York, 1987.

Cohn, Nick, *Broadway – The Heart of the World*, New York, 1993.

Cutler, P., *The Public Landscape of the New Deal*, New Haven, 1985.

Dasnoy, Philip, *20 Million Immigrants*, Paris, 1977.

Davies, Mike, 'Fortress Los Angeles: The Militarization of Urban Space,' in Sorkin, Michael (ed.), *Variations on a Theme Park: The New American City and the End of Public Space*, New York, 1992.

De Boer, Matthijs, 'Stedebouw als strategie – Urban Design in San Francisco,' *Wonen/TABK*, No. 15, Amsterdam, 1985.

Delgado, Annabel, and Roselyne Pirson, *Miami: Architecture of the Tropics*, Brussels, 1993.

Doctorow, E.L., *World's Fair*, New York, 1985.

Dorenbos, L.P., 'Columbia: de geboorte van een nieuwe stad,' *Stedebouw en Volkshuisvesting (October, 1971)*, Alphen aan den Rijn.

Draper, Joan E., 'Paris by the Lake: Sources of Burnham's plan of Chicago,' in Zukowsky, John, *Chicago Architecture 1872-1922: Birth of a Metropolis*, Munich, 1987.

Dunhill, Priscilla, 'An Expressway Named Destruction,' *Architectural Forum* (March, 1967), New York.

Dunlap, David W., *On Broadway. A Journey Uptown over Time*, New York, 1990.

Fabos, Julius Gy., et al., *Frederick Law Olmsted Sr., Founder of Landscape Architecture in America*, Cambridge, Mass., 1968.

Fein, Albert, *Frederick Law Olmsted and the American Environmental Tradition*, New York, 1972.

Fein, Albert (ed.), *Landscape into Cityscape: Frederick Law Olmsted's Plans for a Greater New York*, Ithaca, 1967.

Ferguson, Russell (ed.), *Urban Revisions: Current Projects for the Public Realm*, Cambridge, Mass., 1994.

Fitzgerald, F. Scott, *The Great Gatsby*, New York, 1953.

Fried, William, and Edward B. Watson, *New York in Aerial Views*, New York, 1980.

Frieder, Bernard J., and Lynne B. Sagalyn, *Downtown Inc.: How America Rebuilds Cities*, Cambridge, Mass./London, 1989.

Garreau, Joel, *Edge City: Life on the New Frontier*, New York, 1992.

Giedion, Sigfried, *Space, Time & Architecture: The Growth of a New Tradition*, Cambridge, Mass., 1941.

Gilliam, Harold, *Between the Devil & the Deep Blue Bay: The Struggle to Save San Francisco Bay*, Berkeley, Cal., 1969.

Goddard, Stephen B., *Getting There: The Epic Struggle Between Road and Rail in the American Century*, New York, 1994.

Goldberg, Sheryl, *Waterfronts Compared: A Plan-making Perspective*, Amsterdam, 1990.

Gottmann, J., *Megalopolis: The Urbanized Northeastern Seaboard of the United States*, New York, 1961.

Gunn, Simon, *Revolution of the Right*, New York, 1989.

Hatton, Hap, *Tropical Splendor: An Architectural History of Florida*, New York, 1987.

Heckscher, August, *Open Spaces: The life of American cities (A Twentieth Century Fund Essay)*, New York/Hagerstown/San Francisco/London, 1976.

Huizinga, J., *Mensch en menigte in Amerika*, Haarlem, 1920.

Jackson, John Brinckerhoff, *A Sense of Place, a Sense of Time*, New Haven, 1994.

Jacobs, Jane, *The Death and Life of Great American Cities*, New York, 1961.

Katz, Peter (ed.), *The New Urbanism: Towards an Architecture of Community*, New York, 1994.

Koolhaas, Rem, *Delirious New York*, New York, 1979.

Langdon, Philip, *Urban Excellence*, New York, 1990.

Lynch, Kevin, *The Image of the City*, Boston, 1960.

Martin, Leslie, and Lionel March, *Urban Spaces and Structures*, Cambridge, Mass., 1972.

Martin, Thomas, and Clive Jones, 'Urban Waterfront Development in the United States,' in Reid, Ann (ed.), *Proceedings of Watersite 2000: An International Congress on the Rejuvenation of Waterfronts*, Bristol, 1988.

Marx, Leo, 'The Puzzle of Anti-Urbanism in Classic American Literature,' in Rodwin, Lloyd, and Robert M. Hollister (eds.), *Cities of the Mind: Images and Themes of the City in the Social Sciences*, New York/London, 1984.

MacDonald, Thomas, 'What our Highways Mean to Us,' *Tradewinds*, 1923.

Meyer, Han, 'Een meedogenloos bouwer van de moderne stad. Robert Moses en de wording van de stadstaat New York,' *Archis*, 4-89, Amsterdam, 1989 [III].

'New York. Wanted: A Waterfront,' *Arredo Urbano*, Nos. 27/28, Rome, 1988.

Olmsted, Frederick Law, *Walks and Talks of an American Farmer in England*, London, 1852.

Olmsted, Jr., Frederick Law, and Theodora Kimball (eds.), *Frederick*

*Law Olmsted: Landscape Architect, 1822-1903*, 2 vols., New York, 1922-1928.

Olson, Sheryl H., *Baltimore: The Building of an American City*, Baltimore, 1980.

Plunz, Richard, 'Manhattan Alchemy,' *Arredo Urbano (October, 1988)*, Rome.

Plunz, Richard, 'Water and development in Manhattan,' in Bruttomesso, Rinio, *Waterfronts: A New Urban Frontier*, Venice, 1993.

Porter, Paul R., and David C. Sweet (eds.), *Rebuilding America's Cities: Roads to Recovery*, New Brunswick, N.J., 1984.

Portman, John, and Jonathan Barnett, *The Architect as Developer*, New York/Toronto, 1976.

Raban, Jonathan, *Hunting Mr. Heartbreak*, London, 1990.

Read Shanor, Rebecca, *The City That Never Was: Two Hundred Years of Fantastic and Fascinating Plans That Might Have Changed the Face of New York City*, New York, 1988.

Reps, John W., *Cities on Stone: Nineteenth Century Lithograph Images of the Urban West*, Fort Worth, 1976.

'Robert (I'll Resign) Moses,' *Fortune*, Vol. XVII, No. 6, New York, 1938.

Rodwin, Lloyd, and Robert M. Hollister (eds.), *Cities of the Mind: Images and Themes of the City in the Social Sciences*, New York/London, 1984.

Rose, Edgar, 'Daring to Say That Cities Are Fun,' *Town & Country Planning* (February, 1987), London.

Rosen, Laura, 'Robert Moses and New York: The Early Years,' *The Livable City* (December, 1988), periodical of the Municipal Art Society, New York.

Rosenblum, Robert, et al., *Remembering the Future: The New York World's Fair from 1939 to 1964*, New York, 1989.

Rouse, James W., 'The Case for Vision,' in Porter, Paul R., and David C. Sweet (eds.), *Rebuilding America's Cities: Roads to Recovery*, New Brunswick, N.J., 1984.

Rowe, Colin, and Fred Koetner, *Collage City*, Cambridge, Mass., 1978.

Schuyler, David, *The New Urban Landscape: The Redefinition of City Form in Nineteenth-Century America*, Baltimore/London, 1986.

Schwarz, Jordan A., *The New Dealers: Power Politics in the Age of Roosevelt*, New York, 1993.

Sennett, Richard, *The Conscience of the Eye: The Design and Social Life of Cities*, New York, 1991.

Sennett, Richard, *The Fall of Public Man*, London/Boston, 1977.

Shoret, Alice, and Murray Morgan, *The Pike Place Market: People, Politics, and Produce*, Seattle, 1985.

Smith, Neil, 'New City, New Frontier: The Lower East Side as Wild, Wild West,' in Sorkin, Michael (ed.), *Variations on a Theme Park: The New American City and the End of Public Space*, New York, 1992.

Sorkin, Michael, 'See you in Disneyworld,' in Sorkin, Michael Sorkin (ed.), *Variations on a Theme Park*, New York, 1992 [II].

Sorkin, Michael (ed.), *Variations on a Theme Park: The New American City and the End of Public Space*, New York, 1992 [I].

Strauss, Anselm L. (ed.), *The American City: A Sourcebook of Urban Imagery*, London, 1968.

Sutton, S.B. (ed.), *Civilizing American Cities: A selection of F.L. Olmsted's Writings on City Landscapes*, Cambridge, Mass., 1971.

Tafuri, Manfredo, 'The Disenchanted Mountain: The Skyscraper and the City,' in: Ciucci, Giorgio, et al. (ed.), *The American City*, Cambridge, Mass., 1979.

Talese, Gay, *The Bridge*, New York, 1964.

Vader, Jan Willem, 'Baltimore vs het voorbeeld van succesvolle havenfront-herstructurering,' *Renovatie & Onderhoud*, Vol. 13, No. 9, The Hague, 1988.

Van der Woud, Auke, 'De geschiedenis van de toekomst,' in Van der Cammen, H. (red.), *Nieuw Nederland, onderwerp van ontwerp*, The Hague, 1987 [I].

Van Ermen, Eduard, *The United States in Maps and Prints*, Wilmington, Del., 1990.

Van Leeuwen, Th., *The Skyward Trend of Thought*, The Hague, 1986.

Van Vught, Frans, *Sociale planning – Oorsprong en ontwikkeling van het Amerikaanse planningsdenken*, Assen, 1979.

Venturi, Robert, et al., *Learning from Las Vegas*, Boston, 1977.

Wagner, Jr., Robert F., *New York Ascendant: The Report of the Commission on the Year 2000*, New York, 1987.

Walters, Jonathan, 'After the Festival is over,' in *Governing*, Washington, D.C., 1990.

Warner Jr., Sam Bass, 'Slums and Skyscrapers: Urban Images, Symbols, and Ideology,' in Rodwin, Lloyd, and Robert M. Hollister, *Cities of the Mind: Images and Themes of the Cities in the Social Sciences*, New York/London, 1984.

Warren, James R., and Willam R. McCoy, *Highlights of Seattle's History*, Seattle, 1982.

Webber, Melvin, 'The urban place and the nonplace urban realm,' in Webber, Melvin, et al., *Explorations on Urban Structures*, Philadelphia, 1964.

Weiss, Marc A., 'Skyscraperzoning: New York's Pioneering Role,' *Journal of the American Planning Association*, Vol. 58, No. 2, Chicago, 1992.

White, Morton and Lucia, *The Intellectual Versus the City: From Thomas Jefferson to Frank Lloyd Wright*, Cambridge, Mass., 1962.

Wolman, Harold L., et al., 'Evaluating the Success of Urban Success Stories,' *Urban Studies*, Vol. 31, No. 6.

Wright, Frank Lloyd, *When Democracy Builds*, Chicago, 1945.

Wright, Gwendolyn, *Building the Dream: A Social History of Housing in America*, Cambridge, Mass., 1981.

Zapatka, Christian, 'The American Parkways,' *Lotus International*, No. 56, Milan, 1988.

Zerubavel, Eviatar, *Hidden Rhythms: Schedules and Calendars in Social Life*, Chicago, 1981.

THE NORTHWESTERN EUROPEAN PORT CITY:
ROTTERDAM AND THE DYNAMIC OF THE DELTA

*Planning documents*

ROTTERDAM

Although the names of certain Dutch documents and (government) organizations were translated into English in the main text, to facilitate research activities the following list is given in the original Dutch.

*Basisplan Herbouw Binnenstad Rotterdam*, Adviesbureau voor het

Stadsplan van Rotterdam/Gemeentebestuur Rotterdam, 1946.

*Het nieuwe hart van Rotterdam*, Toelichting op het Basisplan voor de herbouw van de binnenstad van Rotterdam, Gemeentebestuur Rotterdam, 1946.

*Plan 2000 +*, Dienst Stadsontwikkeling, Dienst Gemeentewerken, Gemeentelijk Havenbedrijf Rotterdam, 1969.

*Structuurnota 1972*, Dienst Stadsontwikkeling, 1972.

*Bestemmingsplan Oude Haven*, Dienst Stadsontwikkeling, 1979.

*Nota Herstructurering Oude Havens*, Gemeentebestuur Rotterdam, 1976.

*Structuurplan Rotterdam Binnen de Ruit*, Dienst Stadsontwikkeling, 1978.

*Bestemmingsplan Delfshaven*, Dienst Stadsontwikkeling, 1979.

*Bestemmingsplan Katendrecht*, Dienst Stadsontwikkeling, 1981.

*Binnenstadsplan Rotterdam 1985. Bijstelling van het Basisplan 1946*, Dienst Stadsontwikkeling, Grondbedrijf en Verkeersdienst Rotterdam, 1984.

*Structuurschets Binnenhaven/Spoorweghaven*, Projectgroep Binnenhaven/Spoorweghaven en Dienst Stadsontwikkeling, 1985.

*Ontwerpstudies bebouwingsmogelijkheden van de Landtong op de Kop van Zuid*, prepared by Groosman Partners bv (Manot, B.) for the Dienst Stadsontwikkeling en Dienst Volkshuisvesting, 1987.

*Stedebouwkundige studie Vierhavengebied*, Dienst Stadsontwikkeling 1987.

*De Kop van Zuid, een stedebouwkundig ontwerp*, Teun Koolhaas Associates, 1987.

*Werkprogramma Stadsontwikkeling*, Dienst Stadsontwikkeling, 1987.

*Beleidsplan District Zuid*, Dienst Stadsontwikkeling, 1987.

*Beleidsplan District Centrum*, Dienst Stadsontwikkeling, 1987.

*De Kop van Zuid, uitvoerbaarheidsrapportage*, Tripartite Werkgroep Ministerie van Volkshuisvesting, Ruimtelijke Ordening en Milieu, Provincie Zuid-Holland, Gemeente Rotterdam, 1988.

*Rotterdam Kop van Zuid. Strategie voor aktie*, Enterprise Development Company Inc., 1988.

*Masterplan Structuurschets Kop van Zuid*, Dienst Stadsontwikkeling, 1989.

*Masterplan Wereldhaven. Rotterdam, een toeristisch-recreatieve uitdaging*, Gemeentelijk Havenbedrijf Rotterdam, Grontmij advies- en ingenieursbureau, 1989.

*Masterplan Schiehavengebied*, Alba, Dominique, and Jean Nouvel, 1989.

*Stedebouwkundig plan Müllerpier/Schiehavengebied*, Dienst Stadsontwikkeling, 1989.

*Vierde Nota Ruimtelijke Ordening*, Rijks Planologische Dienst, The Hague, 1990.

*De Kop van Zuid, kwaliteit en beeldvorming*, Projectgroep Kop van Zuid (Achterberg, P., et al.), Dienst Stedebouw & Volkshuisvesting, 1990.

*De Kop van Zuid, buitenruimte*, Dienst Stedebouw & Volkshuisvesting, Rotterdam, 1990-1991.

*Bestemmingsplan De Kop van Zuid*, Projectgroep Kop van Zuid, Dienst Stedebouw & Volkshuisvesting, 1991.

*Project Rotterdam De Kop van Zuid. Historische structuuranalyse*, TU-Delft werkgroep Restauratie (Van Voorden, F.), 1991.

*De Kop van Zuid, Kwaliteitsboek Buitenruimte*, Projectgroep Kop van Zuid (Achterberg, P., et al.), Dienst Stedebouw & Volkshuisvesting, 1991.

*Beleidsplan Buitenruimte Feijenoord. Kop van Zuid*, Projectgroep Kop

van Zuid, Dienst Stedebouw & Volkshuisvesting, 1992.

*Stadsplan Rotterdam. Een visie op de ruimtelijke ontwikkeling van Rotterdam tot 2005*, Dienst Stedebouw & Volkshuisvesting, Gemeentebestuur Rotterdam, 1992.

*De Kop van Zuid, Programmascenario*, Projectgroep Kop van Zuid (Van den Bout, J., and J. van Teeffelen), Dienst Stedebouw & Volkshuisvesting, 1993.

*Rotterdam 2045, visies op de toekomst van stad, haven en regio*, Manifestatie Rotterdam 50 jaar Wederopbouw – 50 jaar toekomst, 1995

AMSTERDAM

*Algemeen UitbreidingsPlan van Amsterdam*, Gemeente Amsterdam, 1934.

*Promenade langs het IJ*, adviesgroep IJ-oevers, 1984.

*Analyse Ideeënprijsvraag Oosterdok*, Gemeente Amsterdam, 1984.

*Verkenningen en Plannen. IJ-oevers en Oosterdok*, Ambtelijke Werkgroep IJ-oevers en Oosterdok, 1986.

*Planaanpassingen/Het Masterplan. IJ-oevers en Oosterdok, Eerste Fase*, Ambtelijke Werkgroep IJ-oevers en Oosterdok, 1987.

*Centrale IJ-oevers Amsterdam, stedebouwkundige verkenning*, Ambtelijke Werkgroep IJ-oevers en Oosterdok, 1987.

*Structuurschets IJ-as*, Dienst Ruimtelijke Ordening, 1987.

*KNSM-eiland Stedebouwkundig Ontwerp*, Buro Jo Coenen, 1989.

*Havenatlas*, Projectgroep IJ-oevers Amsterdam, 1990.

*Stedebouwkundige uitwerking van het Java-eiland te Amsterdam*, architectenbureau Sjoerd Soeters, 1991.

*Structuurplan Amsterdam 1991*, Dienst Ruimtelijke Ordening, 1991-1992.

*Concept Ondernemingsplan*, Amsterdamse Waterfront Financieringsmaatschappij, Rem Koolhaas c.s., 1992.

*KNSM-eiland inrichting openbare ruimte*, Dienst Ruimtelijke Ordening, 1992.

*Java-eiland stedebouwkundig programma van eisen*, Projectgroep Oostelijk Havengebied, 1992.

*Stedebouwkundig Ontwerp Borneo Sporenburg*, Buro West 8, 1994.

*Ontwerp Bestemmingsplan IJ-oevers*, Dienst Ruimtelijke Ordening, 1994.

*Plan Openbare Ruimte IJ-oevers*, Dienst Ruimtelijke Ordening in collaboration with Bureau B&B, Mecanoo, 1994.

*Ontwerp Structuurplan Amsterdam Open Stad*, Dienst Ruimtelijke Ordening, 1994.

*Literature*

Adviescommissie sociaal-economische vernieuwing Rotterdam, *Nieuw Rotterdam – Een opdracht voor alle Rotterdammers*, Rotterdam 1987.

Albeda, W. (ed.), *Nieuw Rotterdam – rapport van de Adviescommissie Sociaal-Economische Vernieuwing Rotterdam*, Rotterdam, 1987.

Amsterdamse Raad voor de Stadsontwikkeling, *Verslag van de expertmeeting over het plan voor de openbare ruimte aan de IJ-oevers*, Amsterdam, 1994.

Andela, Gerrie, and Cor Wagenaar (eds.), *Een stad voor het leven, wederopbouw Rotterdam 1940-1965*, Rotterdam, 1995.

Backx, J.Ph., *De haven van Rotterdam – Een onderzoek naar de oorzaken van haar economische betekenis, in vergelijking met die van Hamburg en Antwerpen*, Rotterdam, 1929.

Bakker, Henk (ed.), *Het IJ geopend, de Binnenstad gedicht. Plancatalogus*

– manifestatie over de oostelijke binnenstad van Amsterdam in oktober 1986, Amsterdam, 1986.

Bang-Andersen, Arne, et al., *The North Sea: Highway of Economic and Cultural Exchange*, Oslo, 1985.

Barbieri, Umberto, et al. (eds.), *Stedebouw in Rotterdam. Plannen en opstellen 1940-1981*, Amsterdam, 1981.

Barbieri, Umberto, and Bert van Meggelen (eds.), *Kop van Zuid. Ontwerp en onderzoek*, Rotterdam, 1982.

Beeren, Wim, et al. (eds.), *Het Nieuwe Bouwen in Rotterdam 1920-1960*, Delft, 1982.

Belderbos, Frank, 'Wederzijds profijt,' in Van den Bout, Jaap, and Erik Pasveer (eds.), *Kop van Zuid*, Rotterdam, 1994.

Blijstra, R., *Rotterdam, stad in beweging*, Amsterdam/Rotterdam, 1965.

Bos, A. (ed.), *De stad der toekomst, de toekomst der stad. Een stedebouwkundige en sociaal-culturele studie over de groeiende stadsgemeenschap*, Rotterdam, 1946.

Bouman, Machteld, and Marike Vierstra, *Maar wie droomt er te Rotterdam! 650 jaar literair leven aan de Maas*, Naarden, 1990.

Bouman, P.J., and W.H. Bouman, *De groei van de grote werkstad – een studie over de bevolking van Rotterdam*, Assen, 1952.

Brautigam, J., *Langs de havens en op de schepen*, Rotterdam, 1956.

Brouwer, Jan, 'Het park in stadsuitbreiding Blijdorp,' *Oase*, No. 12, Delft, 1986.

Brusse, M.J., *Boefje*, Rotterdam, 1924 [II].

Brusse, M.J., *Het rosse leven en sterven van de Zandstraat*, Rotterdam, 1920.

Brusse, M.J., *Onder de menschen*, Rotterdam, 1924 [I].

Brusse, M.J., *Rotterdamse zedeprenten*, Rotterdam, 1921.

Brusse, M.J., *Van af- en aanmonsteren: het leven van den zeeman aan den wal*, Rotterdam, 1899.

Camp, D'Laine, and Michelle Provoost (eds.), *Stadstimmeren, 650 jaar Rotterdam stad*, Rotterdam, 1990.

Centrum voor Grootstedelijk Onderzoek, *Flaneren langs het IJ – een opstel over problemen en pretenties van het IJ-oeverproject*, Amsterdam, 1990.

College van B & W van Rotterdam, *Vernieuwing van Rotterdam*, Rotterdam, 1987.

Damen, Hélène, and Annemie Devolder (eds.), *Lotte Stam-Beese 1903-1988*, Rotterdam, 1988.

Davids, Karel, et al. (eds.), *De Republiek tussen zee en vaste land – Buitenlandse invloeden op cultuur, economie en politiek in Nederland 1580-1800*, Louvain/Apeldoorn, 1995.

De Boer, J.W., and Cas Oorthuys, *Rotterdam dynamische stad*, Rotterdam, 1959.

De Boode, Arij, and Pieter van Oudheusden, *De Hef – biografie van een spoorbrug*, Rotterdam, 1985.

De Goey, M.M., *Geen woorden maar daden – de relatie tussen het bedrijfsleven en de lokale overheid van Rotterdam 1945-1960*, Rotterdam, 1987.

De Graaf, Jan, *Rotterdam 1850-1940*, The Hague, 1993.

De Graaf, Jan, et al., 'Een schone stad – Rotterdam maakt de sprong naar Zuid,' in Barbieri, Umberto, and Bert van Meggelen (eds.), *Kop van Zuid. Ontwerp en onderzoek*, Rotterdam, 1982.

De Jong, A.M., *In de draaikolk*, Amsterdam, 1928.

De Kleijn, Gerard, *De staat van de stadsvernieuwing*, Amsterdam, 1985.

De Klerk, Len (ed.), *Stadsvernieuwing in Rotterdam*, The Hague, 1982.

De Klerk, Len, and Herman Moscoviter (eds.), *En dat al voor de arbeidende klasse, 75 jaar volkshuisvesting Rotterdam*, Rotterdam, 1992.

Demangeon, Alain, and Bruno Fortier, *Les Vaisseaux et les villes: l'Arsenal de Cherbourg*, Paris/Brussels, 1978.

De Ruiter, Fred, et al. (eds.), *Stadsvernieuwing Rotterdam 1974-1984. Deel 1: Beleid*, Rotterdam, 1985. This is Part 1 of a three-part series (Part 2: *Sociale woningbouw*; Part 3: *Woningverbeteringsprojecten*).

De Ruyter-de Zeeuw, Chr.A., *Hendrik Spiekman, de grondvester van de Rotterdamse sociaal-democratie*, Rotterdam, 1971.

Dettingmeijer, Rob, *Open Stad. Planontwikkeling, stedebouw, volkshuisvesting en architectuur in Rotterdam tussen de twee Wereldoorlogen*, Utrecht, 1988.

De Vries, Jan, *Barges and Capitalism*, Utrecht, 1981.

De Winter, Peter (ed.), *Havenarchitectuur*, Rotterdam, 1982.

Dienst Stadsontwikkeling Rotterdam, *Leven in de stad. Rotterdam op weg naar het jaar 2000*, Rotterdam, 1987.

Donia, Henk, et al., *Gemeentewerken Rotterdam 1955-1980*, Rotterdam, 1983.

Eijkelboom, Jan, and Pieter van Oudheusden, *Rotterdam in tekst en beeld*, Rotterdam, 1983.

Fortier, Bruno, *La Metropole Imaginaire – Un Atlas de Paris*, Paris, 1989.

Frijhoff, Willem, 'De stad en haar geheugen,' *Oase*, No. 24, Delft, 1989.

Frijhoff, Willem, et al., *De Rotterdamse cultuur in elf spiegels*, Rotterdam, 1993.

Gall, Stefan, et al. (eds.), *Stedebouw in beweging*, Rotterdam, 1993.

Geurtsen, Rein, 'Rotterdam en het stadsontwerp; dieptepunt discipline en pleidooi voor opwaardering,' *Wonen/TABK*, No. 22, Amsterdam, 1979.

Geurtsen, Rein, and Luc Bos, 'Kopenhagen, dubbelstad. Een bewerkte reisindruk,' *Wonen/TABK*, Nos. 10/11/12, Amsterdam, 1982.

Grassi, Giorgio, 'Architectonisch ontwerp en analyse van de stad,' *Plan*, No. 9, Amsterdam, 1981.

Grimm, Peter (ed.), *Heren in zaken – De kamer Rotterdam van de Verenigde Oost-Indische Compagnie*, Zutphen, 1994.

Heijdra, Ton, *Kadraaiers & zeekastelen, geschiedenis van het Oostelijk havengebied*, Amsterdam, 1993.

Hoogenberk, Egbert J., *Het idee van de Hollandse stad. Stedebouw in Nederland 1900-1930 met de internationale voorgeschiedenis*, Delft, 1980.

Huincks, Paul J.G. (ed.), *Rotterdam in de literatuur*, Rotterdam, 1940.

Initiatiefgroep Open Stad, *Palmen langs het IJ – Hekelschrift over de stad en de IJ-oevers*, Amsterdam, 1992.

Koster, Egbert, *Oostelijk Havengebied Amsterdam: Eastern Docklands, New Architecture on Historic Grounds*, Amsterdam, 1995.

Kraaij, Annenies, and Jan van der Mast, *Rotterdam Zuid, voorstad tussen droom en daad*, Delft, 1990.

Kraaijvanger, H.M., *Hoe zal Rotterdam bouwen?* (second in a series issued by the Rotterdamsche Gemeenschap): 'Hoe bouwen wij Rotterdam?' Rotterdam, 1946.

Kruidenier, Michiel, and Christel Leenen, 'De geboorte van een mythe,' in Andela, Gerrie, and Cor Wagenaar (eds.), *Een stad voor het leven – Wederopbouw Rotterdam 1940-1965*, Rotterdam, 1995.

Lambert, Donald, 'Realisering van het stedebouwkundig plan,' in *Urban Design*, Delft, 1985.

Lombaerde, Piet, 'Antwerpen, Memoria et Utopia,' in Van Reusel, Jef, *Antwerpen ontwerpen*, Antwerp/Bruges, 1990.

Lucas, P., *Overzicht van de bemoeiingen van het Gemeentebestuur Rotterdam met de sanering 1940 t/m 1972*, Rotterdam, 1974.

Maczak, Antoni, *Zycie codzienne w podrózach po Europe w XVI i XVII wieku*, Warsaw, 1978; English translation: *Travel in Early Modern Europe*, 1995.

Mak, Geert, *Een kleine geschiedenis van Amsterdam*, Amsterdam, 1994.

Meiscke, W.A., *Zo groeide Amsterdam*, Amsterdam, 1975.

Meyer, Han, 'Het fragment en de stad. Stedelijke transformatieprojecten in Rotterdam, Antwerpen en Amsterdam,' *Archis*, 6-93, Rotterdam, 1993.

Meyer, Han, *Operatie Katendrecht*, Nijmegen, 1983.

Meyer, Han, 'Veranderingen en konstanten op Zuid,' in Rotterdams Instituut Bewonersondersteuning, *Konferentiemap Kop op Zuid* (February 23, 1990), Rotterdam, 1990.

Meyer, Han, et al., *De beheerste stad – ontstaan en intenties van een sociaal-democratische stadspolitiek: een kritiek*, Rotterdam, 1980.

Meyer, Han, et al., 'Over sociaal-democratie en volkshuisvesting,'in Spiekerman van Weezelenburg, Sonja, and Stef van der Gaag (eds.), *Raderwerk, 10 jaar Projectraad Bouwkunde*, Delft, 1981.

Mik, G. (ed.), *Herstructurering in Rotterdam. Modernisering en internationalisering en de Kop van Zuid*, Rotterdam, 1989.

Ministerie van Landbouw, Natuurbeheer en Visserij, *Visie stadslandschappen*, The Hague, 1995.

Moscoviter, Herman, *Kwetsbare schoonheid, monumenten in Rotterdam*, Rotterdam, 1994.

Moscoviter, Herman, *Want wie niet kan dromen is geen realist*, Rotterdam, 1992.

Nieuwenhuis, Jan, *Mensen maken een stad – uit de geschiedenis van de Dienst Gemeentewerken te Rotterdam 1855-1955*, Rotterdam, 1955.

Nycolaas, Jacques (ed.), *Rotterdam – Praktijk van stedebouw*, Delft, 1988 [I].

Nycolaas, Jacques (ed.), *Rotterdam – Stedebouwkundig ontwerpen*, Delft, 1988 [II].

Palmboom, Frits, *Rotterdam verstedelijkt landschap*, Rotterdam, 1987.

Pfann, H.D., *Amsterdam toen en nu*, Amsterdam, 1974.

Poeth, G.G.J.M., and H.J. van Dongen, *Rotterdam of de noodzaak van een infrastruktuur voor informatie*, Delft, 1983.

Provoost, Michelle, *De stad als verkeersmachine. De ruit om Rotterdam*, Rotterdam, 1994.

Roelofsz. E., *De frustratie van een droom – de wederopbouw van Rotterdam 1940-1950*, Rotterdam, 1989.

Roobeek, Annemieke, 'Main Ports Holland,' *NRC-Handelsblad* (February 12, 1995), Rotterdam.

Rotterdams Instituut Bewonersondersteuning, *De Kop van Zuid en omliggende stadsvernieuwingswijken – naar een programma van wederzijds profijt*, Rotterdam, 1990 [II].

Rotterdams Instituut Bewonersondersteuning, *Konferentiemap Kop op Zuid* (February 23, 1990), Rotterdam 1990 [I].

Rutgers, J., 'De herbouw van Rotterdam, in het bijzonder in verband met de grondexploitatie,' *De Ingenieur* (February 11, 1955).

Seinpost, *Werkgelegenheidsatlas Rotterdam* (investigative report prepared by the Centrum voor Stedelijke Processen, in collaboration with the Faculteit Geodesie, TU Delft, for the Gemeente Rotterdam), The Hague, 1986.

Sigmond, J.P., *Nederlandse zeehavens tussen 1500 en 1800*, Amsterdam, 1989.

Smook, R.A.F., *Binnensteden veranderen*, Zutphen, 1984.

Stedebouwkundige begeleidingscommissie IJ-oevers, *Jaarverslag en commentaar 1992*, Amsterdam, 1993.

Szanto, Katalyn, *Culturele identiteit: Oud-Zuid, Rotterdam*, Restauratie TU Delft (study group), 1992 (unpublished).

Taverne, Ed, *In 't land van belofte: in de nieuwe stad. Ideaal en werkelijkheid van de stadsuitleg in de Republiek 1580-1680*, Maarssen, 1978.

Taverne, Ed, and Irmin Visser (eds.), *Stedebouw, de geschiedenis van de stad in de Nederlanden van 1500 tot heden*, Nijmegen, 1993.

Teychiné van Stakenburg, A.J., *Beeld en beeldenaar – Rotterdam en Mr. K.P. van der Mandele*, Rotterdam, 1979.

Tijhuis, Annet, 'Vergeten stadsbeelden,' in Andela, Gerrie, and Cor Wagenaar (eds.), *Een stad voor het leven. Wederopbouw Rotterdam 1940-1965*, Rotterdam, 1995.

TNO, *Logistiek & Transport*, Delft, 1986.

Uyttenhove, Pieter (ed.), *Tussen kant en wal. De 19de-eeuwse gordel van Antwerpen: elementen voor een cultuur van de stad*, Antwerp, 1993.

Vaandrager, C.B., *De Hef*, Amsterdam, 1975.

Vader, Jan Willem, 'Baltimore vs het voorbeeld van succesvolle havenfront-herstructurering,' *Renovatie & Onderhoud*, Vol. 13, No. 9, The Hague, 1988 [I].

Vader, Jan Willem, 'Centrum Rotterdam verplaatst zich naar Maasoevers,' *Renovatie & Onderhoud*, Vol. 13, No. 9, The Hague, 1988 [II].

Van Campen, José, et al. (eds.), *Financiering & Maatschappij langs het IJ*, Amsterdam, 1990.

Van de Berg, L., *Urban Systems in a Dynamic Society*, London, 1987.

Van den Bout, Jaap, 'Regie van een stedebouwkundig ontwerp,' in Van den Bout, Jaap, and Erik Pasveer (eds.), *Kop van Zuid*, Rotterdam, 1994.

Van der Ploeg, J.G., 'Naar een stadsvernieuwingsbeleid,' in De Klerk, Len (ed.), *Stadsvernieuwing in Rotterdam*, The Hague, 1982.

Van der Woud, Auke, 'De geschiedenis van de toekomst,' in Van der Cammen, H. (ed.), *Nieuw Nederland, onderwerp van ontwerp*, The Hague, 1987 [I].

Van der Woud, Auke, *Het lege land. De ruimtelijke orde van Nederland 1798-1848*, Amsterdam, 1987 [II].

Van Embden, S.J., 'Nieuw Rotterdam. Het herbouwplan voor de Maasstad,' *Bouw* (May, 1946), Rotterdam.

Van Hattum, A.W., et al., 'Stedelijke herstrukturering in Rotterdam, ervaringen en perspectieven,' *Stedebouw & Volkshuisvesting* (November, 1983), Alphen aan den Rijn.

Van Ravesteyn, L.J.C.J., *Rotterdam in de achttiende en negentiende eeuw. De ontwikkeling der stad*, Rotterdam, 1974.

Van Ravesteyn, L.J.C.J., *Rotterdam in de twintigste eeuw. De ontwikkeling van de stad vóór 1940*, Rotterdam, 1948.

Van Reusel, Jef, 'Een bewogen relatie tussen stad en haven,' in Van Reusel, Jef (ed.), *Antwerpen ontwerpen*, Antwerp/Bruges, 1990.

Van Teeffelen, Jan, et al. (eds.), *Omzwervingen door het landschap van de toekomst – Rotterdam 2045, visies op de toekomst van stad, haven en regio*, Rotterdam, 1995.

Van Traa, C., 'Over en om het plan,' *Forum* (April/May), 1953.

Van Traa, C. (ed.), *Rotterdam, de wederopbouw van een stad*, Rotterdam, 1955.

Van Voorden, Frits, 'Historische structuuranalyse,' in Van den Bout, Jaap, and Erik Pasveer, *Kop van Zuid*, Rotterdam, 1994.

Vreugdenhil, A.C., *De Maastunnel*, Haarlem, n.d.

Wagenaar, Cor, *Welvaartstad in wording. De wederopbouw van Rotterdam 1940-1952*, Rotterdam, 1992.

Wattjes, J.G., and W.Th.H. ten Bosch, *Rotterdam en hoe het bouwde*, Rotterdam, 1941.

Weeber, Carel, 'De levende stad bestaat uit breuken. Op de Kop van Zuid valt niets te repareren,' in Barbieri, Umberto, and Bert van Meggelen (eds.), *Kop van Zuid. Ontwerp en onderzoek*, Rotterdam, 1982.

Weeber, Carel, 'Geen architectuur zonder stedebouw,' *Intermediair* (October 19, 1979).

Wentholt, R., *De binnenstadsbeleving en Rotterdam*, Rotterdam, 1968.

URBANIZING INFRASTRUCTURE:
AN URBAN DESIGN PROJECT

*Literature*

Stichting Fort Asperen, *Waterwerk - Visies op steden aan de rivier*, Acquoy/Zwolle, 1995.

Technische Adviescommissie Waterkeringen, *Handreikingen*, Delft, April 1994.

# List of Illustrations

# Index